Mountain Biking

Eastern
New York

Help Us Keep This Guide Up to Date

Every effort has been made by the authors and editors to make this guide as accurate and useful as possible. However, many things can change after a guide is published—trails are rerouted, regulations change, techniques evolve, facilities come under new management, etc.

We would love to hear from you concerning your experiences with this guide and how you feel it could be improved and kept up to date. While we may not be able to respond to all comments and suggestions, we'll take them to heart and we'll also make certain to share them with the authors. Please send your comments and suggestions to the following address:

The Globe Pequot Press
Reader Response/Editorial Department
P.O. Box 480
Guilford, CT 06437

Or you may e-mail us at:

editorial@globe-pequot.com

Thanks for your input, and happy travels!

Mountain Biking
Eastern
New York

Second Edition

Seventy-four Epic Rides from North Jersey and
Long Island to the Adirondacks

Michael Margulis

FALCON®

GUILFORD, CONNECTICUT
HELENA, MONTANA
AN IMPRINT OF THE GLOBE PEQUOT PRESS

To my dad

I go to nature to be soothed and healed and to have
my senses put in tune once more.

—John Burroughs
American essayist and naturalist
(1837–1921)

A FALCON GUIDE ®

Copyright © 1997, 2002 by Michael Margulis

Falcon and FalconGuide are registered trademarks of The Globe Pequot
Press.

Photos credits: Michael Margulis

The previous edition of this book was published as *Mountain Biking New
York.*

ISBN 0-7627-2264-9

Manufactured in the United States of America
Second Edition/First Printing

Contents

List of Maps

Map Legend

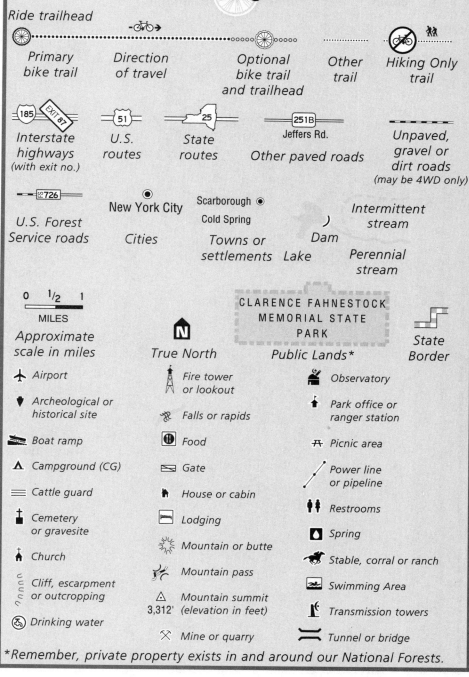

Ride trailhead

- Primary bike trail
- Direction of travel
- Optional bike trail and trailhead
- Other trail
- Hiking Only trail

- Interstate highways (with exit no.)
- U.S. routes
- State routes
- Other paved roads — Jeffers Rd.
- Unpaved, gravel or dirt roads (may be 4WD only)

- U.S. Forest Service roads
- New York City — Cities
- Scarborough / Cold Spring — Towns or settlements
- Dam
- Lake
- Intermittent stream
- Perennial stream

- 0 ½ 1 MILES — Approximate scale in miles
- **N** True North
- CLARENCE FAHNESTOCK MEMORIAL STATE PARK — Public Lands*
- State Border

- ✈ Airport
- ⚐ Archeological or historical site
- Boat ramp
- △ Campground (CG)
- ≡ Cattle guard
- ✝ Cemetery or gravesite
- ♠ Church
- Cliff, escarpment or outcropping
- Drinking water

- Fire tower or lookout
- Falls or rapids
- Food
- Gate
- House or cabin
- Lodging
- Mountain or butte
- Mountain pass
- △ 3,312' Mountain summit (elevation in feet)
- ✕ Mine or quarry

- Observatory
- Park office or ranger station
- Picnic area
- Power line or pipeline
- Restrooms
- Spring
- Stable, corral or ranch
- Swimming Area
- Transmission towers
- Tunnel or bridge

*Remember, private property exists in and around our National Forests.

Ride Locator

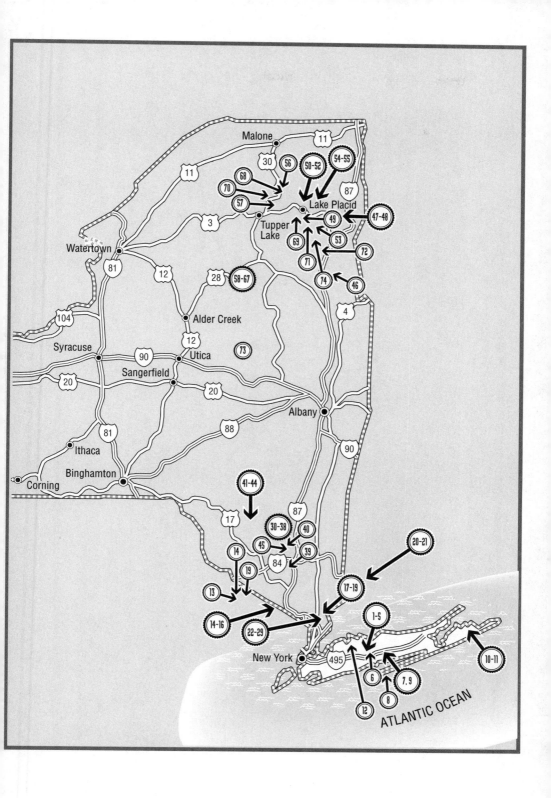

Preface

The key to surviving in the city is to discover nature. I discovered the great outdoors at an early age. My father took our family on trips into upstate New York, luring us to the wilderness, compelled as he was to escape the pressures of urban life, the stress of commuting to work, and the strains of working a long week. This fostered a sense of adventure and appealed to our sensibilities. Time and again we would return to the peace and tranquillity of nature. As a child I didn't sense my father's compulsion, yet I was absorbed in the grand scheme to escape to the country. On the ride up, even before we arrived, I felt that sense of adventure when my father pulled off to the side of the road to take in some panoramic vista. We felt his appreciation as he photographed or painted these panoramas.

We would always learn something from our excursions. We learned a lot about what made us feel good and what we enjoyed, and about the beauty of the environment.

Decades later I have continued the family tradition. I understand why my father brought us into nature and away from all the responsibilities associated with urban living.

Just as he was compelled to escape and seek peace of mind in nature's quiet setting, I am compelled to do the same and share with you my outdoor discoveries through mountain biking.

One of the major challenges of this sport is determining where to ride. Typically we take the trails that are closest or most familiar to us. This is particularly true with those who are not members of mountain bike clubs. The pleasures of mountain biking are greatly enhanced if our choice of trails can be expanded. This is the premise for my book.

There are myriad trails for mountain bikers even within a 100-mile radius of New York City. The last 200 years have left a network of logging, mining, carriage, and old forest routes within the Highland, Ramapo, Shawangunk, and Catskill Mountains as well as the pine barrens of Long Island. My excursions through wilderness tracts have uncovered many great routes of exceptional beauty off the beaten path.

My mountain bike odyssey was enriched as I ventured into woods unknown and found traces and historical remnants of the original trailblazers of hundreds of years before. I rode on dirt roads used by stagecoaches, hunting routes of Native Americans, and escape routes used by the military forces in the American Revolution. Imagine all the purposes these routes served through the centuries for farming, mining, logging, warfare, and hunting. Now this historical network of forested trails provides a great opportunity for mountain biking.

It is surprising that mountain biking is not more popular, considering the region's wealth of wilderness and the soulful high of silently gliding on these pristine trails. It's a thrill finding a new path. The ride becomes a fountain of energy. The day belongs to you.

This book should provide inspiration and enlightenment for those living and working in the metropolitan area and far beyond. It covers a wide variety of trails suitable for riders of all abilities. Mountain biking has provided us with a vehicle to enjoy and explore nature. We must work to preserve nature not only for ourselves, but for our families and for the generations to come.

During the writing of this book, my father passed away. However, I was fortunate to spend hours chatting with him about my riding experiences, which triggered his memories of carrying U.S. Army payroll during World War II. He spent three years motorcycling the jungle trails of New Guinea, all the while dodging the enemy. Though we lived in different times, we shared the same philosophy of life: to get the most out of life, to get out and go, and to get others going. My father always used to say, "Let's take a ride." With those words, I knew we were in for a day of adventure. He would be proud to know his message will be imparted to so many others and that this book will give others a taste of the outdoors he savored.

—Michael Margulis

Acknowledgments

While writing this book, I had much help from a few special people. I would like first to mention my dad, Charles Margulis, who first introduced me to my two-wheeled adventures.

Special thanks go to my lovely wife, Barbara, for making all those sustaining peanut-butter sandwiches, filling my thermos with French cafe, and hiding a Milky Way in my gear bag. And then there were all those times she accompanied me on one of those "I wonder what this trail is like" trips, and all we would do for two hours is carry our bikes on our shoulders. Her understanding and support during the past year were priceless.

My inspiration: My father on his WW II mission—running payroll to the troops in the Philippines in 1942.

Thanks to my little pumpkin Alize, who withstood all those countless bumps in the road in the bike trailer I towed behind. As long as she had Mr. Moose and Bear, a couple of raisins, and a banana, she never complained.

I would like to thank my mom for having the intuition to spot a good trail and for coming with me on my more technical rides. Well, rather than actually ride the demanding trails, she opted to watch my daughter, who complained of too many bumps on the last ride.

I would like to express my gratitude to MARIN Mountain Bikes in Marin County, California, for providing me with their agile, well-crafted, and well-designed "Pine Mountain" mountain bike for my research. My bike was hit by a tree while I was maneuvering down a steep hill and was severely trashed. Fortunately, and as a rule, I was wearing helmet protection. In addition Joannou Cycle in Northvale, New Jersey, supplied my wife with a Jamis mountain bike, a high-performance piece of equipment that provided her with a safe and superior ride.

Many thanks go out to my good friend, David Moin, for his advice and assistance on the text.

And last but not least, I can't forget my faithful companion, Shogun, our Norwegian elkhound, who accompanied me on many of my excursions, keeping pace and frequently sniffing out the direction to take on some of the more poorly marked trails.

—Michael Margulis

Introduction

TRAIL DESCRIPTION OUTLINE

Information on each trail in this book begins with a general description that includes length, configuration, scenery, highlights, trail conditions, and difficulty. Additional description is contained in several individual categories. The following will help you to understand all of the information provided.

Trail name: Trail names are as designated on United States Geological Survey (USGS) or Forest Service or other maps, and/or by local custom.

Length: The overall length of a trail is described in miles, unless stated otherwise.

Configuration: This is a description of the shape of each trail—whether the trail is a loop, out and back (that is, along the same route), figure eight, or if it connects with another trail described in the book.

Scenery: Here you will find a general description of the natural surroundings during the seasons most riders pedal the trail and a suggestion of what is to be found at special times (like great fall foliage or spring flowers in bloom).

Highlights: Towns, major water crossings, historical sites, etc., are listed.

Trail conditions: Trails are described in terms of being paved, unpaved, sandy, hard packed, washboarded, two- or four-wheel drive, singletrack, or doubletrack. All terms that might be unfamiliar to the first-time mountain biker are defined in the Glossary (page 358).

Difficulty: This provides at a glance a description of the degree of physical exertion required to complete the ride and the technical skill required to pedal it. Authors were asked to keep in mind the fact that all riders are not equal and thus to gauge the trail in terms of how the middle-of-the-road rider—someone between the newcomer and Ned Overend—could handle the route. Comments about the trail's length, condition, and elevation change will also assist you in determining the difficulty of any trail relative to your own abilities.

General location: This category describes where the trail is located in reference to a nearby town or other landmark.

Elevation change: Unless stated otherwise the figure provided is the total gain and loss of elevation along the trail. In regions where the elevation variation is not extreme, the route is simply described as flat, rolling, or possessing short steep climbs or descents.

Season: This is the best time of year to pedal the route, taking into account trail conditions (for example, when it will not be muddy), riding comfort (when the weather is too hot, cold, or wet), and local hunting seasons. *Note:* Because the exact opening and closing dates of deer, elk, moose, and antelope seasons often change from year to year, riders should check with the local fish and game department or call a sporting goods store (or any place that sells hunting licenses) in a nearby town before heading out. Wear bright clothes in fall, and don't wear suede jackets while in the saddle. Hunter's-orange tape on the helmet is also a good idea.

Services: This category is of primary importance in guides for paved-road tourers, but is far less crucial to most mountain bike trail descriptions because there are usually no services whatsoever to be found. The author has noted when water is available and has listed the availability of food, lodging, campgrounds, and bike shops. If all these services are present, you will find only the words "All services available in . . ."

Hazards: Special hazards like steep cliffs, great amounts of deadfall, or barbed-wire fences very close to the trail are noted here.

Rescue index: Determining how far one is from help on any particular trail can be difficult because of the backcountry nature of most mountain bike rides. The author therefore states the proximity of homes or Forest Service outposts, nearby roads where one might hitch a ride, or the likelihood of other bikers being encountered on the trail. Phone numbers of local sheriff departments or hospitals have not been provided because phones are almost never available. If you are able to reach a phone, the local operator will connect you with emergency services.

Land status: This category provides information regarding whether the trail crosses land operated by the Forest Service, Bureau of Land Management, or a city, state, or national park; whether it crosses private land whose owner (at the time the author did the research) has allowed mountain bikers right of passage; and so on. *Note:* The author has been careful to offer only those routes that are open to bikers and are legal to ride. However, because land ownership changes over time, and because the land-use controversy created by mountain bikes still has not completely subsided, it is the duty of each cyclist to look for and to heed signs warning against trail use. Don't expect this book to get you off the hook when you're facing some small-town judge for pedaling past a BIKING PROHIBITED sign erected the day before. Look for these signs, read them, and heed the advice. And remember, there's always another trail.

Maps: The maps in this book have been produced with great care, and, in conjunction with the trail-following suggestions, will help you stay on course. But as every experienced mountain biker knows, things can get tricky in the backcountry. It is therefore strongly suggested that you avail yourself of the detailed information found in the 7.5-minute series USGS

2

topographic maps. In some cases the author has found that specific Forest Service or other maps may be more useful than the USGS quads and tell you how to obtain them.

Finding the trail: Detailed information on how to reach the trailhead and where to park your car is provided here.

Sources of additional information: Here you will find the address and/or phone number of a bike shop, governmental agency, or other source from which trail information can be obtained.

Notes on the trail: This is where you are guided carefully through any portions of the trail that are particularly difficult to follow. The author also may add information about the route that does not fit easily in the other categories. This category will not be present for those rides where the route is easy to follow.

ABBREVIATIONS

The following road-designation abbreviations are used:

CR	County Road
FR	Farm Route
FS	Forest Service road
I-	Interstate
IR	Indian Route
US	United States highway

State highways are designated with the appropriate two-letter state abbreviation, followed by the road number. Example: NY 6 = New York State Highway 6.

TOPOGRAPHIC MAPS

The maps in this book, when used in conjunction with the route directions present in each chapter, will in most instances be sufficient to get you to the trail and keep you on it. However, you will find superior detail and valuable information in the USGS 7.5-minute series topographic maps. Recognizing how indispensable these are to bikers and hikers alike, many bike shops and sporting goods stores now carry topos of the local area.

But if you're brand new to mountain biking, you might be wondering "What's a topographic map?" In short these differ from standard "flat" maps in that they indicate not only linear distance, but elevation as well. One glance at a "topo" will show you the difference—"contour lines" are spread across the map like dozens of intricate spider webs. Each contour line represents a particular elevation, and at the base of each topo a particular "contour interval" designation is given. Yes, it sounds confusing if you're new to the lingo, but it truly is a simple and wonderfully helpful system. Keep reading.

Let's assume that the 7.5-minute series topo before us says "Contour Interval 40 feet," that the short trail we'll be pedaling is 2 inches in length on the map, and that it crosses five contour lines from its beginning to end. What do we know? Well, because the linear scale of this series is 2,000 feet to the inch (roughly 2 3/4 inches representing 1 mile), we know our trail is approximately 4/5 mile long (2 inches x 2,000 feet). But we also know we'll be climbing or descending 200 vertical feet (five contour lines x 40 feet each) over that distance. And the elevation designations written on occasional contour lines will tell us if we're heading up or down.

The author of this series warns his readers of upcoming terrain, but only a detailed topo gives you the information you need to pinpoint your position exactly on a map, steer yourself toward optional trails and roads nearby, plus let you know at a glance if you'll be pedaling hard to take them. It's a lot of information for a very low cost. In fact the only drawback with topos is their size—several feet square. I've tried rolling them into tubes, folding them carefully, even cutting them into blocks and photocopying the pieces. Any of these systems is a pain, but no matter how you pack the maps, you'll be happy they're along. And you'll be even happier if you pack a compass as well.

In addition to local bike shops and sporting goods stores, you'll find topos at major universities and some public libraries where you might try photocopying the ones you need to avoid the cost of buying them. But if you want your own and can't find them locally, write to:

USGS Map Sales
Box 25286
Denver, CO 80225

Ask for an index while you're at it, plus a price list and a copy of the booklet "Topographic Maps." In minutes you'll be reading them like a pro.

A second excellent series of maps available to mountain bikers is that put out by the United States Forest Service. If your trail runs through an area designated as a national forest, look in the phone book (white pages) under the United States Government listings, find the Department of Agriculture heading, and then run your finger down that section until you find the Forest Service. Give them a call, and they'll provide the address of the regional Forest Service office, from which you can obtain the appropriate map.

TRAIL ETIQUETTE

Pick up almost any mountain bike magazine these days, and you'll find articles and letters to the editor about trail conflict. For example you'll find hikers' tales of being blindsided by speeding mountain bikers, complaints from mountain bikers about being blamed for trail damage that was really caused by horse or cattle traffic, and cries from bikers about those "kamikaze" riders who through their antics threaten to close even more trails to all of us.

4

The author of this book has been very careful to guide you to only those trails that are open to mountain biking (or at least were open at the time of his research) and without exception have warned of the damage done to our sport through injudicious riding. All of us can benefit from glancing over the following International Mountain Bicycling Association (IMBA) Rules of the Trail before saddling up.

1. Ride on open trails only. Respect trail and road closures (ask if not sure), avoid possible trespass on private land, and obtain permits and authorization as may be required. Federal and state wilderness areas are closed to cycling.

2. Zero impact. Be sensitive to the dirt beneath you. Even on open trails you should not ride under conditions where you will leave evidence of your passing, such as on certain soils shortly after rain. Observe the different types of soils and trail construction; practice low-impact cycling. This also means staying on the trail and not creating any new ones. Be sure to pack out at least as much as you pack in.

3. Control your bicycle! Inattention for even a second can cause disaster. Excessive speed can maim and threaten people; there is no excuse for it!

4. Always yield the trail. Make known your approach well in advance. A friendly greeting (or a bell) is considerate and works well; startling someone may cause loss of trail access. Show your respect when passing others by slowing to a walk or even stopping. Anticipate that other trail users may be around corners or in blind spots.

5. Never spook animals. All animals are startled by an unannounced approach, a sudden movement, or a loud noise. This can be dangerous for you, for others, and for the animals. Give animals extra room and time to adjust to you. In passing use special care and follow the directions of horseback riders (ask if uncertain). Running cattle and disturbing wild animals is a serious offense. Leave gates as you found them or as marked.

6. Plan ahead. Know your equipment, your ability, and the area in which you are riding—and prepare accordingly. Be self-sufficient at all times. Wear a helmet, keep your machine in good condition, and carry necessary supplies for changes in weather or other conditions.

A well-executed trip is a satisfaction to you and not a burden or offense to others.

For more information contact IMBA, P.O. Box 412043, Los Angeles, CA 90041, (818) 792–8830.

HITTING THE TRAIL

Once again, because this is a "where-to," not a "how-to" guide, the following will be brief. If you're a veteran trail rider, these suggestions might serve to remind you of something you've forgotten to pack. If you're a newcomer, they might convince you to think twice before hitting the back-country unprepared.

Water

I've heard the questions dozens of times. "How much is enough? One bottle? Two? Three?! But think of all that extra weight!" Well, one simple physiological fact should convince you to err on the side of excess when it comes to deciding how much water to pack: A human working hard in 90-degree F temperature needs approximately ten quarts of fluids every day. Ten quarts. That's two and a half gallons—twelve large water bottles or sixteen small ones. And with water weighing in at approximately eight pounds per gallon, a one-day supply comes to a whopping twenty pounds.

In other words pack along two or three bottles even for short rides. And make sure you can purify the water found along the trail on longer routes. When writing of those routes where this could be of critical importance, the author has provided information on where water can be found near the trail—if it can be found at all. But drink it untreated and you run the risk of disease (see *giardia* in the Glossary).

One sure way to kill both the bacteria and viruses in water is to bring it to a "furious boil." Right. That's just how you want to spend your time on a bike ride. Besides, who wants to carry a stove or denude the countryside stoking bonfires to boil water?

Luckily, there is a better way. Many riders pack along the effective, inexpensive, and only slightly distasteful tetraglycine hydroperiodide tablets (sold under the names Potable Aqua, Globaline, and Coughlan's, among others). Some invest in portable, lightweight purifiers that filter out the crud. Yes, purifying water with tablets or filters is a bother. But catch a case of giardiasis sometime, and you'll understand why it's worth the trouble.

Tools

Ever since my first cross-country tour in 1965, I've been kidded about the number of tools I pack on the trail. And so I will exit entirely from this discussion by providing a list compiled by two mechanic (and mountain biker) friends of mine. After all, because they make their livings fixing bikes and get their kicks by riding them, who could be a better source?

These two suggest the following as an absolute minimum:
- Tire levers
- Spare tube and patch kit
- Air pump
- Allen wrenches (3, 4, 5, and 6 mm)
- 6-inch crescent (adjustable-end) wrench
- Small flat-blade screwdriver

- Chain rivet tool
- Spoke wrench

While they're on the trail, their personal tool pouches contain these additional items:

- Channel locks (small)
- Air gauge
- Tire valve cap (the metal kind, with a valve-stem remover)
- Baling wire (10 or so inches, for temporary repairs)
- Duct tape (small roll for temporary repairs or tire boot)
- Boot material (small piece of old tire or a large tube patch)
- Spare chain link
- Rear derailleur pulley
- Spare nuts and bolts
- Paper towel and tube of waterless hand cleaner

First-Aid Kit

My personal kit contains the following, sealed inside double Ziploc bags:

- Sunscreen
- Aspirin
- Butterfly-closure bandages
- Band-Aids
- Gauze compress pads (a half-dozen 4" x 4")
- Gauze (one roll)
- Ace bandages or Spenco joint wraps
- Benadryl (an antihistamine, in case of allergic reactions)
- Water purification tablets
- Moleskin/Spenco "Second Skin"
- Hydrogen peroxide, iodine, or Mercurochrome (some kind of antiseptic)
- Snakebite kit

Final Considerations

The author has done a good job in suggesting that specific items be packed for certain trails—rain gear in particular seasons, a hat and gloves for mountain passes, or shades for desert jaunts. Heed his warnings, and think ahead. Good luck.

—Dennis Coello

Long Island Tours

With its proximity to New York City and density of developed towns, Long Island is unlikely grounds for mountain biking. Yet there are twelve remarkable trail systems that range from easy cruising to technically demanding singletracks. The broad spectrum of riding explores the North Shore regions or "Gold Coast," an area of twentieth-century estates and rolling hills, south to the flat meadows and beaches of Long Island's southern shore.

The topography of Long Island shapes the character and quality of the trails and was created over the last million years by several glacial advances. Each glacier sculpted the topography by eroding bedrock and transporting boulders, cobbles, gravel, and sand. The last glacial period, which occurred about 18,000 years ago, settled the 1,000-foot Wisconsin glacier over the region, compressing, transporting, depositing, and reshaping as it advanced and retreated, profoundly affecting the land. During the Ice Age of that same period, much of northern Europe and the northern United States, as well as most of Canada, had been covered by great ice sheets. Geologic features characteristic of glaciation are distinctly different from the features formed by running water. Once recognized, they lead one to appreciate the great extent of glaciation during the Ice Age. From the Matterhorn in Switzerland to the North Shore of Long Island, glaciation has left its mark. When the Wisconsin glacier began to melt, it left behind enormous hills of morainal debris, most of it scoured out of northern New England. Bedrock found in Connecticut is scattered on the North Shore of Long Island as rocks and pebbles. The rides described here wind through and atop this hilly landscape.

Long Island is essentially a 120-mile-long pile of glacial debris representing the southern reach of the last glaciation in the New York/New England region. It is a rich topographical museum of end-glacier features like terminal and recessional moraines, outwash deposits, erratic boulders, and knob-and-kettle terrain. Long Island is not much more than a ridge, or blanket, of direct glacial outwash sediments that almost completely conceal the underlying sedimentary bedrock. The Fire Island tour explores the dynamic shoreline of Long Island, where catastrophic changes are visible with each blink of the eye. Dunes and sandbars are continually swept away and rebuilt from the coastal storms that brew in the Atlantic Ocean.

Long Island's special terrain offers a variety of riding for riders of all levels. Throughout the tours you will be challenged by the hills, charmed by the scenery, invigorated by the wilderness, and soothed by the solitude.

CLIMB (Concerned Long Island Mountain Bicyclists) patrols many of the Long Island tours. Their volunteer mountain bike patrol provides help and answers questions for other riders they encounter on the trail. They promote safety consciousness, from helmets to passing-zone etiquette to first aid. This organization has also helped with fire prevention by riding the trails and scanning for flare-ups throughout the forests. They have participated in numerous search-and-rescue operations, assisting state officials in their searches for missing or overdue hikers and hunters.

The trail patrol members are all certified in first aid and have successfully provided this needed service at a number of Long Island race events. Many of their members are also registered with International Mountain Biking Association's National Mountain Bike Patrol. Mountain bikes have proven that they are an integral component in reaching those in need—they can cover a tremendous distance in a short span of time.

Trains to the trails: Transportation service to the towns where the trails reside can be found on the commuter trains of the Long Island Railroad (LIRR). Traveling on the trains with a bicycle requires a $5.00 bike pass plus the obligatory passenger fare. The bike pass, by the way, is good for life. To acquire a pass call (718) 558–8228. Train service schedules can be found at most train stations, or you can request one by calling (718) 217–LIRR.

Various restrictions apply for individuals portaging bikes on the trains.

There are specific weekend restrictions between Memorial Day and Labor Day. Bikes are prohibited on trains departing from Penn Station between 7:30 and 10:00 A.M.; Saturday arrivals into Penn Station between 8:00 and 10:00 A.M.; and Sunday and Monday holiday arrivals into Penn Station between 4:00 and 6:00 P.M. On the Montauk trains, which service the Hamptons, restrictions apply for arrivals between 3:00 and 10:00 P.M.

Weekday restrictions apply during the rush-hour commuting periods. No bikes are allowed on departing trains from Penn Station between 7:00 and 9:00 A.M. and 3:00 and 8:00 P.M. No bikes are allowed on arriving trains into Penn Station between 6:00 and 10:00 A.M. and 4:00 and 7:00 P.M. For all other questions call the LIRR.

Nassau–Suffolk Greenbelt Trail

In real estate and retailing, location is practically everything. It's what brings up the value and popularity. In some ways the same can be said about this moderately challenging, 16-mile (8 miles one way), out-and-back tour. It makes a straight course through a wooded, protected wilderness corridor in the middle of Long Island, making it quite accessible for most of the local mountain bike enthusiasts.

This special designated mountain bike path is part of the larger 22-mile Nassau–Suffolk Greenbelt trail that practically spans the width of Long Island from Massapequa Preserve on the South Shore to Cold Spring Harbor on the North Shore. The trail offers a refreshing diversity and a welcome contrast to the heavily populated areas it traverses. It parallels the Nassau–Suffolk hiking trail and shares the same rich plant and animal habitat. The trail is in great shape, is generally not too crowded, and provides a great opportunity to sample a variety of terrain. The ride doesn't offer the twists and turns of the Stillwell Woods spaghetti track, but it allows the confident novice to try something more challenging. The length of the ride and the occasional rocks and conspiring roots supply enough gnarls for the average dirthead.

The type of riding and the variety of terrain found on Long Island is closely tied to the region's recent glacial past and the titanic forces associated with the Ice Age. The ride begins in the hilly, wooded northern shore of Long Island at an elevation close to 200 feet. It continues southward, traversing a glacial plain that slopes gently to the broader, flatter, sea-level farmland plains that are characteristic of the southern shore of Long Island. The plain consists mainly of outwash sediments mixed with till and clay that were deposited after the last major glacial period, about 10,000 years ago.

The wilderness corridor you will be traveling remains the home to many types of animals, plants, and trees. As you silently glide through this forested land, try to catch a glimpse of the local wildlife, and I don't mean the helmeted type. The habitat is home to hawks and the elusive fox. If you are lucky you may spot them along the way. As you travel from north to south, notice the hardwood stands of oak, red maple, and beech. These are typically found on the North Shore and differ from the softer conifers of pines found in the pine-barren sections typical of the South Shore. The hardwoods can survive in rockier terrain with less water. The pines grow better in the sandy, moist soils of the South Shore.

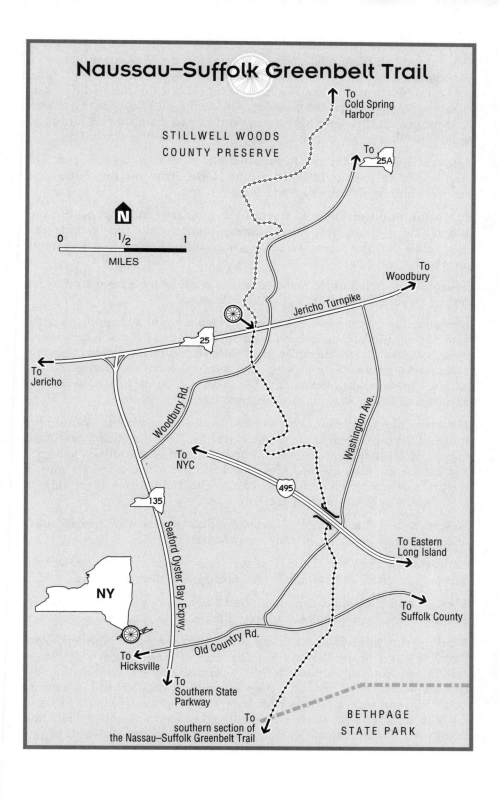

The Long Island Greenbelt Trail Conference, which has helped establish and protect these wilderness corridors, is committed to working with mountain bikers. They work with CLIMB in a coalition that has created and continues to maintain a system of parallel trails that allows hikers and bikers to enjoy these protected wilderness corridors. Thanks to the success of these organizations, we have the opportunity to share the rich forest and animal habitat, a rare commodity in highly populated communities.

General location: On the Nassau–Suffolk border on Long Island. The trail begins on Jericho Turnpike on the North Shore of Long Island and reaches south into Bethpage State Park.

Elevation change: The trail traverses the typically hilly terrain of Long Island's North Shore area, so expect some minor ascents and descents. Farther south the trail levels out as it passes through some old overgrown farmlands.

Season: Year-round usage is available, but keep the trails from eroding too fast by staying off them during wet conditions.

Services: The parking area where you will launch your adventure has a tailgate bike repair stand, and if you wear out your tread they even sell tires. A mall located on Jericho Turnpike just before you reach the parking area provides food services. Often on weekends a refreshment truck parks and dispenses the valuable food stuffs. The Bike Junkie at 272 Broadway in Bethpage offers service and equipment to mountain bikers.

Hazards: This trail tends to be more congested on weekends. Because the usage on the trail is bidirectional (riders travel in both directions), one ought to pay special attention when coming around a blind turn. Erosion and good wholesome use have exposed some roots and rocks, and a few sections of the trail will require minor technical skills. The best times to go are early in the morning or for a sunset ride after dinner.

Rescue index: The trails for hikers and mountain bikers are heavily used, and sometimes help may be only arm's-length away.

Land status: The Long Island Greenbelt was opened in 1978 as a National Recreational Trail and connects state, county, and town parkland.

Maps: The Long Island Greenbelt Trail Conference provides a membership for hikers that includes a full set of maps and a quarterly newspaper.

Finding the trail: Take the Long Island Expressway or Northern State Parkway to the Seaford Oyster Bay Expressway (north) New York 135, to exit 14 east. You will exit onto Jericho Turnpike. Proceed about half a mile east on Jericho Turnpike, past a shopping mall on your left and past a condominium complex known as Woodbury Village. Begin looking for a parking area on your left. There are usually other cars unloading riders and bikes, so it is hard to miss. Turn into the parking lot. The trail begins

Bruce Horowitz picks his line on the rolling singletrack of the Nassau–Suffolk Greenbelt.

directly across from the parking area, which faces south across Jericho Turnpike and can be recognized as a dirt path through some trees.

Sources of additional information:

Long Island Greenbelt Trail Conference
23 Deer Path Road
Central Islip, NY 11722-3404
(631) 360–0753

Concerned Long Island Mountain Bicyclists (CLIMB)
P.O. Box 203
Woodbury, NY 11797
(631) 271–6527
www.climbonline.org

Bicycle Planet
540 Jericho Turnpike
Syosset, NY 11791
(516) 364–4434
www.thebicycleplanet.com

Brands Cycle and Fitness
1966 Wantagh Avenue
Wantagh, NY 11714
(516) 781–6100

The Bike Junkie
272 Broadway
Bethpage, NY 11714
(516) 932–7271

Notes on the trail: The trail is well maintained, and the hard-packed surface of this singletrack makes for a challenging but not too technically difficult trail experience. The path is practically straight and passes through a variety of forest habitats, from hardwoods to pines. You will pass a hillside covered in young oak and go through a dark fern-covered forest floor. As you go farther south, you will pass through the overgrown meadows of abandoned farms.

From the parking area, cross Jericho Turnpike and head south on the singletrack that leads through a small clearing. Whoever is leading the ride should pay attention to what may lie ahead, because this is a bidirectional trail. Shout or use a bell when going around blind turns.

Continue on the trail through a mixed hardwood forest over moderately hilly terrain. After 0.6 mile you will approach a large, steep hill with tracks leading directly up it. Bear left at the trail that crosses the paved Woodbury Road. The trail picks up on the other side of the road. On the top of the hill, which is actually a high ledge, is an old cemetery of early Dutch and English settlers, and some limestone headstones date back to 1803. After some riding you will arrive at a wider dirt road coming from the left. Bear right onto this road. You will come out on the right side of a bridge onto a two-lane roadway. Turn left, cross the bridge, and turn left back into the forest cover as the ubiquitous white-painted blazed trail picks up farther ahead. This is the Nassau–Suffolk Greenbelt Trail. White plastic rectangular blazes on the trees mark the trail after this point. The trail heads into this forest for a short stretch, crosses another paved highway ramp, and leads back into the woods on a small descent over some small, wooden erosion-prevention logs.

After 3.8 miles bear to your right and proceed through an underpass beneath the Long Island Expressway. This barren area resembles the deserted, abandoned-car landscape from the set of *Road Warrior,* from which civilization had disappeared. I kept expecting to see some riders wearing steel armor, riding black mountain bikes with gun turrets. As you emerge from the underpass, continue straight on the main wide path. You will see many tire tracks leading toward the familiar white trail blazes. At the intersection with a paved road, cross and pick up the trail beyond the Interstate 495 sign. Soon you will cross another roadway where the trail picks up across the road, beyond a sparsely treed grassy knoll alongside an overgrown farm meadow. You will soon emerge into a cul-de-sac where the trail wraps back into wooded farm meadow. Proceed along this meadow for a short way and then cross another roadway. By now the terrain has changed from the rolling hilly terrain that is characteristically North Shore to the flatter farmland of the South Shore. At about 6.9 miles you will come into a large, four-way trail clearing. Bear to the right in a southwesterly direction where the triangular white plastic blazes mark the trail's continuation. You will now be entering Bethpage State Park and can hook up with the Bethpage State Park mountain bike network. The trail is fairly straightforward as you must return the way you came.

Stillwell Spaghetti

The little-known Stillwell Woods County Park contains a prime, grade-A mountain bike path and provides many a weekend workout for Long Island's hammerheads and recent converts. Ranked as one of the best singletracks in the East, this custom, well-maintained 5-mile work of art was built by the Concerned Long Island Mountain Bikers (CLIMB). The one-way singletrack loop traverses a hilly wooded landscape on the North Shore of Long Island, which owes its challenging riding to retreating glaciers 10,000 years ago. The park resides on top of an ancient glacial ridge built up from the deposits left behind when the glacier stalled and melted. The result is one gnarly, rocky landscape with many small depressions, gullies, and small hills. As you zip along this trail, climbing in and out of the many gullies, take a moment to look back and ponder the climb and how all this came to be.

From the beginning the trail unravels through an abandoned, regrown farm field and soon takes you through a deep forest of many twists, turns, and miniature loops. The trail has been developed to take full advantage of the hilly terrain and varied woodland that characterizes the North Shore of Long Island. To ride it you need to nurse the front wheel around the tight corners. Shift back and float over roots and branches. Then spin hard down a gully with enough power to ramp up the opposite side. Here's the typical pattern of the trail: Go up 30 feet, down 20, stay flat for 50, and get ready for the next roll. The trails consist mostly of hard-packed singletrack instead of the softer, sandier soils that make up many of the trails in the pine-barren sections of Long Island's southern and eastern woodlands. Serious off-road riding opportunities exist and good bike-handling skills are required throughout the loop. Quick descents and climbs through the many gullies and sections of tight turning constitute hammerhead heaven and demand some adroit handling. The Stillwell Woods County Park trail system also completes the northern end of the Nassau–Suffolk hiking trail and mountain bike path. Sharing the same rich forest and animal habitat, the rider is immersed in the type of primitive wilderness that is a rare sight on the highly populated Long Island.

General location: Near the towns of Woodbury and Syosset, Long Island.

Elevation change: The trail was designed to take full advantage of the moderately hilly terrain. It traverses many gullies and ascends many small

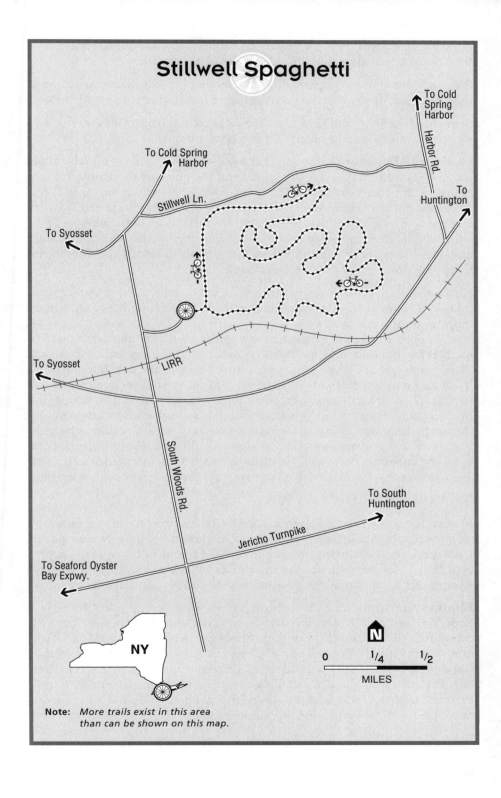

hills. There are very few elevations exceeding 200 feet, but the amount of vertical feet gained during the ride accumulates rapidly.

Season: Year-round except during wet-weather periods. There are signs at the beginning of the ride that advise bikers not to ride if the trail is wet.

Services: The Bike Junkie at 272 Broadway in Bethpage offers service and equipment to mountain bikers. Their phone number is (516) 932–7271.

Hazards: Remember that the trail is a one-way loop. These popular trails are heavily used during the weekends, and the one-way direction prevents many of the hammerheads from hammering their heads together. With collisions out of the way, the next item to pay attention to is the tight twists and turns through trees that are sometimes little more than one handlebar wide. There are some steep sections that you might wish to blast through and ride like a roller coaster. Overall, the main hazard is not having the sufficient skills to handle this great track.

Rescue index: You are never more than half a mile from major civilization, and there is usually some mountain biker passing by every fifteen minutes on the weekends.

My appreciation and respect go out to the members and volunteers of CLIMB for building and maintaining many of the trails on Long Island. Their work parties clean up, repair, and improve the conditions of the trails and develop methods to fight erosion on special sections along the routes. They and all the work party teams that build and maintain the myriad trails described in this book deserve special acknowledgment for the work they are doing to accommodate and minimize the ecological impact of the growing number of mountain bikers. These organizations open up channels of communication between trail users and land management agencies, and they need our support and deserve our cooperation.

Land status: Nassau County Park.

Maps: The Long Island Greenbelt Trail Conference provides a membership for hikers that includes a full set of maps and a quarterly newspaper. Unfortunately these maps do not provide the fine detail you might expect on a USGS topo series map, but the trail is so well marked that it is virtually impossible to get lost if you follow the white triangular markers.

Finding the trail: Take the Southern State Parkway east and take New York 135, Seaford Oyster Bay Expressway, north to exit 14 east. You will exit onto Jericho Turnpike. Continue about half a mile and turn left (north) onto South Woods Road. Look for the entrance to the Stillwell Woods County Park 1.2 miles on your right. Turn into the parking lot. The trail begins past a wooden sign detailing the rules of the mountain bike trail. By train, take the Long Island Railroad to Cold Spring Harbor and proceed north on Route 108 and west on Stillwell Lane.

Sources of additional information:

Long Island Greenbelt Trail Conference
23 Deer Path Road
Central Islip, NY 11722-3404
(631) 360-0753

Bicycle Planet
540 Jericho Turnpike
Syosset, NY 11791
(516) 364-4434
www.thebicycleplanet.com

Bikeworks Ltd.
7 Northern Boulevard
Greenvale, NY 11548-1204
(516) 484-4422

Concerned Long Island Mountain Bicyclists (CLIMB)
P.O. Box 203
Woodbury, NY 11797
(516) 271-6527
www.climbonline.org

The Bike Junkie
272 Broadway
Bethpage, NY 11714
(516) 932-7271

Notes on the trail: The trail is blazed by white plastic triangular markers that are serially numbered based on your progress into the trail and will guide you quite easily through the loop. I will detail the ride below, but it is much easier to just follow the numbered white triangular markers than to keep glancing at this set of instructions for every turn.

Pedal to the south end of the parking area, past the baseball diamonds, and onto a gated gravelly utility road. You will soon see a brown wooden sign marking the Stillwell Woods Mountain Bike Trail. The trail has been created and is currently maintained by CLIMB. A list of courtesy rules includes always wear a helmet, yield to horses and hikers, stay on the trail, follow white markers, and don't ride when trail is wet.

The hard-packed singletrack begins through an old grown-in abandoned farm field traversing about half a mile and soon enters a wooded area, where it zigzags around some mature white pine trees. You will soon pass a trail leading in from your left. Ignore this trail and continue straight on the well-worn singletrack. When in doubt, as a rule, you are in good hands if you stay on the more worn trails. Bear left at the next fork, and soon you will come to another fork with a large white pine bearing the trail's white triangular markers. Bear right at this tree, and enter into a denser wooded

*Miles of singletrack snake through the dense forest of Still-
well Woods.*

forest. As you come into a clearing, make a left at the T intersection, and
take the first right into another wooded area, picking up the number 7
marker. You will know you are on the right trail when the white triangular markers attached to the trails appear soon after a questionable intersection.

Ride through a large forest of oak trees and exit into another open field,
remaining on the well-worn track. At a wooden post with an arrow pointing to the right, turn right into the woods and follow the singletrack. The
trail spirals downhill to another T intersection, where you must turn right.
Notice the number 12 marker. Bear left at the next fork, which is tagged
with the number 13. The trail then climbs steeply through a dry stream
gully; bear left at the top where the trail snakes for another half a mile.
Bear left at the next two forks. At marker number 27, bear right. You soon
will descend into a deep gully; if you are good, let it rip and channel that
momentum to get back up the other side. Before you have time to catch
your breath, you will start another descent to a five-way intersection with

a clearing in the middle. Look for marker number 35 in a westerly direction; it should lead you straight ahead and up the trail. You should encounter marker number 36. If you do not, pedal back to the intersection and try again.

At marker number 45 you come to a T intersection with another trail. Turn right here, and continue straight through the next intersection up a small, steep hill, where you will encounter marker 47. After riding on the plateau for 10 minutes or so, go down and up another gully, and smile at marker number 53. Another gully follows, and then the trail levels out and empties into another clearing. Take the leftmost fork, which is tagged with marker number 58, and hug the left trail, which takes you back into the woods. Ascend a short hill and come into another clearing. Take the middle fork, which is labeled number 61, down and up another gully, and continue straight, ignoring the white painted marker to your right and continuing on the trail marked by white triangles. Even though it may feel like more, at this point you have only gone 3.5 miles.

The trail ends at a wide utility road. Turn left and make a quick right, proceeding through an old abandoned farm field in a westerly direction. At the end of the field, bear left, and then turn right at the first right turnoff. Descend for about 500 feet, bearing left at an abandoned car, and turn right at the next intersection onto the singletrack and up a small hill. You will soon encounter trail marker 84. You will travel through a mature cypress grove that is quite dark and then descend to another intersection and turn right, following the white triangles. You cannot become lost on these well-marked trails. At 5 miles exit where you began, by the wooden sign.

Glacier 8 Trail

This new singletrack has been recently created for the Long Island hammerhead crowd. It is relatively unknown, but it is grade-A material. The Concerned Long Island Mountain Bicyclists (CLIMB) designed, built, and now maintain the 5-mile trail. The trail, which consists of two loops, ranks as one of the newest, most artistically groomed mountain bike trails on Long Island. This trail is a must-do for anyone searching for an easy yet moderately challenging mountain bike experience. The wide singletrack is not technically challenging, and its smoothness, good condition, and gentle, rolling grade facilitate the freedom to have a great ride without much effort. The pine-needle path twists and turns along a gently rolling terrain populated with dense forests of large white pine and oak trees commonly seen along the northern shore of Long Island. The mature stands of conifers and hardwoods provide a canopy for shade that's great for summer riding. This path seems like a small oasis of attractive woodland, particularly after crossing over from one of the paved roadways.

My appreciation and respect go out to the members and volunteers of CLIMB for building and maintaining many of the trails on Long Island. Their work parties clean up, repair, and improve the conditions of the trails and develop methods to fight erosion on special sections along the routes. They and all the work party teams that build and maintain the myriad trails described in this book deserve special acknowledgment for the work they are doing to accommodate and minimize the ecological impact of the growing number of mountain bikers. These organizations open up channels of communication between trail users and land management agencies, and they need our support and deserve our cooperation.

General location: Near Hauppauge, Long Island, approximately 42 miles from New York City and just north of Connetquot River State Park.

Elevation change: The tour is sectioned into two loops: a southern loop that is relatively level, and a northern loop designed to traverse in spaghetti loops and take advantage of the moderately hilly terrain, dropping into gullies and ascending small hills.

Season: This tour has year-round potential. Try to stay off the trails after heavy rains or when they are defrosting from occasional winter storms.

Services: Rocky Point Cycle at 664 Route 25A in Rocky Point offers service and equipment to mountain bikers. Their phone number is (631) 744–5372.

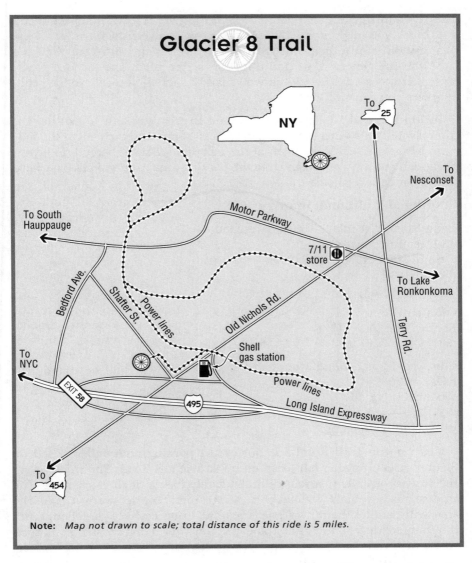

Glacier 8 Trail

NY

To 25

To Nesconset

To South Hauppauge

Motor Parkway

7/11 store

To Lake Ronkonkoma

Bedford Ave.

Shafter St.

Power lines

Old Nichols Rd.

Terry Rd.

To NYC

Shell gas station

EXIT 58

495

Power lines

Long Island Expressway

To 454

Note: *Map not drawn to scale; total distance of this ride is 5 miles.*

Hazards: Remember that the trail is a one-way loop. These popular trails are heavily used during the weekends, and the one-way direction prevents many hammerheads from hammering their heads together. The next item to pay attention to is the busy paved roads. Look both ways when coming out of the woods to cross Old Nichols Road and Motor Parkway.

Rescue index: The land this ride traverses is surrounded by residential areas and crisscrossed by two major roadways. Help can easily be flagged down, if needed.

Land status: New York State.

Maps: Unfortunately there are no USGS topo series maps that provide the fine detail you might expect. There are many small twists, turns, and loops that are difficult to map but great to ride. The map I have supplied will give you the general flow and direction of the route and an idea where things are located. The trail is well marked, and if you follow the white markers you can't get lost.

Finding the trail: Take the Long Island Expressway east to exit 58, Old Nichols Road. Proceed to the end of the exit ramp, and turn left at the light onto Nichols Road. Make a left at the next light (Shafter Street), following the green PARK AND RIDE signs into the parking area. Commuters park here, and the area is available for you, too.

Sources of additional information:

Long Island Greenbelt Trail Conference
23 Deer Path Road
Central Islip, NY 11722-3404
(631) 360–0753

Rocky Point Cycle
664 Route 25A
Rocky Point, NY 11778
(631) 744–5372

Concerned Long Island Mountain Bicyclists (CLIMB)
P.O. Box 203
Woodbury, NY 11797
(631) 271–6527
www.climbonline.org

Notes on the trail: Continue out of the parking area and proceed on Shafter Street, turning left (east) onto Old Nichols Road. The trail crosses the road about 200 feet ahead, immediately past a Shell gas station. The trail begins beyond two metal poles with a metal barrier across them. The trail will parallel the power lines, heading in an easterly direction. After the third solid-structure utility pole, pass another metal barrier. Look for a singletrack trail leading into the woods on your left, in a northerly direction, about 100 feet past this barrier.

Proceed on this singletrack going east for about 500 feet and past some dirt mounds that are used as jumps. Bear left at the next fork, in a northerly direction, and continue past a housing development on your right. You will begin to pick up the white paint blazes on the trees and the mountain bike trail's white triangle. At 0.9 mile you will cross the paved Old Nichols Road.

Cross the road and continue through a young forest of hardwoods. Continue on the singletrack as it winds through a forest of oak and pine. After 0.3 mile of easy singletrack, you arrive at a clearing. Bear left at the green sign with a white arrow pointing in a southwesterly direction. Continue

Shogun searching for a Long Island Iditarod at the Glacier 8 Trail.

for a short distance through thick shrubs and then ascend a short, steep hill. The trail levels out and terminates at the wide, grassy power-line strip. Turn right, and go up another hill. At the top, stop at the paved Motor Parkway. Cross and pick up the trail on the other side, bearing right in the direction of the sign painted green with a white arrow. White triangles mark the trail also. The trail soon turns into a doubletrack and descends along a gully through an oak and pine forest. After your descent the trail traverses a few spaghetti loops, going up and down the hillside. About 3 miles into the ride, you begin the ascent out of this pasta palace and reach the top of a hill marked by an old fire tower.

Continue following the white triangles. The trail stops right next to your entry point into this loop, on Motor Parkway. Continue across the road, proceeding in the same direction you came from before. Go down the grassy slope in a southeasterly direction alongside the power lines until you come to paved Old Nichols Road. Turn right onto Old Nichols Road and right onto Shafter Street to the Park and Ride lot.

4

Pandora's Box

With its close proximity to New York City and density of surrounding towns, one might question the availability of high-quality mountain bike paths in dense townships in this part of Long Island. But in beautiful Bethpage State Park, there are many singletrack surprises locked in the web of trails. This 5-mile loop proves that it's not necessary to travel far to sample some of the best mountain bike adventures in the East.

Perhaps best known for its world-class golf courses, Bethpage State Park is also the deluxe urban playground for the Long Island mountain biker. Only 40 miles from New York City, this 1,475-acre state park offers the mountain biker an endless repertoire of single- and doubletrack trails. Most of the smooth, hard-packed trails include fire roads, bridle paths, and woodland singletracks. These trails wind through a dense, hilly landscape of oak and maple woodland. You can construct numerous riding configurations through this hilly park along a seemingly endless network of paths. The hard, compact conditions of the trails make a pleasant yet challenging ride for advanced beginners. There are plenty of obstacles such as the specially placed logs and large earthen hump jumps, which challenge the advanced wheelhead seeking more technical thrills. The Concerned Long Island Mountain Bicyclists (CLIMB) help maintain and blaze some of the singletracks, using special erosion-control techniques.

As in most of Long Island, much of the hilly terrain and challenging riding of these trails are products of retreating glaciers 10,000 years ago. The park resides on top of an ancient glacial ridge built up from the deposits left behind when the glacier stalled and melted. The result is one gnarly landscape with many small depressions, gullies, and small hills.

This park's reputation is spreading. Long Island mountain bikers are discovering its intriguing and challenging trails.

General location: Near Farmingdale, Long Island.

Elevation change: There are some minor hills to negotiate, but nothing too strenuous. The terrain is a mixed bag of hills and flat woodlands.

Season: Riding opportunities exist year-round, except during wet-weather periods, when it is advisable to remain off the trails. We can help save the trails from further erosion by staying off them during these periods. Wait for them to dry out and then ride. In the fall, one of the better times to ride, the colors are laid on with a bold hand, and the dense woodland glows.

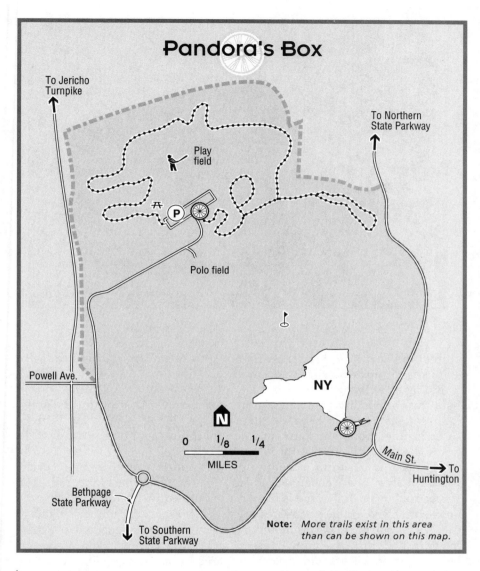

Pandora's Box

To Jericho Turnpike

To Northern State Parkway

Play field

Polo field

P

Powell Ave.

NY

N

0   1/8   1/4
MILES

Bethpage State Parkway

To Southern State Parkway

Main St.

To Huntington

Note: *More trails exist in this area than can be shown on this map.*

Services: This is a great place to have a picnic and do some riding. Those who might not be ready for a singletrack through the woods have the opportunity to ride on an excellent, well-made, two-way paved path. It winds through the park and provides a smooth path for roller blading, jogging, or just strolling. In the large picnic area, you can have a picnic or just throw out a blanket and read a book. Broadway provides loads of shops and is within riding distance of the park. Playfields and tennis courts are also available.

Hazards: Because usage on the trail is bidirectional, one ought to pay special attention when coming around a blind turn. When it is hard to see

A desolate Bethpage State Park on a snowy January afternoon.

around the next turn, take extra care to slow down and signal ahead with a whistle, or just say "Rider approaching."

Riding at Bethpage State Park is a little like a trip to Las Vegas, except here the commodity gambled is time, not money. Many of the trails and intersections are unmarked, so there is a gamble at every turn. In most cases instinct, common sense, and careful following of the route description will suffice to see you through.

The park is beautiful and quite popular and is shared by other users. Occasionally you will encounter horses and hikers on some of the trails. The current policy of trail usage is managed by the individual, and for now the people involved in these activities coexist and respect each other's rights to use this special park. We, as mountain bikers, need to be sensitive while riding here. Let's display a mutual respect and courtesy for each other, and this beautiful park will remain a recreation area for all to enjoy. In my experience a passing hello has always been met with one in return from equestrians and hikers. They are glad to see you enjoying the park also.

Rescue index: The park is a fairly lively one, and help is never far away. I found that other mountain bikers in the park were always willing to lend a hand when I asked for directions or even a patch kit. Most of the bikers I have encountered are very friendly. You may feel this park is easy to become disoriented in, but it is, in fact, hard to get lost. Residential homes surround the park, and this perimeter is usually no more than 1 or 2 miles away.

My appreciation and respect go out to the members and volunteers of CLIMB for building and maintaining many of the trails on Long Island.

Their work parties clean up, repair, and improve the conditions of the trails and develop methods to fight erosion on special sections along the routes. They and all the work party teams that build and maintain the myriad trails described in this book deserve special acknowledgment for the work they are doing to accommodate and minimize the ecological impact of the growing number of mountain bikers. These organizations open up channels of communication between trail users and land management agencies, and they need our support and deserve our cooperation.

Land status: New York State Park.

Maps: A general park map is provided for you at the entrance, or you can mail away for one. This map unfortunately does not detail the mountain bike route. There are also no USGS topo series maps that provide the fine detail you might expect. The many small twists, turns, and loops are difficult to map but great to ride. The map I have supplied will give you the general flow and direction of the route and an idea of where things are located. The trail is well marked, and if you follow the white triangular markers, you can't get lost.

Finding the trail: Take the Southern State Parkway east to exit 31 north (Linden Street), and take the left fork for the Bethpage State Parkway. Take this road all the way to the Bethpage State Park Picnic Area. There is a $3.00 fee for parking. You can take the Long Island Railroad to Bethpage and, from the station, ride east on Powell Avenue into Bethpage State Park.

Sources of additional information:

Bethpage State Park
99 Quaker Meeting House Road
Farmingdale, NY 11735
(516) 249-0701

Long Island State Park Region
Belmont Lake State Park
P.O. Box 247
Babylon, NY 11702
(631) 669-1000

The Bike Junkie
272 Broadway
Bethpage, NY 11714
(516) 932-7271

Concerned Long Island Mountain Bicyclists (CLIMB)
P.O. Box 203
Woodbury, NY 11797
(516) 271-6527
www.climbonline.org

Notes on the trail: The trail begins in the southwest corner of the large Bethpage State Park Picnic Area parking lot. It is a little tricky to find. Stand with the picnic area behind you, and notice the well-worn single-track that diagonally leads into the trees, to the left of the tollbooth. The trail is marked with the white triangle that is used to signify the mountain bike trail. The singletrack goes into the woods immediately before the large sign reading NO PETS, NO ALCOHOL, PARK CLOSES AT SUNSET.

Climb a short hill, and follow along the hard-packed singletrack as it winds through a dense forest of oak. The trail straightens out as it travels along some power lines in a northeasterly direction. At 0.3 mile the trail turns left into the woods, and you will come to a large oak tree with white triangular markers. Bear right at this intersection, and follow some more winding track. A few earthen humps have been shaped and positioned for a quick technical tango, but you can go around them as well. At 0.7 mile you come to another intersection. Turn right, and notice the red paint blazed on the trees with the white triangular markers. You will be heading in a northwesterly direction. After another 500 feet, fork right at a tree with two white triangles. Keep bearing right, ignoring the red-blazed trail. The trail ends in 0.2 mile at a wide, hard-packed maintenance road. Turn right on this road, following the white triangles. In this section you are sharing the bridle path, which is marked with a yellow rectangle and black arrows.

You will soon come to a large wooden piling in the ground placed at the junction of two forks. The bridle path continues along the left fork, but you should take the right fork. After cresting the small hill, the trail crosses the bridle path again and continues past a large oak tree. Bear left at the next fork (as the right fork leads to a paved road), and then turn right at the next T intersection.

This section of the trail is an old semipaved, broken-up path that takes you along the perimeter of the park. After 0.2 mile you come to a large tree. Bear right, following the white triangle–marked semipaved path to descend to the wide bridle path. Turn left, and head in a southwesterly direction. Following the white triangles bear right at the next large fork. In perhaps another 1,000 feet, bear right again as the bridle path forks left. After another 0.1 mile bear left onto a flat, dirt doubletrack. Very soon you will come to a large clearing with trails leading out from all directions. Continue straight through, and then turn right onto the wide bridle path. Soon after notice a pine tree on your left with painted white blazes on it. Turn left onto the singletrack as it enters the woods and ascends a short hill in an easterly direction. You will pick up the white triangles again. After cresting the top of the hill, you will be riding alongside the picnic area to your left. After about a minute of riding, the trail turns right and descends back down into the woods, away from the picnic area. Cross a bridle path and continue through some dense oak and pine woods. The white triangles are well spaced and easy to follow. Turn right at the next wide dirt road, and then make a quick left into the forest. Ascend a short hill for 300 feet and fork left, following the triangles. You will be riding along a ridge that is overlooking a small gully to your left. The ridge is also parallel to NY 135 on your right, and you will be able to hear the sounds of the cars. Ride along this ridge for about ten minutes. Descend off the ridge, and bear left at a small fork onto the bridle path; notice the white triangles ahead. Continue straight, and bear right at the next fork, following the white triangles. Soon after you will come to a piling with the number 13 marked on it. Go past the second piling and up a small hill, in a southeasterly direction. Proceed up the small hill and go straight for about half a mile, where the trail terminates at the paved bike path. Turn left, and take this path down into the parking area.

Rocky Point

Cross-country skiers can pretty much ski anywhere, providing there is the minimum snow ground cover. A well-groomed track can do wonders for a skier's technique, rhythm, and efficiency in covering the distance. Once in the skier's groove, so to speak, there's an enormous sense of freedom to move and enjoy the beauty of the passing scenery, a freedom we mountain bikers share here in warmer weather. Rocky Point Natural Resources Management Area offers a well-planned, 13-mile, groomed, singletrack loop that snakes through an incredibly versatile forest filled with pine barrens, hardwoods, and swamps. If Leonardo Da Vinci was a mountain biker, he would have been proud of the overall design and layout of this trail system. This trail is a work of art. The hard, compact singletrack, sometimes covered with a bed of soft pine needles, has been laid out over 5,000 acres of plains and woodlands. The track's layout is designed to provide the mountain biker with great scenery and action-packed technical hurdles that really put your skills to the test. A network of woodland roads crisscrosses the sandy, wooded pine area and provides ample biking trails. All access is prohibited on Rocky Point lands except under permit from the Department of Environmental Conservation or from the Navy Department.

The development of the trail was made possible by the Concerned Long Island Mountain Bicyclists Club (CLIMB), which is on a mission to preserve and maintain existing paths. My appreciation and respect go out to the members and volunteers of CLIMB for building and maintaining many of the trails on Long Island. Their work parties clean up, repair, and improve the conditions of the trails and develop methods to fight erosion on special sections along the routes. They and all the work party teams that build and maintain the myriad trails described in this book deserve special acknowledgment for the work they are doing to accommodate and minimize the ecological impact of the growing number of mountain bikers. These organizations open up channels of communication between trail users and land management agencies, and they need our support and deserve our cooperation.

There are rules for riding in Rocky Point. Riders must stay on the yellow-marked mountain bike trails. You may ride on the larger dirt roads, but their condition in the sandy terrain may vary and is not always dependable. There is a satisfying range of twists and turns on the 13-mile loop. The trail is one way, so once you begin, you have committed. Helmets and eye protection are also required. Bicycling on marked hiking trails is strictly prohibited.

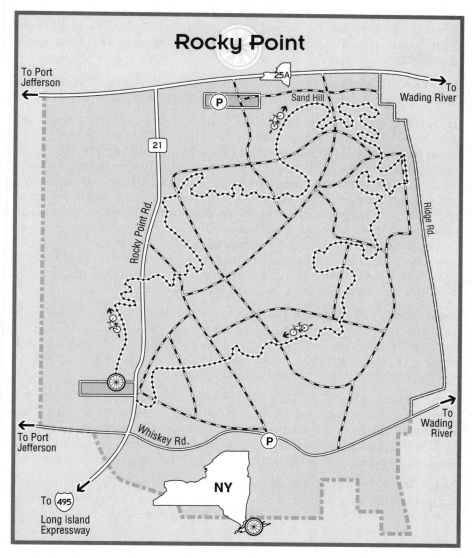

The land was sold to New York State in the late 1970s for $1.00. RCA, which owned the land, owed so much in back taxes that it chose to sell the property for practically nothing to get out of debt. On the trail you'll see many fallen radio towers straddling the steel cables that once held them erect.

General location: Approximately 55 miles east of Manhattan, near Port Jefferson on Long Island's North Shore.

Elevation change: It's mostly flat riding, although the trail has been developed to take advantage of the many variations in the landscape. Several gnarly spaghetti loops carve through the moderately hilly terrain, descending and ascending many small hills and gullies.

Season: Hunters may be present from September 15 to April 16, with the highest concentration from November through January. Call the Department of Environmental Conservation for more detailed information.

Services: Rocky Point Cycle on 664 Route 25A in Rocky Point provides sales, repairs, and equipment. Their phone number is (631) 744–5372.

Hazards: Remember that the trail is a one-way loop. These popular trails are heavily used during the weekends, and the one-way direction prevents many hammerheads from hammering their heads together. With collisions out of the way, the next item to pay attention to is the tight twists and turns through trees that are sometimes little more than one handlebar wide. Then there are some steep sections you might wish to blast through and ride like a roller coaster. Overall the main hazard is not having the sufficient skills to handle this great track.

Watch for ticks during the summer months. It is also advisable to call the New York State fishing and hunting department at (631) 444–0273 for the January deer season dates. Pine needles cover the ground and trails, so be careful about brush fires; they can be easily started.

Rescue index: These trails see their fair share of traffic, and there is usually another rider passing by every fifteen minutes or so. It is hard to become lost because the trail is a loop and will eventually end where it began. As long as you stay on the trail, you will have no problem. You are never more than 2 miles from major civilization.

Land status: New York State Department of Environmental Conservation. A permit is required for access into the preserve. Call to find out details for acquiring the permit. Work parties are an important component in keeping the Rocky Point trail open and are conducted through CLIMB. Trail maintenance is the responsibility of the trail users. This means you!

Maps: New York State Department of Environmental Conservation will supply you with a trail map when you send away for the required permit. The mountain bike trail is well marked with square yellow mountain bike signs. They are posted quite frequently, and you will probably never have to look at a map to find your way.

Finding the trail: Take the Long Island Expressway to exit 66, Sills Road/Yaphank. Make a left onto County Road 101 north, and continue straight toward Yaphank. At the stoplight bear right in the direction of Route 21. You will pass Upper Lake on your left, a small body of water that feeds into Carmans River. There is a convenience store across from it. At the next light bear left, and continue on Route 21. After the intersection with Whiskey Road, you will see a NEW YORK STATE DEPARTMENT OF ENVIRONMENTAL CONSERVATION, ROCKY POINT NATURAL RESOURCE AREA sign. Turn left into the parking area. Park your vehicle, and make sure your permit is in the window. The trail begins beyond the wooden kiosk sign. A park ranger is usually parked in the parking area and will provide extra assistance if needed.

Smooth, face-paced, rolling singletrack at Rocky Point.

Sources of additional information:

New York State Department of Environmental Conservation
SUNY Building 40
Stony Brook, NY 11790-2356
(631) 444-0273 or 444-0310

Concerned Long Island Mountain Bicyclists (CLIMB)
P.O. Box 203
Woodbury, NY 11797
(516) 271-6527
www.climbonline.org

Rocky Point Cycle
664 Route 25A
Rocky Point, NY 11778
(631) 744-5372
www.rockypointcycles.com

Notes on the trail: The directions are simple. The trail is well marked with yellow blazes, and it is virtually impossible to get lost. These yellow markers on the trees guide you for the entire 13-mile loop. This trail has been developed to challenge and satisfy any gonzo dirthead. There are numerous twists and turns and miniature loops that take advantage of the varied, hilly terrain. All you have to do is get on and not get off. If you cannot complete the entire loop, there are bail-out points indicated on the map. You may return by following the yellow markers back to the Rocky Point Road parking lot.

6

Edgewood Oak Brush Plains Preserve

For an easy morning or afternoon ride, set your wheels down on this relatively unknown 3,000-acre preserve. It offers a 4-mile loop-and-other mixture of wide, hard-packed, old abandoned dirt roads and some singletracks. Set in the middle of suburban sprawl, this large piece of land offers basic, no-frills riding and some semblance of solitude—a few trees and not too many people, other than a few members of a dog club who train and clock their Labradors in the act of retrieving fallen game. This may not be a mecca for mountain bikers, but the terrain contains sufficient woodland for some basic off-road riding opportunities. The trails traverse a generally flat, pine-barren forest with spacious fields. The riding provides the novice with a good lesson in basic handling of the bike and offers the average rider some fast-paced doubletrack. Most trails are wide, smooth, and easy to ride. All access is prohibited on the Edgewood Oak Brush Plains Preserve lands, except under permit from the Department of Environmental Conservation or special permit from the Navy Department.

General location: Suffolk County, exit 52 on the Long Island Expressway, near the town of Edgewood.

Elevation change: Negligible. Generally flat terrain.

Season: Year-round riding is available.

Services: Most services are along Jericho Turnpike. Proceed north on Commack Road until it intersects with Jericho Turnpike in about 7 miles.

Hazards: Watch for ticks during the summer months.

Rescue index: Suburbia surrounds the preserve, and help is never more than a mile away.

Land status: New York State Department of Environmental Conservation. A permit is required for access into the preserve. Call to find out details for acquiring the permit.

Maps: New York State Department of Environmental Conservation will supply you with a trail map when you send away for the required permit.

Finding the trail: Take the Long Island Expressway east to exit 52, Commack Road (County Road 4). Go south on Commack Road (CR 4) for about

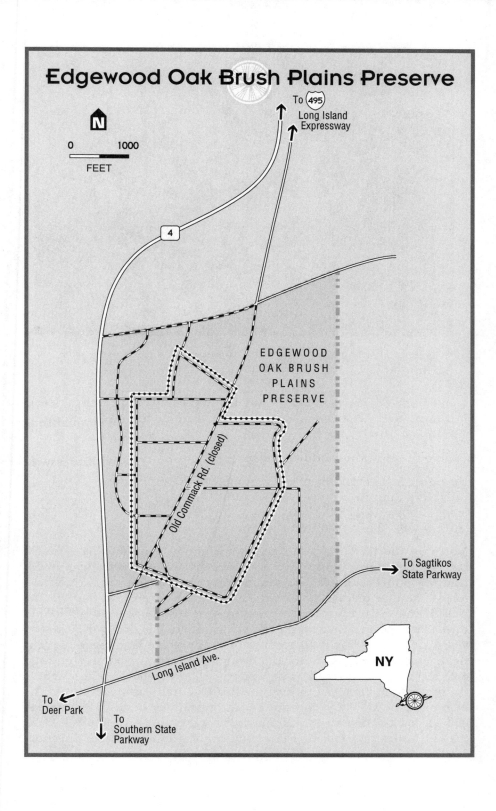

Edgewood Oak Brush Plains Preserve

N

0   1000
FEET

To 495
Long Island
Expressway

4

EDGEWOOD
OAK BRUSH
PLAINS
PRESERVE

Old Commack Rd. (closed)

To Sagtikos
State Parkway

Long Island Ave.

NY

To
Deer Park

To
Southern State
Parkway

"I think we need to discuss frame size." Three-year-old Alize Margulis offers her expertise.

4 miles, and on your left you will see an entrance through a metal fence. It is unmarked, but there is a parking area directly beyond this entrance. Turn in here, and make sure your permit is in your window.

Source of additional information:

New York State Department of Environmental Conservation
SUNY Building 40
Stony Brook, NY 11790-2356
(631) 444–0273 or 444–0310

Notes on the trail: The trail is a basic loop trail with blue blazes marking most of the way. It may be tricky because there are several other woodland roads that intersect with the main course. For this trail description follow the blue-marked trails. Go beyond the wooden pole barrier. The trail begins on your left as a wide sandy dirt road between a row of old trees that appear to have been planted long ago to line the road. This road veers to your right as it approaches the edge of the large plain on your right. Proceed straight ahead in a northerly direction after the turn and onto a grass-covered lane, passing between some low bushes. Turn right at the next intersection, and pick up the first blue trail marker on a tree. The blue markers will be your guide for the remainder of the trip. Proceed down a corridor of white pines. You are now in a pine-barren forest. Make the left at the next four-trail intersection going in a northerly direction, and after a short distance you will see a small break in the trees and a blue marker. Turn right here, and go through some dense cover but remain on the trail. You will soon come onto an old abandoned paved road. This is Old Commack Road, and you may cruise up and down for some additional leisurely riding. Turn right onto the road, and notice the blue markers on the utility poles. After a short distance there will be another break in the trees on your left, with a blue trail marker near that entrance. You will come to a dirt road. Make a right, and you will see the continuation of the blue markers on the trees. Continue past a field on your left, and make a right and then a quick left back into the forest, where the blue markers pick up again. Continue for about a mile, and look for a break in the trees on your right. Turn right, where the blue trail markers appear on the trees. This will take you in a northerly direction. You will come out into a trail intersection of dirt roads. Bear right, and pick up the blue trail on your left. Turn left, and pedal back to the parking area.

7

Southaven County Park

Southaven County Park is an interesting package. It consists of a typical eastern Long Island pine-barren habitat. The dense oak woodlands are interspersed with open fields and picnic areas. The wide, scenic Carmans River forms one of the park's borders. As an extra bonus more than 10 miles of dirt road provide a full supply of off-road opportunities. All that's necessary for enjoyment on this 8-mile loop is a good picnic lunch and a bike that rides. There is enough variety for the beginning rider to learn some basic handling and endurance skills and get an excellent introduction to the sport. There's also some fast doubletrack for the more experienced biker. Seasoned riders can relax and enjoy some easy cruising along a network of secluded bridle paths and wide, hard-packed, unimproved dirt roads. Equestrians, walkers, and bike riders gladly share the trails.

Carmans River establishes the eastern park border, hosts many migrating birds, and is a favorite spot for canoeists. Several paths lead you down to the shore. Park your bikes and cool your heels and wheels at the river's edge. Take a moment just to sit by the sandy shore and watch the waterfowl.

During the high season, between Memorial Day and Labor Day weekends, the bridle paths tends to become chopped up. These trail sections have a sandy consistency and are less stable and resistant to usage. After completing this loop you'll find a great ride along the scenic Carmans River, where it's perfect to stop by the water and have lunch. Bordered on one side by Carmans River, Southaven Park provides fine opportunities for viewing wildlife and reflective moments for gazing at a beautiful river. For the more hardy a brisk morning ride in the off-season is invigorating. Share the park with a few other polar bikers.

The demands for this ride are simple: a drive to the park, some sandwiches and snacks, a couple of bikes and friends or family. Mix for a few hours, and voila!—a recipe for some great fun.

General location: Exit 68 off the Long Island Expressway, near the town of Shirley.

Elevation change: The terrain is generally flat with a few modest hills that climb and descend an ear-popping 40 feet.

Season: If there is no snow on the ground, this is potentially four-season territory. The trails get muddy and unmanageable for riding during wet periods, but it is a great place to get away from the crowds during the

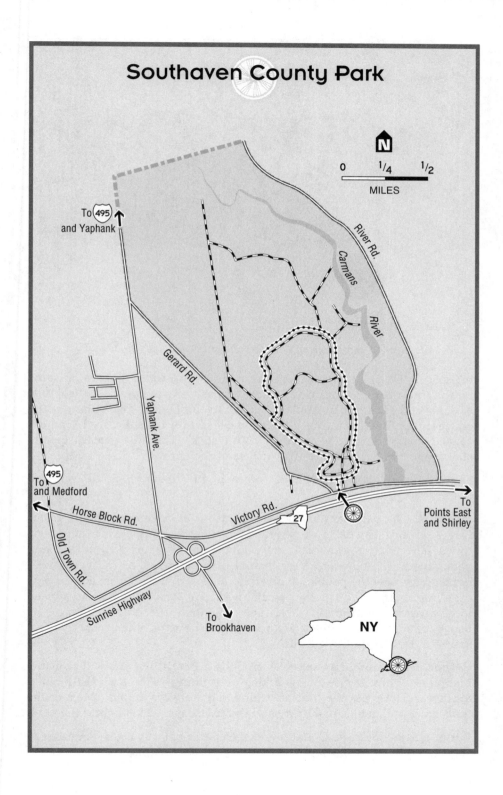

Southaven County Park

0   1/4   1/2

MILES

To 495
and Yaphank

River Rd.

Carmans

River

Gerard Rd.

Yaphank Ave.

495
To
and Medford

Horse Block Rd.

Victory Rd.   27

To
Points East
and Shirley

Old Town Rd.

Sunrise Highway

To
Brookhaven

NY

My wife Barbara and daughter Alize by the western shore of Carmans River.

off-season. During the colder winter months, providing there is no snow on the trails, this park provides a great opportunity to enjoy some solitude and have these popular trails all to yourself. During the summer and warmer months, check your clothing and socks for ticks. Before I head out I usually spray some bug repellent on my socks. The little rascals seem to stay away, but I'm not sure it's because of the spray.

Services: Most services can be found in the towns of Southaven and Shirley.

Hazards: The park sees an increase in use from Memorial Day to Labor Day weekends. Pay extra attention, and ride responsibly during these busy times. The park is beautiful and popular and is shared by hikers and equestrians. The current policy of trail usage is managed by the individual, and for now the people involved in these activities coexist and respect each other's rights to use this special park. We, as mountain bikers, need to be sensitive while riding here. Let's maintain a responsible image. By using commonsense etiquette and having respect for other users, we will assure our place on these trails.

Rescue index: Suburban sprawl surrounds the park, and you will probably bump into someone else riding, hiking, or running on the trails. Park maintenance vehicles use the trails as well and are always helpful. Most of the trails are within a mile of Victory and Gerard Roads, which border the park.

Land status: Suffolk County Parks Department manages Southhaven County Park.

Maps: USGS 7.5-minute series, Bellport quadrangle provides good detail for these unimproved dirt roads.

Finding the trail: Take the Long Island Expressway east to exit 68, and go south on William Floyd Parkway. Just before Sunrise Highway turn right onto Victory Avenue. Turn right at the park entrance sign to gain access into the park. There is a parking area on your right.

Sources of additional information:

Southaven County Park
Victory Avenue
Brookhaven, NY 11796
(631) 854–1414

Cycles Plus
414 New York Avenue
Huntington, NY 11743
(631) 271–4242
www.cyclesplus.com

Suffolk County Parks
Montauk Highway
P.O. Box 144
West Sayville, NY 11796
(631) 854-4949

Notes on the trail: The ride in Southaven Park can be put together as one basic loop. Begin at the park entrance, go past the park maintenance buildings, and bear left onto the wide, well-surfaced, dirt park road through a stand of white pine. In just less than a mile, you will come to a sign that says FIELD TRIAL AREA LARGE UPPER PICNIC AREA 17–22.

Straight ahead is a horse path that travels along the eastern perimeter of the park, paralleling Gerard Road. This trail begins past two wooden pilings with a metal pole going across them. For the shorter loop turn right, and go past several picnic areas. At a fork in the road, you have two choices: The left fork takes you north along a wide horse path past several open fields and leads you back to the parking area in 2 miles; the right fork takes you back to the parking area in just more than a mile.

For the wider loop continue straight through the two wooden pilings, and travel through a mixed hardwood forest for 1.5 miles. Turn right, and continue south on a dirt unimproved road. Follow it for 0.7 mile. A spur trail to your left leads in a northeasterly direction down to Carmans River. In just less than 0.5 mile, turn right, in a westerly direction, onto another spur for a quick 1.5-mile loop. If you choose not to, then just ignore the spur, the fun, the adventure, and continue straight, where in less than a mile you will arrive at the park maintenance buildings. Another less-defined path runs along the western shore of Carmans River. This trail can be reached from the parking area. Just ride to the river, and travel north along a sandy, hard-packed doubletrack for about 1 mile.

8

Fire Island National Seashore

Mountain biking along this flat, hard-packed, unimproved jeep sand trail gives you access to one of Long Island's finest beaches and charming beach communities lining the eastern portion of Fire Island. As another reward stop along the way—providing the weather is warm—park the bike, throw out a towel, and cool off in the Atlantic Ocean. There are more than 14 miles of riding available along this portion of Fire Island.

Generally mountain biking is associated with cruising along old country roads past farm fields or descending from a mountain on singletrack. Riding a mountain bike along one of the flattest sections of Long Island, you'll find that the beaches can qualify as a first-rate off-road experience, too. Novice riders will find the flat road an excellent introduction to the sport and will experience the sense of discovery that accompanies mountain biking, while the seasoned rider can relax and enjoy some easy, pleasant cruising.

Fire Island is a funny place. It's a thin, long strip of land with an incredibly diverse population; depending on the community, it's a summertime mecca for gays, singles, nude bathers, and families. Thousands of Manhattanites arrive by ferries to spend a weekend away from the asphalt jungles. After a weekend there's a mass exodus of sunburned faces heading back to the city to start another week of work.

There is another side to Fire Island that few consider but that lends itself to a pleasurable and meaningful coastal habitat ride. The trail goes past the 1858 Fire Island Lighthouse, which overlooks the Great South Bay and Atlantic Ocean. Stop by the lighthouse visitor center for a history of Fire Island, including its maritime traditions and true stories about life-saving rescues in the ocean. Folklore suggests that land-based pirates built fires at night to lure cargo ships onto shore.

Fire Island is a barrier formed as the glaciers began to melt and recede and currents carried rocks and sediment and deposited them in an east-west direction. Along the ride you will notice the natural sand dunes that create a barrier against the Atlantic Ocean. Through the centuries the island has been bombarded by storms off the ocean. Dunes have been destroyed, creating inlets connecting the Great South Bay to the north with the ocean. About 10,000 waves a day pound and wash away the sand and dunes. Currents drift from the east and carry sands from offshore sandbars and easterly beaches, replenishing the beaches. The dunes begin to grow again as grasses seed the small growing dunes. Notice the small grasses growing on top of and around the dunes. A cycle begins as the

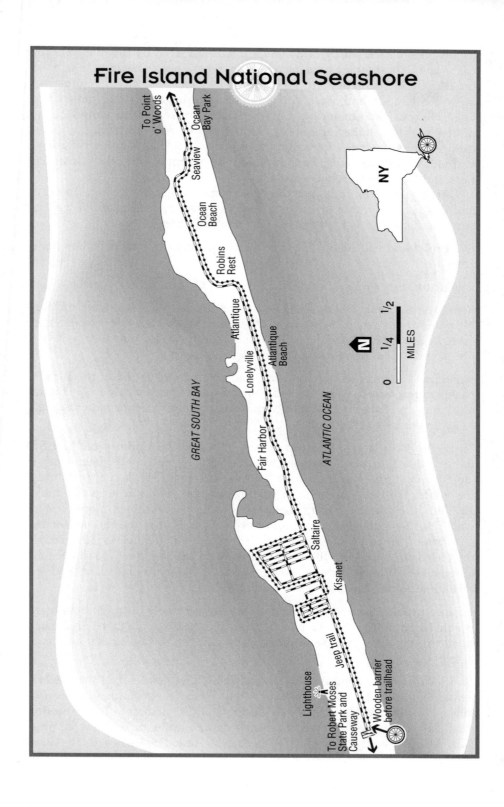

Fire Island National Seashore

To Point o' Woods

Ocean Bay Park

Seaview

Ocean Beach

Robins Rest

Atlantique

Atlantique Beach

Lonelyville

Fair Harbor

GREAT SOUTH BAY

ATLANTIC OCEAN

Saltaire

Kismet

Lighthouse

Jeep trail

To Robert Moses State Park and Causeway

Wooden barrier before trailhead

NY

MILES

0 1/4 1/2

N

dunes become seeded by birds and animals attracted by the grasses; they carry and deposit other seeds. Larger shrub-type plants begin to take hold, building new soil. They are replaced by thickets and then by forests of holly, hardwoods, and pines. Along the trail the stages of this cycle are visible. Without the anchoring roots of beach grasses, there would be no dunes; without sheltering dunes, there would be no forests; and without this precious balance, there would be no island. The island's wealth of seafood, waterfowl, and plants attracted the original Native American settlers and later the European settlers.

Farther along the route are the beach communities of Kismet, Saltaire, and Fair Harbor. These towns have many interesting little roads and paths that crisscross through attractive, charming summer cottages.

General location: South Shore of Long Island near Robert Moses State Park.

Elevation change: Negligible along the flat terrain of the beaches.

Season: Mountain biking along this route can be year-round, except during wet periods when the sandy, hard-packed roads turn into a mush mixture. Winter provides an excellent opportunity to get outside for a few hours and enjoy the solitude of this popular area.

Services: Food stands, picnic areas, and beaches are found in the Field 5 parking area, where you will park your car and begin your ride. The towns of Kismet and Saltaire have village markets and convenience stores as well as some outdoor restaurants.

Hazards: Do not tread on the dunes—they are the primary method for fighting beach erosion. Stay out of tall grasses, because Fire Island has a large population of deer and, as follows, the infamous deer tick. During the winter the deer can be seen grazing near the dunes around the thickets and low grasses. Wear sunscreen during the summer months, and watch out for poison ivy with its three leaflets. Mosquitoes are abundant in summer, so come prepared with bug repellent. Do not speed through the beach communities; there may be walkers heading down to the beach, other bikes, or a car once in a blue moon. All riders are required to carry a bell and a light on their bikes when traveling any of the roads.

Rescue index: It is very easy to find help as you travel through these busy beach communities. Other people use these roads, and there are many homes in the area. In case of emergency, you can always knock on a cottage door.

Land status: The road is used by permit-holding residents of the eastern towns, but it can be used as a bike path as well. The beginning of the ride takes you through National Park Service U.S. Department of the Interior land. You then ride through the beach communities of Kismet, Saltaire, Fair Harbor, Lonelyville, Atlantique, Robins Rest, Ocean Beach, Seaview,

Ocean Bay Park, and Point o' Woods. Ocean Beach does not permit bikes on its roads and paths from Memorial Day to Labor Day weekend.

Maps: Call the National Park Service Headquarters and ask them to send the "Fire Island National Seashore" official map and guide. The USGS 7.5-minute series, Bay Shore East quadrangle provides good detail of this portion of Fire Island.

Finding the trail: This thin, 32-mile-long island can be reached by taking the Southern State Parkway east; exit where you see signs for Robert Moses State Park and Captree State Park. Travel south on Sagtikos State Parkway, which then turns into the Robert Moses Causeway and bridges over the Great South Bay. Go around the rotary, and head in the direction of the Field 5 parking area. There is a $4.00 parking fee, and after you park, you will have to walk your bike along the roadway about 1,000 feet in the direction of the very visible, black-and-white lighthouse. The road begins here. You will see a sign posted: WARNING, NO VEHICLES BEYOND THIS POINT WITHOUT FEDERAL PERMIT. Go right in. It is open to bicycles.

Sources of additional information:

Fire Island Lighthouse
Burma Road
Fire Island, NY 11706
(631) 661–4876

Brands Cycle & Fitness
1966 Wantagh Avenue
Wantagh, NY 11714
(516) 781–6100

National Park Service Headquarters
120 Laurel Street
Patchogue, NY 11772-3596
(631) 289–4810

Notes on the trail: There is a lot to explore. You can ride for 6 miles from the lighthouse in one direction through the towns of Kismet, Saltaire, Fair Harbor, Lonelyville, Atlantique, Robins Rest, Ocean Beach, Seaview, Ocean Bay Park, and Point o' Woods. How far you penetrate into the island depends on the condition of the trail and the distance you wish to cover. Because it is a hard-packed sand trail, it may degrade from storms and extra usage and become difficult to ride on. After 1 mile you reach the town of Saltaire, where the trail traverses along a wooden boardwalk. From Saltaire to Fair Harbor, the next 0.7 mile is part wooden boardwalk and part semipaved. After Fair Harbor you will ride on a jeep trail for about 1.5 miles until you get to the town of Ocean Beach, where again the trail becomes a semipaved road. From Ocean Beach it's another 2 miles until you reach Point o' Woods. The town of Ocean Beach restricts bike riding of any kind during the summer months, from Memorial Day to Labor Day weekend, because of the large crowds of people using the same roads and paths.

About a mile after the lighthouse, past the dunes, turn left on the second street. At the time of this writing, it was unmarked. You'll travel alongside the Great South Bay and through the small town of Kismet. At the end of the road, turn right, and notice the convenience store and restaurant. During the summer you may dine outside, but in the winter both may be closed. Continue through town on the wooden boardwalk, which is characteristic of the roads in these towns. Proceed past a tiny boat basin on your left, turn right at the end, and proceed up the paved road to the dirt road. Turn left onto the dirt road, heading in the direction of Saltaire. There is a sign posted welcoming you in and providing a list of rules you must follow when you are visiting. The 6-foot-wide wooden boardwalks crisscrossing throughout the town of Saltaire are a lot of fun to explore. Turn left onto Surf Street, and pass by some beautiful cottages. Head in the direction of the Great South Bay, and at the end of the path turn right onto Bay Street, which parallels the Great South Bay. Open views of the Robert Moses and Captree Bridges and the bay can be seen from this street. Continue along this street past several boardwalk avenues. There is a village market on Broadway that is generally closed during the winter months. Turn right onto Pacific and then left onto Lighthouse Road. This will take you toward Fair Harbor. Continue straight through Fair Harbor, although you may wish to explore the tiny streets that crisscross through town. The road will change into a jeep trail after Lonelyville. As you pass through the town of Atlantique, visit some stunning beaches half a mile away along the Atlantic Ocean side. Park and lock your bike, and walk a couple of blocks to the ocean on your right. After Atlantique the jeep trail swings north into Robins Rest. Stay on the main jeep trail in an easterly direction. In about a quarter mile, you approach the town of Ocean Beach. At the time of this writing, the roads were semi-paved. Continue through Ocean Beach, and take the last right after the town of Seaview. Make the second left, going east, and then the third right. Turn left at the next path, continue straight through the town of Ocean Bay Park, and end your journey in Point o' Woods. Return the way you came to your car via Lighthouse Street. If you become disoriented by all the roads, just remember to keep heading west.

Navy Cooperative Area Trails

The remote, multiuse Navy Cooperative Area is an extremely popular spot for local hunters. For mountain bikers who do not live in the neighborhood, this little-known area offers an interesting assortment of trail options. The easy riding enables the biker to explore an attractive pine-barren woodscape in a portion of Long Island off the beaten path. Only 60 miles east of New York City, the 1,657 acres of forested land include more than 13 miles of wide, sandy, four-wheel-drive dirt roads. The fairly level riding does not require any special technical skills, enabling beginners to get into some secluded woods and test their emerging skills without being too technically engaged. The more experienced can get in some fast riding and blast along the doubletrack.

The hard-packed paths weave throughout a mixed habitat of typical eastern Long Island pine barrens and oak woodlands. There are several attractive ponds and lakes in the area along the trail. There is no formal entrance, but a multitude of roadside parking areas provide easy access.

All access is prohibited on the Navy Cooperative Area lands except under permit from the Department of Environmental Conservation. Mail away for the permit application. It costs $6.00 and is valid for three years. The area is open to hunters during designated seasons. Call the Department of Environmental Conservation at (631) 444–0273 or 444–0310 to find out dates. During this period, you should try riding elsewhere, or your mountain bike bar-ends could wind up mounted next to some trophy antlers.

General location: Manorville, Suffolk County, exit 69 off the Long Island Expressway.

Elevation change: Negligible.

Season: Hunters may be present from September 15 to April 16, with the highest concentration from November through January. Call the Department of Environmental Conservation for more detailed information.

Services: At exit 70, south on Route 111, there is a service station and some restaurants with great munchies. My favorite is Grace's.

Hazards: The hunting season is usually from November 1 through December 31 and parts of January into February. Call the Department of Environmental Conservation for more detailed information. A few paved-road links require care when traveling on them.

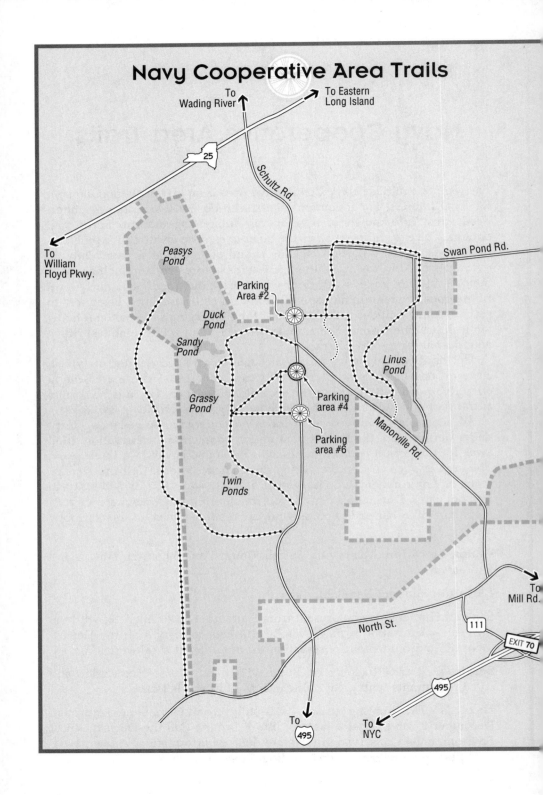

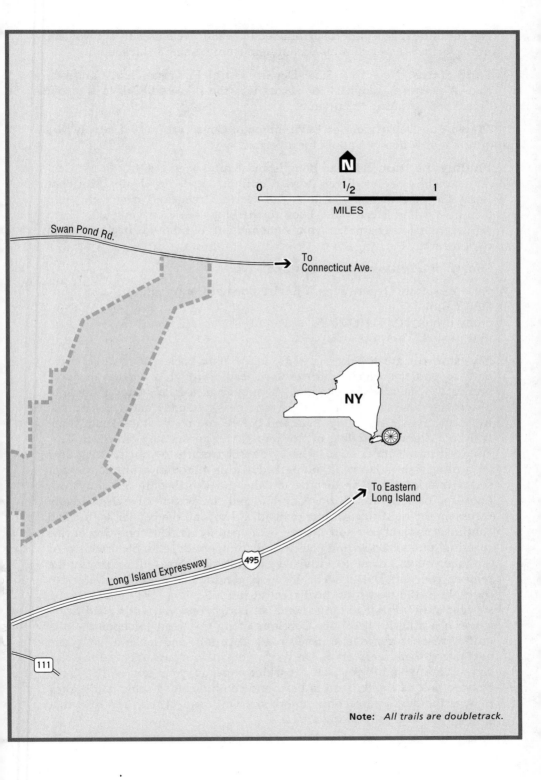

Swan Pond Rd.

To
Connecticut Ave.

N

0   1/2   1

MILES

NY

To Eastern
Long Island

Long Island Expressway   495

111

Note: *All trails are doubletrack.*

Rescue index: The park is surrounded by well-traveled roads, and you are never farther than half a mile from help from passing vehicles.

Land status: New York State Department of Environmental Conservation. A permit is required for access into the preserve. Call to find out details for acquiring the permit.

Maps: The Department of Environmental Conservation will supply you with a map when you apply for a permit.

Finding the trail: Take the Long Island Expressway east to exit 69, Center Moriches/Wading River Road. Continue north on Center Moriches Road. Go past the intersection with North Street, and bear right onto Schultz–Wading River Road. Look for parking area 4 on your left. There are several parking areas on your right and left, but the ride begins beyond parking area 4.

Source of additional information:

New York State Department of Environmental Conservation
SUNY Building 40
Stony Brook, NY 11790-2356
(631) 444–0273 or 444–0310

Notes on the trail: Take the wide, sandy, hard-packed four-wheel-drive path beyond the wooden barrier as it leads through a narrow meadow bordered by stands of white pine. In about half a mile, you will come to a four-way intersection. Turn right, and pass by Sandy and Duck Ponds. Right after you pass Sandy Pond and before you reach Duck Pond, there will be a dirt road leading off to the right in an easterly direction. This will lead into Schultz Road, where you may return to your parking area by turning right—that is, if you parked at area 4. You may link to another set of interior roads by turning left, heading north onto Schultz Road. Look for parking area 2 on your left and the wooden barrier directly across on the right side of Schultz Road. Go beyond the barrier as the road continues straight past some overgrown open fields. The condition of this road is a lot less sandy, and you can rely on more dependable cruising. At 0.2 mile you will come to a four-way intersection. You will return via the road on your left, but to begin this loop, continue straight ahead. Keep to the right at the next fork, bear right at the following fork, and continue straight until you get to Linus Pond. At Linus Pond look for a road heading in a northerly direction. Continue along this road for about 1 mile until it reaches a two-lane paved road. Turn left, and make a left at the next paved-road intersection. On your right you will pass a fenced-in property. Continue until you see a parking area on your left with a large wooden pole as a gate. Turn in here, and continue along some fields. Turn right at the next intersection, where you will connect with the road that you started on from parking area 2.

My daughter Alize is well prepared for a winter's day sojourn at the Navy Cooperative Area.

Across from parking area 6, on the east side of Schultz Road, is a 2-mile out-and-back (1-mile one-way) road. It is worth checking out, so head down for a short spell. Go beyond the wooden barrier, and bear left. There is a short circular dirt road on your right. Try it. After you have completed the tiny loop, look for a road on your left heading in an easterly direction. This 4-foot-wide hard-packed trail leads first through a pine forest; you will notice more hardwoods as you get closer to the swamp, where the trail ends. Some singletrack paths leading off to your left in a northerly direction may be worth exploring if you have the time. Return to Schultz Road along this path.

Surf and Turf

Mountain biking at Hither Hills is a mixed bag through an endless network of trails. Situated between Amagansett and Montauk on far eastern Long Island, the number of off-road opportunities makes up for the long drive it may require to get there. It's 90 miles from the New York City line. The riding includes everything from easy cruising on old, abandoned, semipaved roads and smooth, gentle, grassy doubletracks to tight, twisting, roller-coaster singletrack. Hither Hills is 1,700 acres of playland for hikers, equestrians, mountain bikers, and bathers. A public beach nearby is part of the park and provides a great opportunity to cool off in some surf after hard work in the turf. The hilly terrain of the park stands out in the flat landscape of the agricultural plains of the surrounding countryside and offers epic adventures through its variety of terrain.

A winding singletrack from a dense oak and pine forest skirts the long line of bluffs facing Napeague Bay, offering wide panoramic vistas. Pause a moment, and consider the impression this primeval wilderness might have made on the Native Americans who first discovered it or the first European person who landed on these shores years later.

These bluffs and the surrounding hilly landscape of the park owe their convoluted formation to the glacial moraine that was left behind by the retreating glaciers of the last Ice Age thousands of years ago. The flat land, which was formed by the melting waters of the glaciers, provides a good contrast to the hills. They mark where the glaciers paused and released their huge boulders and glacial debris. Hither Hills was originally an island separated by an open sea. The westward-trending currents of the Atlantic Ocean transported sediments eroded from Montauk Point. A long sleeve of sand extending westward from Hither Hills was built up. This body of land points in the direction of Amagansett, which eventually attached Hither Hills Island to the mainland of Long Island.

The scenery is excellent, the riding is fun yet challenging, and there is enough to fill up an entire day. Water is on all sides. Do not pass up an opportunity to combine a hard, sweaty tour of the hills with a cool, refreshing swim in the Atlantic Ocean. What more could there be?

General location: Eastern tip of Long Island, after Amagansett and before Montauk Point on Montauk Highway.

Elevation change: Elevations rarely exceed 100 feet, but there are many ups and downs throughout the hilly landscape that will challenge the hardy and give a good workout.

Season: Year-round opportunities exist, except when the trails are covered with snow. Don't let winter's cold stop you; just put on more clothing and enjoy the solitude of having popular trails all to yourself.

Services: This state park is a multiple-use area and provides camping and swimming at the adjacent public beach. A campground with 165 sites, showers, rest rooms, and telephones is located along the Atlantic Ocean in the park off Old Montauk Highway. There are some great surf-and-turf restaurants along Montauk Highway just west of the park entrance.

Hazards: Some of the singletrack travels through low underbrush, so if you are wearing shorts and riding during the warmer seasons, give yourself a once-over for ticks. While riding along the route, stay on the trail to prevent tire punctures from the park's many thornbushes.

Rescue index: You are never far from major paved roads.

Land status: New York State Park.

Maps: Pick up a trail map at the park's gatehouse when entering the park on Old Montauk Highway.

Finding the trail: Take the Long Island Expressway east for about 65 miles to exit 70, Manorville. Proceed south on County Road 111 and then go east on Sunrise Highway, New York 27, toward Montauk. Continue through Southampton, Water Mill, Bridgehampton, East Hampton, and Amagansett. The highway splits and forks right onto Old Montauk Highway (Route 27A), where you'll find the campground and beach section of Hither Hills State Park. The left fork takes the direct route into Montauk. Fork left, and after the sign reading OVERLOOK 1,200 FEET turn off Montauk Highway into the parking area on the left.

Sources of additional information:

Bike Hampton
36 Main Street
Sag Harbor, NY 11963
(631) 725–7329
www.bikehampton.com

Hither Hills State Park
50 South Fairview Avenue
Montauk, NY 11954
(631) 668–2554

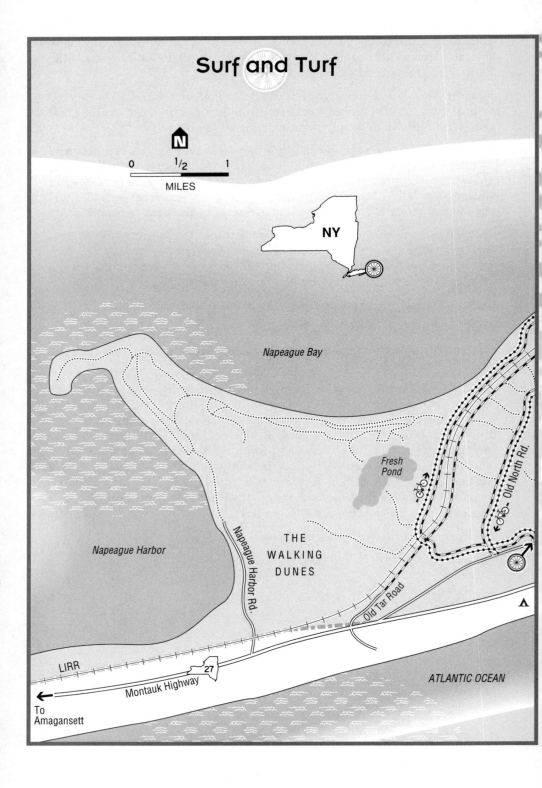

Surf and Turf

N

0   1/2   1
MILES

NY

Napeague Bay

Fresh
Pond

Napeague Harbor

Napeague Harbor Rd.

THE
WALKING
DUNES

Old North Rd.

Old Tar Road

LIRR

27

Montauk Highway

To
Amagansett

ATLANTIC OCEAN

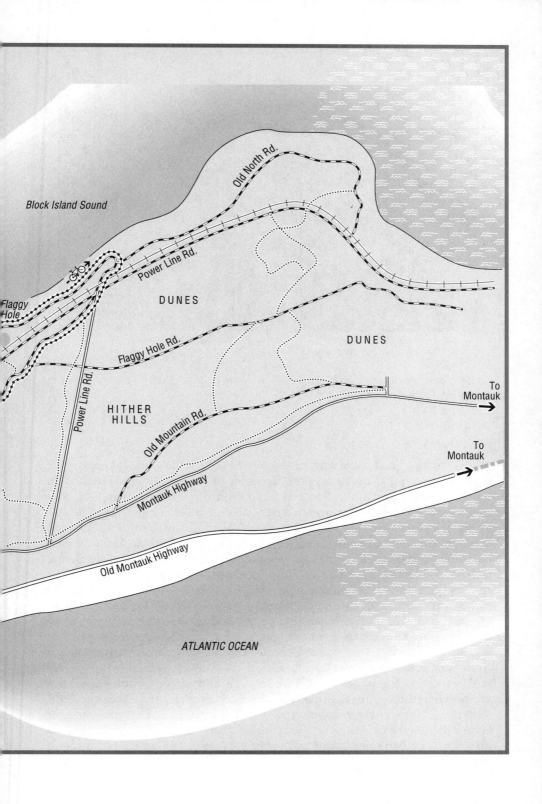

View of Napeague Bay at Hither Hills State Park.

Long Island State Park Region
Belmont Lake State Park
P.O. Box 247
Babylon, NY 11702
(631) 669–1000

Notes on the trail: Standing in the overlook parking area, face the park sign. To your left in a northwest direction lies a small, singletrack path leading down a small hill. Proceed straight through a three-way fork, and then descend a steep hill through a dense wood of small oak trees. The singletrack ends at a sandy, doubletrack dirt road. Turn right, and bear left through some large boulders that block another doubletrack. You will pass by some birdhouses and then end on Old Tar Road in a little more than a mile. You can recognize Old Tar Road because it was originally paved but now is quite broken up. Turn right, and then make a quick left over the railroad tracks. Make sure you look for trains. Proceed into a small opening in the woods on the other side of the tracks. Once you have entered the forest, make the first right onto a singletrack path that runs parallel to the railroad tracks. This portion of the trail is quite pleasant; you can do some nice cruising over rolling, grass-covered singletrack.

After about a mile you will come to a group of four boulders with a white painted blaze marked on one. Proceed through, and make the right onto the dirt road, which soon comes to a T intersection. Continue straight across the wide road onto the singletrack directly in front of you that leads up a small embankment. You will cover some nice rolling terrain through a heavily wooded forest and may catch glances of Napeague Bay to your left. After a steep descent this trail will merge with another from the left. Continue straight where the trail leads to the bay, and make a right after you come out to it. Ride along the trail as it proceeds between wooden stakes with white paint on them. The bay is on your left. You will eventually head back into the forest and climb two steep, sandy hills, one right after another. You have one choice: Walk your bike. Farther ahead a steep downhill will take your breath away, and you will end at a T intersection. Turn right to cross over the railroad tracks. From the four boulders you have covered approximately 2.5 miles. Look for a short, narrow, uphill trail to the left of a birdhouse; take this, and it will empty you onto the doubletrack Old North Road. Take Old North Road for a little more than 3 miles. Continue all the way to a T intersection. Turn left onto Montauk Highway, which lies just east of the overlook parking area.

Northwest by Northwest

This manicured, 4-mile, out-and-back singletrack is a must-do for anyone who travels out to the Hamptons. Located just north of East Hampton off a quiet road, the pine-needle path twists and turns along a gently rolling terrain. The area is populated with dense forests of large white pine and oak, which is characteristic of the northern section of the South Fork of Long Island. These mature stands of conifers and hardwoods provide a high canopy and much-needed shade during the hot summer months. The lack of the thick, low-lying shrubbery that is often prevalent in these forests gives a sense of space, visibility, and freedom for a cerebral experience in the pure pleasures of backcountry bike riding. A different, less pastoral reality returns when you cross a paved road.

The wide singletrack is not technically challenging, and its smoothness, good condition, and gentle, rolling grade facilitates a sort of out-of-saddle experience. On this trail you do not have to try hard to feel great and ride the perfect line. The out-and-back path leads through a thick, primeval forest, and as the pace sets in, as you get into that groove, the maneuvering around the many twists and turns produces a Zenlike sensation, a feeling that's difficult to describe or pinpoint. There's no overbraking and no oversteering, and the tires are carving like skates. You come out of corners with just enough momentum, and it almost feels as though the trail is controlling the bike and you are just along for the ride.

General location: Approximately 90 miles from Manhattan, just north of East Hampton, Long Island.

Elevation change: Small rolling hills take you through elevations of less than 100 feet.

Season: Year-round riding opportunities exist, except when the trails are covered by snow. Do not let winter's cold stop you though; just put on more clothing and enjoy the solitude and satisfaction of having popular trails all to yourself.

Services: Most services can be found along Montauk Highway (New York 27). The village of East Hampton has it all and provides food, window shopping, ice cream, movie theaters, and a busy sidewalk strip of white-shorts-and-sneakers–clad summer vacationers.

Hazards: Although you are not scraping past low undergrowth shrubbery, it is always a good idea to check yourself for ticks. Low pine branches overhang, and you may need to duck under them, so keep your eyes in front of your helmeted head.

Rescue index: Suburban and vacation communities surround the area. Help is never more than half a mile away.

Land status: The trail follows the Northwest Path, which traverses the northwest area in the town of East Hampton.

Maps: The map in this book provides a good view of this singletrack.

Finding the trail: Take the Long Island Expressway east for about 65 miles to exit 70, Manorville. Proceed south on County Road 111, and then go east on Sunrise Highway (NY 27) for approximately 27 miles, until you reach the Village of East Hampton. After you pass signs for the Village of East Hampton, make a left (north) onto Stephen Hands Path. After 2 miles turn left onto Bull Path, and head north. The trail appears on your right as a small dirt path leading through some trees, about 1.5 miles north of your turnoff from Stephen Hands Path. The trailhead begins directly across from address 100 and just before a sign for Fielers Close. A small turnout up ahead from the trailhead provides some parking.

By train, take the Long Island Railroad to East Hampton. Turn right onto Railroad Avenue, right onto Cooper, and left onto Newtown Lane. Proceed for about 1.5 miles, where the road name changes to Long Lane. Turn right onto Stephen Hands Path, and take the next left onto Bull Path. Follow the remaining directions above.

Sources of additional information:

East Hampton Chamber of Commerce
37 Main Street
East Hampton, NY 11937
(631) 324–0362
www.easthamptonchamber.com

Bike Hampton
36 Main Street
Sag Harbor, NY 11963
(631) 725–7329
www.bikehampton.com

Notes on the trail: Yellow triangles posted on trees mark this well-groomed trail. The trail is straight and fairly easy to follow, with few spur trails to confuse you.

The ride begins through a predominantly conifer forest mixed with oak. You will soon come to a detour that was posted to direct mountain bikers to the left. The section of the path that leads off to your right has been temporarily closed because of its crossing private land and a request by the

Northwest by Northwest

N

0   1/2   1
MILES

Alewive Brook Rd.

Scoys Pond

Barcelona Point

NY

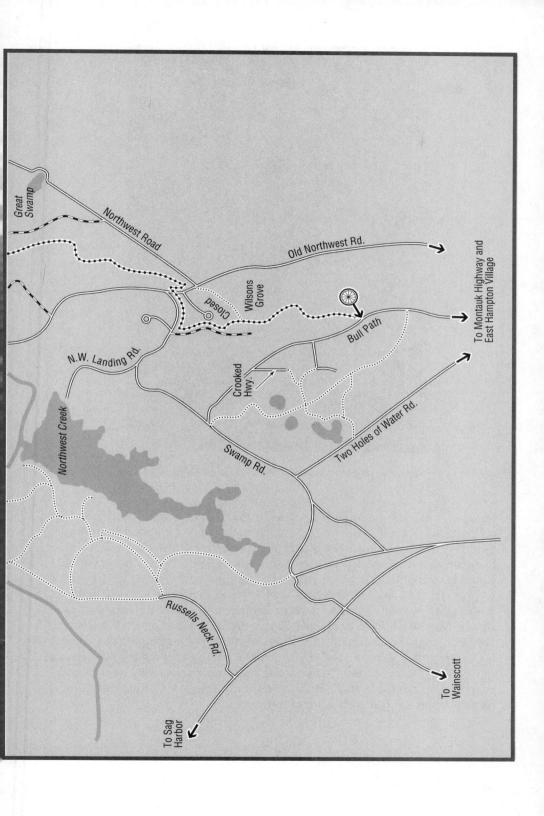

Prime singletrack weaves its way through the Northwest Path.

landowners that the mountain bike traffic bypass their properties. So respectfully, we must bear left. Soon bear right onto a wider doubletrack path that leads you out onto paved N.W. Landing Road. You will be able to reconnect with the Northwest Path by turning right onto N.W. Landing Road. Pass Highland Lane on your left, and then bear right at the next fork to proceed onto Old Northwest Road. After passing Cattle Walk Road on your right, you will come to another intersection. This is where you pick up the Northwest Path that leads diagonally between the two intersecting roads on your left facing north. The half-mile of rolling singletrack ends at a T intersection. After a quick right, make a left, and follow the singletrack to another T intersection. Make a left onto the doubletrack at this intersection, and continue straight. Turn right, and return to Bull Path on the same singletrack trail you were on before.

Caumsett State Park

Seeking a long day of easy riding? Set your wheels down on the secluded former estate of the Marshall Field family for an 8-mile loop. More than 15 miles of hard-packed wide dirt roads and bridle paths form an interesting network on 1,500 acres of rolling terrain. Located at Lloyd Neck in the town of Huntington, the land was purchased in 1921 by Marshall Field III, grandson of the famous department store pioneer. Field built a self-sufficient English-style rural estate that was a combination country club, hunting preserve, and home. Establishing a herd of eighty head of prize cattle, a complete dairy farm, and vegetable gardens, his self-sufficient, self-contained community had its own water and electrical supply. Wood products came from the estate's own stands of oak, pine, dogwood, and locust. Caumsett was originally in the hands of the Long Island Matinecock Indians and is translated as "place by a sharp rock." Situated on a scenic peninsula extending into the Long Island Sound, the state park is bordered by towering bluffs and a sandy pebble beach extending to the water's edge. Several paths lead to the shore, where you can park your bike, jump in the sound, and cool off or just sit on the pebbly beach and watch the boats drift by.

Caumsett State Park has a full spectrum of rides for everybody. Most trails are well maintained, wide, smooth, and a joy to ride. There is enough variety for the beginner to learn some basic handling and endurance skills, and the more experienced rider will find some fast doubletrack. Woodland roads and bridle paths are all available and provide for some great cruising through the park's woodlands, meadows, and salt marshes. This tour consists of an 8-mile loop that will introduce you to the park. Equestrians, walkers, and bike riders gladly share the trails, and only when there is a special equestrian event do the park rangers expect the mountain bikes to stay off the race trails.

General location: Lloyd Neck, town of Huntington.

Elevation change: The paths meander over fairly level ground with some minor hills. The only climbs are when you ascend away from the shoreline to the level of the bluffs, which represent the overall level of the park land.

Season: Year-round could almost be guaranteed if not for the occasional blanket of snow, which makes the area ideal for cross-country skiers.

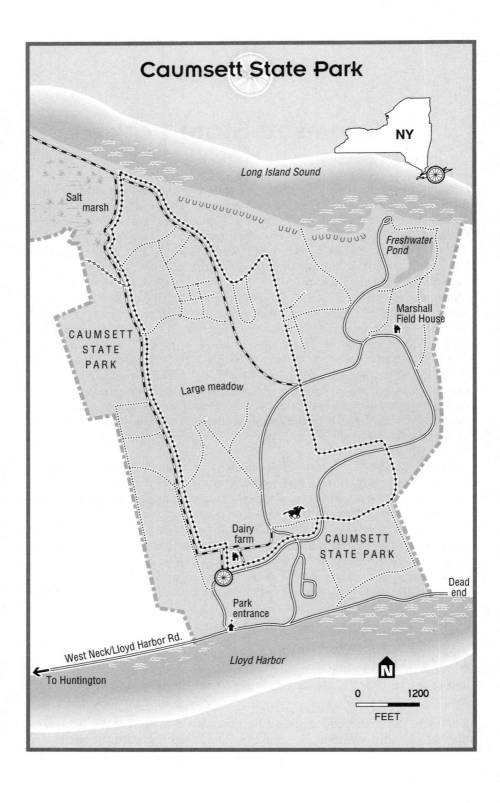

Services: Huntington provides all the services you might need along New York 25A.

Hazards: You will encounter horses and hikers on the same trails, so display a mutual respect and courtesy for them, and this beautiful park will remain a recreation area for all to enjoy. The ticks like mountain bikers, too, and will cling to your clothing or skin regardless of whether they know you or not. There is a large population of ticks, common throughout Long Island. Signs throughout the park indicate this little bugger's presence.

Be careful not to get too close to the 100-foot bluffs that overlook the sound. They continually erode, become extremely unstable, and crash down to the shore.

Rescue index: The park is well traveled, and you are never more than 1 or 2 miles from the parking area. Just find a paved road and take it in any direction, and it will soon lead to one of the estate's buildings or the park office.

Land status: Long Island Region of the New York State Office of Parks, Recreation, and Historic Preservation.

Maps: A well-defined and detailed map is provided at the park entrance before you arrive at the parking area.

Finding the trail: Take Northern State Parkway east to the NY 106/107 exit. Go north on NY 106, and turn right on NY 25A (Northern Boulevard). Take NY 25A past the town of Cold Spring Harbor, and turn left (north) onto West Neck Road at the light; go for approximately 4 miles. Travel over a narrow strip of land that has Oyster Bay on your left and part of Lloyd Harbor to your right. The road will curve to the right, and you should look for the park sign in about a quarter mile. Turn left into the park. The park is open from 8:00 A.M. to 4:30 P.M. daily. There is an entrance fee of $4.00 per vehicle from Memorial Day through Labor Day.

Sources of additional information:

Caumsett State Park
25 Lloyd Harbor Road
Huntington, NY 11743
(516) 423–1770

Bikeworks Ltd.
7 Northern Boulevard
Greenvale, NY 11548-1204
(516) 484–4422

Notes on the trail: Turn right from the parking area. Proceed past the sign AUTHORIZED VEHICLES ONLY BEYOND THIS POINT and a mall kiosk with Caumsett State Park information on it, and turn left onto the cobblestone road that passes between the dairy farm and some maintenance garages.

High bluffs overlook Long Island Sound at Caumsett State Park.

At the end of the road you have two choices. To the left you can take the Fishing Drive for 2 miles north until it reaches the shore of the Long Island Sound. From the shore you can connect with another road that will take you back in a southerly direction to explore the eastern half of the park.

Making a right turn on the trail, after the dairy barn, leads you through the eastern portion of the park. There are several loops worth exploring to your left as you head down the paved road. The park map lays out the basic trail network, and you can just pick out an area and explore it. The trail description I have outlined below is an 8-mile loop and will take you on a grand tour of the park.

At the end of the dairy barn road, turn left where you see the sign for Fishing Drive. The name is derived from the route all the local fishermen take to the shoreline to fish. Continue past open meadows on your left and right. Soon the road curves north, and you gently descend a flat, hard-packed, dirt road for 1.6 miles to the Long Island Sound. The road begins a small climb into a wooded area of beech and oak. You will soon emerge and pass another large meadow on your right. Several bridle paths lead off this main road. They are clearly marked with white signs with a horse in the center. For this grand tour continue straight on the wide road, and enter a dense woodland of vine-enshrouded mature oaks. In half a mile the salt marsh will begin appearing to your left. Stop at the fine lookout point overlooking the marsh before you begin the last descent to the shore. The road ends at the fishermen's parking area. There is an interesting trail to your left beyond a metal fenced gate. You'll ride along a narrow, raised, sandy road that traverses above a marsh and includes tremendous open views of the Long Island Sound to the right. Notice small, sand-colored shorebirds called piping plovers, which scurry along the beach. These tiny birds once nested and thrived along the sandy beaches of the entire Atlantic coast. Human demands for these areas have won the competition for suitable habitat and squeezed out these tiny birds. The road ends in 0.75 mile at a small harbor.

Return along this road to the fishermen's parking area. Notice the tall bluffs and huge boulders dotting the shoreline. Before the glaciers arrived during the last Ice Age, the Long Island Sound was actually a large valley with a stream flowing to the east in it. Glaciation scooped out the river valley and dumped the debris on the surface of the island, building the bluffs and gently sloping land.

Once in the parking area, notice the DO NOT ENTER sign straight ahead in an easterly direction. Proceed in that direction ascending away from the beach up a short, steep hill. The trail levels off in 0.3 mile, and you'll see a small road leading to a bluff overlooking the sound. Be careful not to get too close, as these bluffs continually erode and crash down to the shore.

The riding levels out and passes through a vine-covered forest. After 0.4 mile, you arrive at a fork. Bear left onto the four-wheel-drive jeep road. This connects you to a quadrant of bridle paths. Ironically you will see a sign reading NO HORSEBACK RIDING BEYOND THIS POINT. You soon arrive at a three-pronged fork. Take the middle one. (The left fork leads down to the beach, and the right fork goes to the bridle paths.) The road turns grassy and curves to your right. Continue straight for 0.7 mile through a gentle, rolling, forested landscape. You arrive at an intersection with a well-paved road. Continue over that road and straight down another bridle path. Take this to its end, and turn left onto another four-wheel-drive road. Ride alongside a large field for about 1,600 feet, and at the end of the field you will arrive at a clearing and an intersection with a paved road. Turn right onto the paved road, and take another quick left to descend another bridle path. At the next fork, bear right up a gentle slope ending in a short, steep climb. You will come out onto a paved road. Turn left on the paved road, continue past two intersections, and arrive back at the parking area.

Northern
New Jersey Tours

Those who are not familiar with the state have an image of New Jersey as an industrial wasteland. Far from the oil refineries and heavily industrialized sections are rich, low-lying, forested mountains and an abundance of fine mountain biking trails. Old lumber and carriage roads and single-tracked forest paths lace the northern New Jersey region. These hilly mountains offer a gamut of riding possibilities and a chance to explore the beautiful, historic, rugged woodlands. Some of these old roads and footpaths existed before the acquisition of the land for public use. Some trails date back to the Depression, when a federal program to help unemployment fostered the Civilian Conservation Corps. Public works projects spawned park and recreation facilities as viable today as when they were first constructed in the 1930s.

The beauty of mountain biking in the Garden State lies in its variety of terrain, from the flat, nineteenth-century mining and logging roads to the hilly and rocky highlands in the north. In between are swamps, woods, and grasslands.

Geologists divide the state into four primary regions. In the northwest the Appalachian Ridge and Valley Province contains the highest elevations in the state and cuts a diagonal running southwest to northeast. Here, in what was once a major mountain range (since leveled by erosion), are a series of parallel valleys and ridges composed of sandstones and conglomerates approximately 400 million years old. The Ridge and Valley Province extends more than 1,200 miles from Alabama to Canada and, because of its regularity, is used as a navigational landmark by migrating birds. Hawk sightings along the main ridges are common during the fall migration. Stokes State Forest and High Point State Park together preserve nearly all the mountainous portions of this province.

Southeast and parallel to the Ridge and Valley Province lies the New Jersey Highlands Province. This area is composed of rocks that are 800 million years old—more ancient than those of the Ridge and Valley Province. The flat-topped summits of this province lie a few hundred feet lower than those in the Kittatinny Mountains. This mountain range extends north into New York as the Hudson Highlands and south into Pennsylvania as the Reading Prong. Numerous lakes and reservoirs grace state and county parks, including the large Wawayanda State Park, as well as the vast holdings of the Newark Watershed Conservation and Development Corporation, which supplies drinking water. Both parks have miles and miles of trails.

Sources of additional information:

Ramapo Valley Cycling Club, Inc.
P.O. Box 240
Oakland, NJ 07436
www.rvccmtb.com

New Jersey Division of Travel and Tourism
20 West State Street, CN826
Trenton, NJ 08625-0826
(609) 292–2470
(800) JERSEY7
www.state.nj.us/travel/

Allamuchy Mountain State Park

Allamuchy State Park, with its 12 miles of forest roads and singletrack, is a place worth seeking out. Riding is a mixed bag, including everything from easy cruising on well-graded forest roads to challenging opportunities on an equal number of singletrack.

A convenient network of old farm and lumber roads winds through this secluded and relatively unknown New Jersey State Park, only 50 miles from Manhattan, providing a pleasant mountain biking experience for riders of all levels. Plenty of hills and lively singletracks challenge the average hammerhead, with as much cruising material to go around for the less technically inclined. A wide, hard-packed forest road penetrates the Allamuchy forest and ends at Deer Park Pond just 4 miles later. Several other trails head off into the woods and pass through more densely forested habitat.

The rugged areas of northern New Jersey have a reputation for history, picturesque landscapes, and outdoor recreation opportunities. Allamuchy Mountain State Park is a prime example of this combination of culture, scenery, and activities. The trails pass through more than 4,000 acres of oak hardwood and hemlock-spruce forests and northern marshlands. Replanting projects from thirty years ago have helped certain acreage to regrow and flourish. These areas are known as succession fields and help to retain the natural habitat of the forest. The diversification of wildlife flourishes throughout this rich forest and supports an active population of animals. Deer Park Pond boasts a large group of beavers, and several of their lodges can be seen from the shoreline. Ducks, Canada geese, and osprey nest at the lake as well. A large white-tailed deer population makes this an ideal spot for hunting. Bow hunting is the only sanctioned hunting sport during the regular hunting season.

The first inhabitants of this rugged area were the Delaware Indians. The region was named after their leader, Chief Allamuchahokkingen, whose name translates as "place within the hills." Of course that was a mouthful, and the name of the first settlement in 1715 was changed to Mamuchahoken and then finally to Allamuchy. The majority of the land that composes Allamuchy Mountain State Park was part of the Rutherford and Stuyvesant estates. These families are distinguished as the direct descendants of Peter Stuyvesant, the last governor of New Amsterdam.

A good amount of riding can be done in this park, so gear yourself up and come prepared for a full day of sizzling road and track.

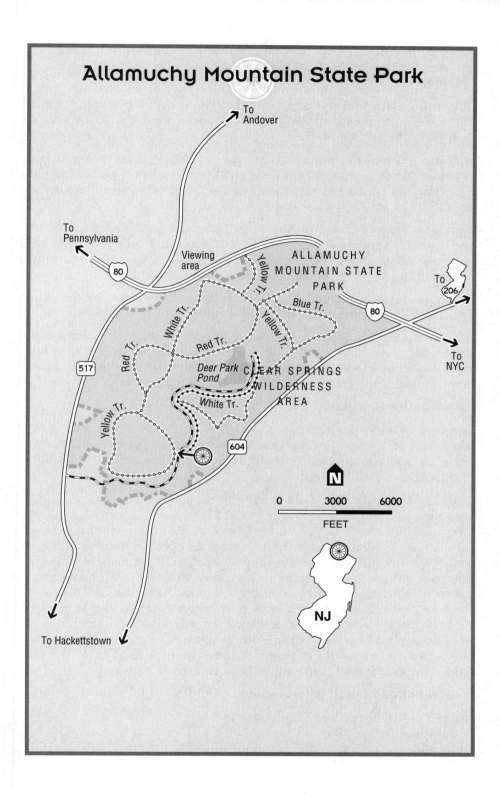

Allamuchy Mountain State Park

To
Andover

To
Pennsylvania

Viewing
area

80

ALLAMUCHY
MOUNTAIN STATE
PARK

To
206

Yellow Tr.

Blue Tr.

White Tr.

Red Tr.

Yellow Tr.

80

Red Tr.

Red Tr.

To
NYC

Deer Park
Pond

517

CLEAR SPRINGS
WILDERNESS
AREA

Yellow Tr.

White Tr.

604

N

0   3000   6000

FEET

To Hackettstown

NJ

General location: The park is approximately 50 miles west on Interstate 80 from the George Washington Bridge and 10 miles south of the town of Andover.

Elevation change: The forest trails traverse up and down with a maximum elevation change of 200 feet. The general elevation of the area is between 800 and 1,000 feet.

Season: The trails in the winter provide excellent cross-country skiing, providing there is snow. Under these conditions, the trails are unrideable. However, once the snow melts, get out there and explore this wonderful park.

Services: Ten miles north of Allamuchy State Park on County Road 517 in the town of Andover is Andover Cycles Center and some food and gas services. Allamuchy Mountain and Stephens State Parks provide fishing opportunities year-round and make a great spot to cast a line.

Hazards: Parts of Allamuchy Mountain State Park are available for hunting. Call the park office for information on the current hunting season.

Rescue index: Some trails receive a fair amount of traffic. Encounters with other trail users may be frequent, especially during the weekend, as this park has become increasingly popular with mountain bikers. A pair of bow hunters helped me get to know the forest trails during one of my visits.

Land status: New Jersey State Park.

Maps: Call the park office to see if they can send you a park map in the mail. This park map provides some good coverage of the area. Allamuchy State Park is also covered by the USGS 7.5-minute series, Tranquillity quadrangle.

Finding the trail: Take I–80 west from the George Washington Bridge and then take exit 19; turn south on CR 517 toward Hackettstown. After about 2 miles on CR 517, look for Deer Park Road, an unimproved dirt access road. It comes up on the left immediately past an Italian restaurant called Mattars. Drive 0.7 mile over some small hills and many potholes to the park entrance, which leads to a parking area. You will see a brown wooden park sign indicating ALLAMUCHY NATURAL AREA, ALLAMUCHY MOUNTAIN STATE PARK. There will be a large grass-covered parking area in another 50 feet. After you have parked and you are ready to roll, put your back to the parking area, and turn to face a small, brown, wooden shed. The yellow-blazed singletrack begins to your right beyond some short trees, and the wider, easier dirt road that leads to Deer Park Pond leads to your left.

Sources of additional information:

Allamuchy Mountain and Stephens State Park
Hackettstown, NJ 07840
(908) 852–3790

Foliage paints the forest of Allamuchy Mountain State Park with a bold hand.

Andover Cycle Center
Highway 206
Andover, NJ 07821
(973) 786–6350

Notes on the trail: Alternate rides can be assembled as you cruise on the easy 3.5-mile main dirt road, which leads down to Deer Park Pond, making this a total of 7 miles out and back. The principal trail that will be described is the main dirt road, but I will mention the other, more challenging rides throughout the description.

Two trails lead from the parking area: an easy, wide dirt road and a more difficult yellow-blazed, singletrack trail, which leads from the northwest section of the parking area. The yellow trail leads into the forest and then reconnects with the dirt road in a little more than 1.5 miles, making a loop.

As you begin your ride at the parking area for the easy ride, face the brown wooden shed, and turn left down the wide dirt road past a wooden sign indicating GREEN ACRES. There is a gradual ascent for about 1 mile through an open forest of oak. In another 0.4 mile you will approach parking area 1. Immediately before that the yellow trail that began from the parking area intersects. Continue on the wide dirt road, and pass by several field regrowth programs, known as succession fields and planted seventy-five years ago. In another 0.7 mile you arrive at the last parking area, 2. Continue straight on the wide road beyond a yellow metal road-bar gate. Immediately past the gate notice a white-painted, blazed trail leading to the north and away from the dirt road. You may take this white trail as it heads north for a little more than 1 mile. When you arrive at a wildlife-viewing area, continue on the white trail in an easterly direction. In a little less than 1 mile, bear right at the next fork. Remain on the white blazed trail, which then leads south. The white trail terminates at Deer Park Pond in about half a mile.

As you continue on the dirt road past this gate, the trail will swing to the east almost immediately. Begin a long, gradual descent through an attractive deciduous forest of oak and maple to Deer Park Pond. The road is marked with white markers on trees. One of the most striking feelings as you proceed through this section of the forest is the openness and the expansiveness of the terrain. The forest floor is nearly all ferns, particularly on the right, and above that is nothing but open space until the lowest branches of some very large trees are reached. As you ride on, a portion of the lake appears through the trees on the left. This is Deer Park Pond. Beavers have built lodges in the area, and the northern shore of the pond was completely denuded several years ago by these tree-felling, bark-chewing little mammals. You will notice some of their lodges around the pond. The road continues down to the pond over a dam and spillway and along the eastern shore. Notice the tall stands of hemlocks and pines right on the water. Thousands of acres of large hemlocks were decimated in the forests of northern New Jersey as well as in New York. Their bark was used for tanning leather products during the nineteenth century. It is rare to come across a stand of mature hemlocks.

The road ends at the lake, but there are several other trails that reach into the hills. Near the spillway the blue trail leads in a northeasterly direction and creates a loop that returns you to the lake. Take the blue trail up a small hill, passing the yellow trail and follow the blue trail for a little more than 1 mile. Take a left at the next T intersection, and go past the next left, turning left at the next white blazed trail, which leads you to the pond in a southerly direction. There is your loop. Return along the main wide dirt road.

14

High Point State Park

This dated north-south forest road trail rests along the crest of the Kittatinny Mountains located in Sussex County in the northwest corner of New Jersey. It passes through a very scenic forest packed with oaks, hickory, red maple, white ash, and young chestnut. The 14,056-acre state park is tantalizing, with its breathtaking scenery and breath-stealing doubletrack. High Point State Park within the Kittatinny Mountains boasts New Jersey's highest peak, High Point, at 1,803 feet, and a challenging doubletrack trail system. The dominating part of this tour is the 5-mile (one-way) Iris Trail (described below), but two other short trails are worth mentioning and exploring. The black-marked Ayers Trail is only 1.5 miles in length, passing an old farm built after the Civil War. The 1-mile, yellow-marked Mashipacong Trail traverses an old farm road lined with the foundations and stone fences of long-gone houses and farms and overgrown apple orchards. The not-too-difficult Iris Trail runs through deep woods on abandoned logging and farm roads that have resulted in rugged trails. The route serves as a popular snowmobile and cross-country ski trail in the winter. This tour is not for the weak of heart. Keep a light touch on the brakes; the trail requires some technical handling as you traverse the rocky surface of the eroded roadbeds.

The trail descends through a varied hardwood forest, crosses springs, and supplies a scenic overlook of picturesque Lake Rutherford. The return trip is demanding. An alternative could be the paved Deckertown Turnpike, County Road 650, and Sawmill Road, which, although just as steep, would avoid the ascent up the rocky Iris Trail.

Cool off during the summer in the spring-fed twenty-acre natural Lake Marcia, almost 1,600 feet above sea level. Lake Marcia also has changing areas, showers, and a food concession.

General location: High Point State Park is located in the extreme northwest corner of New Jersey along the ridge of the Kittatinny Mountains in Sussex County and extends from the New York state line southwesterly 8 miles, where it joins Stokes State Forest. It is approximately 70 miles from Manhattan.

Elevation change: The trail begins at approximately 1,500 feet and descends to Lake Rutherford at an elevation of 1,400 feet over 1.5 miles. The trail continues to descend over the next 3.5 miles to an elevation of 1,200 feet, whereupon you must turn around and head back up the trail.

High Point State Park

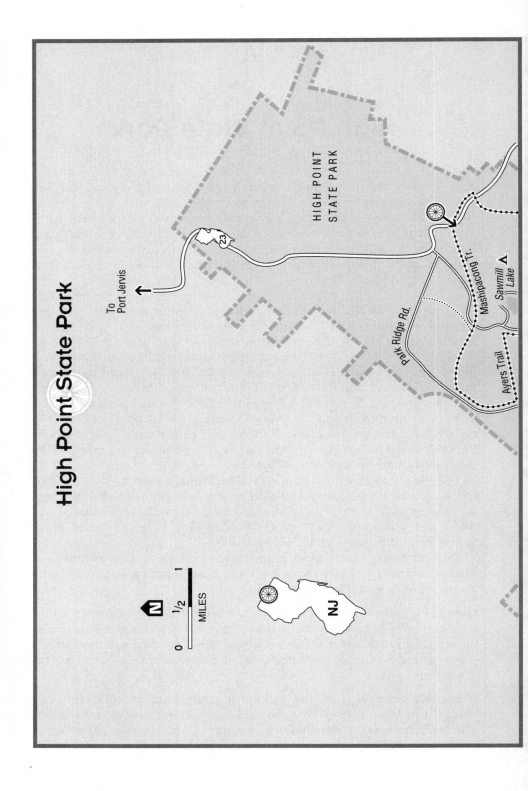

N

0   1/2   1
MILES

NJ

To
Port Jervis

23

HIGH POINT
STATE PARK

Park Ridge Rd.

Mashipacong Tr.

Sawmill
Lake ▲

Avers Trail

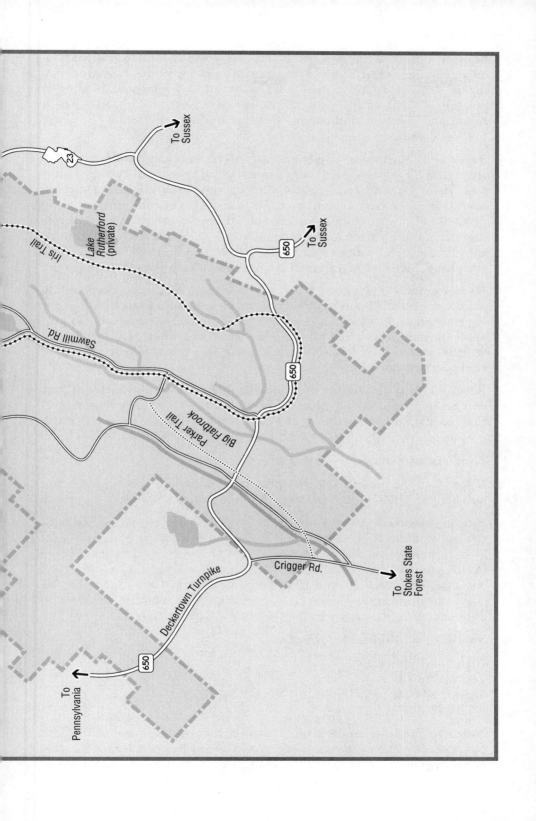

Season: Winter in this section of New Jersey and at these elevations usually guarantees snow, but cold weather has never kept me away from riding in the woods, so if there's no snow, I'd say year-round riding is possible. During early spring the trails tend to get wet from snowmelt runoff and rains, but a quick call to the park office will inform you of the trail conditions.

Services: A concession stand near Lake Marcia and the town of Sussex is located on New Jersey 23, 8 miles before the park, and provides most services. There are some excellent accommodations if you would like to camp overnight in the park. There are more than fifty tent campsites set along Sawmill Lake, with sanitary facilities and drinking water nearby. Reservations may also be made for two remotely located wilderness cabins on the shore of Steenykill Lake which are open from May 15 to October 15. They each have three bedrooms, a full kitchen, and a bathroom with hot water.

Hazards: Even though this is an old forest road, erosion has exposed an abundance of rocks and tree roots, so check your speed when encountering such areas. Ticks can be a problem if you go off the trail, so it is generally recommended that you stay on the trails. These are moderately strenuous trails, so before you set out, make sure you saddle up with some water and energy food.

Rescue index: An increase of activity on these trails occurs between May and September, and help from another trail user is usually available. A first-aid station is open during the summer near Lake Marcia, but it is a good idea to bring a small first-aid kit with you any time you ride.

Land status: New Jersey State Park.

Maps: Call the park to receive a park map in the mail, or wait until you get there and pick up one in the park headquarters building.

Finding the trail: Although far from New York City, the riding possibilities are well worth the trip. The park can be reached by beginning your 70-mile journey on Interstate 80 in New Jersey west from the George Washington Bridge. Take scenic NJ 23 north all the way to the park entrance, and turn left into High Point State Park. Lake Marcia can be reached by turning right into High Point State Park, but turn left into the park and leave your car near the park office headquarters on your left.

Source of additional information:

High Point State Park
1480 Route 23
Sussex, NJ 07461-3605
(973) 875–4800

Notes on the trail: At the southerly end of the parking area near the park office headquarters will be a small, brown, wooden shed used for the storage of firewood. Immediately beyond this shed a yellow-marked trail can

Uh, let's see, the sign says Chicago to the left and Boston to the right.

be seen leading off into the woods. Follow this trail for a short distance until it merges with a trail marked with painted white blazes. Bear right as the trails merge, and after 0.2 mile you will arrive at a three-way inter-section with yellow, red, and white marked trails. Take the leftmost wider trail marked with red disks. As a secondary reference there will also be a 3-foot-high cement marker with IRIS TRAIL painted on it. Secondary insur-ance always helps. The trail follows the rock-studded, eroded roadbed over rolling terrain and passes by Lake Rutherford. As you pass by Lake Rutherford, notice the stumps and rotten logs in and around the lake. These are all that remain from the American chestnut blight of the 1920s, which destroyed the great fruit-bearing chestnut forests of the northeast. The current chestnut tree has been stunted to a height of only 20 feet.

In the next 2.5 miles you will begin a more noticeable gradual descent to Deckertown Turnpike, CR 650. You may turn back the way you came or turn right onto Deckertown Turnpike, and in 2 miles turn right again onto Sawmill Road. Sawmill will take you back to NJ 23 and the park office headquarters. You may also want to try the two alternative rides that can be accessed from Sawmill Road.

The black-marked Ayers and yellow-marked Mashipacong trails are old farm roads that lead off to your left about 4 miles up Sawmill Road, past the second road leading from the Sawmill Lake camping area. Pass the Sawmill Lake camping area, and take a left onto Ayers Trail. The 1.5-mile Ayers Trail cuts through a large hardwood forest filled with oaks, hickory, red maple, and some young chestnut. You will pass through the fields and the site of Ayers farm built after the Civil War. The stone walls and fallen foundations are all that remain today. Take Ayers Trail until you come to a T intersection with paved Park Ridge Road. Turn right onto Park Ridge Road, and then after a mile, turn right onto the yellow-marked Mashipacong Trail, which then travels in an easterly direction. Mashipacong Trail is an old, well-used farm road that takes you through a large overgrown field, fence rows, and apple trees. Follow this trail all the way to NJ 23. It leaves you a short distance south of the park office headquarters.

The Labyrinth

There's a whole day's worth of cruising in the labyrinth of interconnecting trails in the 4,000-acre Ringwood State Park. With any spare time consider a tour of the historic Tudor mansions of Ringwood and Skylands and the botanical gardens.

This trail system, like a maze, consists of hard-packed nineteenth-century carriage roads leading through a beautiful wooded landscape with five attractive ponds. An 8-mile loop trail leads along an interesting yet challenging route that is also beginner friendly. It meanders through a moderately hilly landscape and doesn't require any special technical skills, but it gives the experienced mountain biker a good workout. The ride is also suited for novices ready to try something more demanding than a flat trail but seeking an endurance test on more hilly terrain. What once provided turn-of-the-twentieth-century visitors with a horse-drawn carriage tour through a beautiful woodland forest now enchants the mountain biker with stretches of demanding hill climbs, fast, descending doubletrack, and beautiful scenery.

Ringwood State Park is situated within the Hudson Highlands, a large, ancient mountain range that extends from Pennsylvania to Connecticut in a northeasterly direction. The range was formed more than 1 billion years ago when continents collided and caused a huge mountain system to rise along the North American coast. These mountains once looked similar to the Himalayas in Asia, but 500 million years of erosion have leveled them to their roots, which extend miles deep within the earth. The remaining hills and small mountains are the result of these roots getting pushed up and creating the Highlands.

The Hudson Highlands were mined from the eighteenth to twentieth centuries, bringing great wealth to the industrialists in this region. Forges and furnaces were constructed during the middle of the eighteenth century to supply the metal products crucial to the colonies. George Washington made Ringwood his headquarters on several occasions. Ownership of the land and mansions was passed on for generations. Ringwood Manor, located in the park and on the surrounding land, is a fine example of the splendor and wealth of the ironmasters of the nineteenth century. The botanical gardens were inspired by the classical designs on the grounds of the famous Palace of Versailles in France. Iron for munitions for every major armed conflict from the French and Indian War to World War I was forged here. The Ringwood iron mines operated intermittently from the

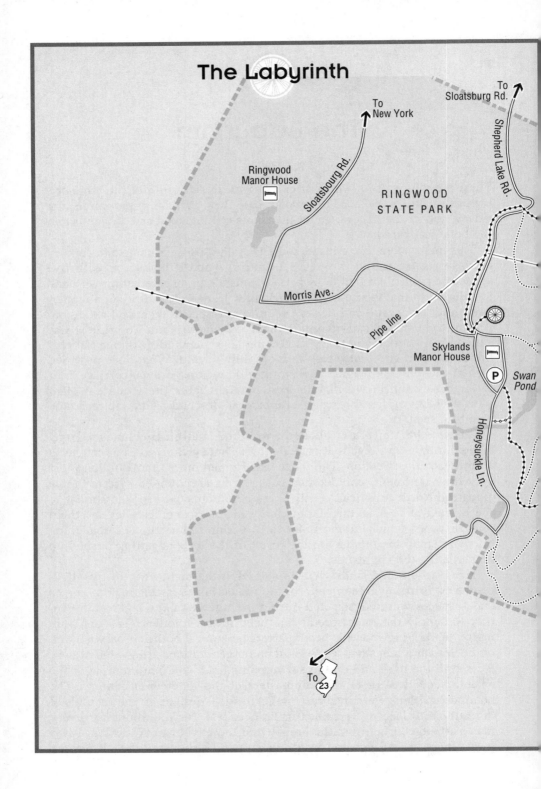

The Labyrinth

To New York

To Sloatsburg Rd.

Sloatsburg Rd.

Shepherd Lake Rd.

Ringwood Manor House

RINGWOOD STATE PARK

Morris Ave.

Pipe line

Skylands Manor House

P

Swan Pond

Honeysuckle Ln.

To 23

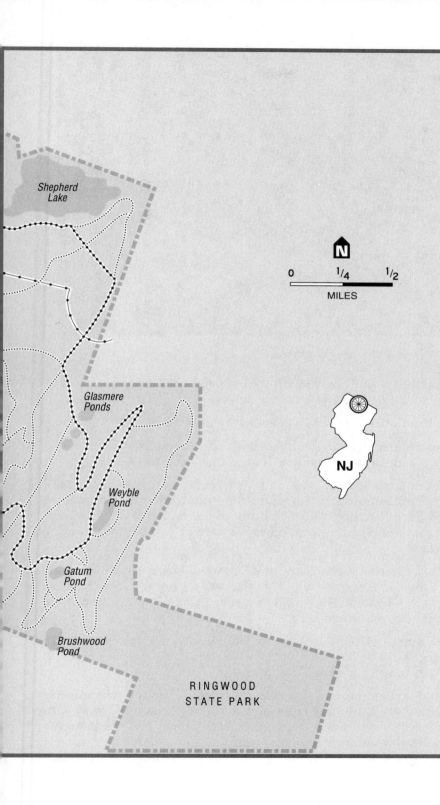

Shepherd
Lake

Glasmere
Ponds

Weyble
Pond

Gatum
Pond

Brushwood
Pond

RINGWOOD
STATE PARK

N

0   1/4   1/2

MILES

NJ

Old stone ruins at Ringwood State Park.

1920s until they ceased operations in 1957. Spend a day exploring the myriad trails, and, if time allows, visit the Ringwood or Skylands mansions.

General location: Northeast Passaic County near the town of Ringwood.

Elevation change: These are mountains. You should expect some hills and valleys with elevations ranging from 600 to 1,000 feet.

Season: The trails are available from late spring until the first snows. After heavy rains or melting snowpacks, the roads tend to get very muddy. Ringwood State Park doesn't prohibit use of the muddy trails. However, use your own discretion as to whether the trails should be ridden during these periods.

Services: Concession services near the Ringwood Manor House are available from Memorial Day to Labor Day weekends. Boating and bathing are available from Memorial Day weekend through Labor Day weekend at the seventy-four-acre Shepherd Lake.

Hazards: Ringwood State Park permits hunting in designated areas. To avoid being in the wrong place at the wrong time, call the park office to get the dates when you should stay away.

Rescue index: In terms of getting lost, many trails are marked improperly or not marked at all. You may feel that it's very easy to lose your way with so many trails, intersections, and choices. Many times I stopped another rider and asked where they had come from and was told that they weren't quite sure, that they had been riding for a few hours but were confident they would end up back at the parking area. On most weekends there will be plenty of trail users to stop and ask questions of, and perhaps they will give you more information than the riders I met. All the trails eventually do lead back to Honeysuckle Lane and the parking areas that are located along it. Stay on the wide dirt roads and keep descending. There are ranger services at the Ringwood Manor House for an emergency. During the hunting season certain areas are off limits, so check with the park ranger for exact details. Sunday is always a day of quietude during hunting season, which means it's a day you should get on the trails.

Land status: The park is managed by the New Jersey Division of Parks and Forestry. There is a $3.00 fee for parking from Memorial Day to Labor Day.

Maps: Call the park office to inquire if they can send you a free park map in the mail. The New York–New Jersey Trail Conference "North Jersey Trails" maps provide good detail as well. The Trail Conference maps sell for $7.95 and are available from most outdoor-type retail stores.

Finding the trail: The park can be reached by taking the New York State Thruway (Interstate 87) to exit 15A. This exit leads you onto New York 17. Take NY 17 north, and turn left (west) onto Sloatsburg Road. Go past Ringwood Manor, and turn left onto Morris Road, going past Hewitt School and Carletondale Road. Skylands Manor House of Ringwood State Park is 1.5 miles up Morris Road at the top of the hill. Go through the tollgate, and try to park at parking area A. If by chance that is full, use parking field B.

Source of additional information:

Ringwood State Park
1304 Sloatsburg Road
Ringwood, NJ 07456-1799
(973) 962–7031

Notes on the trail: Regardless of the parking area, pedal down the park road, and return to the tollgate you passed when you came into the park. After the tollgate turn right, going toward Shepherd Lake. Turn right again at the stop sign; a wide dirt road leads off beyond the area of the boat rental building. Proceed along this route, which is marked with faint red paint blazes. All of these trails are on wide, four-wheel-drive jeep paths used as equestrian bridle paths, mountain bike paths, and hunting vehicle routes. The trail hugs the southern shore of Shepherd Lake, and you will soon come to a three-way fork. The right fork and middle fork eventually merge into one trail. The right fork takes you up a steep hill with a screaming descent, and the left fork leads you on a more gently rolling ride along the shoreline.

From the point at which these two trails merge, continue straight until you come to a clearing. There will be a high-pressure gas pipe indicator made out of white plastic. Here again are another three forks. Take the right fork. You will soon come across two old stone buildings with a stone archway where the trail passes beneath. Go through the archway, continue straight for a short while, and make a left at an intersection with a trail blazed with green paint on the trees. It is about 4 miles to this intersection.

Proceed on a gradual climb on this green-blazed trail until you come to a large intersection. Notice a trail to your left leading in a northeast direction up an incline. This is the continuation of the green-blazed trail. It switches back in the direction you just came, continuing in a steady climb up the mountain. Bear right around the next bend in the trail as the trail continues to climb. At about 6.1 miles you come to another intersection with a trail leading off to your left. Continue straight, and start a descent. Weyble Pond will appear on your left. Bear left at the next fork. Proceed past a small pond on your right, and take a right on the next dirt road immediately past this pond. This trail descends past an old stone wall on your right. Keep descending, and soon you will approach Gatum Pond, where you bear right at a fork that switches you onto a trail marked with white paint blazes. This white trail descends for a short while and intersects with another trail. Turn right, and then make a quick left to remain on the white trail. This intersection is about 7 miles from the start. Fork right at the next intersection, following the white trail markers, and continue straight at the next intersection, always remaining on the white trail. At the next four-way intersection, continue straight up a small steep hill, remain straight, and bear left at the next three forks. You should end up at parking area B, near Swan Pond. This is Honeysuckle Lane. Turn right, and continue past the botanical gardens to parking area A.

16

Wawayanda Yahoo

Wawayanda is a beautiful 10,000-acre state park in the New Jersey Highlands. Laced with centuries-old logging roads and natural beauty, this park provides a wild and magnificent setting for mountain biking. A moderately challenging 8-mile loop trail along a road through the woods leads to a pristine forest of large rock outcrops, evergreens, hardwoods, and wetlands.

Beginners will be put to the test by trails that loop around small hills, dip into creek valleys, climb rolling ridge crests, and skirt major hilltops. Gonzo gearheads, when not blasting along on some smooth doubletrack, may have time to appreciate the interesting natural arena. While riding, notice how the forest changes from the dark, shady evergreens to zones of tall hardwoods. It's a varied and unique woodscape dotted with trees, ponds, boulders, and streams. Up and down the small ravines, the woodscape switches from the conifer-dominant wetland forest of lower valleys to the hardwood sections of the higher plateau.

Because Wawayanda is nestled in the Ramapo Mountains, one expects larger hills and mountains throughout the park, but the 10,000 acres appear to reside on a plateau. It is not a plateau in the geological sense. Rather it's a level mountain top with elevations around 1,200 and 1,300 feet. The riding is challenging, and there are many trails available. Most are fairly level and serve as cross-country skiing routes when there is snow. Another great feature is that Wawayanda Lake provides some great boating and swimming. Mountain bikers should bring their nonbiker friends.

The name Wa-wa-yanda, from the Lenape Indians, means "water on the mountain." It's a reference to both the 255-acre lake with almost 6 miles of wooded shoreline and the other lakes and ponds found on top of the mountain. The park contains a maze of old logging roads that are testament to the heavy logging during the 1940s.

In the beginning of the ride, you'll see an old charcoal furnace—all that remains of New Jersey's iron-ore industry in Wawayanda. Built in 1846, it was used to smelt the iron ore from local mines. It operated continuously for ten years until cheap coal became available in Pennsylvania, making it more economical to transport the ore for smelting to the hotter and more efficient furnaces. On an average day seven tons of iron would be produced from this type of furnace and would be poured off at noon and midnight. Wawayanda iron was of such superior quality that it was used to manufacture railroad car wheels. During the Civil War shovels and swords were forged. During the time of greatest activity, a small village developed

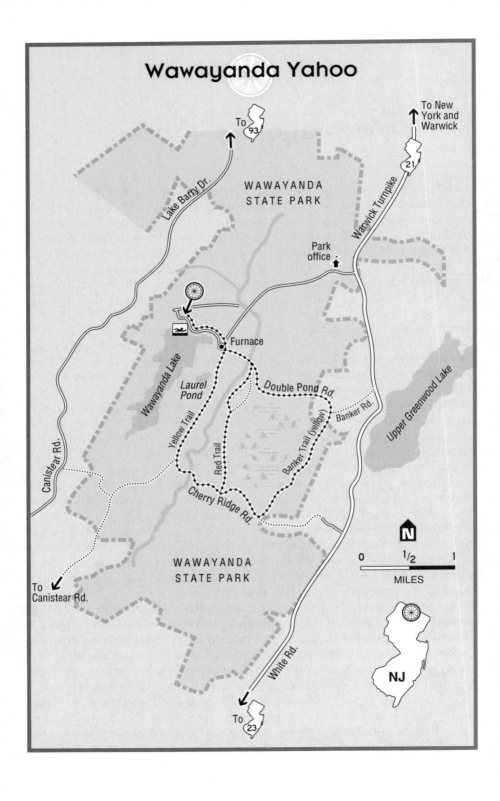

Wawayanda Yahoo

To 93

To New York and Warwick

21

Warwick Turnpike

WAWAYANDA STATE PARK

Lake Barry Dr.

Park office

Furnace

Wawayanda Lake

Laurel Pond

Double Pond Rd.

Banker Rd.

Banker Trail (yellow)

Yellow Trail

Red Trail

Cherry Ridge Rd.

Upper Greenwood Lake

Canistear Rd.

To Canistear Rd.

WAWAYANDA STATE PARK

White Rd.

To 23

N

0   1/2   1
MILES

NJ

in the vicinity to house the workers and provide services such as a post office, store, gristmill, and sawmill. The village has since disappeared, and the chatter of wildlife has brought back the natural solitude of the area. The miles of old logging roads left behind from another era provide an opportunity to access a historic and pristine forest environment. Spend a day at Wawayanda silently gliding through the woods.

General location: The park is located along the New York border in Sussex and Passaic Counties. The main entrance to the park is located on Warwick Turnpike approximately 3 miles north of Upper Greenwood Lake.

Elevation change: The Wawayanda "plateau" is not a geological plateau but rather a flat-topped mountain ridge with elevations ranging from 1,200 to 1,300 feet. The majority of trails described in this ride explore old wooded roads that reside at those elevations.

Season: From mid-April to the first snows. Because of the higher elevation of the Wawayanda "plateau," snows can arrive early. If there is no snow, do not let winter's cold stop you; just put on more clothing, and enjoy the solitude. During the summer months try not to arrive too long after 9:00 A.M. to be sure of a parking space.

Services: Greenwood Lake provides most food and gas services along Warwick Turnpike. During the summer you can cool off in Wawayanda Lake at the lifeguard-protected bathing beach. This picturesque location provides a great rest spot to cool off your tires and grab some concession food.

Hazards: Some equestrians and hikers use these trails as well, so the usual courtesy should be extended to these other trail users. At this point there are no conflicts. Remember that your actions as a rider have a great deal to do with any policy of sharing multiuse trails. On weekends the trails are popular, so exercise some caution when zipping down the hills because other trail users may be zipping down the trail too.

Rescue index: You are within a well-used park. The well-marked trails are within 3 miles of the park office. Help is never too far away.

Land status: New Jersey State Park.

Maps: The New York–New Jersey Trail Conference's "North Jersey Trails" maps provide good detail of Wawayanda Park and are waterproof and tearproof. The two-map set sells for $7.95 and can be found at most outdoor-type stores. USGS 7.5-minute series, Wawayanda quadrangle also provides coverage.

Finding the trail: Take Interstate 80 west from the George Washington Bridge to exit 53, which will lead to Route 23. Take Route 23 north for about 16 miles, and turn right onto Echo Road (New Jersey 513). Follow NJ 513 north to its end, and turn left (west) onto Macopin. Continue for about 4 miles, and bear left at a fork onto Union Valley Road. The fork is obvious but landmarks are the gas station on the right and the small shopping center on the opposite side. At the next fork bear left onto White Road. You will see a sign for Wawayanda State Park. This road will end at a stop sign and intersection with Warwick Turnpike. Turn left onto Warwick Turnpike, and continue to the Wawayanda Park entrance on your left. Enter the park. Between Memorial Day and Labor Day weekends, a parking fee of $5.00 for weekdays and $7.00 for weekends and holidays is charged. Continue past the tollbooth, and take the park road until you see the large parking area near the beach. Turn left into this parking area. There is a park office at the entrance if you need additional maps or other information.

Source of additional information:

Wawayanda State Park
885 Warwick Turnpike
Hewitt, NJ 07421
(973) 853–4462

Notes on the trail: If you have parked near Wawayanda Lake beach area, the trail begins beyond the wooden barrier between the beach and the parking area. There are usually people walking, riding, or running on this portion of the trail. Turn left onto this trail, and follow it as it passes through another parking area for boat rentals. Keep hugging the lake's shoreline, and continue straight and a bit to the left as you pass a stone dam at the end of the lake. You will soon come to the remnants of the old charcoal furnace at a four-way intersection. It had been used at Wawayanda for the manufacture of shovels and railroad car wheels. Continue across the road. You will be returning from the trail that leads off to your right.

Cross a wooden bridge, and fork right as you enter a small campground. Turn right at the next turn, and then make another quick right; you'll notice a green metal barrier with a beautiful forest road leading beyond it. Go past the green barrier, and pick up a trail that is marked by yellow paint blazes on the trees. This trail is known as Double Pond Road. Proceed up a small incline. The wide road soon levels out through an attractive hemlock forest. After about 1.5 miles cross a small wooden bridge spanning a small stream. This is one of the many streams that carve and drain south from the New Jersey Highlands. Soon after the bridge turn right at the next intersection onto a red-marked trail. Take this trail south through an attractive hemlock forest. If you would like to add another 4 miles onto this loop, do not turn right onto the red trail but continue along the yellow-marked Double Pond for about another 1.5 miles. You will arrive at a parking area. Turn south onto another yellow-marked trail known as Banker Trail. Take this south for another 2 miles, where it ends at the wider four-wheel-drive Cherry Ridge Road. Turn right onto Cherry Ridge Road, and follow it in a general northwesterly direction. You will soon come to the exit point to which the red trail leads you.

So now let's continue down the red-marked trail. After a while you will come to a fork where the red trail seems to go left and right. Bear right at

92

Somewhere in the middle of Wawayanda's glorious nowhere.

this fork. Ride for a bit more, then come out of the hemlocks into a clearing, where again the red trail goes left and right. Turn right, continuing in a southerly direction. At about 3 miles from the beginning of the ride, you will come to a fork. The red trail leads to your left and returns to Double Pond Road. Bear right onto the unmarked trail in a southwesterly direction. In about 0.3 mile a stream will appear on your right with a small rock bridge across it. Carry your bike over this rock bridge, and continue on the unmarked trail as it picks up on the other side of the stream. A singletrack leads up and away from the stream and eventually opens up into a four-wheel-drive trail. In a little less than a mile, you come to a T intersection with the wider Cherry Ridge Road.

Turn right onto Cherry Ridge Road. At 0.2 mile turn right at the T intersection, heading in a northerly direction. Ride for another 0.4 mile, and arrive at a larger intersection. The yellow-blazed Laurel Pond Trail leads north through a beautiful forest of beech, elm, and hemlock. The trail descends for a small distance, levels off, and then begins a steady climb to an elevation of about 1,370 feet. You will pass a large ravine on your right lined with huge boulders. They have been split and fractured many times and now have trees growing in their cracks. Notice the 1,375-foot rocky ridge of an unnamed peak farther ahead to your left. It's all downhill from this point on. Pass a small blue-marked trail leading to your left. Continue straight on the yellow trail, which eventually leads into the four-way intersection where the old furnace is located. At the furnace turn left, and head up the hill between two wooden fence posts. This will return you to the Wawayanda Lake beach parking area.

Westchester Area Tours

As you cycle along the many paths throughout the parks and wilderness regions of Westchester County, it's hard to believe that the Native American Algonkian tribes or European Dutch settlers encamped along the same routes you will explore on these tours. Native Americans cut trails through the primitive forests for the purpose of establishing seasonal hunting routes. The European pioneers built dirt roads for transporting supplies and linking their tiny settlements to the larger populated city of New York.

Imagine yourself as an adventurer, a modern-day Henry Hudson, who in 1609 sailed up the river that now bears his name. There were no million-dollar homes, no highways, no corporate headquarters in Westchester back then. Just beautiful hills and valleys, fertile lands, and the promise of a bountiful future.

By 1664 others had sensed the area's great opportunities. The imperialist English took over the region from the Dutch, and settlements grew as the Royal Governor granted large tracts of land, known as lordships or manors, to ambitious pioneers and settlers. Westchester County became a magnet for settlers forming small villages, manors, and subsistence farms, the precursors of today's towns and localities. It became the most prosperous county in the colony of New York, and ultimately, as centuries passed, one of the wealthiest counties in the United States.

The setting, however idyllic through most of its history, became war torn on 18 October 1776, when the British army and the American Revolutionaries fought at the Battle of Pelham. The earlier Native American and pioneer encampments became those of the British and American troops. General George Washington camped for six weeks in Westchester as part of his strategy to defeat the British.

With the war ending the small farms of Westchester returned to productivity, taverns and inns opened their doors to weary and hungry travelers, and the county's charm was restored. One unusual industry that developed in northeastern Westchester in the 1820s was the traveling animal menagerie. The area was the birthplace of the American circus of Barnum and Bailey. The county began to change from an agricultural to an industrial economy after 1850 as factories were built along the Hudson and Bronx Rivers and along the Long Island Sound. The iron industry developed in Croton and Peekskill, employing large numbers of immigrant laborers from central and eastern Europe. The need for water by New York City led to the county's huge dam and aqueduct projects, built primarily by Irish and Italian laborers.

Southeastern New York is dominated by the Hudson River, which flows past the wonders of its cities and industries. At the same time the river touches some of the state's wilder lands, where the mountain biker can quickly escape the centers of civilization that dot the Hudson's banks. This area includes a variety of rides that will introduce you to the best of southeastern New York's wild lands not far from the Hudson.

Trains to the trails: Transportation service by rail to some of the towns where the trails reside can be found on the commuter trains of the Metro North Railroad. Traveling on the trains with a bicycle requires a $5.00 bike pass and the obligatory passenger fare. The bike pass, by the way, is good for life. To acquire a pass go to Window 27 at the Grand Central Terminal or call (212) 340–2176 to request an application. Train service schedules can be found at most train stations.

Various restrictions apply for individuals portaging bikes on the trains.

Bikes cannot be carried on the trains during New Year's Eve, New Year's Day, St. Patrick's Day, Mother's Day, Rosh Hashanah Eve, Thanksgiving Eve, Thanksgiving Day, Yom Kippur Eve, Christmas Eve, and Christmas Day, or between the hours of noon and 8:00 P.M. on the Fridays or day before Memorial Day, July Fourth, and Labor Day weekends.

Weekday restrictions apply during the rush-hour commuting periods. No bikes are allowed on departing trains from Grand Central between 7:00 and 9:00 A.M., and 3:00 and 8:00 P.M. No bikes are allowed on arriving trains into Grand Central between 6:00 and 10:00 A.M., and 4:00 and 7:00 P.M. For all other questions call Metro North, (212) 340–2176.

Bedford Country Road Ramble

This ride tours the hilly, hard-packed country backroads that weave through the village of Bedford in Westchester County. It's of medium difficulty. Perhaps it's a blessing that it's not a technical ride because of the wonderful scenery—the working horse farms, magnificent country estates, nineteenth-century homesteads, and historic landmarks along more than 25 miles of wide roads. The beauty of this New England–type village and surrounding countryside is better appreciated with an easy cruising ride like this. It's classic New England countryside down country lanes that intersect and tempt further exploration. This tour consists of a variety of roads, which form an 11-mile loop.

Many of these roads double as bridle paths and are labeled with yellow markers on trees. These markers have a black arrow pointing in the direction that the bridle path follows and are marked with the letters BRLA for Bedford Riding Lanes Association. Because cars travel on these roads, keep your eyes and ears open when rounding a blind curve. When approaching horses be careful not to spook them by riding too close to them or by coming up fast on them from either direction on the road.

These country roads were once part of a parcel of land that had been purchased from Chief Katonah in 1680. Old Post Road passes by the town common, a small triangular park in front of the post office, which was the original center of the village. Several village streets date back to this period. Bedford was one of the most important towns in northern Westchester during the American Revolution. American Revolutionary forces marched through Bedford to defeat the British at Yorktown.

Many old wood paths penetrate pristine wilderness areas and make great mountain biking routes. Moreover, these routes are unique. They have a rare, heavy historical flavor extending 300 years into the past.

General location: Approximately 30 miles north of Manhattan; exit 4 off Interstate 684.

Elevation change: Although the roads are hard and compact, the riding is made more challenging by the short, steep climbs up the many hills throughout the area. However, the scenic rewards and sense of history are well worth the effort.

Season: This is an all-season territory, and with a little snow blanketing the ground, the serenity of these old houses is splendid.

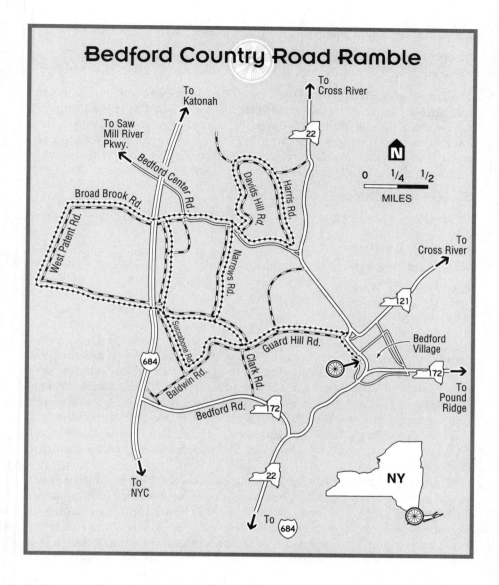

Services: Most services can be found in the town of Bedford. If you're in the mood for some snacks and home-baked cakes and brownies, stop by the deli facing the town common on Old Post Road.

Hazards: These roads are shared by people out for a stroll, groups of equestrian riders, bicycles, and cars. If you intend to tuck and burn down a hill with all that wind rushing past your ears, pay close attention around the turns, for you may not be able to hear the cars.

Rescue index: The roads are well traveled, and you might be able to flag someone down. Bedford Village is never more than 2 miles away.

Land status: Town roads in the village of Bedford.

Maps: Hagstrom's "Upper Westchester County," which costs $3.95, provides sufficient detail for this ride and is available in most bookstores.

Finding the trail: Take the Hutchinson River Parkway north to I–684 and take exit 4. Turn right (east) onto New York 172 and left (north) onto NY 22, proceeding into Bedford Village. Park anywhere that allows parking. Take your bike and get back onto NY 22 going north. Shortly after the town you will come to the intersection of NY 22 and NY 121. Begin your tour with a left onto Guard Hill Road directly across from NY 121.

Sources of additional information:

Westchester County Department of Parks, Recreation and Conservation
25 Moore Avenue
Mt. Kisco, NY 10549
www.westchestergov.com/parks/main2.htm

Briarcliff Bike Works
1238 Pleasantville Road
Briarcliff, NY 10510
(914) 762–7614

Notes on the trail: Head down Guard Hill Road, passing beautiful old farms and estates and bearing right at the first intersection. Continue up a small hill, and turn right onto Narrows Road. Take that fine country road for about 1 mile to its end at Bedford Center Road. For a small 3-mile detour, turn right and then left at Davids Hill Road, bearing right until it ends at Harris Road. Turn right onto paved Harris Road, heading downhill. At its end turn right onto Bedford Center Road. You have just made a small detoured loop.

Continuing on Bedford Center Road, pass Davids Hill Road (which you just took for this loop), and in less than a mile, bear left onto Broad Brook Road as you come to a bend in the road that bears right. Continuing on Broad Brook Road, you may make a left onto Succabone Road to shorten the 11-mile loop by 3 miles, or continue straight ahead and turn left at West Patent Road. Both these roads lead back to Guard Hill Road, which you can then take all the way back to where you started.

Take some extra time and explore Succabone Road, Clark Road, Clinton Road, and Fox Lane. They all pass through magnificent countryside.

18

Clarence Fahnestock Memorial State Park

There are a variety of trails in this 6,500-acre state park, located in the northern half of the Highlands, only 50 miles north of Manhattan. The rolling terrain is crisscrossed by forest roads, bridle paths, and nineteenth-century railroad beds, and is sprinkled with several picturesque lakes. If you wish to get off the trails and into the water, Canopus Lake offers a beautiful sandy beach and boating facilities. This state park offers something for everyone. The four trail systems described in this chapter provide a wide range of riding opportunities. You can cruise on wide, hard-packed dirt roads and blast down some awesome singletrack descents.

This wild and heavily wooded countryside consists of deep forests of tall hemlocks and maple stands among numerous lakes and marshes. Deer are numerous, and beaver can be spotted in the swamps. The trail runs along the railroad beds built in 1862 to carry ore from the Sunk Mine to the Greenwood mine in Harriman Park. This ore was used for the Union Army artillery during the Civil War. The entire area was once the site of considerable activity, and evidence of early settlements and overgrown wood roads, cellar holes, and stone walls can be seen along the routes. Iron ore attracted miners in the early part of the nineteenth century. Mining survived until 1873. The surrounding land was purchased by Dr. Clarence Fahnestock in 1915 and then given to the state as a gift in 1929 by his son, Dr. Alfred Fahnestock, in memory of his father.

General location: Approximately 50 miles north of Manhattan, about 8 miles east of the historic town of Cold Spring.

Elevation change: The terrain is rolling with some short, steep hills.

Season: Because of the higher elevation of this park, there is greater exposure to snowstorms and cooler weather than the surrounding areas. Some fine riding can be found from late March to the first snows. If there is no snow on the ground in the winter months and you come prepared with warm clothes, the solitude on these trails is unparalleled. The extra effort it might take to get here on a cold morning will be worth the exhilarating experience.

Services: Canopus Lake offers a concession stand, locker room, shower, and toilet facilities. Tent and trailer camping are available for those wishing to camp overnight. Boat rentals are also available. Main Street in the town of

Clarence Fahnestock Memorial State Park

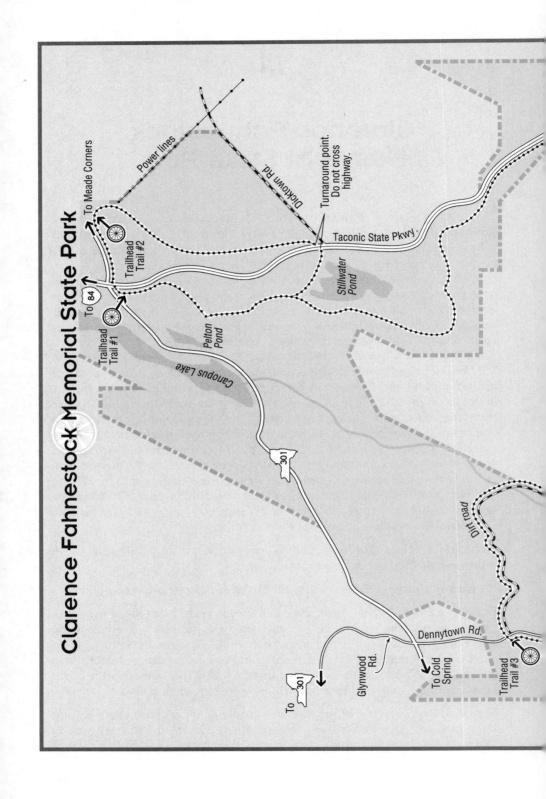

To Meade Corners

Power lines

Dicktown Rd.

Turnaround point.
Do not cross
highway.

Taconic State Pkwy.

Trailhead
Trail #2

To 84

Trailhead
Trail #1

Pelton Pond

Stillwater
Pond

Canopus Lake

301

Dirt road

Dennytown Rd.

Glynwood
Rd.

To Cold
Spring

Trailhead
Trail #3

To 301

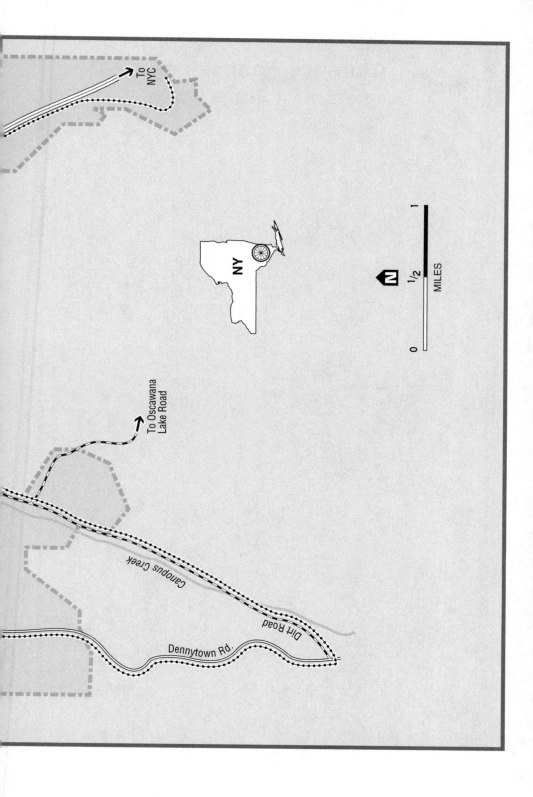

Clarence Fahnestock
Memorial State Park

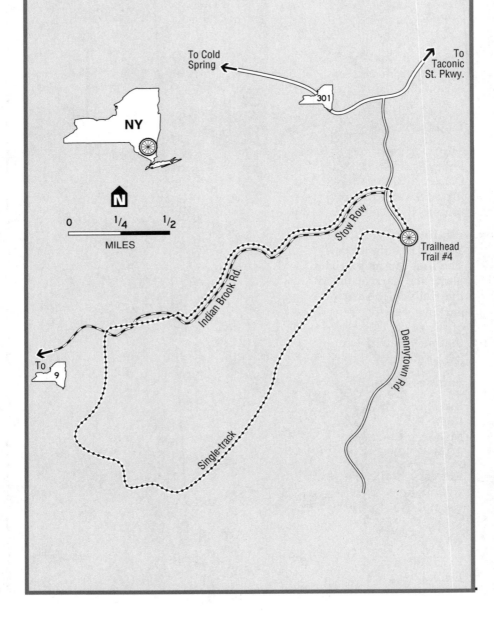

Cold Spring has some restaurants and delis. Mountain bike rentals, trail information, and supplies can be found at the Wheel and Heel bike shop in Fishkill.

Hazards: There is an unstated courtesy expected on multiuse trails such as the bridle paths. Hikers, equestrians, and mountain bikers at this point coexist in relative harmony. Let's keep it that way. When approaching horses be careful not to spook them by riding close or fast from either direction on the road. Raccoon rabies are present in this area of New York, so do not approach or feed these animals in the park. If you do see an animal behaving strangely, please contact a member of the park staff.

Rescue index: The park receives a lot of visitors and is very popular with equestrians, hikers, and other bike riders. You are bound to run into someone on a trail. You will be only about 2 miles from the well-traveled paved roads that surround the park.

Land status: New York State Park.

Maps: A park map is available free from the park. The New York–New Jersey Trail Conference's "East Hudson Trails, #3" provides good detail of Clarence Fahnestock State Park and is waterproof and tearproof. It sells for $8.95 and can be found at most outdoor-type stores. The USGS 7.5-minute series, Oscawana quadrangle also provides coverage.

Finding the trail: Take the Taconic State Parkway north and exit at New York 301 going west. There are two different parking locales in the park. The first can be reached just after you get onto NY 301. Turn left into the park, and park at the end of the campsite road. This gives you access to the trails in the northern half of the park. The second locale offers two parking areas on Dennytown Road, which divides the lower southern half of the park. This gives you access to Sunk Mine Road and the horse trails that penetrate the southern half. I have listed four trails below, but there are numerous other possibilities for assembling your rides.

Sources of additional information:

Bikeway
Route 6
Mahopac, NY 10541
(914) 621–2800

Clarence Fahnestock Memorial State Park
RFD 2, Route 301
Carmel, NY 10512-9802
(914) 225–7207

Wheel and Heel
2275 Route 9
Fishkill, NY 12524
(914) 896–7591

Notes on the trail: The trails available throughout the park for biking are independent of each other and do not necessarily interconnect. I have listed four distinctive trails worth exploring. They each offer a little different terrain and scenery.

To reach the northern locale, turn left into the park entrance just after you exit the Taconic Parkway onto NY 301.

Trail 1: From the parking area head back out to NY 301 and east for about 500 feet and turn right, into the campgrounds. Proceed through the campgrounds, and the trail begins past campsite number 50. The out-and-back mountain bike–designated trail is roughly 2 miles in length, making it 4 miles total. It passes along the west shore of Stillwater Pond. This ride can be extended by turning left at its termination at the T intersection. Continue on the same horse trail for another 4 miles as it meanders in a southerly direction along the eastern spur of the park property. Fortunately horses and mountain bikers understand each other in this state park, and a mutual respect of each other's rights on the trails is evident from encounters.

Trail 2: Get back onto NY 301 and turn right (east). Go 0.9 mile past the Taconic Parkway intersection with NY 301, and start looking for a bridle/snowmobile path on your right leading in a southerly direction. If you pass the power lines, you have gone too far. This bridle and snowmobile trail is a little more than 2 miles in length. It goes over moderately hilly terrain and ends on Dicktown Road. Turn around, and return the way you came.

To reach the southern locale, take NY 301 south and turn left onto Dennytown Road. There is a parking area just past Sunk Mine Road on your left.

Trail 3: This 8-mile loop tour follows along a 16-foot-wide, hard-packed, dirt town road called Sunk Mine Road, descending and winding through the midsection of the park. There is an interesting spur trail 0.9 mile from the start. It appears as a doubletrack trail on your left just after the small pond and follows a meandering brook. This abandoned mining road ascends to Sunk Mine. About 1.7 miles from the start, turn right onto the dirt Bell Hollow Road. Take this for about 2.5 miles as it follows along the Canopus Creek through a beautiful rugged ravine. Dennytown Road will come in from the north at an angle, so turn north and follow it for 2.7 miles to your parking area.

Trail 4: This trail begins on Sunk Mine Road, across from Dennytown Road. Look for the circular, yellow, horse trail markers. This 5-mile loop includes 3 miles of singletrack on a yellow-marked horse trail with a 2-mile return along a scenic backcountry road. The trail takes you through quiet stands of pine, young tree growth, and mountain laurel. There are some small climbs along the horse trail, but the scenery is well worth the effort.

Indian Brook Road Loop

Hard-packed country roads supply ample mileage to explore some of Putnam County's rolling terrain. Three country roads can be connected to form a 9-mile loop with a detour at an eighteenth-century tavern for a full-course meal. The Bird and Bottle Inn was established in 1761 before the Revolutionary War. It was an important stagecoach stop along Old Albany Post Road. The inn still retains the ambience of the Colonial era, with wood-burning fireplaces, beamed ceilings, wide plank floors, and authentic antiques. Call ahead to reserve a table for brunch. Work off your eats by finishing the last leg of the trip. Pass by scenic ponds and stop by the Taconic Outdoor Education Center. Call to find out what programs are being sponsored. On one occasion there were lectures on drawing sap from trees to make syrup.

General location: Approximately 50 miles north of Manhattan, about 8 miles east of the historic town of Cold Spring.

Elevation change: The terrain is rolling with some short, steep hills to climb, but mixed in are a fair share of reciprocal, well-earned descents.

Season: These roads are great in all seasons, and if the cold doesn't bother you, saddle up and get on the trail. These are wide, hard-packed dirt roads that provide access to many homesteads. Plowing during winter is almost always performed, and the compacted roads barely show a dent or any rutting during wet periods. If you can brave the cold, don't hesitate to get out there and enjoy a brisk morning ride, followed, of course, by some warm cider at the local tavern.

Services: Overnight lodging is available at the Bird and Bottle Inn (1123 Old Albany Post Road, Granton, NY 10524; 800–782–6837 or 845–424–3000, info@birdbottle.com or www.birdbottle.com). Each room is furnished with a working fireplace and is decorated with furnishings of the eighteenth century. The neighboring town of Cold Spring provides some restaurants and delis on Main Street as well as attractive antique and craft shops.

Hazards: These roads are not well traveled. However, there is the occasional vehicle here and there, so take care on blind turns and listen for oncoming cars.

Rescue index: You will always be able to flag down a car if needed, or you can ask for help at one of the residential homes along the way.

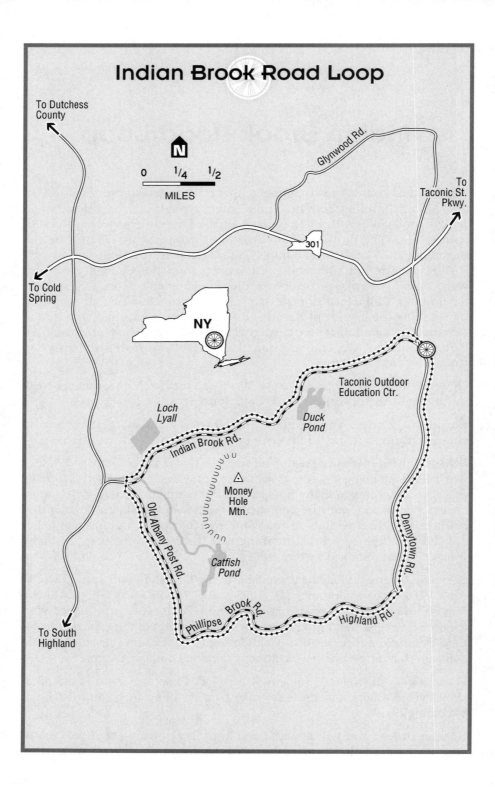

Indian Brook Road Loop

To Dutchess County

N

0   1/4   1/2
MILES

To Taconic St. Pkwy.

Glynwood Rd.

301

To Cold Spring

NY

Taconic Outdoor Education Ctr.

Loch Lyall

Duck Pond

Indian Brook Rd.

Money Hole Mtn.

Old Albany Post Rd.

Catfish Pond

Dennytown Rd.

Phillipse Brook Rd.

Highland Rd.

To South Highland

Ah, solitude. January on the Indian Brook Road Tour.

Land status: County roads.

Maps: USGS 7.5-minute series, Oscawana quadrangle.

Finding the trail: Take the Taconic State Parkway north and exit at New York 301 going west. Look for Dennytown Road on your left in just less than 4 miles, and turn left. Parking can be found on your left in three-quarters of a mile.

Sources of additional information:

New York–New Jersey Trail Conference
156 Ramapo Valley Road
Mahwah, NJ 37430
(201) 512-9348
www.nynjtc.org

Hickory and Tweed
410 Main Street
Armonk, NY 10504
(914) 273-3397
www.hickorytweed.com

Notes on the trail: After you park your car, return to Dennytown Road the way you came and turn left on Indian Brook Road. You will pass the Taconic Outdoor Education Center and Duck Pond. After about 3 mostly downhill miles, turn left at the stop sign; the Bird and Bottle Inn is directly on your right. A quick left onto Old Albany Post Road begins your return. The 0.6-mile ascent of Old Albany Post Road is a little demanding after having stopped at the inn, but the lovely homes will help distract you and keep your pedaling in good form as you climb the long, steady hill. When you reach the top after 1.5 miles, turn left onto Phillipse Brook Road, which at the time of this writing was marked with a road sign, and pass by an old farm with sheep. Though the road name changes to Highland Road, take it to its end, where it meets up with Dennytown Road. Turn left, and proceed uphill for 0.2 mile. You should recognize the parking area coming up on your right.

20

The Mianus Maze

This unique trail system, located in the Mianus River Park near Greenwich, Connecticut, is a maze of singletrack and hard-packed old carriage roads, a tantalizing network of mountain bike trails suitable for beginners and intermediates. It's all wrapped up in a primeval, densely forested park of only 220 acres, although the wealth of trails adds up to more than 14 miles in linear distance. The 5-mile loop trail described here is just one of the many configurations that can be created from this vast network of trails. There is just enough trail variety here to initiate the novice and invigorate the archetypal, total-bent dirthead. The moderately hilly singletrack has become a popular destination for local mountain bikers. Novices can cruise on the easy carriage roads through the park, and the more technically inclined will find enough streambeds, rocks, and logs to cross and maneuver around. It makes for a full afternoon of riding. The scenery is packed with dense hardwood and conifer forests, and the trout-filled Mianus River runs through the park for more than 1 mile.

Once in the park, the suburban sprawl that surrounds it is quickly left behind, and this urban oasis takes on the dimensions of a full-scale wilderness with a large variety of flora and fauna. Large rock ridges and outcrops are found throughout the park, and the forests consist of white pine, hemlock, willow, hickory, ash, birch, maples, and oak. At least twenty-two varieties of birds—including owls, hawks, and herons—live in these woods. Red fox, chipmunks, squirrels, and the white-tailed deer call this dense habitat home.

As you glide silently along the trails, think about the rich and colorful events that took place in the area that encompasses Mianus River Park. The river hosted the primitive cultures that settled and thrived in this region. Native Americans lived on the lands that surround the Mianus River long before the arrival of English and Dutch settlers in the seventeenth century. Fertile meadows stretched for miles along the river north and south of the Mianus Gorge, inviting settlements and leading to the creation of towns and villages.

Spend an afternoon riding the trails in Mianus River Park, and share in this primeval wilderness.

General location: Greenwich, Connecticut.

Elevation change: There are some minor hills to climb and descend as you go over the ridges and into the stream valleys, but none exceeds 100 feet.

The Mianus Maze

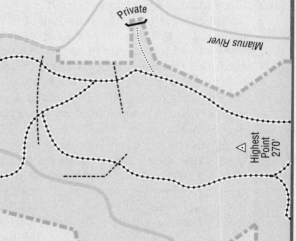

Note: ----------- = Stone Wall

Private

Mianus River

Highest
Point
270'

NY

CT

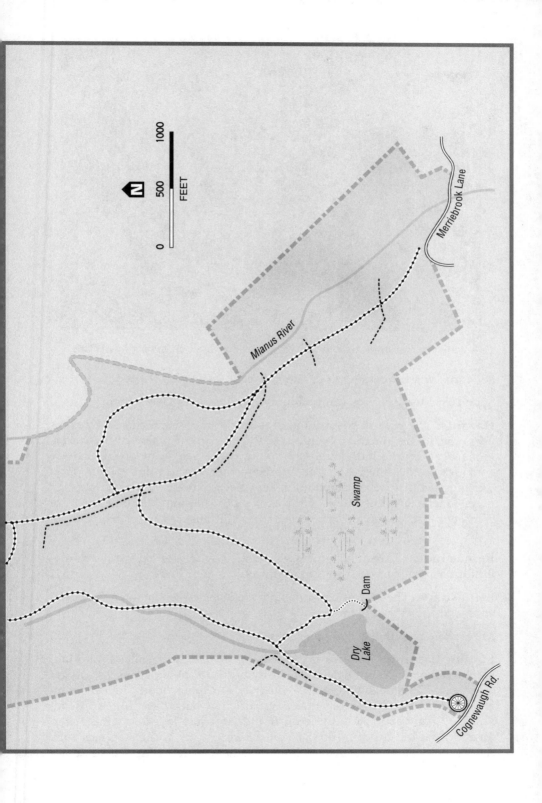

A variety of landscape features shape the primeval forest of Mianus River Park.

Season: This is four-season territory, except during snow cover.

Services: Most services can be found in the town of Greenwich.

Hazards: The park is beautiful and quite popular and is shared by other users, including hikers and equestrians. The current policy of trail usage is managed by the individual, and for now the people involved in these activities coexist and respect each other's rights to use this special park. This implies that we, as mountain bikers, need to be sensitive while riding here. So let's keep the image of the eco-respectful mountain biker and use commonsense etiquette, and perhaps we will ensure our place on these trails.

Rescue index: This small park is surrounded by residential areas, and civilization is never more than 2 miles away.

Land status: The park is on municipal land shared by the town of Greenwich and the city of Stamford.

Maps: The map that accompanies this tour is one of the best for this park.

Finding the trail: The park is located approximately 40 miles from Manhattan. Take the New England Thruway north for about 24 miles and get off at exit 5/Riverside and Old Greenwich, in Connecticut. The exit ramp winds around and over the thruway. Turn left onto East Putnam Road, Route 1, going south. Continue on Route 1 for just less than a mile, and turn right at the third traffic light onto River Road. At the stop sign turn right onto Valley Road. After about a mile turn left onto Cognewaugh

Road. Take Cognewaugh Road for 2 miles to a circular gravel parking area on the right side, just after Shannon Lane.

Sources of additional information:

Town of Greenwich, Division of Parks and Trees
101 Field Point Road
Greenwich, CT 06836-2540
(203) 622–7824

Hickory and Tweed
410 Main Street
Armonk, NY 10504
(914) 273–3397
www.hickorytweed.com

Danny's Cycles
644 Central Avenue
Scarsdale, NY 10583
(914) 723–3408
www.dannyscycles.com

Notes on the trail: At the time of this writing, the trails were not marked; there is quite an array of interconnecting trails, so try to follow the route description below.

A wide carriage road leads beyond a metal barrier in the northeast section of the parking area. It's hard to miss. The carriage road soon passes by a swamp on your right, and at 0.4 mile you should bear left onto a wide, hard-packed singletrack. The fork to your right is the trail you will be returning on. In 0.2 mile cross a small streambed, and bear left in a westerly direction up a steep hill. Ignore the trail to your right that parallels the streambed. As the trail levels out, you begin a small descent, fork left, pass a small pond on your left, and continue straight, ignoring a small trail to your right. Bear right at the next fork up a small switchback. There are many trails in this portion of the park, so pay attention to all the forking going on.

Bear right at the next fork and then left at the fork immediately after. The trail descends to a swampy area, crossing a small stream and generally heading in a northeasterly direction. Bear left at the next fork, and ride parallel with the streambed. You will notice some houses up on a hill to your left. The trail begins to turn away from the stream; at the T intersection turn right, and head up a small incline. Bear right at the next fork and turn left at the next T intersection, which brings you to the wider carriage road at 2.1 miles. Turn right onto the carriage road. In another 0.2 mile, take the leftmost fork, and soon after fork right. You will ride along the Mianus River to your left. Notice a small path leading to your right; this can connect to the Service Road carriage trail. Continue straight, and pass a large eastern hemlock grove on the river's edge to your left.

At 2.8 miles you reach an intersection with another carriage road. Bearing right will send you back, but bear left to continue cruising on this picturesque path. The park is home to about a mile of the Mianus River and is known for brook, rainbow, and brown trout fishing. You pass several fishing spots. After 0.4 mile you reach a gate. Turn around, head back, and bear left at the intersection that brought you this way.

Pass two smaller singletracks on your left, and then turn left at the four-way intersection with a wooden post in the ground, proceeding in a southwesterly direction. This carriage road leads you over some minor hills, and at the top you'll pass a large stone barrier and bear right. Continue straight until you reach another fork in about 1,000 feet. Bear left to return to the parking area, or bear right to do the loop again, but as a different configuration.

Babcock Preserve

This park has rugged sections along its network of hiking and bridle paths set upon abandoned roads, but the trails are not overly difficult. An intermediate 6-mile loop is described in this ride, but many other configurations can be created by analyzing the map and connecting the trails.

This tour is technically tricky along some portions of the rocky trail, but there is enough smoother doubletrack to whisk you through and quicken the pace. The trails are fairly level and gently roll over an interesting terrain of primitive wilderness habitat hosting a wide variety of birds and small mammals. Nature is your companion, and serenity prevails in these woods as you travel over old, eroded, and overgrown forested roads that now serve as hiking and equestrian trails. There are many sections of smooth trail, as well as a fair portion of rocky trail that will jar your teeth and keep you busy. The trail is seldom used by mountain bikers, and perhaps it's been decades since it served as a road.

General location: Just north of the town of Greenwich on North Street.

Elevation change: There are minor hills to climb, but the trail follows a gently rolling terrain.

Season: This is four-season territory except when the trails are covered with snow. Then you might consider taking out your cross-country skis.

Services: Most services can be found throughout the town of Greenwich.

Hazards: The trails are shared with equestrians, so yield to the larger of the beasts and give them the right of way. The park is beautiful and may be popular on weekends. The current policy of trail usage is managed by the individual, and for now the people involved in these activities coexist and respect each other's rights to use this special park. We, as mountain bikers, need to be sensitive while riding here. So let's keep a positive image and use commonsense etiquette, and perhaps we will ensure our place on these trails.

Rescue index: The park is very small in terms of acreage, but it is always possible to get disoriented. The trails are well marked, with posted wooden signs indicating the direction you should take to return to one of the two parking lots. The ride described here will park you at the North Street parking area. Numerous private homes also border the park, so in the worst-case scenario, knock on a door.

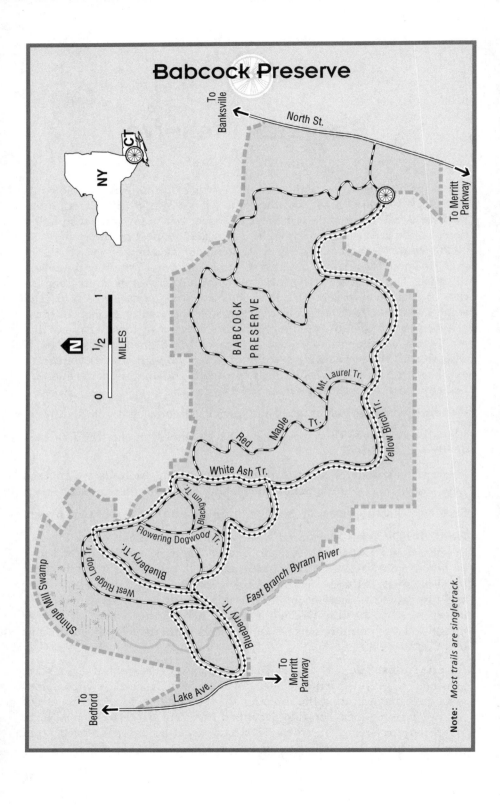

Babcock Preserve

To Banksville

North St.

To Merritt Parkway

BABCOCK PRESERVE

Mt. Laurel Tr.

Yellow Birch Tr.

Red Maple Tr.

White Ash Tr.

Blackgum Tr.

Flowering Dogwood Tr.

Blueberry Tr.

West Ridge Loop Tr.

Blueberry Tr.

Shingle Mill Swamp

East Branch Byram River

To Merritt Parkway

Lake Ave.

To Bedford

N

0   ½   1

MILES

NY   CT

Note: *Most trails are singletrack.*

Land status: The preserve is maintained and owned by the town of Greenwich.

Maps: An Eagle Scout project by Boy Scout Troop 37 completed a comprehensive map of the preserve; it hangs on a board beside the beginning of the trail on North Street.

Finding the trail: Take the Hutchinson River Parkway north, and then follow signs for the Merritt Parkway. Take the Merritt Parkway and the North Street exit. At the end of the exit ramp, turn left, and go about half a mile. The entrance to the parking area for the Babcock Preserve is on your left. Turn in, and take the bumpy dirt road to its terminus. Park your car here, and notice the wooden bulletin board erected to hold the preserve's map. Directly to the left of that, beyond a metal barrier and over a stone bridge, the trail will begin.

Sources of additional information:

Town of Greenwich Chamber of Commerce
45 East Putnam Avenue, Suite 121
Greenwich, CT 06830
(203) 869–3500
www.greenwichchamber.com

Town of Greenwich Division of Parks and Trees
101 Field Point Road
Greenwich, CT 06836-2540
(203) 622–7824

Danny's Cycles
644 Central Avenue
Scarsdale, NY 10583
(914) 723–3408
www.dannyscycles.com

Notes on the trail: The ride begins on a wide, hard-packed, dirt utility road crossing a stone bridge over a small stream and ascending a moderate hill in a westerly direction. This is Yellow Birch Trail, marked by yellow disks and square yellow tree markers. At the top of the hill, bear right at the fork. The trail follows a gently rolling terrain, first through an open oak forest and then through a dense undergrowth of huge mountain laurel. Turn right at a T intersection, descend into a small, shallow gully, and then climb out of it. Fork right at the next intersection, and remain on Yellow Birch Trail. At 1.3 miles you come to a metal, barbed-wire fence. Notice several signposts indicating these trail crossings. To the right the White Ash trail follows the length of the metal fence. Bear left, continuing on the Yellow Birch Trail, which becomes more singletrack. Soon you come to another intersection with the Flowering Dogwood Trail. Remain straight on the Yellow Birch Trail. After another 1,000 feet, you come to a fork. The left path leads to a sign indicating the trail is closed, so bear

Self-portrait at Babcock Preserve.

right, and then at the next forked intersection, bear left onto the blue-marked Blueberry Trail, which will lead you through the remains of an old stone boundary wall. You have now gone 1.8 miles. The Blueberry Trail is marked with round, wooden, blue disks that are very easy to follow. In 0.1 mile cross a stream and continue straight, ignoring the small path leading off to your left. Descend a hill to a paved road. Turn right onto a single-track called the West Ridge Loop Trail. In about 100 feet a trail leads to your right, but continue straight through the remains of a stone fence and down a small incline, bearing right and then continuing straight on the trail that parallels a small brook to your right. Pass a small singletrack leading to your left. This is the continuation of the West Ridge Road, which leads later into Red Maple Trail. Ascend a small hill, and you will arrive at a clearing bordered by a stone wall. Bear right, and then make a quick left to pick up the blue Blueberry Trail. Bear left at the next fork. The trail to your right is the Black Gum Trail, which leads back to the Yellow Birch Trail and the parking area.

At 2.8 miles you come to a four-way intersection with Flowering Dogwood Trail. Continue straight on the Red Maple Trail. Bear left at the next T intersection after traversing some large rocks in the trail. Bearing right at the next fork will place you on the White Ash Trail, which will proceed along the metal fence. At the intersection with Yellow Birch Trail, near the opening of the fence, turn left. That will lead you back to the parking area. This loop is about 6 miles.

Taconic–Hereford MUA

The Taconic–Hereford Multiple Use Area, one of the largest MUAs in Dutchess County, has been set aside for its great upland game hunting and other outdoor activities. It's a 909-acre oasis for mountain bikers and generally is not known as a mainstream mountain bike area. It's a gem and will fulfill anybody's wanderlust, with its easy yet stimulating 11 miles of four-wheel-drive roads and singletrack.

More than 8 miles of well-maintained, hard-packed, four-wheel-drive roads loop through a low, hilly terrain. The trail is fast-paced, exhilarating, and a joy to ride. Some spur trails take off and wind through an attractive, dense hardwood forest as singletrack. The terrain consists of rolling hills with somewhat steep slopes, but none of the routes for riding require technical handling skills. Don't think. Just ride. These trails are perfect for easy or fast cruising, depending on your mood or how much caffeine you've imbibed.

The Taconic–Hereford MUA is composed almost entirely of deciduous hardwood forest and offers a compact and robust habitat for a variety of upland game animals like grouse, squirrel, woodcock, and rabbit. Throughout the ride are innumerable opportunities to view the cherished wildlife that flourishes here.

An MUA provides recreational options for a variety of sportsmen and outdoor enthusiasts. Area use regulations allow individuals to hunt, fish, and even trap game. Access throughout these MUAs is usually via networks of four-wheel-drive roads that, during winter, provide suitable snowmobile routes. The great concept here is that these roads provide some fine mountain biking paths as well, and during seasons when hunting is banned, the place is wide open to exploration by bike.

General location: Dutchess County in the town of Pleasant Valley. The Taconic–Hereford MUA is located along the eastern side of the Taconic State Parkway and south of Tyrell Road.

Elevation change: The 8-mile loop traverses a low, hilly terrain and provides for some easy riding. The more challenging riding takes place on the singletrack spur trails.

Season: From April to September you're safe. I have been told by the New York State Department of Environmental Conservation to wear orange

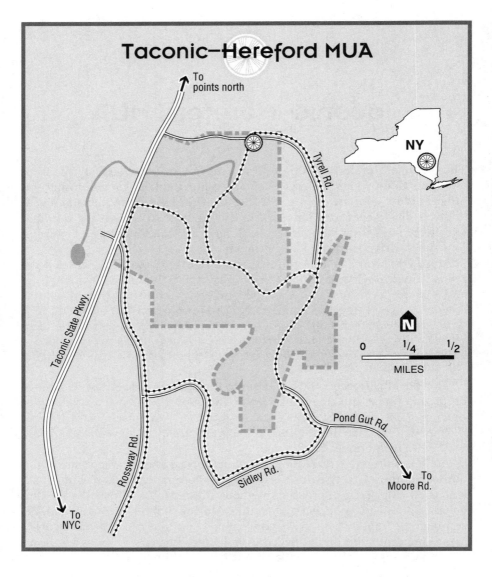

Taconic–Hereford MUA

To points north

Tyrell Rd.

NY

Taconic State Pkwy.

N

| 0 | 1/4 | 1/2 |

MILES

Pond Gut Rd.

Rossway Rd.

Sidley Rd.

To Moore Rd.

To NYC

during the hunting season to avoid being mistaken for a large squirrel or deer with a helmet on.

Services: The towns of Pleasant Valley along U.S. Highway 44 and Millbrook on New York 44A provide most services. In nearby Millbrook is a 250-acre Chinese-style garden called Innisfree Garden, with streams, waterfalls, and terraces. It is located on Tyrell Road. If you have time, it's worth checking out.

Hazards: This is a popular destination for hunters, and hunting seasons start at the end of September and end sometime in March. The area is available for riding around those dates. Call the Department of Environmental Conservation for exact dates and details.

Rescue index: You will not find the crowds you might encounter in southern Westchester County, so be smart and travel safe, tell friends or family where you are going, and carry a compass and a whistle (for scaring the bears). Even though the area is only 909 acres, you might get disoriented. But not to worry; if you head long enough in one direction on any of the four-wheel-drive roads, you will reach a paved road in less than 4 miles, at which point you may flag down a passing motor vehicle and explain your predicament.

Land status: New York State Department of Environmental Conservation manages the forest as a multiple-use area.

Maps: The Department of Environmental Conservation will supply you with a general map for this MUA, along with several other MUAs in Dutchess County, in a small brochure.

Finding the trail: Drive north on the Taconic State Parkway. There are two access points, one of which is directly off the Taconic State Parkway. I have found, however, that as one travels at 55 mph, the entrance comes up a bit too fast, and I am always missing it. I usually take the second exit, Tyrell Road. Turn right onto Tyrell Road, which turns into a dirt road. You will soon come to the Department of Environmental Conservation sign for the Taconic–Hereford MUA. There is parking immediately to your left.

Sources of additional information:

New York State Department of Environmental Conservation, Region 3
21 South Putt Corners Road
New Paltz, NY 12561-1696
(845) 256–3000

Wheel and Heel
2275 Route 9
Fishkill, NY 12524
(914) 896–7591

Notes on the trail: The four-wheel-drive road heads in a southerly direction into the woods. Notice two singletrack spurs, one on your left and one on your right, that lead off into the woods about 200 feet into the ride. These paths are worth investigating and follow a perimeter path around the area. For now just remain on the four-wheel-drive path. You will pass by a few doubletrack paths leading off to your right in a westerly direction, but continue straight. At a T intersection with another four-wheel-drive road, turn left in an easterly direction. At the next intersection you may do one of two things: You can turn left and head in a northerly direction to end up on Tyrell Road, where you will just have to turn left again, and you will have returned via a loop to your parking area. Or you can bear right and head in a southerly direction. After crossing a small bridge, the road turns into Pond Gut Road. Turn right at the next road, Sidley Road. Turn right again at the next road, which is parallel to a stream. At the next intersection, Rossway Road, turn right, and head north to the Taconic Parkway. Travel for a short distance north on the side of the Taconic, and you will soon reach the first entrance into the Taconic–Hereford area, which I have always missed by car. Turn into the woods on the wide four-wheel-drive road, and at the next intersection with a four-wheel-drive road, turn left in a northerly direction toward your parking area near Tyrell Road.

Ye Olde Croton Aqueduct

The Old Croton Aqueduct, although no longer supplying water to New York City, provides an enjoyable passage for the mountain bike family seeking an easy ride along a wide, hard-packed dirt road. It's great for those new to mountain bike riding who don't have the technical skills necessary for different terrain. The generally flat path is 3 miles (one way) and provides easy, pleasant cruising. Often the twists, turns, and maneuvering that more technical trails demand serve to distract from gazing upon the scenery. The riding in this tour, however, allows attention to be focused on the woodland and distant scenery of the Hudson River and surrounding valley.

What makes this ride so interesting is the history that rounds out the package. This path was part of a project to bring lifesaving fresh water into a desperate New York City in 1830. Diseases from filth and contaminated drinking water were claiming lives across all social and economic classes. During these times fires raged throughout the city, and there was not enough water to fight them. The decision to import water into Manhattan led to the design and construction of the Old Croton Aqueduct. It drew water from the Croton River through a masonry-enclosed structure that ran 41 miles into New York City. Gravity pulled the water along. The scope of this engineering project was massive yet not innovative—the Assyrians and Romans had long ago built similar aqueducts using much of the same basic technology. Construction began in 1837 and was completed by 1842 with the help of 4,000 immigrant Irish laborers earning a mere seventy-five cents for a ten-hour day. The water filled the Yorkville Reservoir (now the Great Lawn in Central Park) and the Murray Hill Reservoir (now the site of the New York Public Library at 42nd Street and Fifth Avenue). Although designed to last for centuries, the aqueduct was discontinued in 1890. By 1925 the Great Lawn of Central Park had filled in to become the vast playground and outdoor concert setting of today. Spend a morning or afternoon riding along this path. It's another opportunity to enjoy a setting with a unique place in history.

General location: Town of Cortlandt in northern Westchester County, only 4 miles from Croton.

Elevation change: Generally flat and wide with some gradual grades.

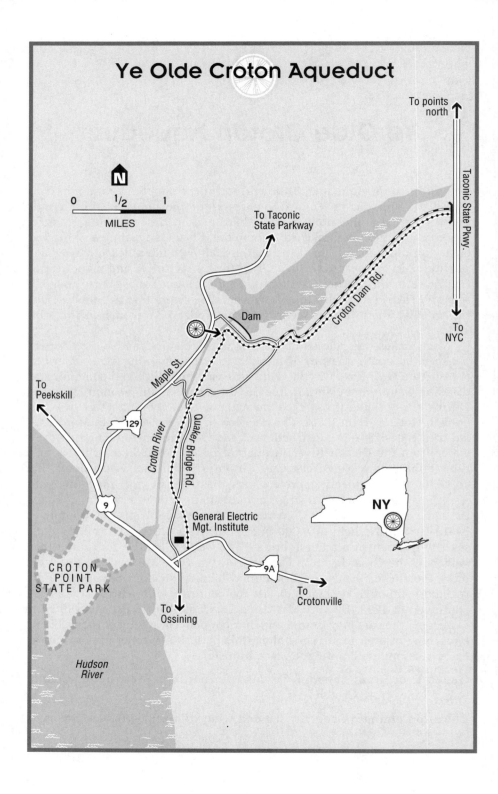

Ye Olde Croton Aqueduct

Season: The trails are available year-round, but when snow arrives and covers the trail, cross-country skiing becomes the sport. It's a good idea to stay away from the trails during wet weather, as they have a tendency to become muddy.

Services: The town of Croton provides most services. There is a small deli on Quaker Bridge Road as the trail nears its turnaround point at the General Electric Management Institute. Mountain bike rental, trail information, and supplies can be found at the bike shops below. Group rides are also organized each weekend.

Hazards: Keep an eye out for walkers, and watch for motor vehicles when the trail crosses a paved road.

Rescue index: The park is situated in a residential area. The route sees a fair amount of traffic from walkers and other bike riders, so help is usually close at hand.

Land status: New York State Park. There will be a sign calling this area OLD CROTON TRAIL WAY STATE PARK.

Maps: The path is fairly straightforward, and the map I have drawn should provide enough detail.

Finding the trail: Take the Taconic State Parkway north to the Underhill Road exit, just past the bridge that crosses the New Croton Reservoir. Proceed west on Underhill Road to where it ends at Route 129, Croton Lake Road. Turn right on Route 129, and after 3.5 miles turn left into Croton Gorge Park in the town of Cortlandt. There is a $6.00 parking fee. You can also turn left onto Croton Dam Road before the park, cross the dam, and find parking for your vehicle in a small parking area on your right directly after the dam.

Sources of additional information:

Old Croton Aqueduct State Historic Park
15 Walnut Street
Dobbs Ferry, NY 10522
(914) 693–5259

Bicycle Julio
45 South Bedford Road
Chappaqua, NY 10514
(914) 238–1312

Yorktown Cycling Center
1889 Commerce Street
Yorktown Heights, NY 10598
(914) 245–5504
www.yorktowncycle.com

Danny's Cycles
644 Central Avenue
Scarsdale, NY 10583
(914) 723–3408
www.dannyscycles.com

Notes on the trail: If you have left your car in the small parking area on Croton Dam Road, the white stone gravelly path begins just beyond the metal fence. An alternative would be to leave your car in the parking area of Croton Gorge Park. Take the maintenance road past and behind the rest rooms. It is visible from anywhere in the parking lot. This road makes a few switchbacks as it reaches the level of the aqueduct path. Keep bearing left until you reach the top, where the white gravel road you are on swings left. Take a sharp right in a southeasterly direction onto the aqueduct path. The path to the left leads you to a metal, fenced gate that leaves you on Croton Dam Road. If you are geared up for another tour, look up the Croton Dam Road tour, another ride in this book.

The 10-foot-wide, hard-packed dirt road leads you through an attractive and covered hardwood forest with rock outcroppings along the way. You will soon encounter a large, cylindrical stone structure. There are several along the route. These ventilator shafts were built to aerate the flowing water within the underground aqueduct and to maintain the water's fresh flavor and prevent if from being pressurized. The water traveled through the conduit at about 1.5 miles an hour, and the ventilators were originally placed every mile.

The path crosses the paved Quaker Bridge Road several times and skirts the north edge of Gerlach Park in Crotonville, following a grassy trail until you near the Indian Creek Culvert. You may turn around when you reach the General Electric Management Institute that looms in front where the path ought to be.

After you have turned back and returned the way you came, if you have some extra time, continue on the aqueduct trail until it reaches Croton Dam Road. Turn right on Croton Dam Road and follow it around for about 4 more miles of riding. This wide country road provides for some pleasant riding accompanied by great views of the surrounding countryside and Croton Reservoir.

Blue Mountain Nirvana

A magnificent network of designated mountain bike trails winds through some spectacular scenery in the Hudson Highlands. Blue Mountain Reservation in Peekskill, New York, is one of the rare Westchester County parks that still allow mountain biking. One can travel more than 7 miles of reasonably challenging carriage roads and singletrack that comb through 1,600 acres of hilly park. There is something here for every level of rider. Novices can enjoy the scenery along the gently rolling carriage roads. The more advanced rider can take on the tough hills that climb through a densely wooded landscape. The trails are strictly cardiovascular, not technical, and the rewards are in the fast-paced and well-controlled descents. The park has rules about riding at speeds that are out of control or threatening to hikers, plants, or wildlife. Remember to ride courteously and responsibly. It's the best way to ensure that these mountain bike nirvanas will long be available to us. Spend a complete day wandering past spectacular rock outcroppings and scenic ponds, exploring the eclectic terrain of this primeval forested park.

The region went through extensive geological faulting, in which sections of bedrock thrust hundreds and even thousands of feet up, causing extreme placement of the mountains and valleys. This type of faulting caused the steep-sided, narrow-topped ridge rising to Blue Mountain and Spitzenberg Mountain to grow to a height of more than 700 feet from the sea-level Hudson River. As you ride throughout the park, notice the other parallel gullies that run north-south as well. After these ridges were pushed up to these heights, they were intensely eroded by the gigantic continental ice sheets of the last Ice Age, which at times were more than 1 mile high. Many of the rock outcroppings on the trails include trees growing on the top or clinging to the sides with the roots set in the cracks. These distinctive characteristics of the terrain are the result of faulting and friction from the gigantic continental ice sheets of the last glacial period.

General location: A little more than 40 miles north of Manhattan, located in the town of Peekskill in Westchester County.

Elevation change: This part of Westchester County is known for its hilly and rocky terrain. A robust mixture of ascents and descents awaits the rider. None are too long or steep, and elevation changes rarely exceed 400 feet, but they may be rigorous.

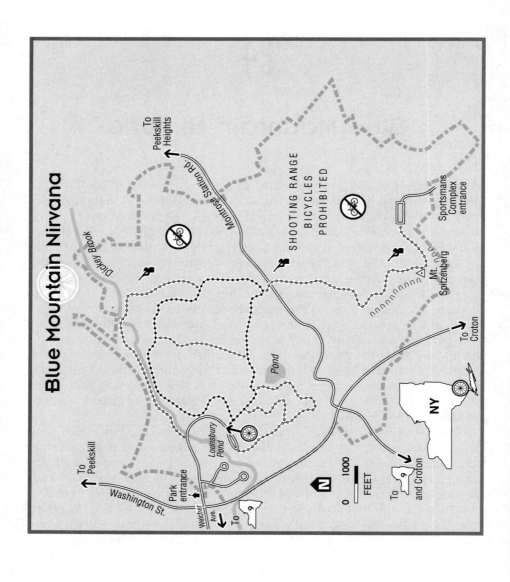

Blue Mountain Nirvana

SHOOTING RANGE
BICYCLES
PROHIBITED

To Peekskill Heights

Montrose Station Rd.

Dickey Brook

Pond

Lounsbury Pond

Washington St.

To Peekskill

Park entrance

Welcher Ave.

To

Mt. Spitzenberg

Sportsmans Complex entrance

To Croton

To 9 and Croton

N

0   1000

FEET

NY

Season: Year-round riding is available seven days a week from dawn to dusk. A parking fee of $6.00 will be collected at the park's gate. If there is no snow, get onto the trails. Do not let winter's cold stop you; just put on more clothing and enjoy the solitude.

Services: The town of Peekskill provides most services. Mountain bike rentals, trail information, and supplies can be found at the bike shops below. Group rides are also organized each weekend.

Hazards: Hikers and horses can be found on the trails, and there is a Cyclist Responsibility Code that requires you to yield the right-of-way to them. If they find you riding at out-of-control speeds, stomping on plants, menacing hikers, or running over wildlife, you will be removed from the park. Courteous and responsible conduct will assure the mountain biker's presence in this park. When approaching hikers or horses, be careful not to spook them by riding close or fast from either direction on the trail.

Rescue index: The compact trail system never takes you too far from your parking area, and usage from other recreational users puts you in close contact, in case you need it. The park is surrounded by the residential community of Peekskill.

Land status: Westchester County Department of Parks, Recreation and Conservation. Special thanks to the Westchester County Department of Parks for their effort in laying out all the trails and providing maps and accommodating the mountain-biking sport. If you are interested in helping out, contact Westchester County Department of Parks at (914) 242–PARK or join a club.

Maps: The park provides a well-detailed trail map with the designated rider-level mountain bike paths. You may call and ask the Westchester County Department of Parks (914–242–PARK) to send you a map.

Finding the trail: Take the Taconic Parkway north to the Briarcliff Manor exit. Route 9A will merge with Route 9. Turn right onto Welcher Avenue, and proceed east to the park entrance.

This park can be reached by the Metro North Railroad, Hudson Division Line. Disembark at the Montrose Station. Cross the tracks, take Montrose Station Road for 1 mile, and then make a left onto Washington Street. Remain on Washington Street for 1 mile, and then turn right onto Welcher Avenue into the park.

Sources of additional information:

Blue Mountain Reservation
Welcher Avenue
Peekskill, NY 10566
(914) 737–2194

Hickory and Tweed
410 Main Street
Armouk, NY 10504
(914) 273–3397
www.hickorytweed.com

Peekskill-Cortlandt Chamber of Commerce
1 South Division Street
Peekskill, NY 10566
(914) 737–3600

Bikeway
692 Route 6
Mahopac, NY 10541
(914) 621–2800

Danny's Cycles
644 Central Avenue
Scarsdale, NY 10583
(914) 723–3408
www.dannyscycles.com

Yorktown Cycling Center
1889 Commerce Street
Yorktown Heights, NY 10598
(914) 245–5504
www.yorktowncycle.com

Westchester County Department of Parks, Recreation and Conservation
25 Moore Avenue
Mt. Kisco, NY 10549
(914) 242–PARK

Notes on the trail: Continue past the park gate and bear left to the last parking area. You will notice a wide carriage road leading past a yellow triangular sign adjacent to a sign listing the rider responsibility codes. Begin your ride here.

Ride a short, steep pitch, and you will soon encounter a yellow-marked trail on your left; continue straight. One very pleasant aspect of riding at the Blue Mountain Reservation is that the trails are color coded and easy to follow. The coding system indicates three levels of riding skills. Yellow is for beginner, orange and green are for intermediate, and red is for advanced. The colors are painted on the trees. Don't be scared off by the red trail. If you are a beginning or intermediate rider, it will not be long before you master the required gnarliness.

Continue straight on the orange and green trail, and bear left at the next intersection with a trail on your right. Keep bearing left at the next intersection with a small trail leading off to your right. Bear left again at the next intersection. Remain on the green trail and ignore the red trail leading off

Mature sugar maples sentinel along a divine section of Blue Mountain doubletrack.

to your right. You will soon come to a T intersection. Bear right onto the orange and green trail. Turning left onto the red trail will take you back to the parking area. Continue on the orange and green trail, and climb a short, steep, rock hill that levels out soon. As you come to a large blowdown, take the small blowdown-influenced singletrack on your left that soon rejoins the trail. After passing through some magnificent rock outcroppings, you will exit the forest into a small field with a swamp to your right. Take a sharp left up a small hill. If you were to continue straight ahead, the orange and green trail would take you up toward Mount Spitzenberg. The path soon reenters the forest, where the blazes become blue. Proceed over some rocky terrain. Notice a yellow arrow on a brown sign at the next intersection, and bear left at the fork.

Descend along a moderately rocky trail through a beautiful hemlock forest. Several major rock outcroppings line both sides of the trail. You are in a general descent mode and will be for about half a mile. It's a nice reward for all the climbing you did before. Descend two long switchbacks and pass by five 100-year-old maple trees on your left. The forest you are traveling through at this point is all maple trees. Fork left at the red trail, and you will soon come to another fork; bear right. From this point on it's mostly singletrack marked with blue and orange V blazes on the trees. You will soon emerge onto a paved road. Turn left, and in about 50 feet turn left again back into the woods. Descend a steep hill and continue straight, ignoring the trail on your right. Continuing on this rolling section of trail, you will emerge into a parking area. Turn left at the clearing, and continue along the trail that runs along the left side of the lake. At the end of the lake will be a red wooden building. Make a left onto a small trail, and bear right at the next fork, which leads you down to a carriage road. Turn left onto the carriage road. Make another left at the next intersection, and continue down a hill over a small bridge. The singletrack changes into a carriage road and ends at a road. Return to your parking area from here, or head back in for another loop.

25

Alberto's Favorite

The North County Trailway is great for the beginner mountain biker and the entire family. I learned about it from Alberto, an attendant at a gas station near the town of Ossining. I inquired about directions, and Alberto observed my mountain bikes on top of my car. He asked me where I was biking. I told him I was looking for routes, and he shared one of his favorites, which was just off New York 9 not too far from where we were.

This trailway comprises 10 miles (5 miles one way) of out-and-back fun. It provides a great opportunity to bring the young ones who want to ride through the woods with a minimum of exertion or technical prowess. Because the trail is paved, it's a confidence builder for those new to the sport looking to break in and get accustomed to their new machine before graduating to the mightier challenges of doubletrack and singletrack. The trailway passes through an oasis of woodlands amid the urban sprawl. Fall is splendid in this setting, and the foliage at peak periods is intense.

This path runs mostly over the right-of-way of the former Putnam Railroad that was in service from 1881 to 1958. It was also the old stagecoach route that ran north from White Plains and into the many northern hamlets of Westchester. At full operation the Putnam Railroad served twenty-two stations, some of which still exist today. Thanks to the National Trails System Act of 1983, the rails-to-trails program converts abandoned railroad tracks into public, recreational trailways throughout the United States.

General location: This tour is about 34 miles from Manhattan in northwest Westchester near Eastview and Tarrytown.

Elevation change: The trail travels over a railroad grade but is nevertheless quite smooth and slightly inclined.

Season: This is four-season territory, except when the trail is covered with snow.

Services: Most services can be found in Tarrytown along NY 9.

Hazards: In the beginning of the ride the path crosses Saw Mill River Road, and one should take care to look for cars coming in both directions because they will be coming around turns. Another hazard I should mention is that this path tends to be busy on weekends. Runners, roller bladers, and bikes going faster than they should are often seen darting

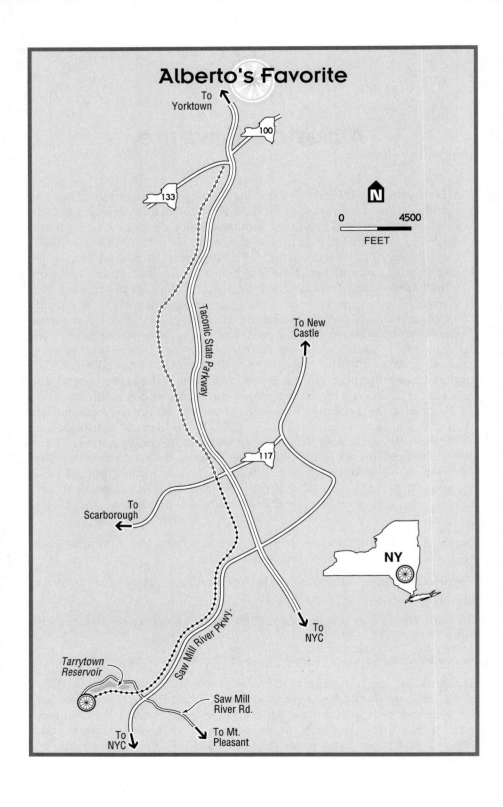

Easy cruising along the North County Trailway.

around on the path. Pay attention, and stay alert to these obstacles. You do not often have the solitude on this trail that you might have in the woods on some quiet doubletrack.

Rescue index: The trailway receives a fair amount of use, and there is usually someone who can provide assistance. The trailway is also surrounded by residential areas and is in close proximity to help if needed.

Land status: The trailway is managed by the Westchester County Department of Parks, Recreation and Conservation.

Maps: The Westchester County Department of Parks will send you a general map of the trailway system, but the paved trail is straightforward, goes in one direction, and is easy to follow. Unless you ride with your eyes closed, it's almost impossible to become lost.

Finding the trail: Take the Saw Mill River Parkway north to exit 23. The sign says SAW MILL RIVER ROAD, EASTVIEW. Turn left, and go 1.5 miles around the Tarrytown Reservoir. Look for the parking area on your right. Turn up Sunnyside Road, perpendicular to the parking area, and turn left onto the North County Trailway.

Sources of additional information:

Westchester County Department of Parks Recreation and Conservation
24 Moore Avenue
Mt. Kisco, NY 10549
www.westchester.com/parks/main2.htm

Bicycle Julio
45 South Bedford Road
Chappaqua, NY 10514
(914) 238–1312

Notes on the trail: The path is very straight, with few turns. It starts by skirting the Tarrytown Reservoir through a dense wooded corridor with sufficient canopy to block summer's midday sun. After 1 mile the path reaches the reservoir's pump station and ends on Saw Mill River Road. Cross the road, and continue up a short, steep hill and then down another short, steep hill, bearing left at the bottom of the hill. From this point on you will be on a gradual incline. This is characteristic of the old rail bed, which was designed to rise no more than two degrees from level. This portion of the ride continues for another 4 miles to the turnaround point. Return along the trailway toward where you began.

26

The Old "Put" Path

This is an exciting and easy trail wrapped in the beautiful pastoral landscape of Westchester County and its history. Although not technically challenging this partially paved and wide, hard-packed cinder trail is ideal for beginners testing out new equipment but also a lot of fun for novices. It's a great opportunity to bring the young ones in tow on a child seat or on small bikes. Spin some tales about what might have taken place in history along this very same route. This path is along the North County Trailway, which passes through an attractive and protected woodland corridor. In the fall the foliage is breathtaking. From the parking area described below, you can pedal south for 8 miles or north for about 13 miles. The path is fairly straight and easy to follow. It is mostly paved, except for a 4-mile segment in the northern section, which is encountered approximately 2 miles north of the parking area.

The path travels over the former Putnam Division Railway right-of-way. The old "Put" line of the New York Central Railroad ran from 1881 to 1958, connecting more than 56 miles of track and serving twenty-two stations. Some still exist. Through a nationwide rails-to-trails program, created in 1983 by the National Trails System Act, many abandoned railroad tracks have been converted to recreational paths. It has been said that the route was used for carrying George Washington's wounded to nearby Chappaqua following the battle of White Plains in October 1776. The French General Rochambeau also marched his forces along the route on his way from Newport, Rhode Island, to Yorktown, Virginia, in 1781. Your ride begins in the hamlet of Millwood, named after a local grain mill.

The old "Put" trail not only provided a means of transportation, it made for a pleasant day in the country. The railroads spurred the development of Chappaqua and Millwood, creating opportunities for commerce in the region. Although the line was primarily used for passengers, local farmers also used the old Put to ship milk, cider, apples, and other produce to the New York markets. The Millwood station was constructed in 1880. More development ensued, and there was extensive acquisition of watershed lands and the construction of the network of reservoirs and aqueducts for the New York Water Supply System. Within Westchester the development of this system involved the construction of three aqueducts, six reservoirs, and seven major dams starting in the 1830s and continuing into the early 1950s. In a number of locations, the railroad lines were built along or near the reservoir's watershed or the aqueduct's right-of-way lands, thereby

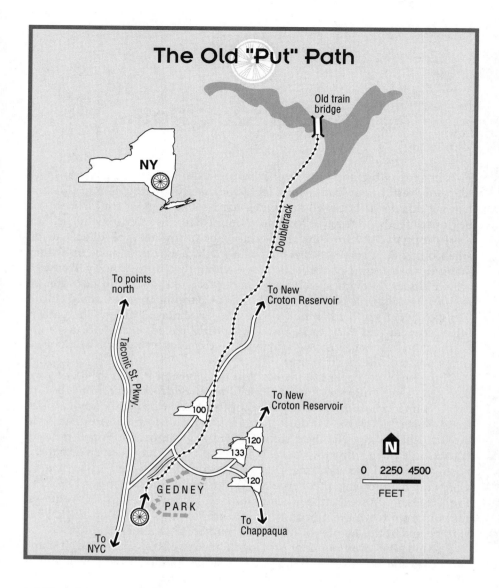

The Old "Put" Path

Old train bridge

NY

Doubletrack

To points north

To New Croton Reservoir

Taconic St. Pkwy.

To New Croton Reservoir

100

120

133

120

GEDNEY PARK

N

0   2250 4500

FEET

To NYC

To Chappaqua

taking advantage of the spectacular views. Your ride covers one of these paths.

General location: Northwest Westchester. This tour is about 40 miles from Manhattan near the towns of Millwood and Chappaqua.

Elevation change: The trail travels over a railroad grade and is quite smooth and slightly inclined.

Season: This is four-season territory, except when the trail is covered with snow.

Services: Most services can be found in Tarrytown along New York 9.

Hazards: This path tends to be busy on weekends. Runners, roller bladers, and bikes going faster than they should are often seen darting around on the path. Pay attention, and stay alert to these obstacles. You do not often have the solitude on this trail that you'd find in the woods on some quiet doubletrack.

Rescue index: The trailway receives a fair amount of use, and there is usually someone who can provide assistance. The trailway is also surrounded by residential areas and is in close proximity to help if needed.

Land status: The trailway is managed by the Westchester County Department of Parks, Recreation, and Conservation.

Maps: The Westchester County Parks Department will send you a general map of the North County Trailway system, but the trail is very straightforward and easy to follow. The trailway is paved and travels in one direction. Many other trail users can be seen on the trail, and unless you ride with your eyes closed, it's almost impossible to get lost.

Finding the trail: Take the Taconic State Parkway north to the Millwood exit, NY 100/NY 133. At the end of the exit ramp, turn left, and then turn right at the stop sign onto NY 100/NY 133. Go to the traffic light (Mobil service station), and take a right turn onto NY 133. Look for a parking area in 0.25 mile on your right. Park there; the path begins directly in front of the parking area.

Source of additional information:

Westchester County Department of Parks Recreation and Conservation
25 Moore Avenue
Mt. Kisco, NY 10549
(914) 864–7000, (914) 864–7275 (twenty-four hour hotline)
www.westchestergov.com/parks/main2.htm

Notes on the trail: The path is straightforward, with few turns. This chapter describes the section of the pathway that leads 13 miles in a northerly direction. An optional 8-mile section lies south of the parking area, too.

Begin your journey by turning left onto the special paved North County Trailway path that will take you in an easterly and then northerly direction and will soon cross Millwood Road. The paved portion of the trail extends for about 2 miles and terminates alongside a small pond. Look for a small dirt singletrack leading to your right. Continue down a small dip that will cross a wet section of trail, and then climb above the small rock retaining wall, where you will find the continuation of the trail. The trail becomes more singletrack at this point, but it is wide and smooth and takes on the level of the original railroad grade. One small section of the path where the trail surface undulates reminded me of a roller coaster.

The path soon enters a densely wooded forest with such a thick canopy that it feels like riding through a tunnel of trees. You will emerge from the woods in front of the railway trestle bridge that carried the trains over the Croton Reservoir. It is quite a sight and a great place to stay a while and take in the scenery. You can cross the bridge and continue on a singletrack for another 5 miles, passing through the old stations of Yorktown Heights, Amawalk, and Baldwin Place. To return face the direction you came from, and start to pedal. It is that simple.

Ninham Mountain MUA

A multiple-use area (MUA) is a parcel of land that provides recreational options. Area use regulations allow individuals to hunt, fish, and even trap game. Networks of four-wheel-drive roads often provide the transportation pathways necessary for accessing MUA resources. Hunters use these roads during the fall. During the winter these routes are often used as snowmobile trails. For mountain bikers these dirt roads mean an opportunity to gear up and get out. During seasons when hunting is banned, these unique wilderness areas are wide open to explore on bike.

This particular MUA is located in the town of Kent, just north of the West Branch Reservoir and about 3 miles east of the village of Carmel. There are approximately 8 miles of four-wheel-drive roads through 1,023 acres. Two major dirt road systems begin from the parking area and wind through a mixed hardwood forest. There's a 4-mile, out-and-back route with one road ascending for 1 mile with a 2-mile singletrack (1 mile, one way) linked at its end. The other dirt road descends for 2 miles and terminates at Boyds Road on the West Branch Reservoir. From that point it is a 5-mile return to the parking area, forming a 7-mile loop.

The rolling plateau and steep, densely wooded slopes of the Ninham MUA make for challenging terrain that is not terribly technical but requires good stamina. The 1-mile climb along the dirt road ascending Ninham Mountain is a real lung stretcher and worth attempting. A 1.5-mile singletrack traverses a ridge near the summit, and then the return descent deals the payback. The second road winds through another section of the MUA. You are east of Clarence Fahnestock Park and close to some of the rides detailed in that park. New York 301 connects both areas.

The mountain is named after Daniel Ninham, a member of the Wappinger Indians tribe and a devoted friend of the people who settled the area.

General location: Putnam County, near the town of Carmel.

Elevation change: There is only one serious hill climb, and that is the 1-mile, four-wheel-drive road on the right side of the last parking area. There may not be enough oxygen in the air to fill your lungs going up, but the return descent will put a smile on your face as you blast your way down.

Season: April to September provides the best riding opportunities. Call the Department of Environmental Conservation to get details of the hunting season. Wet weather does not affect or rut the hard-packed dirt roads, so a day after a rain shower should be no problem for riding.

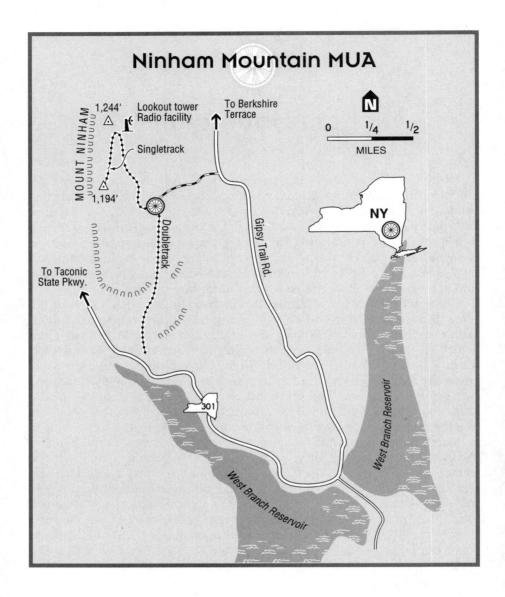

Ninham Mountain MUA

MOUNT NINHAM

1,244'
Lookout tower
Radio facility

To Berkshire
Terrace

Singletrack

1,194'

Doubletrack

To Taconic
State Pkwy.

Gipsy Trail Rd.

N

0   1/4   1/2
MILES

NY

301

West Branch Reservoir

West Branch Reservoir

Services: Services can be found in Lake Carmel and Kent Corners.

Hazards: Hunting seasons start in the beginning of October and end in March. The area is available for riding around those dates. Call the New York State Department of Environmental Conservation for exact dates and details.

Rescue index: This is not one of your mainstream mountain biking areas, so you will probably not see too many other bikers; carry an extra tube, water, and snacks. If you become disoriented just head downhill. This will eventually lead you to NY 301, which has a substantial amount of vehicular traffic on it.

Land status: New York State land. The New York State Department of Environmental Conservation manages this state land as an MUA. These state-owned parcels of land have been set aside to provide a place for hunters and other recreationalists who may not be affiliated with a hunting club or own suitable acreage for such activities. Hunting is often not permitted in many of the counties that are within easy driving distance of New York City. These lands are therefore inaccessible to the urban hunter.

Maps: The USGS 7.5-minute series, Lake Carmel quadrangle provides sufficient detail of this area.

Finding the trail: Take the Taconic State Parkway north, and exit at NY 301. Turn right, and head east on NY 301 as it follows along the West Branch Reservoir. Just before you reach the road that passes over the dam of the West Branch Reservoir, turn left onto the unmarked Gipsy Trail Road. You will see signs for Putnam County Park at this intersection. Follow this road to the Department of Environmental Conservation sign for the NINHAM MULTIPLE USE AREA, turn left, and continue to the end of the dirt road, which terminates at a circular parking area. There will be two barriers, one to the left and the other—with a stop sign posted on it—to the right. The Ninham Mountain ascent begins beyond the barrier on your right and the second, lower road begins beyond the left barrier.

Sources of additional information:

New York State Department of Environmental Conservation, Region 3
21 South Putt Corners Road
New Paltz, NY 12561-1696
(845) 256–3000

The Bicycle Shop, Inc.
Route 44, Main Street
Pleasant Valley, NY 12569
(845) 635–3161

Bikeway
692 Route 6
Mahopac, NY 10541
(914) 621–2800

Wheel and Heel
65 Gleneida Avenue
Carmel, NY 10512
(914) 228–1206

Notes on the trail: Start by passing the barrier on the right side and begin the gradual but steady climb. After 1 mile of a steady climb, the abandoned lookout tower will be within your sights. Just before you reach the top, look to your left and notice the large, three-pole utility platform. Just to the right of that is a small, overgrown, grass-covered, two-wheel-drive road. The trail gradually descends through a primitive forest for 0.8 mile and degrades into an unnegotiable singletrack. Turn around, and head back the way you came. As you get back to the lookout tower, catch your breath, and get ready for that lip-stretched descent on the mile-long hill you came up earlier.

The second dirt road leading from the parking area descends 2 miles to the West Branch Reservoir. After reaching the reservoir turn left, and proceed 5 miles to the parking area. Just before you reach the road that passes over the dam of the West Branch Reservoir, turn left onto the unmarked Gipsy Trail Road. You will see signs for Putnam County Park at this intersection. Follow this road to the Department of Environmental Conservation sign for the NINHAM MULTIPLE USE AREA. Turn left, and continue to the end of the dirt road, which terminates at the circular parking area.

28

Hubbard–Perkins
Conservation Area

More than 9 miles of abandoned, well-maintained wooded country roads traverse a serene and unpopulated wooded landscape in the middle of Putnam County. The main course consists of a 7-mile (total) out-and-back, hard-packed road, and two short spur trails serve as the dessert on this full-course mountain bike meal. These roads flow through beautiful meadows and open forests and along a meandering stream. The trail passes by an undisturbed valley some 4 miles long and 2 miles wide and crisscrosses several streams. It is bordered by stone walls and full-grown, mature trees. Land parcels are delineated by these walls. The walls of the valley are steep, wooded slopes that rise 1,100 feet. Extensive stands of hemlock and mountain laurel are noticeable at the higher elevations.

Bike-handling skill requirements are minimal. The easy grades and good cruising, except for one long climb at the end of the main route, make this an ideal ride for beginners who are ready to start advancing their skills. For the more experienced dirt disciple, this tour is remote and secluded, with lots of wildlife and an opportunity to get in some fast doubletrack.

Thanks to the Open Space Institute, a nonprofit land preservation organization, the estates of Helen Fahnestock Campbell Hubbard and the adjacent Perkins estate (comprising approximately 4,000 acres of undeveloped mountains and woods) were combined. The lands were acquired for the preservation of open space in the Hudson Highlands.

The house at the entrance to the area belongs to Willie Conklin, who serves as caretaker on the lands. He removes blowdowns, maintains the trails, and is knowledgeable about the area. He said that around April the coyotes go into mating and do a lot of hooting. The area is plentiful with deer, and Willie says there are bears in the hills as well.

General location: The tour is located in Putnam County just west of Clarence Fahnestock Memorial State Park, near the intersection of New York 9 and NY 301.

Elevation change: The first 2 miles are fairly level at 500 feet, but the last 2 miles climb to an elevation of 1,100 feet.

Season: The trails should dry out by mid-April and provide good riding through December. If there is no snow on the trails, and if you do not

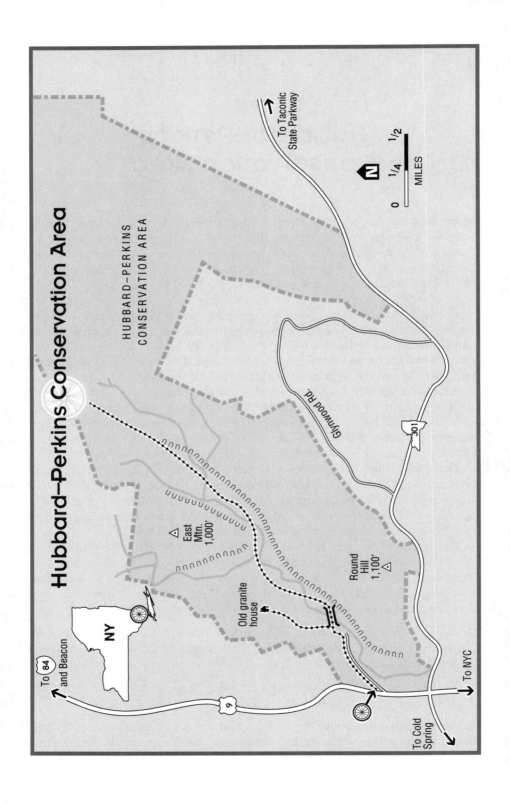

Hubbard–Perkins Conservation Area

HUBBARD–PERKINS
CONSERVATION AREA

East Mtn.
1,000'

Round
Hill
1,100'

Old granite
house

Glynwood Rd.

301

To Taconic
State Parkway

N

0   1/4   1/2
MILES

NY

To 84
and Beacon

9

To Cold
Spring

To NYC

mind the cold, get out there and enjoy the solitude and quiet of a winter day.

Services: Cold Spring offers most services along its popular Main Street.

Hazards: Raccoon rabies are present in this area of New York State, so do not approach or feed these animals in the park. The eastern deer tick spreads Lyme disease, so use insect repellent on your clothing and around your ankles and shoes.

Rescue index: At most you will be about 4 miles from the well-traveled NY 301.

Land status: New York State Office of Parks and Recreation, the Taconic State Park and Recreation Commission.

Maps: New Jersey Trail Conference's "East Hudson Trails," Trail Map 2 provides complete coverage of this trail and the surrounding area and is waterproof and tearproof. It sells for $8.95 and can be found at most outdoor-type stores. USGS 7.5-minute series, West Point quadrangle also provides detail.

Finding the trail: Take the Taconic Parkway north and exit at NY 301 going west. Continue on NY 301, and turn north on NY 9. About a quarter of a mile on your right, the trail begins. Park along the stone wall, but do not block the driveway.

Sources of additional information:

Bikeway
692 Route 6
Mahopac, NY 10541
(914) 621–2800

Cold Spring/Garrison Area Chamber of Commerce
P.O. Box 36
Cold Spring, NY 10156
(845) 265–3200

Wheel and Heel
2275 Route 9
Fishkill, NY 12524
(914) 896–7591

Notes on the trail: You will begin on an old, wide, paved road bordered by stone walls and old-growth trees. Families built their homes along this road, and the remains of the foundations of their homes can be seen along the sides of the trail. You will come to a fork in the road with a lesser road leading off to your right, blocked by a metal fence. Bear right onto this road, traveling over some metal bridges and crossing several brooks and streams. In about half a mile, you will pass by the remnants of an old stone

Bridge crossing a stream through the valley of the Hubbard-Perkins Conservation Area.

entrance. That spur-trail road to your left leads uphill to the site of an old granite house that was buried for unknown reasons. Continue straight on the wide, four-wheel-drive jeep road. At 1.5 miles an open clearing provides you with good views on your right of the 1,100-foot Round Hill and the smaller unnamed hill just north of it. The road climbs along the west bank of the stream for 0.1 mile and levels out. After about 2 miles, a fork to the right begins a steep ascent to the end of the trail.

Franklin D. Roosevelt State Park

Franklin D. Roosevelt State Park is evidence that good things, even places to mountain bike, come in small packages. This state park is not deep in the heart of wilderness. It's not hammerhead heaven or the holy training grounds for technique. What this compact urban park does offer is some relaxing family riding, picnicking, boating on a picturesque lake, swimming in a large outdoor pool, and Italian ices. The well-maintained roads and trails make it an ideal place for a beginner mountain biker to venture off road. The wide gravel roads provide a good surface for someone new to off-road riding and first getting the feel of a bike on surfaces other than pavement.

A 5-mile loop of hard-packed dirt roads winds its way past two pleasant, scenic lakes (Crom Pond and Mohansic Lake) and through attractive hardwood and conifer forests. There is a "family-style" singletrack that children can attempt, but if you need to bail out, switch to the wider dirt road that runs parallel to it.

Boat rentals are available at Mohansic Lake, and a large swimming pool is open during the summer; you can cool off here and enjoy some nearby refreshments. Franklin D. Roosevelt State Park has something for everyone and provides a full day of diverse family fare.

General location: The park is approximately 30 miles north of Manhattan off the Taconic Parkway.

Elevation change: The trail follows fairly level grades with no strenuous hill climbs.

Season: These trails are great in any season, and if you do not mind the cold, dress warmly and enjoy the solitude of a popular park.

Services: Yorktown is next to the park and offers some services. Two concession stands are located in the park; one is near parking area 1, and the other is located near the swimming pool.

Hazards: During the weekends the paths might be crowded with walkers and other bikers, so drive cautiously and courteously. Raccoon rabies are present in this area of New York State, so do not feed, touch, or approach them. If you see one acting a bit strange, contact park personnel and inform them of its whereabouts.

Rescue index: Because this is an urban park, people are always around, and park personnel can be found at the park office near the entrance.

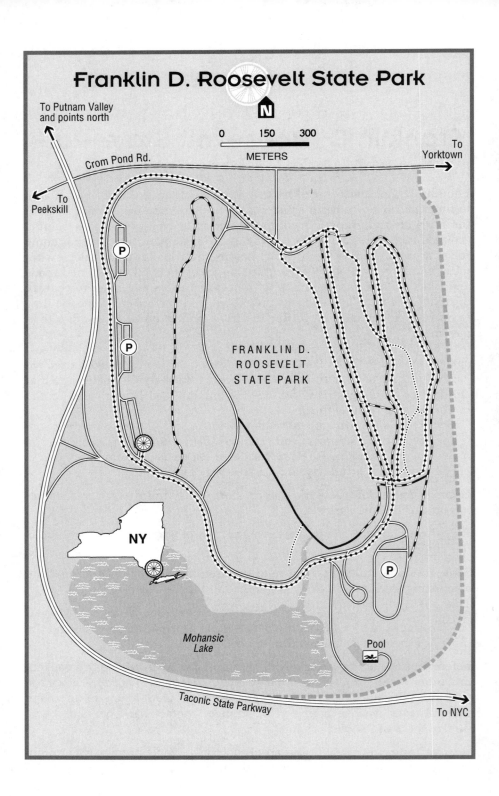

Land status: New York State Park.

Maps: A park map is available by paying the $3.00 entrance fee into the park, and it provides very good coverage of the trails.

Finding the trail: Take the Taconic Parkway north until you see signs for Franklin D. Roosevelt State Park. Exit the Taconic, pay at the park entrance, turn into the park, and bear left for parking area 1.

Source of additional information:

Franklin D. Roosevelt State Park
2957 Crom Pond Road
Yorktown Heights, NY 10598
(914) 245–4434

Notes on the trail: Park at area 1, return to the park road, and turn left. A small, narrow, paved path to the right of the park's roadway runs parallel to it. Get onto that path, and soon views of Mohansic Lake open up. This path ends at the park road, which leads to the boat-launching site. Do not turn right here, but rather continue straight ahead toward the swimming pool parking area up a short hill. Bear left at the fork near the parking area's entrance, and ahead on your right look for a brown sign labeled Nature Trail.

Turn right, and take the hard-packed, wide dirt road. The trail descends and comes to a T intersection with another wide, well-surfaced trail. Turning right will take you into the pool zone. Turn left onto the fairly level path, which soon ascends a small hill. As the path turns a corner, keep bearing left as you pass through a conifer forest of hemlock and spruce. You will see some other paths leading into the main trail you are on; however, continue straight ahead in the southerly direction you have been maintaining since rounding the bend.

The trail ends where you began in 1.4 miles. Cross the paved park road directly across from this "nature trail" and look for a small singletrack leading into the woods. Turn onto this trail and bear right. This is a great singletrack to try the kids on, and it will take you through an attractive, dense forest for 1.5 miles. It ends at a well-built wooden bridge that spans a small brook. Cross the bridge, and turn right onto a gravelly paved road. This road will continue around a bend and proceed south. Continue straight up a small hill and past a low wooden barrier fence that runs alongside a picnic area and playing field. Turn right at the next intersection. If this path looks familiar, it should, as you have been down it once before. For the sake of a good full ride, let's do it again. Take it to its termination at the paved park road, and turn right onto the wide, gravelly park road. Take this to its end, and then return to parking area 1 or ride to one of the other attractions in the park.

Shawangunk
Mountain Tours

Ninety miles north of Manhattan lies one of the finest mountain bike trail systems in New York. This trail system, composed of mostly nineteenth-century carriage roads, is spread throughout 24,000 magnificent acres in the Shawangunk Mountains. The area includes a state park, private preserves, and the Mohonk resort property. The area is quite popular with hikers, equestrians, cross-country skiers, and mountain bikers. The charming college town of New Paltz caters to the needs of the outdoor set, and the grandeur and beauty of mountains and cliffs have attracted people primarily from the metropolitan New York and New England regions for more than a century. There are many attractions. New Paltz has some of the oldest streets in America. Take a stroll down Huguenot Street, where several stone houses evoke a rural European village. They were built by homesick French Huguenot families 300 years ago. Several wineries, apple farms, and pumpkin patches in the area are worth visiting, too.

The Shawangunk creation bears some very important geologic history. Hundreds of millions of years ago, a great landmass called Appalachia stretched from what is now Maine to Alabama. Erosion wiped out its identity, and the region was submerged under a sea. Massive quantities of eroded material accumulated and gradually cemented together. After a great upheaval the landmass was lifted out of the sea to great heights and folded into fantastic shapes. This mountain-building era is known to geologists as the Appalachian Revolution and is currently represented in the Appalachian Mountains. There are many different names to portions of this range. The 30-mile section in New York, where Lake Minnewaska and Lake Mohonk lie, was called Shawangunk by the Native Americans. Sedimentary rocks, made up of fragments of other rocks and eroded materials deposited under water, form the Shawangunks. Three general types of rocks are found in this area and are readily identified. The first is quartz conglomerate, which is very hard and resistant and contains many different materials from silt particles to pebbles. The second is sandstone. The third is shale, which is much older than the other two. The last period in this creation story is the Ice Age, beginning perhaps 125,000 years ago and ending possibly 10,000 years ago. The glaciers of this period acted as nature's gigantic bulldozer. They moved from northeast to southeast, gouging out deep ravines in the mountains and scattering thousands of boulders of immense proportions. The glaciers left a chain of lakes: Mohonk, Minnewaska, and Awosting, among others.

A maze of several mountain bike paths winds through the impressive terrain of Minnewaska State Park Preserve. This beautiful park is characterized by unique and sensitive environments, valuable for their many rare geologic and ecological features. The park is situated on the dramatic Shawangunk Mountain ridge, which rises more than 2,000 feet above sea level. The ridge dominates the park and its immediate environs as well as the rolling agricultural landscape of the surrounding towns and hamlets below.

The Mohonk Mountain House, a sprawling 125-year-old Victorian castle, sits on 2,200 acres and offers a few spectacular bike trails (and other trails that are equally impressive and designated for hiking). The Mohonk Mountain House is a national historic landmark. The building complex and surrounding land are included in the landmark designation. The Mohonk Preserve, which adjoins the resort, provides an additional 5,500 acres of woodlands and trails.

The mountain bike possibilities in the Shawangunk Mountains are nearly endless. Day rides from New York City usually entail an early start and a late return. Consider staying overnight at one of New Paltz's many bed-and-breakfast inns or motels, and make it a long, memorable weekend.

30

Bonticou Road Tour

Roughly 10 miles of hard-packed carriage roads traverse the unique mountain ridges of the scenic and spectacular Shawangunk Mountains. More than 5,600 acres of precipitous, craggy cliffs, glens, mountain lakes, and mixed forests cover the land, which is part of the Mohonk Preserve.

Some of the most spectacular and scenic doubletrack can be found in these mountains on this 10-mile loop tour. It's easy to spend hours and hours cruising along nineteenth-century carriage roads that were built for vacationers of past eras who visited these mountains often. These trails are considered among the finest in the East. Beginning in the early nineteenth century, America entered the Romantic period, during which renewed emphasis was placed on the arts and nature. A good view was held in high regard. The aristocracy and intelligentsia of New York, who often took the long trip up the Hudson River by boat, found this an area of abundant natural beauty and prime meeting grounds.

Along these pleasant trails are great panoramic views of the distant pastoral farmland of the Wallkill. The expansive Roundout River Valley lies below. These carriage roads generally follow the contours of the land and do not require any great stamina or special technical skills. The exception is the steep Link Trail, which connects the Mohonk Preserve Visitor Center parking area to the beginning of the Bonticou carriage road.

What once provided turn-of-the-twentieth-century visitors with a horse-drawn carriage tour through a beautiful woodland forest now benefits mountain bikers with stretches of gentle hill climbs and beautiful scenery. A tour at Bonticou makes for a day of memorable riding.

General location: Travel about 90 miles north of Manhattan on the New York State Thruway (Interstate 87) to exit 18, New Paltz.

Elevation change: The trail begins at a little higher than 900 feet and gradually climbs to 1,100 feet. The route then levels out and follows the contour of the mountain. There are some ascents to Guyot Hill and some descents as you go down Cedar Drive, but nothing too taxing.

Season: Fall is absolutely breathtaking, with colors filling the surrounding valleys. Winter usually brings snow, but if there is no snow on the trails, put some extra layers of clothing on and enjoy the popular trails for yourself. Late spring and summer are excellent, with warm breezes convecting up from the valleys.

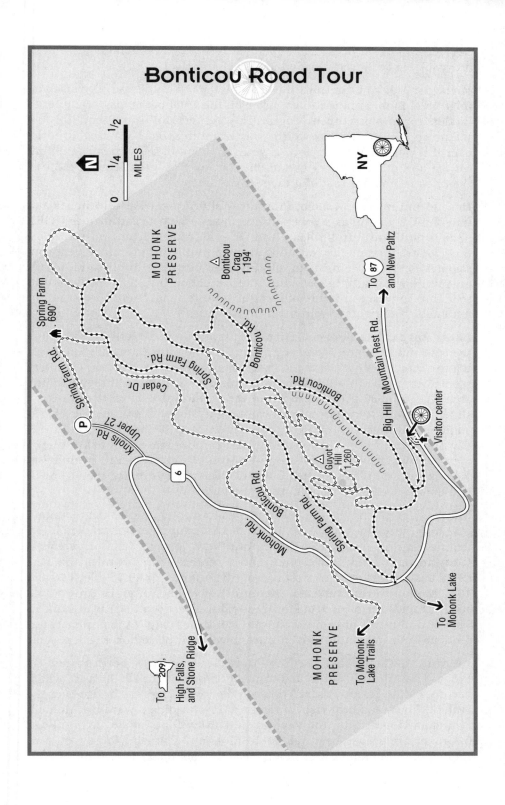

Bonticou Road Tour

MILES
0 1/4 1/2
N

NY

MOHONK PRESERVE

Bonticou Crag 1,194'

Spring Farm 690'

Spring Farm Rd.

Cedar Dr.

Spring Farm Rd.

Bonticou Rd.

Bonticou Rd.

P

Knolls Rd.
Upper 21

6

Bonticou Rd.

Mohonk Rd.

Spring Farm Rd.

Guyot Hill 1,260'

Bonticou Rd.

Big Hill

Mountain Rest Rd.

To 87 and New Paltz

Visitor center

To 209, High Falls, and Stone Ridge

MOHONK PRESERVE

To Mohonk Lake Trails

To Mohonk Lake

Services: Most services can be found at New Paltz. Mountain bike rentals are available at Bicycle Depot and Wheel and Heel.

Hazards: Many of the trails traverse the tops of flat ledges. Because you might feel more inclined to go faster on the level paths, pay attention to hidden turns along open ledges. This respect for speed and for the unknown beyond may be worth your while to avoid becoming airborne over the Wallkill Valley below. If you are riding in the winter, watch out for ice and other slippery conditions that may be prevalent on the carriage roads. You are required to wear a helmet.

Rescue index: The Mohonk Preserve Visitor Center has telephones and first aid. On weekends a volunteer mountain bike patrol known as GORP (Gunks Off-Road Patrol) rides a beat. They provide help and answer questions for other riders they encounter on the trail. They promote safety consciousness, from helmets to passing-zone etiquette to first aid. This organization has also helped with fire prevention by riding the trails and scanning for flare-ups throughout the forests, and it encourages other mountain bike riders to join them.

Land status: The Bonticou Road and its network of trails pass through the Mohonk Preserve. Mohonk Preserve is a nonprofit organization working to protect the natural lands in the Shawangunk Mountains. There are special programs in environmental education and tours throughout the area. These 5,500 acres are open to the public from dawn to dusk for a small fee. A $10 yearly seasonal-use pass is charged for each bicycle. In addition a day-use fee of $5.00 (weekdays) or $7.00 (weekends and holidays) is charged each time you ride. You can become a Mohonk Preserve member, which will cut down the day-use charges if you're planning to visit frequently. Whatever the cost, a wonderful day's outing awaits you in this unique setting of mountains, forests, and lakes.

Maps: After paying the day fee at the visitor center, ask for the mountain bike map. Take along hiking maps, too, as they supply more detailed information on the trails. The New York–New Jersey Trail Conference's "Shawangunk Trails" waterproof and tearproof map provides the best detail and can be found at most outdoor-type stores for $9.95. Maps 10 and 10A, Mohonk Preserve, Lake Mohonk Resort and Virginia Smiley Preserve, provide the most detail for these rides. These roads are well marked. Bicycle trail blazes are posted on trees along the route. At important intersections the name of the road you are traveling is posted on wooden signs.

Finding the trail: Take the New York Thruway (I–87) north to exit 18. Proceed past the tollbooths, and turn left onto New York 299 (west), which becomes Main Street. Proceed through the town, cross the bridge over the Wallkill River, and bear right at the next fork heading toward the Mohonk Mountain House. After the town of New Paltz, continue on County Road 6. Cross a bridge, and bear right at the Mohonk Mountain House sign, continuing onto Mountain Rest Road. Head up this road for 1.75 miles until you see the Mohonk Preserve Visitor Center on your right. Directly across from the center is the parking area. You can park here and ascend the 0.2-mile Link Trail that climbs from the parking area and intersects with Bonticou Road. The other option is to continue on CR 6 and park in the parking area just after the entrance to Mohonk Mountain House. There is a $6.00 fee for this parking area. Both alternatives lead to Bonticou Road.

Sources of additional information:

Ulster County Tourism and Public Information Office
10 Westbrook Lane
Kingston, NY 12402
(845) 340–3566

New Paltz Chamber of Commerce
124 Main Street
New Paltz, NY 12561
(845) 255–0243

Wheel and Heel
116 South Plank Road
Newburgh, NY 12550
(845) 567–1740

Mohonk Preserve
P.O. Box 715
New Paltz, NY 12561-0715
(845) 255–0919
www.mohonkpreserve.org

Mohonk Mountain House
1000 Mountain Rest Road
New Paltz, NY 12561
(845) 255–1000 or (800) 772–6646 (reservations)
www.mohonk.com

Bicycle Depot
3 Church Street
New Paltz, NY 12561
(845) 255–3859
www.bicycledepot.com

Notes on the trail: From the visitor center take the Link Trail (yellow-marked) a short distance up a steep hill to the Bonticou carriage road. You will ascend from an elevation of about 950 feet to 1,100 feet in 0.4 mile. The Link Trail comes to an end at Bonticou Road. Turn right at the intersection. Bonticou Road is a wide, exquisite, level, hard-packed road that passes through forests of maple, oak, and hemlock and provides great views of the pastoral farmland of the Wallkill River Valley to the east. After 1.3 miles a four-way intersection offers two options.

The family chariot gliding along Spring Farm Road.

Turning to the left will take you uphill along the Guyot Hill loop trail to an elevation of 1,260 feet. This small loop passes a small, picturesque pond and returns you to the same intersection with Bonticou Road. You can also take this loop to return to the visitor center, because there is a connection at the western end of the loop linking back down into Bonticou Road. Guyot Hill is unique. The Shawangunks are mostly made up of a hard conglomerate rock that covers the other rocks. This small hill is the highest mound of soft shale in the mountains not covered by the conglomerate. Guyot Hill and Bonticou Crag served as hiding grounds for militia during the Revolutionary War.

Continue on Bonticou Road by following the posted wooden sign reading BONTICOU ROAD. Farther along the road you will come across the tremendous blocklike boulders that make up the "talus" of the Bonticou Crag. These huge rock fragments, sometimes the size of a house, have fallen from the face of the cliff as a result of faulting, fracturing, and erosion. You are looking at rock that should be horizontally laid out, but the tremendous pressures from beneath the earth's surface have caused these landmasses to be pushed up vertically through a process called faulting. As you ride along views of the fallen rocks of Bonticou Crag come into view. Consider taking a short, vigorous rock scramble up the Crag to the summit where beautiful mountaintop views of the surrounding valleys and Catskill Mountains can be had.

A quarter-mile later you will come to another intersection. Let's become oriented and stand at the intersection with our noses facing north. Continue to your right down Cedar Drive as it leads off in a northerly direction through a mature hemlock forest. Cedar Drive takes you downhill to an intersection with Spring Farm Road. Continue on the main carriage road bearing left. Turn left uphill at the intersection with Spring Farm Road.

Continue up Spring Farm Road, bearing left at the intersection with Bonticou Road. The right fork will take you away from your parking at the visitor center, but it will link you from Bonticou Road into the Mohonk Lake trail systems. Spring Farm Road, the left fork, will take you back to CR 6, the Mohonk tollgate, and the Mohonk Preserve Visitor Center parking area.

Land of Oz

Imagine riding along smooth, wide, hard-packed, dirt carriage roads and traversing precipitous, craggy ledges that rise up hundreds of feet with magnificent views of distant farmland and river valleys. Does it sound like a mountain biker's dream? Perhaps, but it is within your reach. Just click your heels and get an early morning start for a full day of riding. Then take in 14 miles of carriage roads that weave along this unique mountain plateau in the scenic and spectacular Shawangunk Mountains.

The trails on this 14-mile loop encircle the Lake Mohonk area, whose landscape was sculpted by the last Ice Age. Mohonk, a Native American name meaning "top of the sky," towers above the nearby valleys and can be seen as a long ridge of high cliffs running in a north-south direction. Ironically they were once a landmass submerged deep within a large sea. Forces deep in the earth pushed this landmass out of the sea to great heights and creased it into bizarre shapes. Freezing water fractured the vertical cliffs, causing large boulders to plummet down the escarpment. The mile-high continental ice sheets from the last Ice Age became nature's bulldozers and gouged out deep clefts in the mountains, scattering thousands of tons of boulders of immense sizes and shapes across the landscape. The glaciers carved out a ravine on the top of this ridge along a fault line and created a chain of lakes, among them Mohonk and Minnewaska. About this time one of the glaciers pushed tremendous quantities of rock and debris into the south end of Lake Mohonk. When the ice melted the materials settled into a solid mass, preventing any water from passing through. Rains that fell on these mountains seeped through the landscape and fed underground streams that built up the lake through hidden channels and replenished its waters.

Visit the nineteenth-century Mohonk Mountain House overlooking the lake. It was purchased as a rundown tavern in 1869 by the Smiley brothers and has evolved into a 305-room hotel. It's still owned by the Smiley family. Surrounded by the Mohonk Preserve, the environs of the area reflect the lifestyle of leisure and elegance of bygone eras. Cruise along the faultless carriage roads and meander through the exquisite Shawangunk Mountains, with their exposed, craggy rock ledges and thick hemlock forests. A century ago horse-drawn carriages rode along the same trails. Park your bikes near the Mohonk Mountain House, and stroll through the nearby gardens and around the spring-fed half-mile-long mountain lake in front of this huge Victorian castle.

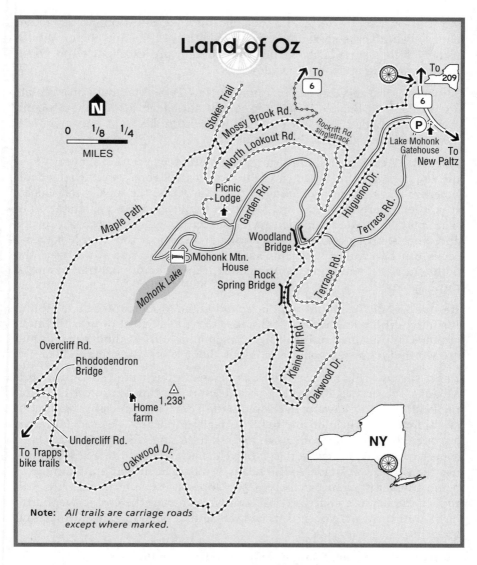

Land of Oz

N

0   1/8   1/4
MILES

Stokes Trail

Mossy Brook Rd.

To 6

To 209

Rockrift Rd. singletrack

North Lookout Rd.

Lake Mohonk Gatehouse To New Paltz

Maple Path

Picnic Lodge

Garden Rd.

Huguenot Dr.

Terrace Rd.

Woodland Bridge

Mohonk Mtn. House

Mohonk Lake

Rock Spring Bridge

Terrace Rd.

Overcliff Rd.

Rhododendron Bridge

Kleine Kill Rd.

Oakwood Dr.

Home farm

1,238'

NY

Undercliff Rd.

To Trapps bike trails

Oakwood Dr.

Note: *All trails are carriage roads except where marked.*

General location: About 90 miles north of Manhattan on the New York State Thruway to exit 18, near the town of New Paltz.

Elevation change: The ride begins at the Mohonk House parking area, elevation 1,100 feet, near the gatehouse. The trail basically follows the contour of the land, with some moderate hills punctuating the route. The long, traversing ascent along Kleine Kill Road at the end of the tour will be the most rigorous climbing you have to do. Once at the top it's all level riding with one last long downhill ride to the parking area.

Season: In the winter cross-country skiers can be found on the groomed tracks. If there is no snow, get your bike out, dress warmly, and take in the views. Don't forget to grab a hot chocolate at the Mohonk Mountain House. Fall fills the surrounding valleys with breathtaking colors. Winter usually brings snow. Late spring and summer are excellent, with warm breezes moving up from the valleys.

Services: Most services can be found at New Paltz. Mountain bike rentals are available at Bicycle Depot and Wheel and Heel. Within the Mohonk area, Picnic Lodge, a visitor center located 1.5 miles from the gatehouse, has a snack bar, gift shop, and picnic area.

Hazards: Weather conditions can make routes icy, wet, and slippery along the edge of the cliffs. Tread carefully, and control your speed when conditions are less than secure. Many of the trails travel the tops of flat ledges. If you feel more inclined to go faster on the level paths, pay attention to what may lie beyond a hidden turn. During the winter watch out for ice and other slippery conditions. In spring and summer the open ledges and rocks can be sunning spots for snakes. During one ride we crossed the path of a 5-foot slithering friend making his way across the trail to one of those spots.

Rescue index: Telephones can be found at the Mohonk Mountain House. It's fairly difficult to become lost since most trails end at or near the main grounds. Trail names and road signs are abundant throughout the tour and are worthwhile when you are in doubt about which direction to take.

Land status: This network of trails passes through the Mohonk Resort. Mohonk Preserve is a nonprofit organization working to protect the natural lands in the Shawangunk Mountain. There are special programs in environmental education and tours throughout the area. These 5,500 acres are open to the public from dawn to dusk for a small fee. A $10 yearly seasonal-use pass is charged for each bicycle. Each time you ride, a $5.00 day-use fee ($7.00 weekends and holidays) is charged. If you are planning to come frequently, you can become a Mohonk Preserve member. It will reduce the day-use charges considerably. Whatever the cost, a wonderful day's outing awaits you in this unique setting of mountain, forests, and lakes.

Maps: A bicycle map is supplied when you stop by the visitor center to pay the day fees. Take along their hiking maps too, as they supply a little more detailed information on the trails. The New York–New Jersey Trail Conference's "Shawangunk Trails" waterproof and tearproof map provides the best detail and can be found at most outdoor-type stores for $9.95. Maps 10 and 10A, Mohonk Preserve, Lake Mohonk Resort and Virgina Smiley Preserve, provide the most detail for these rides. These roads are well marked, with bicycle trail signs and the name of the road you're traveling on posted on trees. Things could not get much better than this.

Finding the trail: Take the New York Thruway (Interstate 87) north to exit 18. Proceed past the tollbooths, and turn left onto New York 299

Craggy cliffs, once buried under a large sea, tower above the trails in the Mohonk Preserve.

(west), which becomes Main Street. Proceed through town, cross the bridge over the Wallkill River, and bear right at the next fork heading toward the Mohonk Mountain House. After the town of New Paltz, continue on County Road 6, cross a bridge, and bear right at the Mohonk Mountain House sign onto Mountain Rest Road. Head up this road for about 2 miles until you see the Lake Mohonk Gatehouse on your left. Turn in here. There is a $6.00 fee for parking. Return to CR 6 and turn left, pedaling down a steep hill for about 200 feet. Look for a carriage road on your left leading into the forest. This is Bonticou Road west. Begin your journey there.

Sources of additional information:

Ulster County Tourism and Public Information Office
10 Westbrook Lane
Kingston, NY 12402
(845) 340–3566

Bicycle Depot
3 Church Street
New Palz, NY 12561
(845) 255–3859
www.bicycledepot.com

New Paltz Chamber of Commerce
124 Main Street
New Paltz, NY 12561
(845) 255–0243

Wheel and Heel
116 South Plant Road
Newburgh, NY 12550
(845) 567–1740

Mohonk Preserve
P.O. Box 715
New Paltz, NY 12561-0715
(845) 255–0919
www.mohonkpreserve.org

Bryan's Bikes
240 Main Street
Cornwall, NY 12518
(845) 534–5230
www.bryansbikes.com

Mohonk Mountain House
1000 Mountain Rest Road
New Paltz, NY 12561
(845) 255–1000 or (800) 772–6646 (reservations)
www.mohonk.com

Notes on the trail: This portion of Bonticou Road continues on the west side of CR 6 and is a continuation of the Bonticou Road tour found in this book. It connects several other carriage roads to form a 14-mile loop through the Lake Mohonk area.

This portion of the hard-packed carriage road takes you through mature stands of hemlocks and past a hillside dotted with fallen talus from the Shawangunk conglomerate ledges. The landscape is interesting and unique, and the carriage roads are easy to cruise on, leaving you time to focus on the scenery and not on the difficulties of a trail. At 0.7 mile a trail comes in from the right; keep bearing left on the main carriage road. You will soon come to an intersection with North Lookout and Rockrift Roads. Bear right onto Rockrift Road; there are signs indicating that bicycles are not allowed any farther on North Lookout Road, so you can only turn right at this point. Descend past more large rock crevices, and bear left onto

Cedar Drive. Bear left at the intersection onto Mossy Brook Road. Each of the roads has signs indicating which route it is.

There is a half-mile steady climb up the four-wheel-drive Mossy Brook Road. Turn right when you reach the intersection with singletrack Maple Path, indicated by blue markers on a tree. Ascend Maple Path a very short distance, and turn left where the trail levels off along some utility lines. In about 50 feet you come to an intersection with Stokes Trail; bear right to continue on Maple Path. The trail ascends and travels through a forest with an understory of mountain laurel and past more open ledges. Some sections of Maple Path are uncharacteristically rockier than what is found along the other carriage roads, but the remaining trails are in excellent condition. The final descent from Maple Path takes you through a huge arena of broken rock known as Rock Pass and down to the Laurel Ledge carriage road. Turn right toward the Rhododendron Bridge. Laurel Ledge Road is a wide, fairly level carriage road. It passes along the base of a great broken-up talus slope. The placement of these huge boulders has created a unique landscape that has become a home for plant and animal communities to thrive in. After 1.5 miles along Laurel Ledge Road, you will come to an area filled with huge rhododendrons. You will notice a road higher up on a ridge to your right. That is Overcliff Road. Keep bearing left to the bridge that spans a small stream. This is Rhododendron Bridge. Proceed over the bridge, and make a right onto Oakwood Drive. Take this carriage road bearing left. At a large intersection with Duck Pond Road, Kleine Kill Road, and Oakwood Drive, take Kleine Kill Road, and climb heartily for 0.7 mile toward Rock Spring Bridge, past great views of Sky Top along this wide, hard-packed, dusty road. Continue straight toward Woodland Bridge and Huguenot Drive. When you reach the paved Huguenot Drive, a turn to the right will bring you back to the parking at the Mohonk Gatehouse. Turning left will take you up toward Mohonk Lake and the Mohonk Mountain House and picnic area.

32

The Trapps

This area of the Mohonk Preserve is popular with hikers, mountain climbers, and cross-country skiers. The 5-mile loop consists of two wide, hard-packed dirt roads known as the Undercliff and Overcliff Roads. The tour of the Trapps should not be left out of any mountain biker's itinerary of the Shawangunk Mountains. The scenery is awesome. These two roads encircle dizzying, craggy ledges that rise hundreds of feet, with panoramic views of distant farmland and river valleys. This fairly level ride is not technically challenging, and its smoothness, good condition, and gentle rolling grades provide opportunities to shift your gaze from the ground and peer out across the landscape. This area has a universal appeal to bikers of all skill levels. Beginners will be exhilarated by the accessibility of such scenery. The more experienced rider will appreciate the opportunity to get in some fast doubletrack riding. You can also network into the Mohonk Lake area's trail system, readily accessed via the Rhododendron Bridge at the end of Undercliff Road.

Undercliff Road follows the 2,000-foot Shawangunk Mountain Ridge with wide-open views of the Wallkill River Valley and all its wineries and farms. Millions of years ago sediments, eroding and washing down from the Shawangunk Mountains, filled the valley to the east. These soft sediments were then carved out by streams and rivers flowing from the higher, surrounding mountains. The glaciers from the last Ice Age finished the job. They bulldozed a tremendous trough running north-south along the eastern side of the Shawangunk Range, creating the present-day fertile lowlands of the Wallkill River Valley.

Undercliff Road, built in 1903, is considered an engineering feat because it crossed a talus slope of rock fragments varying in size from pebbles to house-size boulders. These tremendous blocks of white conglomerate rock were wedged loose by ice and growing plants and tumbled down the face of the cliffs, settling as talus. Notice the talus blocks that are more angular. These are the newer blocks that have recently fallen. The older blocks are more rounded.

Undercliff Road traverses one of the most popular mountain climbing regions in the eastern United States, called "The Gunks." As you ride past these vertical cliffs and steep faces, notice all the climbers suspended from or attempting an ascent up the ledges. The rock is unusually solid and trustworthy and provides excellent handholds and footholds in tiny ledges and horizontal cracks.

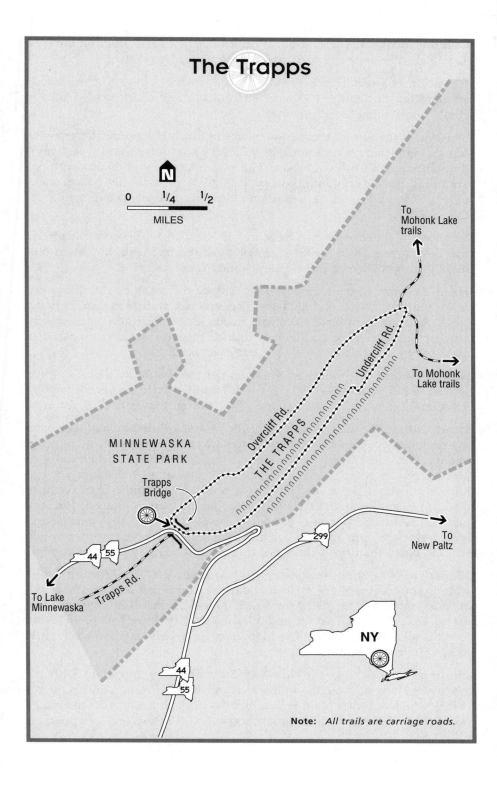

The Trapps

N

0   1/4   1/2
MILES

To Mohonk Lake trails

To Mohonk Lake trails

Overcliff Rd.

Undercliff Rd.

THE TRAPPS

MINNEWASKA
STATE PARK

Trapps
Bridge

44 55

To Lake
Minnewaska

Trapps Rd.

299

To
New Paltz

44

55

NY

Note: *All trails are carriage roads.*

General location: Travel about 90 miles north of Manhattan on the New York State Thruway to exit 18, near the town of New Paltz.

Elevation change: This loop basically follows the contours of the land at an elevation of about 1,000 feet. There are a few short, graded hills to climb, but nothing too strenuous.

Season: In the winter cross-country skiers can be found on the groomed tracks; but if there is no snow take your bike out, dress warmly, and enjoy the solitude of a fresh winter day. Fall is absolutely breathtaking with colors filling the surrounding pastoral valleys. Winter usually brings snow. Late spring and summer are excellent, with warm breezes coming up from the valleys.

Services: Most services can be found at New Paltz. There is a sandwich and beverage truck in the parking area near the trailhead. Mountain bike rentals are available at Bicycle Depot and Wheel and Heel.

Hazards: Most of the riding is along ledges, and weather conditions can make routes icy, wet, and slippery. The area is beautiful and quite popular. Expect considerable traffic from hikers and other riders in the beginning of the ride. Ride courteously and defensively, and be prepared to drastically reduce your speed on a busy weekend.

Rescue index: Telephones and a small deli can be found near the intersection of NY 55 and NY 299. Undercliff and Overcliff Roads are popular trails, and there are usually Mohonk Preserve rangers patrolling the area.

Land status: The Trapps are part of the Mohonk Preserve, and the roaming park rangers require a daily-use fee. Mohonk Preserve is a nonprofit organization working to protect the natural lands in the Shawangunk Mountains. There are special programs in environmental education and tours throughout the area. The area is open to the public from dawn to dusk for a small fee. A $10 yearly seasonal-use pass is charged for each bicycle. Each time you ride, a day-use fee of $5.00 ($7.00 weekends and holidays) is charged. You can become a Mohonk Preserve member, which will cut down the day-use charges, if you're planning to visit frequently.

Maps: The New York–New Jersey Trail Conference's "Shawangunk Trails" waterproof and tearproof map provides the best detail and can be found at most outdoor-type stores for $9.95. Maps 10 and 10A, Mohonk Preserve, Lake Mohonk Resort and Virginia Smiley Preserve, provide the most detail for these rides. The loop consists of only carriage roads. It is hard to become lost.

Finding the trail: Take the New York State Thruway (Interstate 87) north to exit 18. Proceed past the tollbooths, and turn left onto New York 299 (west), which becomes Main Street. Proceed through town, cross the bridge over the Wallkill River, and bear left, staying on NY 299. The road provides a good perspective of the Shawangunk Ridge as the mountains fill up your front windshield. Turn right at the intersection with NY 55. After the hairpin turn begin looking for available parking anywhere along the side of the road. Because of the area's popularity, you will probably see many other vehicles parked along the side too. People get there early to begin climbing. After you have parked along the road, proceed to the small pedestrian bridge that crosses NY 44. This is Trapps Bridge. The trail begins on the northeast side of NY 44 or the right side coming from New Paltz.

Sources of additional information:

Ulster County Tourism and Public Information Office
10 Westbrook Lane
Kingston, NY 12402
(845) 340-3566

New Paltz Chamber of Commerce
124 Main Street
New Paltz, NY 12561
(845) 255-0243

Mohonk Preserve
P.O. Box 715
New Paltz, NY 12561-0715
(845) 255-0919
www.mohonkpreserve.org

Wheel and Heel
116 South Plank Road
Newburgh, NY 12550
(845) 567-1740

Bryan's Bikes
240 Main Street
Cornwall, NY 12518
(845) 534-5230
www.bryansbikes.com

Mohonk Mountain House
1000 Mountain Rest Road
New Paltz, NY 12561
(845) 255-1000 or (800) 772-6646 (reservations)
www.mohonk.com

Bicycle Depot
3 Church Street
New Paltz, NY 12561
(845) 255-3859
www.bicycledepot.com

Notes on the trail: Pedal up the steep embankment to the top of the bridge, and take Undercliff Road leading off to the right. The road passes under the cliffs where you will see many climbers and their gear hanging from the crevasses and ledges.

Stay on Undercliff Road until you come to a four-way intersection at about 2.5 miles. If you feel like extending your loop, you can network with the Mohonk-area bike trails. Take a right over the Rhododendron Bridge onto Oakwood Drive, which connects with Old Stage Road. Then return to the intersection. Refer to the map for better detail of this loop extension.

To continue on the Trapps loop, take the farthest left-hand road and ascend a short hill to Overcliff Road. Take this wide carriage road back to Trapps Bridge. If you are charged up and would like to continue riding, pedal across the bridge and continue along the hard-packed road known as Trapps Carriage Road. This wide dirt road continues for another 3.5 miles.

33

Shangri-La

Minnewaska State Park Preserve is a mecca for mountain bike riders. This area may not be a dirt disciple's technical dream because the trails are wide, hard-packed, dirt carriage roads. However, once your knobbies touch down on this 11-mile loop, it's a rider's taste of heaven. Hammerheads may not find many steep, narrow, and twisting trails that stretch the limits of their abilities. So what? They will find miles of old carriage roads that seem to have been divinely created just for cruising on a mountain bike. The network of trails is situated on the Shawangunk Mountain Ridge, which rises more than 2,000 feet above sea level. There are overlooks and panoramic vista points of incredible beauty along the trails, which roll through the evergreens and hardwoods bordering the 1,500-foot dazzling white craggy cliffs. Dense thickets of laurel and azalea, blooming in May, are abundant along the carriage roads. Ride through a unique habitat. The Shawangunk Mountain Range displays a transition in flora between the northern boreal forests of the Catskill high peaks and the southern forests that are distinguished by hardwoods, oak, hickory, and pitch pine. The Shawangunk ridge is used as a corridor for animal migrations. Hawks, falcons, and vultures use these migration pathways or flyways and can be seen soaring above the warm updrafts rising above the escarpment.

After a day of warm-weather riding, cool off or picnic around the two beaches set among the gemlike Lake Minnewaska or Lake Awosting. Nestled among the craggy cliffs of dazzling white conglomerate bordered with evergreens and hardwoods is the clear, deep, blue-green Awosting Lake. This "Shangri-La" bears incredible beauty. The Shawangunks were once the bed of a large sea. Forces deep within the earth forced this landmass out of the sea to great heights and into bizarre shapes. Freezing water fractured the vertical cliffs, causing large boulders to plummet down the escarpment. The mile-high continental ice sheets from the last Ice Age scoured the land and carved deep clefts in the mountains, scattering thousands of tons of boulders. The glaciers carved out a ravine in the top of this ridge along a fault line, forming the Mohonk, Minnewaska, and Awosting Lakes, and many more. Lake Awosting lies within one of these fault zones and is replenished from underground springs that channel the rains falling on these mountains and seeping into the landscape. This land has much to offer.

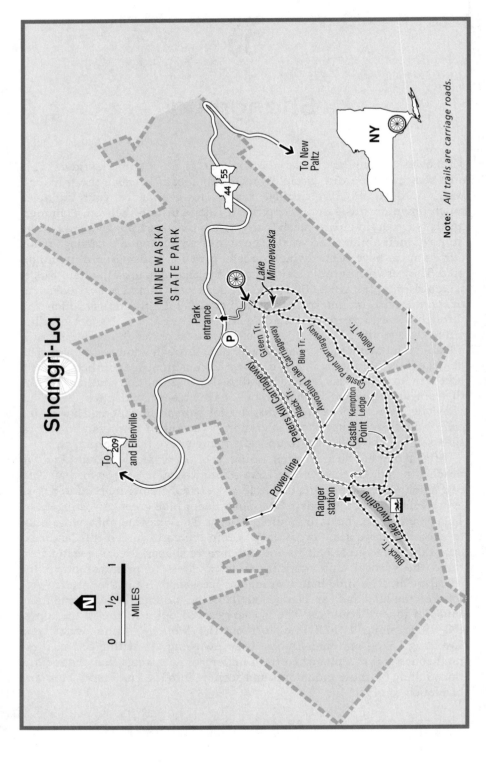

Shangri-La

N

0   1/2   1
MILES

MINNEWASKA
STATE PARK

To 209
and Ellenville

44 55

To New
Paltz

Park
entrance

P

Lake
Minnewaska

Green Tr.

Blue Tr.

Peter's Kill Carriageway

Black Tr.

Awosting Lake Carriageway

Castle Point Carriageway

Yellow Tr.

Castle
Point

Kempton
Ledge

Power line

Ranger
station

Lake Awosting

Black Tr.

NY

Note: *All trails are carriage roads.*

General location: Travel about 90 miles north of Manhattan on the New York State Thruway (Interstate 87) to exit 18, near the town of New Paltz.

Elevation change: The carriage roads gradually climb from 1,200 feet to 2,000 feet and drop to about 1,800 feet during the course of the ride. There are short ups and downs, but nothing too strenuous, as well as a fair share of level riding.

Season: In the winter cross-country skiers can be found on the groomed tracks, but if there is no snow take your bike out, dress warmly, and enjoy the solitude of a winter day. Fall is absolutely breathtaking, with colors filling the surrounding pastoral valleys. Late spring and summer are excellent, with warm breezes rising from the valleys.

Services: Most services can be found at New Paltz. There is a sandwich and beverage truck in the parking area near the trailhead. Mountain bike rentals are available at Bicycle Depot and Wheel and Heel. There is an energy-supply truck with sandwiches, coffee, and cool, refreshing beverages in the parking area near Lake Minnewaska. Portosans, those friendly mobile toilets, can be found below the parking area near the lake. During the summer there is also a swimming dock by the lake.

Hazards: Most of the riding is along ledges, and weather conditions can make routes icy, wet, and slippery. The area is beautiful and quite popular. Expect considerable traffic from hikers and other riders at the beginning of the ride. Ride courteously and defensively, and be prepared to drastically reduce your speed on a busy weekend. The hiking trails are off limits to bikers, so if you are looking for singletrack, try somewhere else. Horseback riding is allowed on the carriage roads, so as a courtesy pull to the side and allow them to pass. There is currently no conflict between equestrians and mountain bikers, and all share and enjoy the same trails. Be careful not to spook horses by riding close or fast from either direction on the trail. Fall weekends during peak foliage make for difficult parking. Get there between 9:00 and 10:00 A.M.

Rescue index: There is a ranger station next to Lake Minnewaska. There is also considerable people traffic on the carriage roads during the busier seasons. Help is never too far away.

Land status: The Palisades Park Commission manages this New York park. The park is open daily at 9:00 A.M., and closing hours, which are posted, may vary throughout the seasons. An entrance fee of $5.00 per person is charged to enter the Lake Minnewaska area.

Maps: The New York–New Jersey Trail Conference's "Shawangunk Trails" waterproof and tearproof map provides the best detail and can be found at most outdoor-type stores for $9.95. Map 9, "Minnewaska State Park/Ice Caves Mountain," provides the most detail for these rides.

Finding the trail: Take the New York Thruway (Interstate 87) north to exit 18. Proceed past the tollbooths, and turn left onto New York 299 (west), which becomes Main Street. Proceed through town, cross the bridge over the Wallkill River, and bear left, staying on NY 299. The road provides a good perspective of the Shawangunk Ridge as the mountains fill up your front windshield. Turn right at the intersection with NY 44/NY 55. Continue on this road for about 5 miles until you see a sign posting the park entrance. Turn left into the Minnewaska park, and pay the individual entrance fees.

Sources of additional information:

Ulster County Tourism and Public Information Office
10 Westbrook Lane
Kingston, NY 12402
(845) 340-3566

Bicycle Depot
3 Church Street
New Paltz, NY 12561
(845) 255-3859
www.bicycledepot.com

New Paltz Chamber of Commerce
124 Main Street
New Paltz, NY 12561
(845) 255-0243

Wheel and Heel
116 South Plank Road
Newburgh, NY 12550
(845) 567-1740

Minnewaska State Park Preserve
P.O. Box 893
New Paltz, NY 12561
(845) 255-0752

Bryan's Bikes
240 Main Street
Cornwall, NY 12518
(845) 534-5230
www.bryansbikes.com

Notes on the trail: Leave the parking area, and head toward the north end of Lake Minnewaska. You will see some picnic tables overlooking the lake. Descend to the lake. There will be several signs with trailhead names and mileage posted. Several loop configurations can be created within this park. For the sake of choosing one, I am going to propose the following route, which offers the most diversity, fun, and scenery.

Centuries of weathering scar the plateau of the Shawangunks.

Our goal is to picnic or snack at Lake Awosting. Lake Awosting, Lake Minnewaska, and Mohonk Lake are surrounded by a very tough and durable, quartz-pebble conglomerate wall of rock. The lakes are thought to lie along a fault zone where the bedrock was broken up. The Ice Age glaciers scooped up and carried off the rocks, leaving a basin to be filled by the melting glaciers.

Look for the blue-blazed Castle Point carriage road trail. This wide, hard-packed road takes you along a very scenic escarpment with many panoramic viewpoints. The 3 miles of gradual ascent needed to reach the downhill trail to Lake Awosting will go unnoticed because you will become lost in the natural beauty that appears around every turn. There are some gazebos built along the ledges for resting and taking in the scenery. Take a moment to sit in one and look out over the landscape. A very unusual and interesting feature along the route is the huge blocks of rock that have split off the cliffs and tumbled down to lean against each other. The wide crevasses in the ledges you see along your ride are the beginnings of the jointing and fracturing of these rocks. At about 4.3 miles from Lake Minnewaska, you will come to an intersection with the yellow-blazed Hamilton Point carriage road trail. If you wish to return at this point or create a shorter ride, make a left onto this path, and continue straight until you reach the parking area in about 3 miles.

To continue to Lake Awosting, make a right at Castle Point's trail junction with Hamilton Point and descend to the lake. Fork left, and you will be on the black-marked Awosting Lake carriage road loop. Take the loop and stop at the stone swimming beach located along the middle of the lake. If it's summer, this is a great place to stop, rest, and swim. There are two more great places for stopping. A little farther on, two rock promontories jut into the water, which is more secluded and is situated in a beautiful setting.

Make your way around the lake. At the end of the lake a black-blazed road comes in from your left. Stay to your right, and cross the small dam at the north end of the lake. Bear left onto the green-marked Awosting Lake carriage road, and return to the parking area, which is more than 3 miles away. If you are riding in the winter, you will see some very large frozen falls created by water seeping over the cliffs along this road.

Wallkill Valley Rail Trail

This beautiful, 12-mile hiking and biking trail (6 miles one way) passes through two quaint seventeenth-century villages, skirts farms, passes through woods, and crosses over rivers and streams. The elevated rail bed provides a view of the surrounding area, including woodland ponds, the Wallkill River, and the Shawangunk Mountains in the distance. Wood turtles, woodcocks, songbirds, broadwing hawks, great horned owls, fox, white-tailed deer, and raccoons are frequently sighted.

The well-maintained cinder trail is essentially flat. It can be ridden as an out and back or as a loop by returning to the start via one of twenty-one paved roads that cross the trail. The trail passes through the New Paltz Historic District, which features seventeenth-century stone houses and the old railroad station that served the trains on this former Conrail route. There is also a Mexican restaurant, a bistro, a bakery, and several pizza parlors to top off a leisurely ride.

General location: The ride begins in the town of New Paltz, 15 miles south of Kingston and 1.5 miles from the New York State Thruway (Interstate 87).

Elevation change: Negligible.

Season: The best riding is from late spring to midfall.

Services: All services, including two bike shops and rentals, are available in New Paltz. Gardiner has several bed-and-breakfast inns.

Hazards: Parts of the southern section of the trail are frequently covered with water after heavy rain. The bridge over the Wallkill has been slated for repair; if the work is not completed before your visit, take special care.

Rescue index: Help can be flagged down on the paved roads that cross the trail or from nearby residences.

Land status: The linear park is jointly owned by the village of New Paltz and the Land Trust of Wallkill Valley.

Maps: The New York–New Jersey Trail Conference's "Shawangunk Trails" waterproof and tearproof map provides the best detail and can be found at most outdoor-type stores. Map 10, Shawangunk Trails–North, has the most detail. The USGS 7.5-minute series quadrangles are Gardiner and

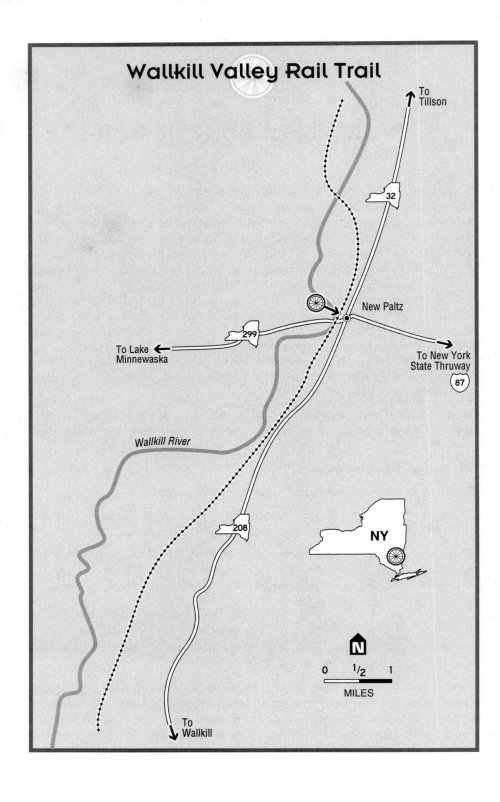

Wallkill Valley Rail Trail

To Tillson

32

New Paltz

299

To Lake
Minnewaska

To New York
State Thruway

87

Wallkill River

208

NY

N

0   1/2   1
MILES

To Wallkill

Rosendale. Brochures of the trail include a map and are available at the Town Hall on North Chestnut Street in New Paltz (914–255–0100).

Finding the trail: Take the New York State Thruway (I–87) north to exit 18. Proceed past the tollbooths, and turn left onto New York 299 (west), which becomes Main Street. At 1.5 miles from the exit, the Wallkill Valley Rail Trail crosses the road. Park on a side street in the village or in the lot near the historic district.

Sources of additional information:

Wallkill Valley Rail Trail Association
P.O. Box 1048
New Paltz, NY 12561-1048

Bryan's Bikes
240 Main Street
Cornwall, NY 12518
(845) 534–5230
www.bryansbikes.com

Wheel and Heel
116 South Plank Road
Newburgh, NY 12550
(845) 567–1740

Notes on the trail: From the parking area the path leads in both a northerly and southerly direction. You have the option of traveling in either of those directions.

Catskill Region Tours

Within the sprawling, 700,000-acre Catskill Park region lies the state-protected Catskill Forest Preserve, which includes the Catskill Mountains. This range is west of the Hudson River, which carves the valley running north-south through eastern New York. Actually the Catskills are not true mountains. Rather, the Catskills are eroded portions of a plateau millions of years old. Four hundred million years ago this area was beneath a shallow ocean. The region was pushed up as the earth's continental plates collided and merged. The Ice Ages, whose glaciers covered the northern half of North America, weathered this plateau into the many valleys and mountains visible today.

These mountains offer virtually unlimited possibilities for rugged, scenic biking. I have included ten tours that sample some of the best terrain. Endless miles of dirt roads also crisscross this beautiful landscape. The forests are laced with dirt roads, jeep trails, and singletrack hiking trails. The Catskill Forest Preserve is dotted with campsites and offers diverse recreational activities for all who visit.

Exploitation of the mountains began in the early nineteenth century. Decades upon decades of relentless, uncontrolled cutting and burning left the 250,000-acre preserve denuded and wasted in the latter half of the nineteenth century. It was a wilderness thought to be inexhaustible, but full-grown majestic hemlocks, maples, and oak trees were reduced to stumps. Green pastures became barren dirt fields. When one sees the verdant mountains today, it's hard to imagine that long ago they were just studded with stumps.

Unlike the White Mountains of New Hampshire and the Green Mountains of Vermont, the Catskills were protected from exploitation well into the nineteenth century and stayed unchanged until the forces of the Industrial Revolution ravaged the land. The forests of this great park were initially exploited for their bountiful supply of hemlock bark, used in the process of turning animal hides into leather. Massive numbers of trees across the valleys and mountainsides were leveled.

Hunter, now a popular ski resort town, was the site of the first tannery. It thrived, and soon after more tanneries were built, and then more, and they all thrived on surrounding hemlock forests and ample water supplies. The industry continued to grow until shortly after the Civil War, when all reachable tracts of hemlocks were gone and the demand for the Catskill-tanned leather, which played a large role in outfitting the Union troops, dried up.

Today a virgin hemlock grove is a rarity. The few surviving trees are spotted only by those hikers or woodsmen who venture deep into the wilderness or have a sharp eye, or perhaps a mountain biker pausing at just the right spot. The forests of New York became the bastion of several industries that came and went over the decades. As tanneries sprang up, so did quarries for the excavation of bluestone. However, close to the end of the nineteenth century, the quarries became obsolete with the discovery of the less expensive Portland cement.

Logging, another mountain industry, continues today, as does the tourist industry with its growing legions of hikers, mountain bikers, and nature lovers. It's an industry with roots traceable to the early 1800s, when America acquired a renewed appreciation for the arts and nature.

As we enter the twenty-first century, despite the ravaging of the land and pockets of poverty, the Catskills remain rich in beauty and history. Generations of the well-to-do and famous came to the large hotels, which over the decades changed ownership, were renovated, or simply closed during hard times. The region's golden era stretched from the 1940s to the 1960s; it became the vacation paradise for families and the weekend retreat for singles looking for that perfect someone long before the Hamptons was the in spot.

Europeans escaping the world wars immigrated to America for sanctuary and then made summer migrations from the cities to the Catskills for vacations. Small Catskill towns became havens for Irish, Italians, Germans, and Eastern European Jews. Railroad and steamship lines, originally laid down for industrial purposes, were now transporting populations of new Americans to the mountains.

It was the great escape from the industrial age, the strife of the city, and the problems of the past. Many owe it all to the 1885 creation of the Catskill Forest Preserve. It reshaped the land and charted the future as a major source of year-round recreational activities and miles and miles of excellent hiking, cross-country ski, and snowmobile trails. The rich history of this region is an attraction, especially for mountain bikers. Old lumber and carriage roads provide many miles of potentially awesome mountain bike experiences.

Sources of additional information:

New York State Department of Environmental Conservation, Region 3
21 South Putt Corners Road
New Paltz, NY 12561
(845) 256–3000

New York State Department of Environmental Conservation, Region 4,
Stamford Sub-Office
Route 10
Stamford, NY 12167-9503
(607) 652–7365

Fats in the Cats Bicycle Club
61 John Street
Kingston, NY 12401
(914) 331–9800

35

North Lake Trails

The setting for this moderately challenging 5-mile-out, 5-mile-back trail is the unique and natural habitat of the Catskill Forest Preserve's North Lake area. The tour includes spectacular views of the Hudson Valley and explores an area steeped in nineteenth-century Catskill history. The legendary Catskill Mountain House once stood here and played host to an assemblage of famous people. A combination of horse and wood roads, set on top of an elevated plateau, gently traverse the eastern face of the 2,000-foot escarpment. The trail passes through a forested habitat and features plants and trees from three geographic forest types. This is the only area in the Catskills where pitch pine (common to southern forests), maple and beech hardwoods (northern forests), and spruce and firs (mountain summits) can be found in the same place. On a clear day, five states can be seen from the rocky, flat ledges that make up the eastern edge of the Catskill escarpment.

What once provided turn-of-the-twentieth-century visitors with a horse-drawn carriage tour through a beautiful woodland forest now enchants mountain bikers with stretches of demanding hill climbs and fast, descending doubletrack. The great views and mysterious, craggy mountains make for a day of captivating riding. Camp overnight at the North-South Lake Campground, and ride for a second day if you can't do it all in one.

For centuries the Catskills were Native American hunting grounds. Native Americans lived and fished in the fertile river valleys and hunted in the dark, hemlock-filled valleys and wooded slopes of the mountains they called Onteora, or "land in the sky."

Beginning in the early nineteenth century, America entered the Romantic period, when the arts and nature took on greater significance. A good view was held in high value. Despite the ravaging of the land from the lumbering and tanning industry during this time, the Catskills still held abundant natural beauty. The aristocracy and intelligentsia of America sought out this area as a prime meeting ground. Grand hotels with spectacular mountain views were built for the rich and famous, who flocked to the Catskills. From the midnineteenth century to the turn of the twentieth century, two large hotels, the Catskill Mountain House and Hotel Kaaterskill, built right on the escarpment, had guest registers that included presidents, entertainers, industrialists, and other celebrities. The views from the escarpment inspired famous painters, poets, and writers. The

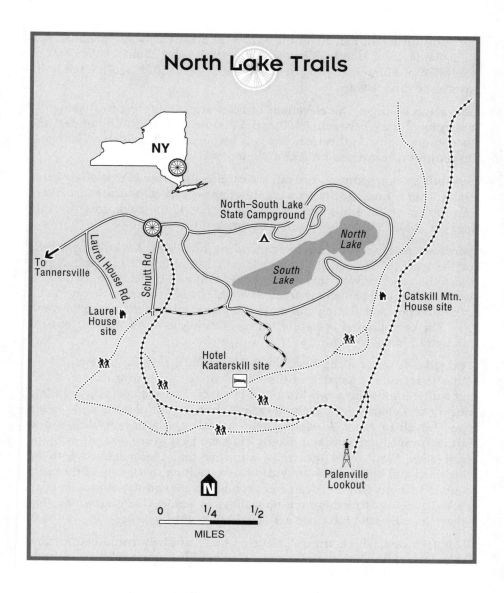

North Lake Trails

NY

North–South Lake
State Campground

North
Lake

South
Lake

To
Tannersville

Laurel House Rd.

Schutt Rd.

Laurel
House
site

Catskill Mtn.
House site

Hotel
Kaaterskill site

Palenville
Lookout

N

0   ¼   ½

MILES

North Lake area's reputation made it the place to be for New Yorkers downriver. Carriage roads were built into and on the escarpment to bring guests to the most spectacular vantage points. Take your time at North Lake. There is a lot to see, and one of the best ways to get it all in is to camp out in the North-South Lake Campground.

Although I have not had the pleasure of riding this trail, it is strongly recommended by two friends. John Lowe and his son Mathew rode the trails and fell in love with them. As you silently glide through miles of bridle paths and wood roads, enjoy the history and the pristine forest environment.

General location: Exit 20 off the New York State Thruway (Interstate 87), near the town of Haines Falls and Tannersville and about 9 miles east of the town of Hunter. If you package it as a weekend, it will certainly be worth the time it takes to get there.

Elevation change: The elevations of horse trail and forest road along the escarpment vary between 2,400 and 1,800 feet. If you continue past the turnaround point on this ride, you will keep descending to about 700 feet. To return you have one heck of a climb back.

Season: Spring, summer, and fall are excellent seasons to ride along these trails. This region usually sees plenty of snow and cold weather. If there is no snow on the trails and you feel like braving the cold, dress warmly and get out on the trails for one very brisk ride.

Services: Most services can be found along New York 23A in Haines Falls or the town of Hunter. The North–South Lake public campground provides the base for your travels and offers tent and trailer sites, two lakes, two beaches, and two picnic areas with tables and fireplaces. Rowboat and canoe rentals and fishing complete the gamut of recreational opportunities. The campground opens for spring camping in mid-May and remains open until late October.

Hazards: It tends to be busy on the weekends, so keep an eye out for other trail users. A portion of the trail is shared by equestrians. You will encounter equestrians and hikers on the same trails, so display a mutual respect and courtesy for each other, and these beautiful trails will remain open for all to enjoy. A passing hello has always been met with one in return from equestrians and hikers. They are glad to see you enjoying the park also. Most share the trails, knowing that these lands are to be respected and enjoyed. I would also like to caution that many of the trails contain sections that are located along high ledges and sometimes on open rock. In most places there are no railings or fences. Do exercise caution when the views get too close and look too good to be true.

Rescue index: These are well-traveled trails and help could be available from one of the other trail users. Campground personnel are usually around most times of the day.

Land status: New York State Department of Environmental Conservation manages the New York State Forest Preserve lands of the Catskills.

Maps: The New York–New Jersey Trail Conference's "Catskill Trails," Trail Map 40 provides complete coverage of this region and is waterproof and tearproof. It sells for $13.95 and can be found at most outdoor-type stores. Another trail map is usually available in the North–South Lake campground area near the registration booth.

Finding the trail: Take the New York State Thruway (I–87), north to exit 20, Saugerties. Turn north onto County Road 32 for approximately 6 miles and then west on NY 23A. Stay on NY 23A to the village of Haines Falls. Make the first right turn in Haines Falls onto CR 18, and continue north for 2 miles to the end of the road. Just before you reach the campground entrance, turn right onto Schutt Road. You will find a parking area to your immediate right.

Sources of additional information:

North–South Lake Campground
P.O. Box 347
Haines Falls, NY 12436
(518) 589–5058

Performance Pedal
830 Broadway
Ulster Park, NY 12487
(845) 340–1334

Greene County Tourism Association
Box 332
Cairo, NY 12413
(800) 781–4492

Notes on the trail: Facing east away from the parking area, look for and get on the blue-blazed Escarpment Trail. The trail turns south and intersects with the red-blazed Schutt Road Trail in about half a mile. Bear left (south) on the Schutt Road Trail. After 0.3 mile bear right onto a yellow-blazed trail, and in another quarter-mile, fork left onto the horse trail, marked with yellow horse-trail disks with a black horse head in the middle. Follow this trail for another 0.7 mile. Continue past a trail leading north, and soon you will reach a T intersection. Turn left onto the forest road. Turning right will continue to lead you on the horse trail and down the face of the escarpment and eventually to NY 23A. You then will be faced with the agonizing climb back up 1,700 feet.

Continue left onto the forest road for a little more than half a mile, where you arrive at another T intersection. Turn right onto a short spur trail to the Palenville Lookout. Continue back up the trail and straight on the forest road for another 2 miles, passing over the old railroad grade that brought visitors up to the Catskill Mountain House. This tour only covers 2 more miles past the Palenville Lookout. Then you approach an intersection with another forest road. The forest road that lies beyond is not documented on this tour, so turn back at this point.

Travel for 2 miles, and make a right onto the forest road at the T intersection. Continuing straight will take you out to the Palenville Lookout. After another half-mile you will come to the intersection with the horse trail. Continue northwest on the horse trail back to the parking area.

Overlook Mountain Ascent

This ride is not for the weak of heart. Just outside the town of Woodstock lies a graded, wide jeep road that ascends the 3,100-foot Overlook Mountain. Not many roads reach a summit in the Catskill Mountains. Although this nontechnical climb demands great stamina and lung capacity, the rewards of cresting this mountain with a bike are incomparable. The effort to climb the summit is more than compensated by the views from the top. Additional rewards are a remote wilderness lake and a gonzo, turbo-charged descent. At the summit are spur trails on open ledges facing the Hudson Valley. There is also a fire tower at the summit providing some spectacular views after a short climb up the stairs.

The 9-mile (total mileage), out-and-back, wide, smooth jeep road passes the ruins of the historic Catskill Hotel site. Beginning in the early part of the nineteenth century, America entered the Romantic period, when arts and nature became priorities. A good view was held in high regard. Despite the ravaging of the land at the time, the Catskills still held much natural beauty. The region became a magnet for the aristocracy and intelligentsia. Grand hotels with glorious mountain views were built for the rich and famous, who flocked to the Catskills. As the West was discovered, the Catskill crowd thinned, and the great hotels closed one by one. Built in 1870 the Overlook Mountain House, which housed about 300 guests, was situated at an elevation of more than 2,900 feet, the highest of them all.

After reaching the summit explore a rocky jeep trail that descends 2 more miles to the secluded and picturesque Echo Lake. It's a great place to rest, feast, snooze, and meditate.

General location: Just outside the village of Woodstock in the Catskill Mountains from exit 20 on the New York State Thruway (Interstate 87).

Elevation change: The ride up Overlook Mountain climbs about 1,400 feet in a little less than 3 miles and will whip you into shape.

Season: Spring, summer, and fall are excellent seasons to climb the summit. This region usually sees plenty of snow and cold weather. The hard-packed dirt road doesn't get too soft after rains and can be ridden in wet weather, but traction on the rocky jeep trail descending to Echo Lake can be slippery.

Services: The village of Woodstock is basically an artist community of painters, writers, and musicians and is an interesting place to visit. The village has a great variety of restaurants and unusual shops.

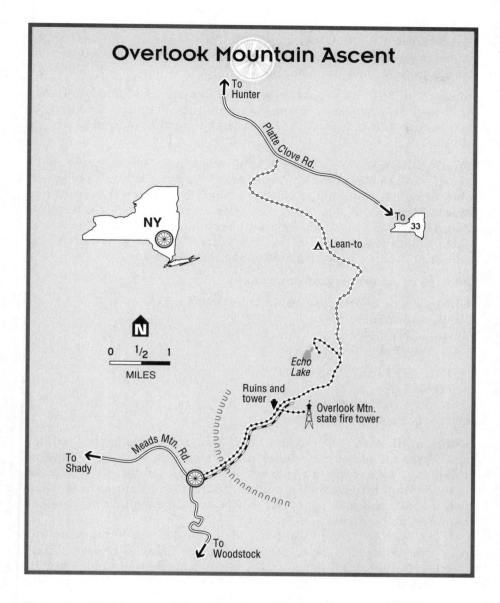

Overlook Mountain Ascent

To Hunter

Platte Clove Rd.

To 33

NY

▲ Lean-to

N

0   1/2   1

MILES

Echo
Lake

Ruins and
tower

Overlook Mtn.
state fire tower

Meads Mtn. Rd.

To
Shady

To
Woodstock

Hazards: The descent from the summit may entice you to exceed the speed limit. It is nice to bomb down the road, but remember that hikers and other bikers may be coming up. Exercise control in case you have to stop or move to the side for another trail user. Try not to ride any faster than you can handle. At the summit use caution on the ledges where rattlesnake dens have been spotted.

Rescue index: Other bikers and hikers use this popular trail often and could be a source for help, should the occasion arise. Becoming lost is not an issue because it is one road in and one road out.

Land status: New York State Department of Environmental Conservation manages the New York State Forest Preserve lands of the Catskills. The trail is on New York State land.

Maps: The New York–New Jersey Trail Conference's "Catskill Trails," Trail Map 41, provides complete coverage of this trail and is waterproof and tearproof. It sells for $13.95 and can be found at most outdoor-type stores.

Finding the trail: Proceed north on the New York State Thruway (I–87) to exit 20. Take New York 212 west toward Woodstock. Turn right (north) onto County Road 33 in the village of Woodstock, which then turns into Meads Mountain Road. Ignore the intersection with Glasco Turnpike, which is also labeled CR 33, and continue on Meads Mountain Road. After about 2 miles past the intersection with Glasco Turnpike, on Meads Mountain Road, look for a parking area on the right. Park here.

Sources of additional information:

Ulster County Tourism and Public Information Office
10 Westbrook Lane
Kingston, NY 12402
(845) 340–3566

Performance Pedal
830 Broadway
Ulster Park, NY 12487
(845) 340–1334

Notes on the trail: The red-blazed jeep trail, referred to as the Overlook Spur Trail, leaves the trailhead at the parking area and begins to climb steadily for 2.5 miles in a northeasterly direction. After reaching the site of the ruins of the Overlook Mountain House, follow in an easterly direction a short, half-mile spur trail that leads to the summit of Overlook Mountain and the State Fire Tower.

If you wish to ride to Echo Lake, return on the spur to the ruins, and bear right down a blue-blazed trail known to hikers as Overlook Trail. Descend for about 1.5 miles, and turn left onto the yellow-blazed Echo Lake Trail for another 0.8 mile. You can hang around the lake, relax, take in some lunch time, snooze a bit, and then commence your climb out of this serene setting. Retrace your steps, bearing right on the blue-blazed trail up to the summit of Overlook Mountain, and then descend the red-blazed jeep trail to the parking area.

37

High Point Kanape Brook Trail

The rewards of this ride are twofold. This journey ascends gently through a secluded and attractive valley of the Kanape Brook. The ride terminates 3 miles later at the 2,000-foot forested saddle between High Point and Mombaccus Mountains. Kanape Brook flows along a rock-and-boulder-studded streambed and passes through a typical Catskill forest of beech, birch, and maple. Once there take an optional hike up to the 3,000-foot High Point Mountain, with its panoramic views. Stay for lunch and soak in the scenery.

The trail parallels the Kanape Brook for most of its length and is an old, hard-packed, dirt and gravel road. The road is in very good condition even though it receives no maintenance. It seems to survive the tremendous erosional forces of the mountains. Trail erosion results from poor drainage along the route. Rains wash down a trail, eventually exposing some of the rocks and roots beneath the roadbed. The object of some trail maintenance programs is to divert some of this runoff and preserve the surface of the trail. An effort was made a long time ago to divert the water flowing down the mountain through several stone culverts that had been constructed to lead the water beneath the trail. An encroaching, growing forest can cause trails to disappear. Along the ride notice the many old stone walls and ditches that were constructed. This helps to keep the forest from growing over the trail. The trails have a history and require upkeep. Do not take this fact for granted. Giant efforts are required to maintain trails for all of us who want to enjoy them.

Although I have not had the pleasure of riding this trail, it is strongly recommended by my friend and riding companion, Bruce Horowitz. We have logged many miles together on our bikes in our quest for the ultimate singletrack.

General location: Southeastern Catskills, near Kingston.

Elevation change: The ride gradually ascends from an elevation of 1,200 to 2,000 feet, to the height of land. The optional hike to High Point covers another 1,000 feet over 1 mile and reaches the summit of High Point at 3,000 feet.

Season: Late spring, summer, and early fall. The Catskills usually get a blanket of snow after Thanksgiving, but it can snow earlier.

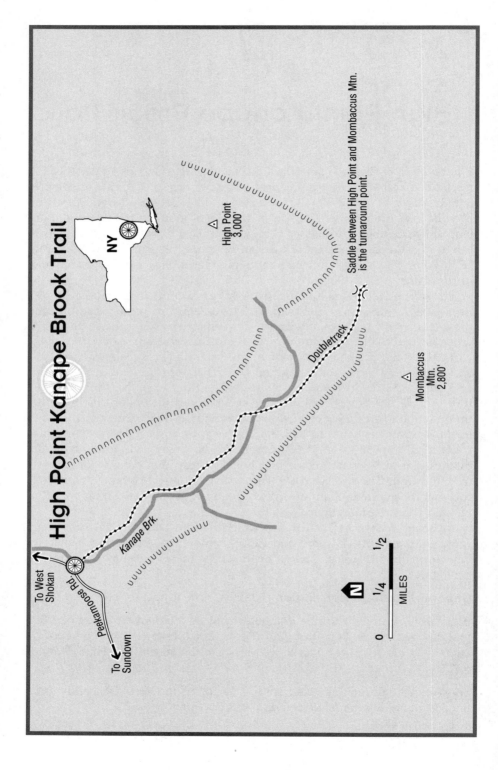

High Point Kanape Brook Trail

NY

To West
Shokan

To
Sundown

Peekamoose Rd.

Kanape Brk.

Doubletrack

High Point
3,000'

Mombaccus
Mtn.
2,800'

Saddle between High Point and Mombaccus Mtn.
is the turnaround point.

N

0   1/4   1/2

MILES

Catskill rocks require good shocks.

Services: Services can be found along New York 28, west of Kingston.

Hazards: This is not a mainstream mountain bike trail. It is secluded and seldom used. Hikers use these trails to gain access to the climb up High Point Mountain. If you are riding near hikers, slow down. If you are approaching from behind, let them know of your presence with a whistle or a friendly greeting.

Rescue index: These are not well-traveled roads, but to get out of this wilderness, all you have to do is pedal downhill toward Peekamoose Road, where several country homes are located.

Land status: The trail is on New York State land. New York State Department of Environmental Conservation manages the New York State Forest Preserve lands of the Catskills.

Maps: The New York–New Jersey Trail Conference's "Catskill Trails," Trail Map 43 provides some detail of this trail and is waterproof and tearproof. It sells for $13.95 and can be found at most outdoor-type stores.

USGS 7.5-minute series, West Shokan quadrangle also provides decent coverage.

Finding the trail: Take the New York State Thruway (Interstate 87) north to the Kingston exit and get on NY 28 west. In a few miles fork left onto NY 28A. Take that road around the southern shores of Ashokan Reservoir. Follow 28A to County Road 42 (Peekamoose Road). Proceed through the town of West Shokan, and look for a small parking lot in about 3 miles on your right. Notice the state land and forest preserve signs. Pedal across the road, and go over the wooden bridge across Kanape Brook. The trail begins beyond a large, open, grassy area on the other side of a wooden bridge.

Sources of additional information:

Ulster County Tourism and Public Information Office
10 Westbrook Lane
Kingston, NY 12402
(845) 340–3566

The Downtube
466 Madison Avenue
Albany, NY 12208
(518) 434–1711

Notes on the trail: Take the trail southeast along the brook. It travels uphill through the beech, birch, and maple forest and slowly climbs up and away from Kanape Brook on your right. Notice the stone culverts you cross over, which are used to divert water from the mountainside. Bear right at the next fork, staying on the more established trail. You will soon cross Kanape Brook into a clearing, where the brook forms a large pool. The area is surrounded by a conifer forest, and as you continue on the trail, balsam fir and hemlock begin to appear. Follow this wide trail and ascend about 500 feet in 1 mile. The height of land between Mombaccus Mountain and High Point, elevation 2,050 feet, is reached with little effort. Here an unmarked hiking trail starts up to High Point. The hike is only forty-five minutes and 1 mile in length. The panoramic view from the small rock ledge summit is a place worth seeking out and is well worth the trip. Views from east to southwest open up. The Ashokan Reservoir, Shawangunk Mountains, and Hudson Highlands can be seen. From the saddle turn back and return the 3 miles, all downhill.

Vernooykill Falls Trail

One of the commodities mountain bikers can be thankful for is that snow-mobilers know a good trail when they see one. This 8-mile, out-and-back (4 miles one way), old town road doubles as a snowmobile trail in the winter and remains one of the best-kept secrets in Ulster County for mountain bikers. It's secluded, quiet, and interesting to explore for a few hours. The trail passes through a tall, attractive forest of beech and hemlock. At the end of the ride, you might want to visit Vernooykill Falls, which can be reached by following the turquoise paint blazes on the trees. Lock up your bike and take a hike. The series of cascades is part of the Vernooy Kill, which flows south toward the Rondout Reservoir. The falls make a superb location to sit down and munch some of the food you should bring along. Walk and follow the falls for a short distance south, where a sturdy wooden footbridge crosses the creek and provides great views of this area.

This is not a strenuous ride, but sections of the rough, washed-out, old town road require some basic technical skills to maneuver through the eroded, exposed rock bed of the trail. Beginner-intermediate riders will feel their confidence building as they tackle these minor obstacles along the rolling terrain. Learning to work the rocks on a steep hill is more difficult because you have other impediments—like fear—which cause you to stop prematurely and perform an end-over.

Along this four-wheel-drive road, you will come across a half-mile spur leading to a remote beaver pond in a primitive wilderness setting known as Balsam Swamp. There are even a few campsites on the road down to the pond. It's quite interesting to see how the beavers have colonized this pond.

If you get an early start, you can do this tour and one of the other nearby southeastern Catskill tours such as Willowemoc, Flugertown Road, or Denning Road.

General location: Ulster County in the southeastern Catskills, near Kerhonkson.

Elevation change: The old road travels over rolling terrain with some minor hills, but nothing too hard to handle. There is a half-mile descent to Balsam Swamp.

Season: Late spring, summer, and early fall are the best seasons. The fall foliage is superb and laid on with a heavy hand.

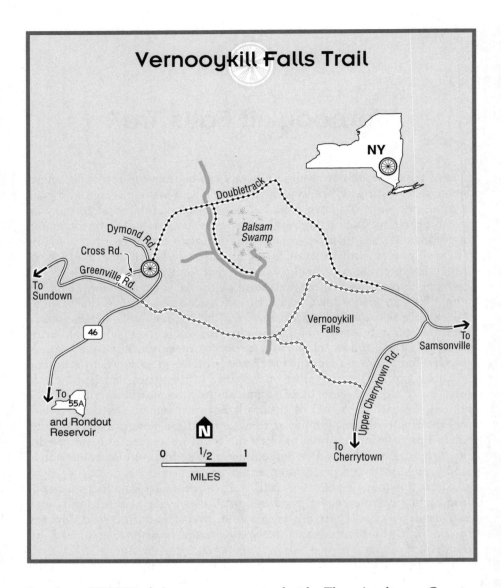

Vernooykill Falls Trail

Doubletrack

Balsam
Swamp

NY

Dymond Rd.

Cross Rd.

Greenville Rd.

To
Sundown

Vernooykill
Falls

To
Samsonville

46

Upper Cherrytown Rd.

To
55A

and Rondout
Reservoir

To
Cherrytown

N

0   1/2   1

MILES

Services: BYOWB—bring your own water bottle. There is a bar on County Road 55 past the Rondout Reservoir. Ellenville is a large town with gas, stores, and even a bike shop known as Moto-Mark Cycles.

Hazards: During foliage season leaves may cover up some rocks protruding on the trail. Be aware that these rocks become slippery during wet periods. Though this is not a well-traveled path, keep an eye out for other trail users. When I was there, a jeep came up the road.

Rescue index: This is not a well-traveled path, but you are only within a few miles of CR 46, which has residences and traffic.

Wide hardpack along the Vernooykill Falls tour.

Land status: The trail is on New York State land. The New York State Department of Environmental Conservation manages the New York State Forest Preserve lands of the Catskills.

Maps: The USGS 7.5-minute series, Kerhonkson quadrangle provides coverage for this area.

Finding the trail: Take the New York State Thruway (Interstate 87) north, and exit at New York 17/U.S. Route 6 West. Take NY 17 north and exit at Ellenville/NY 209. Turn right onto NY 209, going north. Proceed past Ellenville, and take CR 55 north. Bear right at the fork with CR 55A. This takes you on the northeast side of the Rondout Reservoir. You will ride along this attractive body of water at an elevation of 1,440 feet. Turn right at the intersection with Ulster CR 46, and continue north. There are some amazing views along this road to your east. Look for Greenville Road, which intersects from the left at the end of CR 46. Turn left onto Greenville Road, and you will soon notice a wide town dirt road leading off to your right. This is Cross Road, the beginning of your ride. Look for a small turnout that will serve as parking a short distance past Cross Road on your right.

Sources of additional information:

The Downtube
466 Madison Avenue
Albany, NY 12208
(518) 434–1711

Performance Pedal
830 Broadway
Ulster Park, NY 12487
(845) 340-1334

Ulster County Tourism and Public Information Office
10 Westbrook Lane
Kingston, NY 12402
(845) 340-3566

Moto-Mark Cycles
Route 209
Ellenville, NY 12428
(845) 647-6068

Notes on the trail: Take Cross Road a short distance to its end at Dymond Road. At the intersection continue straight ahead onto the designated snowmobile trail. Two brown New York State Department of Environmental Conservation trail signs indicate that the trail type is a snowmobile trail. Cross Dymond Road, and head into the forest on the four-wheel-drive road. The trail follows a gently rolling terrain with some rocky and wet sections where water runoff has eroded the roadbed and exposed the rocks. Many drainage streams tumble down these mountainous slopes and cross the trail at points.

A little after 1 mile, you will start picking up blue markers on the trees. Bear left at a fork. You reach the end of the trail in 3 miles. The right fork will lead you down to Balsam Swamp in about half a mile.

39

The Holy Land

The operative word on this huge parcel of land is *diversity*. Seven thousand acres on the Stewart Airport property in Newburgh have been packaged as a cooperative area, available for hunters and other outdoor enthusiasts. This domain is the "holy land" to the local mountain biking community because of its excellent and competitive singletrack trail system over a variety of challenging terrains. The cooperative area is composed of a combination of active and abandoned farmland, apple and pear orchards, and second-growth forestland. Ponds and marshes dot the landscape, along with several small streams. Twelve miles of wide, gravelly, hard-packed dirt roads crisscross the hilly interior, providing long, sweeping descents from hills. These roads are perfect for the novice or experienced rider hungry for some genuine fat-tire fun.

For the more serious riders and technicians, there are wads of intermediate and advanced high-tech singletracks. These trails traverse what seems to be an unlimited supply of hills and tight turns punctuated by myriad jumps. They can be attacked aggressively or handled slowly. The lunar, 10-mile, jackhammer, singletrack loop described below is for dedicated hammerheads with a purpose. Good bike handlers will get an excellent workout. Sections of the ride are actually banked and pitched at an angle, keeping you off the brakes and moving fast. As you navigate through the many twists and turns of the trail, the riding begins to take on a Zenlike quality. You're not overbraking or oversteering, and the tires seem to carve like skis. You come out of corners with just enough momentum, as if the trail is controlling the bike and you're just along for the ride.

The Stewart Airport Cooperative area, aka "the holy land," is a great place to come with a group of people with different riding skills. There is plenty of track for those who would like some easy peddling through scenic countryside. For the dirt disciples who are not happy unless they have shredded some rock and come back bruised and battered and have conquered every hill, this is heaven.

General location: Located in northeastern Orange County between the city of Newburgh and the village of Maybrook. The area is bounded on the north by Interstate 84, on the east by the New York State Thruway (I–87), and on the south by New York 207.

Elevation change: The topography is generally flat and gently rolling. The layout of the singletrack loop takes full advantage of the hilly terrain

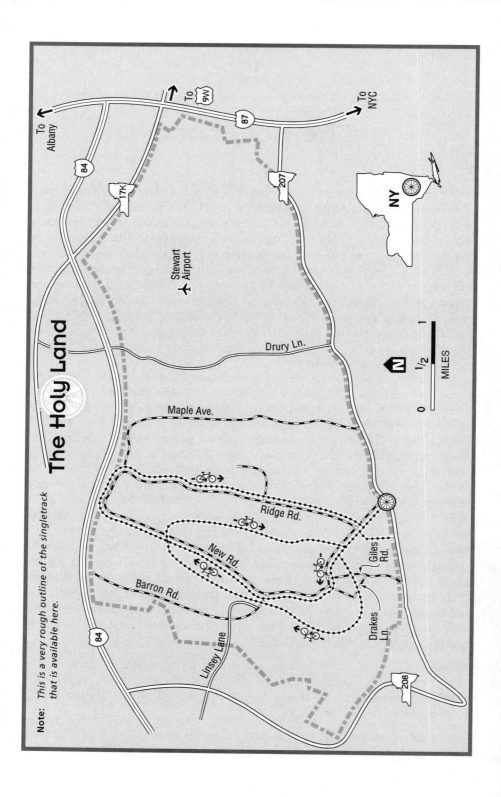

The Holy Land

Note: This is a very rough outline of the singletrack that is available here.

Stewart Airport

Drury Ln.

Maple Ave.

Ridge Rd.

New Rd.

Barron Rd.

Giles Rd.

Drakes Ln.

Linsey Lane

To Albany

To 9W

To NYC

NY

MILES

0   ½   1

and varied woodland, including as many short-haul ascents and descents as can fit into the trail's 10 miles. There are no major long hauls up any mountain, just lots of tiny hills. The doubletrack rolls gently along the interior dirt roads with no appreciable gain or loss in elevation.

Season: Because of its use as a hunting area, the "safe" season is from April 1 to September 30. It's a good idea to check with the New York State Department of Environmental Conservation for exact dates and any other relevant information about the area.

Services: Many service stations and convenience stores are located on NY 207. Nearby Newburgh will make up for the rest, with other general services.

Hazards: Hunting seasons start in the beginning of October and end in March. The area is available for riding in this period. Call the New York State Department of Environmental Conservation for exact dates and details. I would also like to mention that becoming lost while doing the singletrack routes is a real possibility. Unless you frequent this area and are familiar with the myriad trails that interlace this terrain, stay on the route described here. I was warned by veterans. The general condition of the singletrack is good, but sections are blemished occasionally with roots and rocks to keep it challenging. Some sections of trail are pitched at an angle to keep you off the brakes and moving fast.

Rescue index: If you do become lost and you do not have a compass, watch for airplanes overhead departing or arriving at nearby Stewart Airport. The landing and takeoff patterns are usually in an east-west line. Just keep heading in the direction of the landing aircraft, which is east. However, do not follow it after takeoff! As you head in the direction of the airport, you will eventually reach a paved road called Drury Lane. No matter where you are in the 7,000 acres, the distance to Drury Lane is no more than 3 miles. On Drury Lane turn right, going in a southerly direction to reach NY 207. Turn right onto NY 207, west, back to the parking area.

Land status: The land is owned by the New York State Department of Transportation, but the New York State Department of Environmental Conservation manages the forest as a cooperative multiple-use area.

In 1957 the New York State legislature passed the Fish and Wildlife Management Act. It established a set of standards to provide for good fish and wildlife management practices on private lands and waters and to ensure the orderly use of them. The act establishes a cooperative effort between New York and the private land owners. It helps to protect and enhance fish and wildlife resources, to provide hunting and fishing opportunities for the public, to improve landowner and sportsmen relations, and to safeguard the interests and rights of landowners. The cooperative agreement provides public access on these lands through permit stations where fees and permits may be collected. The landowners, in return for sharing their land, receive services such as general maintenance and cleanup, free shrubs and trees, as well as some law enforcement provided for by the Department of Environmental Conservation. Cooperative agreements provide for orderly public recreational access while protecting the interests of the landowner.

Maps: There is no accurate map of this area. The Department of Environmental Conservation map supplied to you when you pick up your permit indicates the major dirt roads that are part of the doubletrack trail option described below. Unfortunately it does not detail the incredible network of singletrack. Bring a compass! There are also no USGS Topo Series maps to provide the fine detail you might need. There are zillions of small twists, turns, and loops that are difficult to map but incredible to ride. The map our cartographer and I have supplied will give you the general flow and direction of the route and an idea of where things are located. The trail is well marked, and if you follow the markers you can't get lost.

Finding the trail: You must first pick up a permit, good for one season of riding in the area, from the Stewart Airport administrative building. From there it's only a few minutes to the parking area. Take the New York State Thruway (I–87) north to the Newburgh exit. After the exit ramp follow the signs for Stewart Airport, which will eventually land you on NY 207. Turn into Stewart International Airport off NY 207, and follow the signs for the terminals. Turn right at the terminal sign, go past the terminal, and turn right on First Street. You will find the Stewart Airport administrative building on your right in the second-to-last brick building. There will be a yellow sign outside reading RECEPTIONIST. Go inside and present your driver's license, and then the "receptionist" will issue you a two-part permit, one to keep in the car and one to keep on your person. You are now on your way.

Go back out to NY 207 and turn right. At 3.7 miles down NY 207, you will turn right at the STEWART AIRPORT COOPERATIVE HUNTING AREA, STATE OF NEW YORK DEC sign. Parking can be found right in front of the gate.

Sources of additional information:

New York State Department of Environmental Conservation, Region 3
21 South Putt Corners Road
New Paltz, NY 12561-1696
(845) 256–3000

Bryan's Bikes
240 Main Street
Cornwall, NY 12518
(845) 534–5230
www.bryansbikes.com

Notes on the trail: The easy, cruising doubletrack and the advanced singletrack briefly described above are detailed below.

Advanced Singletrack: Continue past the parking gate down a wide, gravelly, paved road. Pass some cornfields on the left and a brown wooden shack on your right. Continue through a four-way intersection with New Road (not a new road) and Ridge Road. Continue for 0.2 mile, and on your left will be the singletrack. Usually orange streamers are tied around the trees where the path goes through. This route is occasionally used as a race route and is marked with spray paint or streamers, which helps in navigating your way. Continue through an apple grove and then into a dense hardwood forest. After about 2 miles cross a paved road, and head back into the forest on the singletrack. There are several sections of exposed roots from trail use and natural erosion. Because this singletrack is used as a race course, many banked turns are built up. This gives you the freedom to get into the rhythm of the course. Once your pace is set, you and your bike are swept into one turn after another. There are some rocky sections where it might be necessary to portage your bike, but you will soon turn into the hard-packed singletrack that is prevalent throughout the course.

At 3.2 miles you will come to another singletrack intersecting from the right, but just remain straight. You start hitting some demanding small hills at the 4-mile mark, with one major ascent out of a gully that will shame us all and require a dismount. For the next half-mile the course runs along a ridge and skirts some magnificent corn- and farm fields. At about 4.9 miles, you pass by a small pond on your left, and bear right as another road joins it from the left. Continue on the wide dirt road between some cornfields. Some trails will lead off it, but keep straight on the main wide road. At 5.7 miles fork left onto the main wide dirt road. At about 6 miles make a left at the T intersection with another dirt road, and then make a quick right into the woods. The trail climbs through a hardwood forest for a short distance and then descends to a four-way intersection. Continue straight. In another mile you will come into a clearing; continue to your right. Bear left at the next fork, and proceed up a short hill. At the top bear right into the forest. When you get to the top of another hill, bear right where the orange streamers could and should be, if they are still clinging to the trees. At 7.5 miles turn right at another intersection. After descending a short hill, you will see an orange arrow spray-painted on a tree. Bear right at this fork, riding along solid rock, which runs for a short distance along a ridge. Shortly you will descend sharply to your left down a steep hill. After two more sharp descents, bear left at another fork and up another hill to a long rock ledge. If you are not Arnold or Superbike-man, you will probably have to walk and push the bike up and over. Another orange arrow spray-painted on the rocks indicates the direction to take. At the next four-way, singletrack intersection, continue straight, and at 8.4 miles bear right at the next T intersection. At about 9 miles you will merge with another four-wheel-drive road; continue straight, bearing left through an overgrown pear orchard. Finish your ride at 10 miles on the same old paved New Road where you started. Turn left to return to the vehicle parking or try the loop again if you dare. The pros do it three times in one race.

Beginner Doubletrack: Continue past the parking gate down a wide, gravelly, paved road. Pass by some cornfields on the left and a brown wooden shack on your right. Continue through a four-way intersection with New Road and Ridge Road. Ridge Road will be the road you return on. Continue north on New Road. In less than a mile, you approach a clearing with another wide dirt road. The road leading off to your left is Giles Road, which continues onward to NY 207. Remain on New Road. Shortly after that turnoff pass Drakes Lane and then another road on your left; continue on New Road. You will soon pass some cornfields and arrive at another intersection with Linsey Lane on your left. Linsey Lane could be a candidate as an additional country road to tour on, but for now just remain straight. Climb gently and notice several singletracks crisscrossing New Road. It just gives you a hint of the extent and amount of singletrack out there. Continuing straight ahead on New Road, the wide, gravelly road turns paved, starts making a turn toward the southeast, and runs parallel to I-84. At 5.5 miles you approach a four-way intersection after what seems like a long climb. To your left will be a gate and bridge that goes over I-84. Straight ahead is Maple Avenue. Turn right at this intersection onto the wide Ridge Road. The road turns gravelly as you descend a small hill. Climb gently up another hill over a paved section of road. It gets a little steeper before it levels out and earns its name as the "Ridge." The views are great, and you can see for miles. Cruise for another mile, and soon you will pick up the scent of apples from an abandoned apple orchard on your left. At a little past 9 miles, you reach the intersection with New Road. Turn left to reach the vehicle parking area.

40

Bashakill

This trail runs along an abandoned railroad corridor and is graded for comfortable riding. The tracks have long since been removed, and the wide path is flat and level and travels through a fascinating wildlife area known as the Bashakill Wildlife Management Area. In total, more than 10 miles of riding are possible on the old railway bed, providing a perfect opportunity to experience this unique resource. More than 5 miles run along the eastern side of the 2,175 acres, and there's more mileage after the path leaves the northern edge of this multiple-use area.

The operative word is *cruising.* There will not be a lot of steep, winding singletrack to test your skills, just a long straight path through the natural beauty of a lowland freshwater wetland, the largest in southeastern New York. The long wide valley is geologically known as the Port Jervis Trough. It is banked by views of the Allegheny Plateau to the west and the steep Shawangunk Ridge to the east. The ridge rises almost 700 feet. This ridge is part of the same mountainous ledges found around the Lake Minnewaska and Mohonk bike trails. The trough is a depression in the land that began when the Shawangunk Mountains were lifted and pushed up from the valley floor. Streams and rivers flowed through the valley, guaranteeing the erosional pathway. The arrival and departure of the glaciers during the last continental glaciation, which reached as far south as Pennsylvania, caused the valley to be wide and flat. This freshwater wetland is home to a diverse biotic community, resulting in a variety of fish and wildlife. White-tailed deer, grouse, rabbit, turkey, fox, raccoon, beaver, muskrat, and many species of waterfowl provide great opportunities for wildlife observation and photography. While traveling on the rail path, notice the many birdhouses built in the marshy waters. These houses are used to study wood ducks and bluebirds. Wildlife management programs protect and maintain habitat diversity through construction of these structures. You will also see some nesting platforms, used to attract osprey.

General location: In southeastern New York approximately 65 miles northwest of New York City, south of New York 17.

Elevation change: The trail travels over a railroad grade that is slightly inclined.

Season: From April to September.

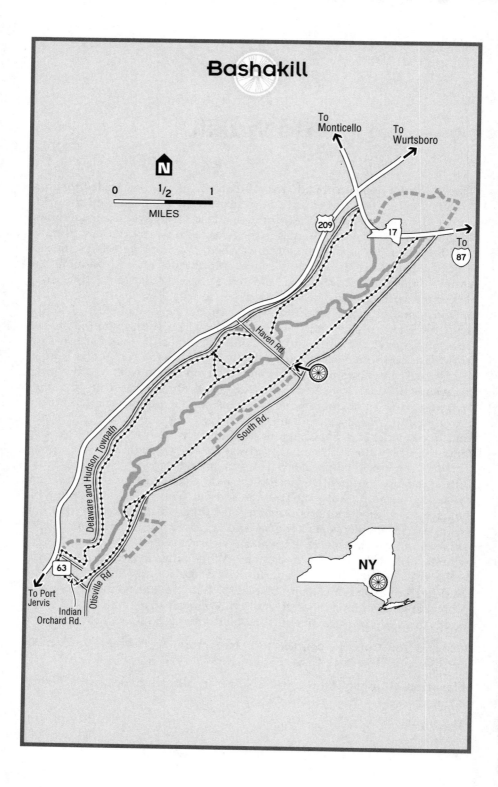

Services: Most of the exits off NY 17 have gas and convenience stores. The nearest large towns are Wurtsboro and Monticello.

Hazards: Hunting seasons start in the beginning of October and end in March. The area is available for riding around those dates. Call the New York State Department of Environmental Conservation for exact dates and details.

Rescue index: U.S. Route 209 is a heavily traveled road, and help can usually be flagged down from passing motorists.

Land status: The New York State Department of Environmental Conservation manages the state-owned forest as a multiple-use area. The land was purchased in 1980 as part of the Environmental Quality Bond Act to preserve unique wilderness areas.

Maps: The Department of Environmental Conservation provides a Bashakill Wildlife Management Area brochure with a basic map of the area. It contains sufficient detail to follow the trail.

Finding the trail: Take the New York State Thruway (Interstate 87) north, and exit at NY 17/US 6 West. Take NY 17 north, and exit at Ellenville/NY 209. Turn left after the exit ramp, and after 2.2 miles turn left onto Haven Road. One-third mile down this road is the first access parking area for the Bashakill. Continue down the road, crossing a small bridge that spans the wetland, and you will soon come to the second access parking area. Turn left down a wide dirt road, and the parking will be on your right. The trail exists in both directions to the northeast and southwest of the parking area beyond some barriers.

Sources of additional information:

New York State Department of Environmental Conservation, Region 3
21 South Putt Corners Road
New Paltz, NY 12561-1696
(845) 256–3000

Wheel and Heel
116 South Plank Road
Newburgh, NY 12550
(914) 567–1740

Notes on the trail: From the parking area you can proceed to the right in a northeasterly direction beyond the barrier or southeasterly by crossing Haven Road and continuing beyond the concrete barrier. Both paths run parallel along the open wetland. The eastern side of the trail faces an upland mixture of forests, old fields, and abandoned orchards.

The trail that leads south can be made into a loop. Follow it for 3.4 miles. Exit onto Otisville Road, and then turn right onto paved County Road 63. Take that a short distance to US 209. Turn right onto US 209, and then take another right onto an unmarked road. You will enter an open field. Look on your left for another unmarked doubletrack trail. If you reach the stream you have gone too far. Turn north (left) onto this wide trail. After 0.4 mile look for a hard-packed, doubletrack trail on a ridge beyond a line of trees. This is the old Delaware and Hudson towpath. Horses would pull floating barges and work their way down the path. The trail is slightly elevated above the landscape and provides good views. Continue on the tow path to Haven Road. Turn right on Haven Road to return to your parking area.

Flugertown Road

Combine 8 miles of easy cruising along a beautiful, forested country road. Add another 8 miles of singletrack through the dense hemlock forests in the New York State Catskill Forest Preserve. Throw in a campground, many small ponds, and some marshmallows, and it's a recipe for a great weekend. The rolling Flugertown Road is wide and semipaved and turns into an old wood road that runs through a tall, dense, hardwood and conifer forest along the Willowemoc Creek. Beginner riders will be pressed by the winding, 4-mile (one way), up-and-down dirt road. The more experienced will want to tackle a rolling, 4-mile (one way), narrow singletrack leading to the Mongaup Pond State Campground. Adventurers will be charmed by this secluded singletrack as they are immersed in a dense Catskill forest of mature conifers and hardwoods. The entire area teems with plant and animal life. Silently glide through this pristine wilderness setting. Take a moment to assimilate the surroundings. The large Mongaup Pond awaits at the end of the ride.

Take your time. There is a lot to see. One of the best ways to get it all in is to camp overnight at a campsite by a brook or stream. There is a lean-to on the edge of Long Pond stationed 0.9 mile from Flugertown Road in a secluded, primitive wilderness setting. It is an ideal campsite. Look for beaver lodges and dams near the outlet at the southern end of the pond. If you are camping, drive your car up Flugertown Road and park by one of the campsites near the Department of Environmental Conservation signs. You can then ride along Flugertown Road and tackle some of the singletrack described below.

General location: North of Monticello off New York 17, on the border of Ulster and Sullivan Counties in the southeastern Catskills, about 100 miles from New York City. If you package it as a weekend, it will certainly be worth the time it takes to get there.

Elevation change: Flugertown Road is fairly level with some minor hill climbs. The 4-mile singletrack along the snowmobile trail leading to the Mongaup Pond campground climbs to about 400 feet, levels off, and then drops 300 feet. The singletrack to Long Pond begins steeply but levels out as it reaches the pond. The unnamed road that leads to Sand Pond is fairly level, with some minor climbs.

Season: Late spring, summer, and early fall provide the best riding opportunities.

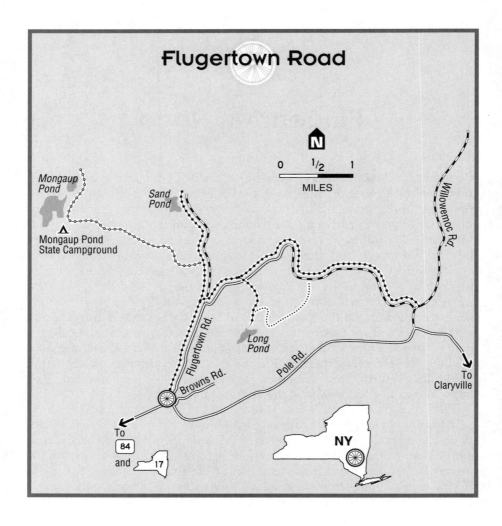

Services: Liberty is about 15 miles south of this area, but overall there is not much in the neighborhood, so come prepared and carry what you will be using during your stay.

Hazards: Mongaup Pond State Campground is a popular area during the summer months. It sees its fair share of crowds, but as you head out on the trails, the din of tents and trailers will diminish. Slow down if you are approaching hikers so you won't surprise them.

Rescue index: This area seems remote, but the popular trails are well used and you will usually encounter other individuals camping or hiking. Becoming lost should not be a problem because the routes described in this ride are not part of any network or loop and are one-direction, out-and-back paths.

Land status: The trail is on New York State land. New York State Department of Environmental Conservation manages the New York State Forest Preserve lands of the Catskills.

Maps: The New York–New Jersey Trail Conference's "Catskill Trails," Trail Map 43 provides complete coverage of this area and is waterproof and tearproof. It sells for $13.95 and can be found at most outdoor-type stores.

Finding the trail: Take the New York State Thruway (Interstate 87) north, and exit at NY 17/U.S. Route 6 West. Take NY 17 north, and exit at Parksville/Cooley, exit 98. The exit is actually a stoplight. Make a right onto County Road 85. If you need to fuel the car or yourself, do it at the convenience store at the corner of this stoplight because there is not much up ahead. The road turns into CR 84 after the intersection with Cooley Mountain Road. After about 8 miles you will reach an intersection with a stop sign; continue straight. You will soon come to a small bridge, where you will pick up the intersection of Flugertown Road and CR 84. Make a left onto Flugertown Road, and take the left fork. You can park on the left side in a small turnout and take your bike up Flugertown Road. There is also the option of driving farther up Flugertown Road to the New York State Department of Environmental Conservation signs. If you choose the latter, you will miss out on the fun and beauty of Flugertown Road. If you are camping you will need to haul in your equipment. In this case drive up Flugertown Road to the Department of Environmental Conservation signs, and park closer to one of the campsites in the area.

Source of additional information:

New York State Department of Environmental Conservation, Region 3
21 South Putt Corners Road
New Paltz, NY 12561-1696
(845) 256–3000

Notes on the trail: There are four riding opportunities in this tour. Continuing on Flugertown Road, the paved section ends and the wide dirt country road begins after about 1 mile. You will soon come to an open field on your left. There will be a four-wheel-drive, unmarked path leading off to your left before the field. It proceeds in a northeasterly direction to Sand Pond. Two miles in length, it makes an excellent spur trail to explore one of the unique ponds that exists on these lands. This double-track intersects with the yellow-blazed, Mongaup-Willowemoc Trail in about 1 mile. Turning left in a westerly direction will lead you to Mongaup Pond and its campgrounds. Turning right in a northwesterly direction leads out to an intersection farther up on Flugertown Road. Continue straight on the unmarked Sand Pond Trail, cross a small brook, and reach the pond in 1.5 miles.

   If you have just returned from Sand Pond and are standing on Flugertown Road, pedal along the wide, hard-packed Flugertown Road past open land. You will soon pass an attractive country house on your left. Continue straight ahead into a dense portion of woods beneath a canopy of hardwoods. You will soon come to the New York State Department of Environmental Conservation sign for the Long Pond Trailhead. The red disks indicate the snowmobile trail that leads to your right and ascends to Long Pond in 0.9 mile. It requires a short, steep climb until you get to the level of land near the pond. After the second wooden bridge, fork right, and ascend steeply to Long Pond. The Long Pond lean-to is off a spur from this path.

Turning back to Flugertown Road, continue down the road. Another Department of Environmental Conservation sign will be on your left. This is the 4-mile, one-way Mongaup-Willowemoc Trail. It begins along the snowmobile trail, which is marked with red disks nailed on trees, and then veers to the left along a trail marked with yellow disks.

You can continue on Flugertown Road; bear right in a northeasterly direction until you see the private road signs posted by the Peters Hunting Club. This trail description ends here, but Flugertown Road continues for another 4 miles and intersects with Willowemoc Road. According to the Department of Environmental Conservation, these roads are public and you can ride on them. If you are riding during the fall hunting season, pay attention at this point on the road, because this is a hunting club and they post signs. You might want to turn around here during hunting season.

Willowemoc Road

This strenuous, 6-mile (total), out-and-back, wide, country dirt road is for tough bikers. Its climb demands great stamina and lung capacity. But the rewards are there, as you pass a wilderness of mature hemlock, old abandoned apple orchards, and clearings with some great mountain views. Need I mention the turbo-charged, fireball descent?

The road traverses the Beaver Kill Range, which consists of two 3,300-foot summits. They rise to the north and offer open vistas of a large, densely forested valley with streams feeding the West Branch River that joins the Neversink River.

Willowemoc Road can be ridden in conjunction with the Flugertown Road tour by continuing on Flugertown Road to its termination at Willowemoc Road.

General location: North of Monticello off New York 17 on the border of Ulster and Sullivan Counties in the southeastern Catskills, about 100 miles from New York City. It's a good idea to combine this ride with the Flugertown Road tour.

Elevation change: The general trend of this tour is up, but oh my, what a ride down. There is about a 500-foot elevation gain over 3.5 miles.

Season: Late spring, summer, and early fall are the prime seasons. The hard-packed dirt road does not get too soft after rain and can be ridden in wet weather.

Services: Liberty is about 15 miles south of this area, but overall there is not much in the neighborhood, so come prepared and carry what you will be using during your stay.

Hazards: Watch for vehicles coming and going on the road. There are a few hunting lodges as you get closer to the top of your ride. Club members and visitors contribute to the small amount of vehicular traffic on the road. Pay close attention around the turns as you descend, as there are often vehicles coming up the road.

Rescue index: There are several residences along the road, and in case of emergency a knock on a door may be an option.

Land status: Ulster County secondary road.

Willowemoc Road

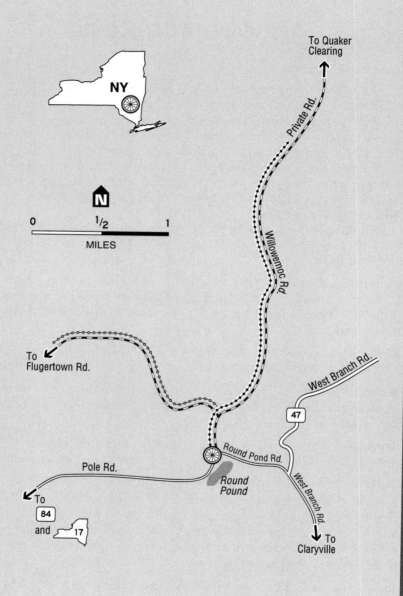

Willowemoc Road leads through a dense primeval forest.

Maps: The New York–New Jersey Trail Conference's "Catskill Trails," Trail Map 43 provides complete coverage of this area and is waterproof and tearproof. It sells for $13.95 and can be found at most outdoor-type stores.

Finding the trail: Take the New York State Thruway (Interstate 87) north and exit at NY 17/U.S. Route 6 West. Take NY 17 north, and exit at Parksville/Cooley, exit 98. The exit is actually a stoplight. Make a right onto County Road 85. If you need to fuel the car or yourself, do it at the convenience store at the corner of this stoplight, because there is not much up ahead. The road turns into CR 84 after the intersection with Cooley Mountain Road. After about 8 miles you will reach an intersection with a stop sign; continue straight. You will soon come to a small bridge where you will pick up the intersection of Flugertown Road and CR 84. Ignore the intersection with Flugertown Road, and keep bearing right. You will be continuing on Pole Road. As you approach an intersection with another road on your left you will see the New York State Department of Environmental Conservation sign for Long Pond and Balsam Lake Trails. This is across from a small body of water called Round Pond. Make a left, and about 500 feet on your right is a parking area.

Source of additional information:

New York State Department of Environmental Conservation, Region 3
21 South Putt Corners Road
New Paltz, NY 12561-1696
(845) 256–3000

Notes on the trail: If you are approaching Willowemoc Road from the Flugertown Road tour, continue to the end of Flugertown Road. The intersection with Willowemoc Road is approximately 4 miles past the PETERS HUNTING CLUB sign. Turn left, heading north on Willowemoc Road.

If you are beginning from the parking area, turn right onto Willowemoc Road, and in less than a quarter-mile, you will come to a fork. The fork to your left is actually the alternate end of the Flugertown Road tour and is blazed with red disks, indicating a snowmobile trail known as Basily Road. It will eventually connect with Flugertown Road.

Bearing right at the fork, continue up a long, gradual incline for about 2 miles. You first proceed through a mature hemlock forest and then into a forest of beech as you get to the higher elevations. In 0.7 mile you pass an abandoned apple orchard, and views start opening up to the east of some 3,000-foot mountains. The valleys you look across are the drainage basins for the Fall Brook stream networks, which all flow into the West Branch River, which joins the Neversink River farther south.

At about 3 miles, you will see a sign indicating that the road ahead is private. It passes through the Wild Meadows Game Preserve and belongs to the Shannon Hunting Club. You have to turn around at this point. The ride down should be a real screamer.

43

The Denning Trail

This great Catskill tour follows the scenic Denning Road for 5 miles. The 10-mile (total), out-and-back country road passes along old meadows bordered by 100-year-old sugar maples and dense woodland. The easy riding cuts through an area that is part of the primitive wilderness of the Catskills, partially settled long ago. The countryside resembles old but well-maintained country estates. The gently rolling, semipaved road parallels the wide East Branch of the Neversink River and passes through the Neversink River flood plain, which deposited rich soils long ago. The result: beautiful, fertile meadows for apple orchards and farms that have existed for more than 200 years. For centuries the Catskills were hunting grounds for Native Americans. They lived and fished in the fertile river valleys, and hunted in the dark, hemlock-filled valleys and wooded slopes of the mountains they called Onteora, or "land in the sky." American farmers shared these woods with the Native Americans of the Northeast and began searching the mountainous region for rare, flat parcels of land to farm. This flood plain provided a fertile piece of land in the rocky, craggy Catskill Mountains and was a prime location to grow an orchard or cultivate a small farm.

Try to imagine the impressions this land made on those who discovered it. Beginner and advanced riders can share and embrace the rich history that embodies these mysterious woods and surrounding lands. One cannot help but feel the exhilaration when riding through this rich, forested land.

General location: North of Monticello off New York 17 on the border of Ulster and Sullivan Counties in the southeastern Catskills, about 100 miles from New York City.

Elevation change: The ride is fairly level, and the elevation change is minimal.

Season: Late spring, summer, and early fall are great seasons to ride. The winter brings snow. The hard-packed dirt road does not get too soft after rain and can be ridden in wet weather.

Services: Liberty is about 15 miles south of this area, but overall there is not much in the neighborhood, so come prepared and carry what you will be using during your stay.

Hazards: Watch for other vehicles on the road. Getting lost is not a problem because the road is straight.

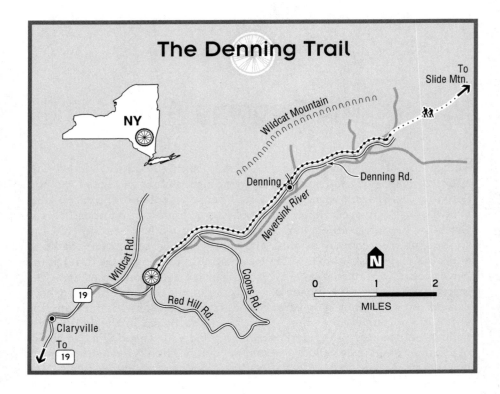

The Denning Trail

Rescue index: Denning Road passes some country homes, and a trailhead at the end of Denning Road is used by hikers. There are always some vehicles on their way to the trailhead or to one of the country homes.

Land status: This is a town road surrounded by private and state land.

Maps: The New York–New Jersey Trail Conference's "Catskill Trails," Trail Map 43 provides complete coverage of this area and is waterproof and tearproof. It sells for $13.95 and can be found at most outdoor-type stores.

Finding the trail: Take the New York State Thruway (Interstate 87), and exit at NY 17/U.S. Route 6 West. Take NY 17 north to the Liberty exit. Take County Road 55 for about 12 miles, and then turn left, going north on CR 19 toward Claryville. Look for parking near the intersection of Red Hill Road and Denning Road, or anywhere along Denning Road.

Source of additional information:

New York State Department of Environmental Conservation, Region 3
21 South Putt Corners Road
New Paltz, NY 12561-1696
(845) 256–3000

216

Notes on the trail: The ride begins on the paved section of Denning Road. After a short distance the road degrades to a wide, hard-packed country road, and you will pass by some charming homesteads. Climb a short hill for about a quarter-mile, and then descend to the level of the Neversink River. Continue past the DEAD-END signs for another 3 miles. Do not turn right onto New Road Hill. At a fork bear right. You will pass by a Japanese-style house with peaked roofs and rock gardens that was built at the turn of the twentieth century. The estate was and is still owned by the Tison family. The parking area for the Denning hiking trailhead is reached soon after at about the 5-mile mark. This will be your turnaround point.

Vertigo at Plattekill

On a remote road in the Catskill Mountains, a rustic ski center provides lift service for you and your mountain bike up Plattekill Mountain. Forty miles of novice, intermediate, and advanced single- and doubletrack trails crisscross and descend the mountainous terrain. Cross-country ski trails run along the ridges that encircle the ski center and provide rolling singletrack trails through dense conifer and deciduous forests. Wild raspberries grow freely along the trails.

Plattekill Mountain attracts a lot of serious riders. Don't stand in the middle of any path on a busy weekend. You might encounter one of these fully armored and padded road warrior–style bikers bulleting down on a full-suspension mountain bike. For a relatively short chairlift ride, you have access to a variety of trail options. Wide, steep switchbacks across the ski runs and hard-packed, sometimes rocky singletrack lead down the mountain. A group of cross-country trails at the top of the mountain provide rolling, singletrack terrain.

Laszlo Vajtay is the owner of Ski Plattekill, the small, 1,000-vertical-foot slope outside of Roxbury. The mountain biking center on the premises is run solely by Vajtay. He has encouraged the building of stimulating routes. His staff and volunteers have creatively hacked out and constructed singletrack trails and high-speed switchbacks through the dense hardwood forests.

The easy novice-rated trails are wide and gently sloping and use the beginner downhill ski trails. The intermediate trails are steeper and narrower and include the singletrack. The advanced trails are for the aggressive rider seeking technical, race-quality, extreme, and vigorous downhill and singletrack. All-day, long-distance rides are also available, as are instructions and guided tours for riders of all levels.

General location: Approximately 40 miles west of Kingston in the western Catskill Mountains.

Elevation change: The mountain provides 1,000 feet of vertical. An all-day lift ticket allows you to pile up many descents.

Season: The area is open to mountain biking from Memorial Day weekend through Thanksgiving Day weekend, weather permitting.

Services: Don't be fooled by the ski center's rustic appearance. Prices are on the high side for rentals and lift tickets. Good-quality, Gary Fischer

The way to master the vertical on Plattekill Mountain is to go along with it.

front-suspension and full-suspension bikes are available; at the lodge you can kick back, chat, and drink some cold ones.

At the time of this writing, an all-day lift ticket was $18. This does not include mountain bike rentals. Rigid bikes go for $20, front-suspension bikes go for $30, and full-suspension bikes are priced at $40. Add another $5.00 for a helmet, and it might be wiser to purchase a mountain bike before going. On weekends it is a good idea to call in advance and reserve a bike.

Hazards: Sections of the single- and doubletrack trails that descend throughout the terrain can be classically Catskill rocky. Caution is advised on all descents, as the rocks cause your tires to skip and lose traction. After a few runs you become acquainted with this kind of riding. There are some sharp turns throughout the forested trails; these, too, require some caution.

Rescue index: Help can be found on the premises. A first-aid station can be found at the lodge.

Land status: Ski Plattekill is owned by Laszlo Vajtay.

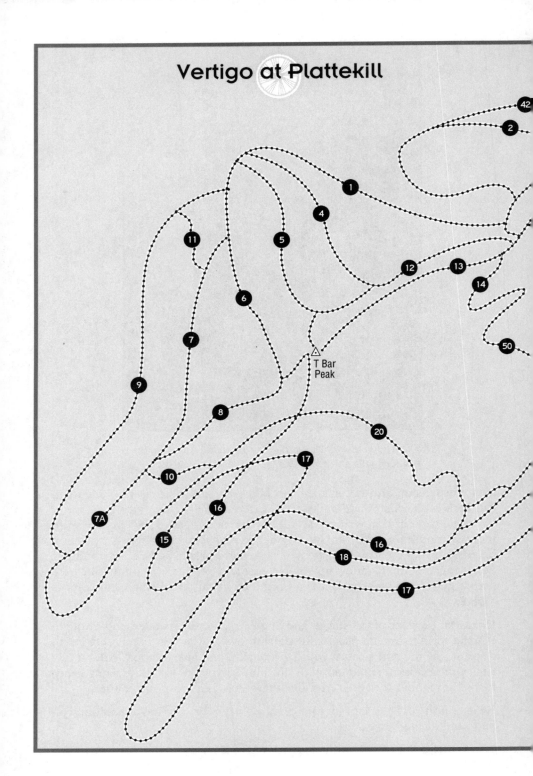

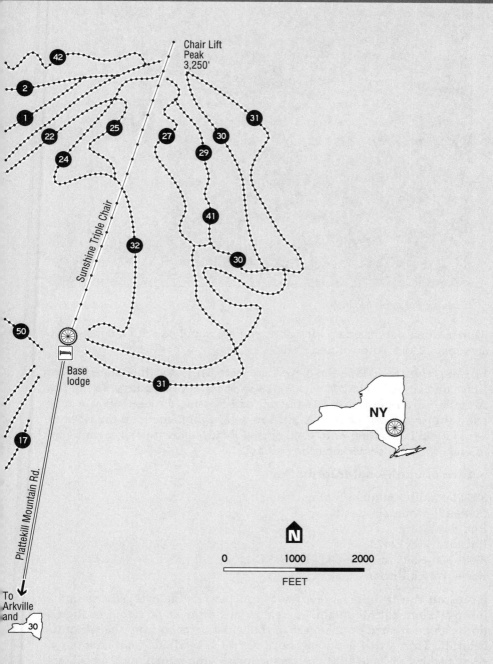

Chair Lift
Peak
3,250'

Sunshine Triple Chair

Base
lodge

Plattekill Mountain Rd.

To
Arkville
and

NY

N

0   1000   2000

FEET

Note: *More trails exist in this area than can be shown on this map. Maps are available at the mountain. All trails are numbered.*

Climbing Plattekill Mountain.

Maps: Upon purchasing a lift ticket, you are supplied with a comprehensive map of the ski bowl and trails.

Finding the trail: Take the New York State Thruway (Interstate 87) and Kingston exit 19. Follow New York 28 west for approximately 35 miles to Arkville. Turn right just before the railroad crossing. Proceed about 1 mile, and turn right (north) onto NY 30. You will begin picking up the signs for Ski Plattekill. Turn left onto Cold Spring Road, follow the signs, and park in one of the ski center's parking areas.

Source of additional information:

Ski Plattekill Mountain Biking Center
Plattekill Mountain Road
P.O. Box 187
Roxbury, NY 12474
(607) 326–3500 or (800) GOTTA–BIKE
www.plattekill.com

Notes on the trail: A large array of trails awaits the energetic mountain biker at Plattekill Mountain. A tremendous number of riding configurations can be created on the maze of trails that descend from the top of the chairlift. They will fill up an entire day of bike riding and exploration. After picking up your lift ticket at the lodge, grab a map, pick a trail, and just begin riding. Most of the routes are marked as they appear on the map. If you do get lost, just keep descending. All trails lead to the lodge and chairlift.

The D & H Heritage Corridor

This is an exciting and easy trail wrapped in the beautiful pastoral landscape of historic Ulster County. The 6-mile (one way) hiking/biking rail-trail connects two quaint seventeenth-century villages: Hurley and High Falls. The well-maintained, level path passes through a dense, deciduous woodland, paralleling tranquil farmland and crossing over rivers and streams. It's a splendid setting, particularly in the fall, and the foliage at peak periods is intense. Although not technically challenging, this wide, hard-packed cinder rail-trail is ideal for beginners and gently paced for riders seeking placid terrain and scenery. In total there are 12 miles of out-and-back fun. Only a minimal amount of exertion and technical prowess is required. This route passes through the attractive and protected woodland area known as the Delaware and Hudson Canal Corridor.

What was the former Ontario & Western rail bed now provides a two-wheeled passage through history. The trains, which ran until 1957, hauled coal and local farm products.

This can be an out-and-back ride or a loop (by returning to the start via one of the paved roads that cross the trail). The trail begins near the historic village of Hurley, which features eighteenth-century stone houses. It terminates near High Falls, settled in 1669.

In Hurley the past comes to life as you pass along the main street lined with stone houses. The Van Deusen house, built in 1723, served as the temporary capitol of the state after the burning of Kingston in 1777. The Esopus-Minisink Trail passes through town. This Native American trail connected the Delaware Valley with the Hudson River and was used before and during the American Revolution. While riding you pass the Old Guard House, used to hold a British spy, Lieutenant David Taylor, who was hanged from an apple tree on 18 October 1777. In High Falls you can walk or ride down to the scenic Rondout Creek. Nearby and across from the historic Depuy Canal House Restaurant and tavern on NY 213 is the old stone aqueduct built in 1825 by the D & H Canal Company. The Depuy Canal House Restaurant is housed in a stone building built in 1797 by S & A Depuy, which also kept a tavern there. To this day the menu is great. The canal was completed in 1828 and abandoned in 1889. The 108-mile canal was conceived in 1823 as a means of transporting coal from Honesdale, Pennsylvania, to Eddyville, New York, and became an important source of much-needed energy. The coal was then carried to New York City on barges floated down the Hudson River.

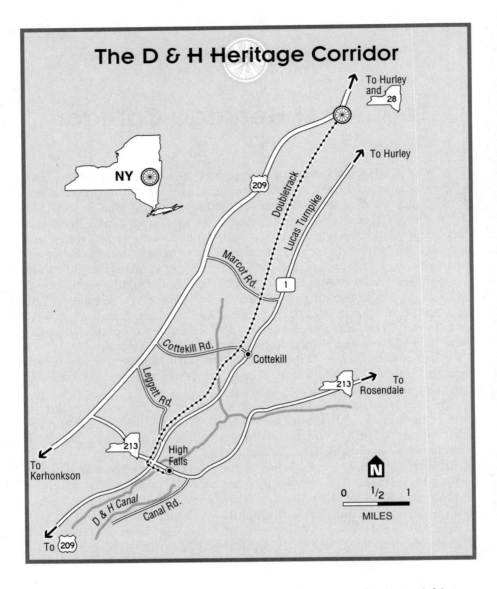

The construction of the rail path began with support from special interest groups and the Environmental Quality Bond Act Fund, which provides monies for parks and recreation throughout several state counties. Thanks to the efforts of a group of local bicyclists and the Delaware and Hudson Canal Heritage Alliance, the path is maintained and kept in very good condition.

Now get out there and ride. Ride with an effort to protect the trail and the environment. Riding in muddy conditions hastens erosion. Be thoughtful about sharing the trails with others, including hikers and joggers, and maintain proper etiquette while enjoying the beauty of this path.

Rondout Creek.

General location: Travel about 90 miles north of Manhattan on the New York State Thruway (Interstate 87) to exit 19, Kingston.

Elevation change: The smooth trail travels over a flat and generally rolling grade.

Season: Fall is absolutely breathtaking, with colors filling the surrounding valleys. Winter usually brings snow, but if there is no snow on the trails, get some extra layers of clothing on and enjoy hearty cold-weather riding.

Services: Services are available at Hurley and can be reached off U.S. Route 209 or at High Falls on New York 213. Stewart Shops in Hurley is a convenience store and gas station.

Hazards: You may at times share the path with hikers, joggers, and other bike riders. Extend the usual courtesy when approaching from behind, and let other users know that your presence is near. Be thoughtful about sharing the trails with others so mountain bike riders can enjoy the use of beautiful trails like these.

Rescue index: The trail receives a fair amount of use, and there is usually someone who can provide assistance. The path is also surrounded by residential areas and therefore in close proximity to help if needed. Further help could be found in High Falls or along US 209.

Land status: The path passes through the Hudson Valley Greenway Countryside Corridor/The D & H Canal Heritage Corridor. The Rail-Trail Park marks the beginning of the trail. The D & H Canal Corridor extends between the Catskill and Shawangunk Mountains.

Maps: The trail is easy to follow, and the map I have drawn up provides the best detail. USGS 7.5-minute series, Kingston East quadrangle and St. Regis quadrangle provide good detail for these unimproved dirt roads.

Finding the trail: Take the New York State Thruway (I–87) north to exit 19, Kingston. You must bear right (west) on NY 28, and then follow the signs for US 209. After traveling for 3.2 miles on US 209, look for a blue trailhead sign on your left that reads 1986 ENVIRONMENTAL QUALITY BOND ACT, THE HURLEY-MARBLETOWN O & W RAIL TRAIL THROUGH THE D & H CANAL HERITAGE CORRIDOR. Turn off US 209, and find a small, gravel-covered parking area before the trailhead that is marked with a small, wooden, informational kiosk.

Sources of additional information:

Ulster County Tourism and Public Information Office
10 Westbrook Lane
Kingston, NY 12402
(845) 340–3566

Bicycle Depot
3 Church Street
New Paltz, NY 12561
(845) 255–3859
www.bicycledepot.com

Kingston Cyclery
1094 Morton Boulevard
Kingston, NY 12401
(845) 382–2453 or 382–BIKE

Notes on the trail: The path is straightforward with few turns. Begin your journey by pedaling beyond the metal gate and the wooden informational kiosk. The wide, hard-packed dirt path proceeds in a southwesterly direction through a dense woodland for about 2 miles, followed by a long, narrow wetland area. Cross Marcot Road at 3.5 miles, and begin pedaling on a wide, hard-packed singletrack. The next road you cross is Cottekill Road. You have now covered 4.5 miles. Continue across the road, and pass some farm fields and attractive pine plantations. At 6.4 miles the path terminates on Leggett Road.

You may turn back at this point to the parking area, making this about a 13-mile round-trip. You can also continue your ride into High Falls. To do so head east (left) onto Leggett Road, and then make a quick (0.2-mile) right (south) onto Lucas Turnpike. Turn left (east) at the next intersection with NY 213. Cross the bridge spanning Rondout Creek, and proceed into High Falls. Be sure to check out High Falls Historic Park on NY 213 and the D & H Canal Museum in town on Mohonk Road.

Adirondack
Region Tours

Adirondack Park is simply enormous. With more than 6 million acres of public and private lands in the northern third of New York, the park could practically cover the entire state of Vermont. Established in 1892, it remains the largest state park in the nation.

Despite its vast, original, natural beauty, the Adirondacks for decades was largely taken for granted and abused by industrial interests. During the midnineteenth century legions of lumberers and loggers pounced on the landscape, denuding it of virgin timberland as the nation's demand for wood grew. New York became the nation's leading lumber-producing state. Majestic white pines—strong and straight as telephone poles—were logged while hemlock was left to rot on the forest floor after having been stripped of bark used for leather tanning. The spruce trees made the finest pulp for paper and were relentlessly cut down. Erosion from rains and snow meltwater washed over the barren hillsides, and these remote, primitive forests became a memory.

Fortunately the massive abuse did not go unnoticed forever. Conservationists forced the government to establish in 1885 the New York State Forest Preserve. As a result ten years later 900,000 acres of land were protected. The area within the preserve was declared "forever wild."

Forty-two percent of this land is public; 58 percent is private. Most of the state land is designated as "wilderness" or "primitive" and is off limits to bicycles and motorized vehicles. That's one giant step for protecting the environment, but not good news for off-road bike riders. However, in 1985, the State Land Master Plan allowed access throughout the preserve on land that was designated as "wild forest." Any foot trails, dirt roads, and horse and snowmobile trails on these particular lands labeled as "wild forest" became open for bicycling. This wild forest amounts to about 1.2 million acres of backcountry wilderness mountain bike yahoo potential, with the exception of routes posted closed. In effect Adirondack Park provides the most extensive mountain biking opportunities in the eastern United States.

All-terrain biking began in the Adirondacks at the end of the nineteenth century and soon became popular. A local biking club was formed in Keene Valley in 1897. Many of its members had to ride over rough roads with sections filled with tree stumps and logs and without the benefit of today's modern suspension systems.

Many of the routes throughout the Adirondacks were once in a primitive state. The early roads, literally hacked out of the dense woodland, were later paved with logs, making for a very bumpy ride. The waterways, ancient paths of least resistance, were the first travel corridors and became the preferred method of travel. Native Americans and early explorers, hunters, and trappers paddled the lakes and rivers by canoe. Before the sixteenth century not many year-round residents chose the Adirondacks for settling and raising a family. The Native Americans avoided the densely forested mountains and preferred to settle in the gently rolling Champlain Valley, where they engaged in agriculture. The Adirondack region proved to be excellent hunting territory, which attracted Native Americans, hunters, and trappers. Bear, moose, deer, mountain lion, and wolf were plentiful, and the 2,800 lakes and ponds and 6,000 miles of rivers and streams were well stocked for fishing. The region was also a popular tribal warground. There were numerous skirmishes among the Iroquois from the south and the Algonquins and Hurons from the north.

Heavy settlement of the region didn't begin until the latter part of the eighteenth century, after the Adirondack Mountains were discovered to be a tremendous source for lumber. Recreation began after the Civil War, and from 1870 to 1910 the area became the preferred location for many vacationers. The burgeoning tourist industry spawned hotels, rustic guides, and roads. At the beginning of this period, steamships and other boats were used to transport people in and out. The railroad came next. The tracks and trains that were built to haul lumber became a convenient way to bring tourists. It wasn't until the twentieth century, with the advent of the automobile, that roads were built and improved. I have included some rides that follow along these ancient corridors of travel.

The Adirondack Mountains are a wilderness that beckons explorers and adventurers of any age or era. And that includes mountain bikers. Snowmobile routes, forest roads, and singletracks are abundant in the Adirondacks and make for prime two-wheel travel rides for all levels of riders.

The Adirondacks evokes the deep meaning of wilderness. To quote Edward Abbey in his book, *Desert Solitaire:*

> Wilderness invokes nostalgia, a justified not merely sentimental nostalgia for the lost America our forefathers knew. The word suggests the past and the unknown, the womb of earth from which we all emerged. It means something lost and something still present, something remote and at the same time intimate, something buried in our blood and nerves, something beyond us and without limit. Romance—but not to be dismissed on that account. The romantic view, while not the whole of truth, is a necessary part of the whole truth.
>
> But the love of wilderness is more than a hunger for what is always beyond reach; it is also an expression of loyalty to the earth, the earth which bore us and sustains us, the only home we shall ever know, the only paradise we ever need—if only we had the eyes to see.

Happy trails.

Johnson Pond—Paradox Tour

Tucked above the small hamlet of North Hudson lies a 22-mile loop through a mixed hardwood and evergreen forest. This hearty feast of a ride requires about a good half day. If you take your time, you could fill up a whole day. Get an early start, and explore these mostly hard-packed dirt roads. After finishing this tour exit north on Interstate 87 to the Lake Placid and Keene Valley area, and sample some of the great tours available there. North Hudson resides in a quiet corner of the Champlain Valley and offers a mixture of paved and dirt roads. The historic settlement is just north of the popular and attractive Schroon Lake and Lake George. Views of ponds, forests, and hillsides add to your ride's delight.

General location: Thirty-eight miles north of Lake George near the village of North Hudson in Essex County, in northeastern New York.

Elevation change: The terrain is rolling, and there are some gradual climbs, but nothing very steep. This tour is primarily a challenge based on distance versus a mountain bike technical dream.

Season: These routes are rideable providing that they are not covered with deep snows and that they have dried out after the spring thaws. The approximate dates are early May through November. However, it always depends on the severity of the winter and the amounts of snow that fall.

Services: There are better options for food and shops 6 miles south in Schroon Lake. Gear up and fill up there before you tour.

Hazards: During mud season, which begins from the first thaws and lasts until late April, the roads are deceptively moist and soft. The roads are frozen with water during the winter, and when they begin to thaw out, riding on them is like riding on quicksand.

Rescue index: You are riding along seldom-traveled roads. Some summer residences are scattered along the roads, though. During my first jaunt along these routes, I had to ride back down to New York 9 before I could find some assistance.

Land status: The route travels through the pristine Hammond Pond Wild Forest on public roads.

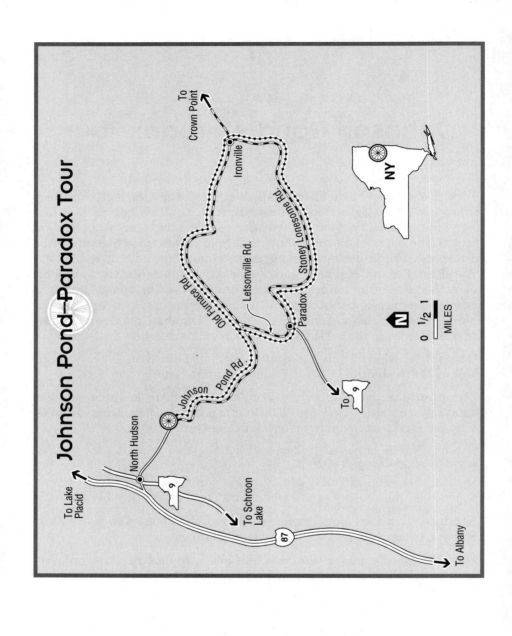

Johnson Pond–Paradox Tour

Maps: The New York State *Atlas and Gazetteer,* published by DeLorme Mapping Company, provides some topographical detail as well as route layout. The topographic details shown on the maps include 160-foot contour intervals. The popular atlas is available at most bookstores in the Northeast.

Finding the trail: Take the New York State Thruway (I–87) north to exit 24 (Albany). Take I-87 north to Newcomb/North Hudson, exit 29. After the exit ramp, turn right at the stop sign to pick up NY 9 north. Follow it for 0.3 mile, and turn right onto Johnson Pond Road (Essex County Road 2). Park your car anywhere along the road. To avoid a major steep section, drive your car 0.6 mile, and park anywhere along the road soon after it levels out.

Source of additional information:

Lake Placid/Essex County Convention and Visitors Bureau
216 Main Street
Lake Placid, NY 12946
(800) 447–5224
www.lakeplacid.com

Notes on the trail: I know the beginning is painful, but once out of the way, the remaining passage is a piece of cake. The first 0.6 mile climbs steadily up the semipaved, rough road. It does level out and pass through an evergreen forest. Catch your breath, and take a moment to admire the raging stream that tumbles alongside the road. Johnson Pond Road (CR 2) changes into a dirt road soon after passing Johnson Pond on your right. After pedaling 5 miles from NY 9 along Johnson Pond Road, turn left (northeast) at the intersection with Old Furnace Road. Paradox Creek and the 600-foot Bald Pate and Moose Mountain will accompany you on your left to the north. This 5-mile leg leads you to Ironville, the location of the Penfield Museum.

From Ironville pedal south, winding along the western shore of Penfield Pond. In just less than 2 miles, turn right onto Stoney Lonesome Road. Continue another 5 miles, passing Flemings Pond on your left. You can turn left onto Letsonville Road to reach Paradox Lake and NY 74. Turn right onto Letsonville Road, and connect with Johnson Pond Road in just less than 2 miles. If you are riding in the summer, make sure you stop to swim at Paradox Lake near the state campsite.

The Wild One

In the High Peaks region of the Adirondacks is a rugged valley surrounded by spectacular scenery and the site of a unique and challenging mountain bike trail. Old Mountain Road traverses the valley, located northwest of Pitchoff Mountain. This 6-mile (one way) route passes through meadows and mixed woodlands with spectacular views of the rocky northern cliffs and crags of nearby Pitchoff Mountain. The ride provides an excellent intermediate-level, doubletrack trail. Except for trail erosion exposing a few rocks along the route and some small hills, this trail is ideal for those who would like to challenge themselves and experience true mountain-pass scenery. As you pedal along, you will pass numerous beaver ponds. They often flood the trail and may require a small detour with a carry.

The ride follows one of the original pre–eighteenth-century routes across the Adirondacks. The route connected Lake Champlain to the St. Lawrence Valley and was known as the Northwest Bay Road. This section, which ran from Keene to Lake Placid, was long considered to be the most difficult and treacherous. Stagecoach passengers often had to get out and help push their coach through the 2,350-foot pass. By the midnineteenth century stagecoaches traveled along the present New York 73 route through Cascade Pass. Ironically, the severe winter weather in Cascade Pass often made people prefer Old Mountain Road. From 1810 to 1860 this route was the only direct roadway from Keene and the east to North Elba and the west. Cars passed along the same route until 1930. After 1930 the eroded route was only passable by four-wheel-drive vehicles. And then came the mountain bike, opening up this exciting route for two-wheel travel and discovery.

General location: Near the village of Keene, about 14 miles south of Lake Placid in the High Peaks area of Adirondack Park in northeastern New York.

Elevation change: Heading east from Alstead Mill Road, the elevation begins at 1,800 feet, rises to 2,350 feet at the pass, and descends to 2,100 feet as the trail leads into NY 73.

Season: The trails are available almost year-round, and if there is no snow cover, winter is an ideal time in these primitive woods, providing the ground is frozen (sans ice) and there is no snow. The route follows a deep

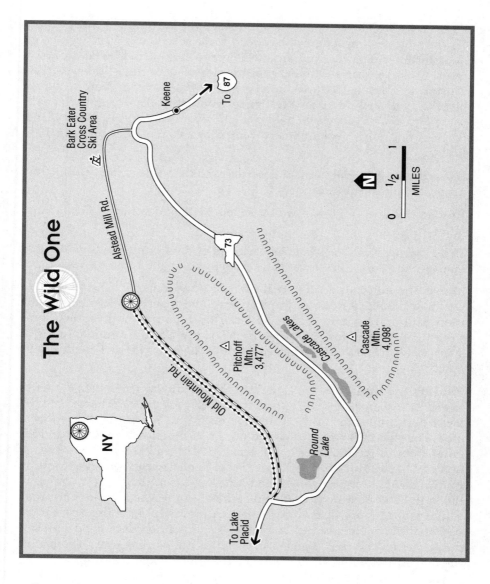

valley within a high mountain notch and can be muddy and flooded in sections during wet weather. The blackflies can be fierce in late spring, so bring some repellent. Try to avoid mud season, which begins after the first thaws in March and can last until early May.

Services: We stayed at the Bark Eater, a true country inn, located on Alstead Mill Road. The inn provides the mountain bike rider with a base camp to launch several bike excursions along the miles of trails just beyond the Bark Eater's perimeters. Originally a stagecoach stopover, the

Bark Eater Inn has been in operation since the early nineteenth-century. The farmhouse atmosphere still reflects these early times with wide-board floors, stone fireplaces, and antiques everywhere. It is located on a spacious, 350-acre farm in the heart of the Adirondack High Peaks. Joe Pete Wilson—a former Olympic and world competitor in Nordic skiing, biathlon, and bobsledding—welcomes mountain bikers year-round. His experienced staff is eager to help you enjoy your time there. Placid Planet Bicycles and High Peaks Cyclery rent and sell mountain bikes in Lake Placid.

Hazards: An 800-foot vertical descent awaits the rider after reaching the height of land at the pass.

Rescue index: NY 73 is a well-traveled route and is never more than 5 miles away.

Land status: New York State Department of Environmental Conservation manages the Forest Preserve land through which the route passes.

Maps: The Adirondack High Peaks Region Area Map published by Plinth, Quoin & Cornice Associates provides excellent topographical detail of the route and surrounding terrain and can be found at most outdoor-type stores in New York for $5.00. It is based on the USGS 15-minute series, at a scale of 1:62,500 and a contour level of 20 feet, where 1 inch = 0.98 mile.

Finding the trail: Take the New York State Thruway (Interstate 87) north to exit 24 (Albany). Take I-87 north to exit 30. Pick up NY 9 north, and follow it for 2 miles to NY 73. Continue on NY 73 toward the Lake Placid area. The start of the tour is located on NY 73, 9 miles from Keene and 5.8 miles from the traffic light in Lake Placid. The end point is the termination of Alstead Mill Road in Keene. From Keene's center proceed west on NY 73, and turn right onto Alstead Mill Road. Turn left after 1.4 miles at the Bark Eater Touring Center, and continue straight to the top of the road at 3.9 miles. You will notice a small parking area in a pretty meadow beside three buildings that are used for an Adirondack guide service organization. The trail begins at the end of the parking area. The end of the tour is located on NY 73, 9 miles from Keene and 5.8 miles from the traffic light in Lake Placid. If you are shuttling, park your car in the small lot near the intersection of Old Military Road (on the maps as Old Mountain Road) and NY 73 (half a mile east of Cascade Ski Touring Center). You can also just ride up to the pass and back down again.

Sources of additional information:

The Bark Eater Inn
Alstead Mill Road
Keene, NY 12942
(518) 576–2221
www.barkeater.com

Panoramic views surround you along Alstead Mill Road.

Placid Planet Bicycles
51 Saranac Avenue
Lake Placid, NY 12946
(518) 523-4128
www.placidplanetbicycles.com

High Peaks Cyclery
331 Main Street
Lake Placid, NY 12946
(518) 523-3764

Adirondack Park Agency
P.O. Box 99, Route 86
Ray Brook, NY 12977
(518) 891-4050

New York State Department of Environmental Conservation, Region 5
P.O. Box 296, Route 86
Ray Brook, NY 12977
(518) 897-1211

Lake Placid/Essex County Convention and Visitors Bureau
216 Main Street
Lake Placid, NY 12946
(800) 447-5224
www.lakeplacid.com

Notes on the trail: This tour can be as short as a 6-mile jaunt over a mountain pass if someone is willing to park a second car at the end of the route, or an 18-mile loop if you have to make it back to your starting point by yourself.

Proceed past the parking area onto forested, grassy doubletrack. The trail follows the Nichols Brook. You will soon cross a wide plank bridge just above the convergence of two streams. Begin a gradual climb of 1 mile, and come out of the woods near a large, stump-filled beaver pond. Look to your south to take in Pitchoff Mountain. After half a mile the route narrows to singletrack. Pass by another three small beaver ponds. Try to catch a glimpse of some of their lodges amid the stumps and fallen dead trees. Just before the last pond, look for the deep valley to your south. You are ascending along its side, and just a few feet to the left, the ground seems to fall away into this valley. You will soon begin a short descent to the last pond.

The last pond is 2.8 miles from the parking area and is a great spot to take in the tree-enshrined cliffs of Pitchoff Mountain. Proceed west on the trail. It may be wet in spots, but just take the higher route, which lies north of the trail. It is a well-defined herd path. A gentle descent through a birch, beech, and hemlock forest delivers you to the western trailhead. Continue straight (west) to NY 73. You are now 0.8 mile northwest of the Mount Van Hoevenberg Ski Center, which hosts another 25 miles of trail.

The Bark Eater Backroads

A menagerie of old country roads winds through farm and forest and provides a good half day of pleasurable riding. The hard-packed dirt Bartlett Road is 6 miles in one direction. Connect it with two other dirt roads, and it forms a 16-mile loop around the Bark Eater Inn. The steep descents and hearty climbs along Limekiln and Lacy Roads provide some challenging but not impossible riding. The rewards unfold as you pass through beautiful beech and hemlock forests and pass in and out of mountain farms and meadows. Gushing, babbling brooks crisscross your path under bridges and alongside roads. Forests, horse farms, and meadows combined with the mountain backdrop of the Hurricane Mountain Primitive Area to the east make for some spectacular scenic mountain bike riding.

General location: Near the village of Keene, about 14 miles south of Lake Placid in the High Peaks area of Adirondack Park, in northeastern New York.

Elevation change: There are some great descents, but the price is some steep climbs. Elevations range from 800 feet at New York 73 to 1,500 feet, the height of land on Bartlett Road. The greatest climb is along Limekiln Road heading south and up toward its intersection with Alstead Mill Road.

Season: The trails are available year-round, and if there is no snow cover, winter is a time of solitude on these roads. If the roads are firm, free of snow, and not spongy from spring thaws, winter to spring is a great time to explore these backroads.

Services: We stayed at the Bark Eater, a true country inn, located on Alstead Mill Road. The inn provides the mountain bike rider with a base camp to launch several bike excursions along the miles of trails just beyond the Bark Eater's perimeters. Originally a stagecoach stopover, the Bark Eater Inn has been in operation since the early nineteenth century. The farmhouse atmosphere still reflects these early times with wide-board floors, stone fireplaces, and antiques everywhere. It is located on a spacious, 350-acre farm in the heart of the Adirondack High Peaks. Joe Pete Wilson—a former Olympic and world competitor in Nordic skiing, biathlon, and bobsledding—welcomes mountain bikers year-round. His experienced staff is eager to help you enjoy your time there. Placid Planet Bicycles and High Peaks Cyclery rents and sells mountain bikes in Lake Placid.

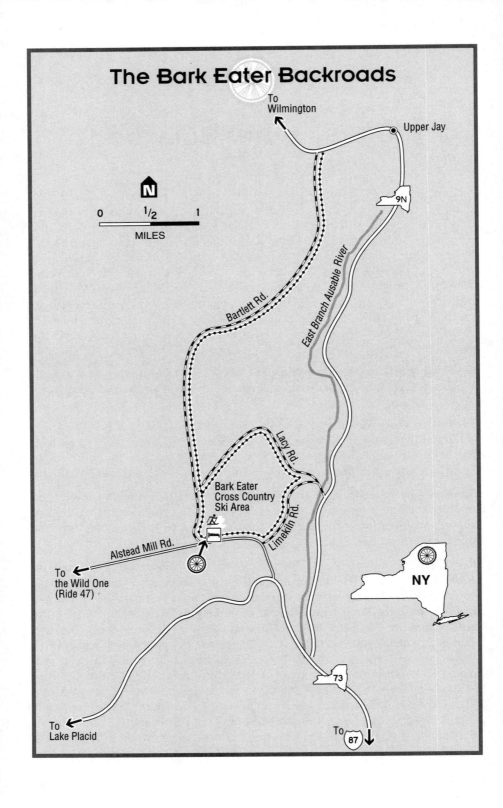

The Bark Eater Backroads

To Wilmington

Upper Jay

9N

East Branch Ausable River

Bartlett Rd.

Lacy Rd.

Bark Eater
Cross Country
Ski Area

Limekiln Rd.

Alstead Mill Rd.

To
the Wild One
(Ride 47)

To
Lake Placid

73

To
87

N

0   1/2   1
MILES

NY

Hazards: An 800-foot vertical descent awaits the rider after reaching the height of land at the pass.

Rescue index: These roads are not too remote—only about 1 to 2 miles from well-traveled NY 73. There is usually someone around the Bark Eater Inn who can provide a phone or some aid.

Land status: These are public roads.

Maps: The Adirondack High Peaks Region Area Map published by Plinth, Quoin & Cornice Associates provides excellent topographical detail of the route and surrounding terrain and can be found at most outdoor-type stores in New York for $5.00. It is based on the USGS 15-minute series, at a scale of 1:62,500 and a contour level of 20 feet, where 1 inch = 0.98 mile.

Finding the trail: Take the New York State Thruway (Interstate 87) north to exit 24 (Albany). Take I-87 north to exit 30. Pick up NY 9 north, and follow it for 2 miles to NY 73. Continue on NY 73 toward the Lake Placid area. After the village of Keene, turn right onto Alstead Mill Road. Look for signs for the Bark Eater Inn. You may park along Alstead Mill Road, or if you are staying at the Bark Eater Inn, just go out your door and start pedaling.

Sources of additional information:

The Bark Eater Inn
Alstead Mill Road
Keene, NY 12942
(518) 576–2221
www.barkeater.com

Placid Planet Bicycles
51 Saranac Avenue
Lake Placid, NY 12946
(518) 523–4128

High Peaks Cyclery
331 Main Street
Lake Placid, NY 12946
(518) 523–3764

Adirondack Park Agency
P.O. Box 99, Route 86
Ray Brook, NY 12977
(518) 891–4050

New York State Department of Environmental Conservation, Region 5
P.O. Box 296, Route 86
Ray Brook, NY 12977
(518) 897–1211

The scenic Bark Eater back roads.

Lake Placid/Essex County Convention and Visitors Bureau
216 Main Street
Lake Placid, NY 12946
(800) 447–5224
www.lakeplacid.com

Notes on the trail: Begin your ride on Alstead Mill Road, and turn right (north) onto Bartlett Road. After about half a mile, notice a dirt road to your right. This is Lacy Road, which you will turn down after returning from the one-way Bartlett Road. Turning left leads you to Clifford Falls. You can take Bartlett Road for about 6 miles and then turn around. On your way back, turn left (east) onto Lacy Road, which descends toward the East Branch of the Ausable River and NY 73. At a yield sign you may continue straight to the river or turn right and ascend Limekiln Road. Take Limekiln Road more than 1 mile to its T intersection with Alstead Mill Road. Turn right onto Alstead Mill Road to wherever your car is parked.

49

The Mystery of Pine Pond

The 12-mile, round-trip (6 miles one way), hard-packed, doubletrack route leading toward scenic Pine Pond, on the northern edge of the High Peaks Wilderness Area, is one of Lake Placid's most popular trails. Because of the restrictions on riding in designated wilderness areas, this trail travels through the state's "Wild Forest" zone and is permissible and ideal to ride.

Pine Pond, a tiny, isolated gem rimmed by stands of old-growth white pine on its wide, sandy shores, is beautiful in all seasons. The pond was formed when a large chunk of Ice Age ice fell off one of the glaciers. The ice surrounding this large piece melted faster than the chunk. The result is that sand filled in around the sides of this chunk of ice, and when it finally did melt, a large hole in the ground remained. Naturally over time this hole filled with water. Pine Pond is known as a kettle hole.

The Adirondack landscape has been extensively sculpted by the glaciers that dominated North America during the Ice Ages. The glaciers, which were sometimes 1,000 feet thick, completely covered the mountains.

Your trip into Pine Pond will be exciting, easy, and scenic. This well-worn trail is easy to follow and a must-do for all ability levels.

General location: Northeastern New York, Adirondack Park. The trailhead is located within minutes of the village of Lake Placid.

Elevation change: The grade of the trail going to the pond is a gradual descent, with the exception of the initial climb. A few rolling hills are thrown in for fun, and the trip back from the pond will nevertheless be generally uphill. The most technical part of the ride is at the beginning, an uphill with rocks to maneuver around followed by a rocky downhill. After this the trail is rolling and has several areas with mud holes that may be deceptive in depth. Don't forget to allow for adequate time and energy for the longer return uphill. Once darkness falls what was first an easy trail can quickly become an evening's nightmare.

Season: The blackflies can be fierce in late spring, but the trail can be ridden in most seasons except when there is snow on the ground.

Services: Most services can be found in Lake Placid, which is full of lodging, restaurants, and shops. Placid Planet Bicycles rents and sells mountain bikes.

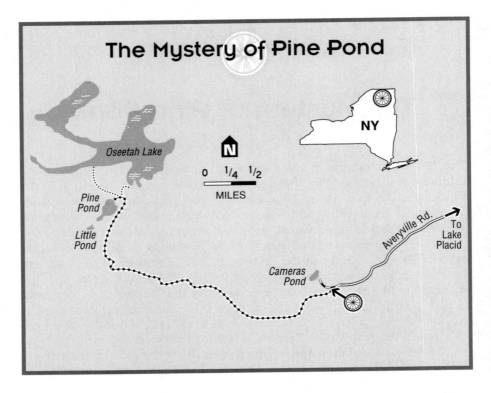

The Mystery of Pine Pond

Oseetah Lake

Pine Pond

Little Pond

NY

0   1/4 1/2
MILES

Cameras Pond

Averyville Rd.

To Lake Placid

Hazards: This is a popular trail among cyclists, hikers, horses, four-wheelers, hunters, and a variety of wildlife. Follow and respect the rules of the trail; treat these other users the way you want them to treat you, and use of special trails like these will continue.

Rescue index: The trail is fairly worn, straightforward, and hard to get lost on. You are never more than 6 miles from Lake Placid, and there are usually other trail users in the vicinity.

Land status: New York State Department of Environmental Conservation manages the Forest Preserve land.

Maps: The Adirondack High Peaks Region Area Map published by Plinth, Quoin & Cornice Associates provides excellent topographical detail of the route and surrounding terrain and can be found at most outdoor-type stores in New York for $5.00. It is based on the USGS 15-minute series, at a scale of 1:62,500 and a contour level of 20 feet, where 1 inch = 0.98 mile.

Finding the trail: Take the New York State Thruway (Interstate 87) north to exit 24 (Albany). Take I-87 north to exit 30. Pick up New York 9 north, and follow it for 2 miles to NY 73. Continue on NY 73 for 28 miles to the Lake Placid area. In Lake Placid take Old Military Road, also known as Old Mountain Road (near ski jumps), to Averyville Road (note the

Rocky stream in the Adirondack High Peaks region.

Northville–Placid Trail sign). Turn left (south) onto Averyville Road, and follow this until the pavement ends; continue past a barn and through a farm field. Upon entering the woods continue until you find parking at the side of the road.

Sources of additional information:

Placid Planet Bicycles
51 Saranac Avenue
Lake Placid, NY 12946
(518) 523–4128
www.placidplanetbicycles.com

Adirondack Park Agency
P.O. Box 99, Route 86
Ray Brook, NY 12977
(518) 891–4050

New York State Department of Environmental Conservation, Region 5
P.O. Box 296, Route 86
Ray Brook, NY 12977
(518) 897–1211

Lake Placid/Essex County Convention and Visitors Bureau
216 Main Street
Lake Placid, NY 12946
(800) 447–5224
www.lakeplacid.com

Notes on the trail: The trail is fairly straightforward and easy to follow. Stay on the most worn path, and don't stray onto any errant deer paths. The route is actually a continuation of Averyville Road and passes through potato fields and then enters the woods. Once in the woods you will begin to pick up the state's red snowmobile markers, which blaze the trail. Proceed through the hardwood forest for about 1 mile. The next mile, along a sometimes washed-out logging road, is a steep, rocky descent; the exposed rock can be slippery when wet or when covered with fallen leaves. The track then narrows to about 4 feet, and the forest changes to pine and hemlock. The final portion of the trail is mostly pine needle–covered trail with tree roots to maneuver over. Cold River enters from the left, and the trail follows its banks for a few hundred yards before intersecting a T junction. A left turn takes you to Pine Pond's north shore, and a right takes you to Oseetah Lake. Return to your car by the same route.

50

McKenzie Mountain Loop

This challenging 4-mile loop climbs a doubletrack (cross-country ski trail) that ascends to the saddle between McKenzie Mountain (elevation 3,861 feet) to the north and Haystack Mountain (2,878 feet) to the south and goes through a pristine forest. Mountain bikers are not allowed up near the pass because it lies within the wilderness designation, but a turnoff before the forbidden zone provides safe passage through friendly territory and loops back to the trailhead. Sections of the trail may be difficult to ride because of exposed rocks from the weathered trail bed, but the riding is exciting and the scenery rewarding. The forest has been left in its natural state and saved from the infamous logging of the nineteenth and early twentieth centuries. New York was the leading lumber-producing state in the nation by 1850. The nation's demand for wood escalated in the early part of the nineteenth century, and lumber barons established logging operations throughout the Adirondacks. They stripped the forests of the majestic white pines that were valued for their strength and straight grain. Rivers were used to transport the logs, and roads were cut throughout the woodlands. Fortunately, due to the donations of the Shore Owners Association of Lake Placid, the land was bought by the state before the former owners, the International Paper Company, could log it. The Shore Owners Association, which began in 1893, maintained trails in and around this small wilderness area. The association was formed to fight the massive fluctuations of the levels of water in Lake Placid. These fluctuations were caused from logging near the lake. Eventually the association won control.

During the winter this trail is part of the extensive Jackrabbit Cross Country Ski Trail System that extends from Keene Valley west to Lake Placid and Saranac Lake. The Jackrabbit Ski Trail was constructed in 1986 to improve the cross-country skiing in the Lake Placid–Saranac Lake area. It is named in memory of Herman "Jack Rabbit" Johannsen, who laid out many of the trails himself. He was a pioneer of Lake Placid skiing from 1916 to 1928 and died in 1987 at age 111.

The extension of this trail to the pass beside McKenzie Mountain has great potential as a grade-A mountain bike trail, but until that section of the trailway becomes accessible and sanctioned for mountain bikers, we must keep to the lower regions of the trails and stay out of the wilderness area. I have confidence that one day this beautiful recreational resource can be shared with our trail-conscious mountain biker community.

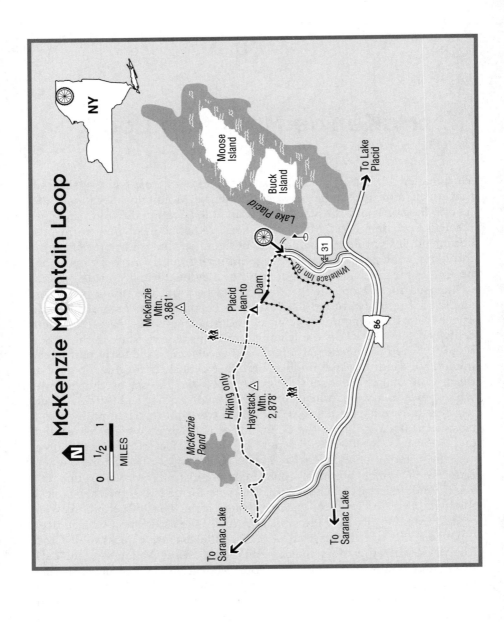

McKenzie Mountain Loop

NY

MILES
0   1/2   1

McKenzie Pond

McKenzie Mtn. 3,861'

Haystack Mtn. 2,878'

Hiking only

Placid lean-to

Dam

Lake Placid

Moose Island

Buck Island

Whiteface Inn Rd.

31

86

To Lake Placid

To Saranac Lake

To Saranac Lake

General location: Just west of the village of Lake Placid in the High Peaks area of Adirondack Park, in northeastern New York.

Elevation change: The first 0.3 mile rises sharply along an eroded road from approximately 1,900 to 2,400 feet. The trail then levels out and begins to descend back to the trailhead.

Season: The trails are usually dried out after spring thaw around the middle of May and are good to ride on until the first snows appear. This abandoned tote road gets very wet and soggy for a high-pass route.

Services: Placid Planet Bicycles is located on the corner of Whiteface Inn Road and Saranac Avenue and rents and sells mountain bikes and supplies.

Hazards: There is one awesome descent after reaching the height of land at the pass. Care should be taken if the trail is wet and/or covered with leaves.

Rescue index: The route passes through a wilderness that is not far from condominiums near Whiteface Landing on Whiteface Inn Road, and the well-traveled New York 86 is only a mile away.

Land status: New York State Department of Environmental Conservation manages the Forest Preserve land.

Maps: The Adirondack High Peaks Region Area Map published by Plinth, Quoin & Cornice Associates provides excellent topographical detail of the route and surrounding terrain and can be found at most outdoor-type stores in New York for $5.00. It is based on the USGS 15-minute series, at a scale of 1:62,500 and a contour level of 20 feet, where 1 inch = 0.98 mile.

Finding the trail: Take the New York State Thruway (Interstate 87) north to exit 24 (Albany). Take I-87 north to exit 30. Pick up NY 9 north, and follow it for 2 miles to NY 73. Continue on NY 73 for 28 miles to the Lake Placid area. Proceed west from Lake Placid on NY 86. Turn right (north) onto Whiteface Inn Road (Essex County Road 31) toward the Whiteface Inn Resort. After 1.2 miles there will be parking on your left. Across the road from the golf course entrance on the left are signs for the Jackrabbit Trail. Take the second trailhead about 200 feet farther down the road to access the beginning of this old logging road. There will be two large stones about 75 feet in on the trail. A New York State Department of Environmental Conservation sign specifies the routes' destinations. The McKenzie Pond Road is 5.5 miles and Saranac Lake is 7 miles.

Sources of additional information:

Placid Planet Bicycles
51 Saranac Avenue
Lake Placid, NY 12946
(518) 523–4128
www.placidplanetbicycles.com

Adirondack Park Agency
P.O. Box 99, Route 86
Ray Brook, NY 12977
(518) 891–4050

New York State Department of Environmental Conservation, Region 5
P.O. Box 296, Route 86
Ray Brook, NY 12977
(518) 897–1211

Lake Placid/Essex County Convention and Visitors Bureau
216 Main Street
Lake Placid, NY 12946
(800) 447–5224
www.lakeplacid.com

Notes on the trail: The route proceeds steeply along the old, eroded logging road and levels off after 0.3 mile. The trail is washed out with cobblestones but is rideable. The forest changes from old-growth beech and birch to a mixed second-growth forest with evergreens. You will soon reach a dam. Walk your bike across, because the drop-off is dangerous and painful, and continue 0.5 mile. A small path leads off to the left in a southwesterly direction. This path will loop back to the trailhead and avoid the illegitimate regions. Continuing onward along the doubletrack to the pass beside McKenzie Mountain is illegal.

51

Scarface

The following description was adapted from the Placid Planet Bike Shop's trail brochure:

Only 4 miles from Placid Planet in the metropolis of beautiful Ray Brook are the access trails to Scarface Mountain. At 3,088 feet Scarface Mountain stands out; its sheer rock face can be seen while driving on New York 86. The trails up the actual mountain itself are not suitable for riding, and you are requested to abstain from riding up Scarface. You are encouraged to stash your bike in the woods and hike up. An awesome 8-mile network of trails winds through a dense spruce and white pine–forested wilderness. The route traverses a combination of single- and doubletrack trails. The undulating terrain is pure heaven for mountain biking. There is a touch of the surreal as you ride over pine needle–covered singletrack through dense plantations of conifer woodland and things become eerily quiet.

Rumor has it that these trails were reconditioned for a European cross-country ski team to train for the 1980 Olympic Games in Lake Placid. Whatever the reason for their existence, they are a great ride—not too technical but fun for riders of most abilities. In late summer the wild blueberries are wonderful. Keep in mind that this area is very popular with hunters; dress appropriately in season. This tour was high on the Placid Planet Bicycle staff's favorite mountain bike ride list and is a must-do if you're visiting the area.

General location: Just west of Lake Placid in the village of Ray Brook, located in the High Peaks area of Adirondack Park, in northeastern New York.

Elevation change: The terrain is mostly rolling with one major ascent from the bridge crossing the pond into which Ray Brook flows. The ascent is from 1,600 to 1,700 feet in half a mile.

Season: The trails are available year-round, and if there is no snow cover, winter is an ideal time in these primitive woods. The blackflies can be fierce in late spring. Many trails throughout Adirondack Park are wet and unrideable until mid-May, but these trails are very dry. The peaty composition of the ground is very absorbent, and there are rarely any muddy spots.

Services: The village of Ray Brook, located farther west on NY 86, has a great barbecue takeout restaurant. An ice cream store and some wood

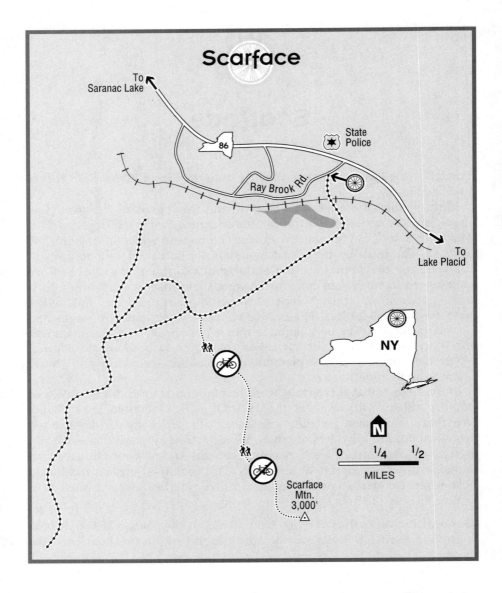

Scarface

To
Saranac Lake

86

State
Police

Ray Brook Rd.

To
Lake Placid

NY

N

0   1/4   1/2
MILES

Scarface
Mtn.
3,000'

craft stores and cottage lodging round out this rural town's occupancy in the wilderness.

Hazards: The trails are fun to ride, and the tight turns demand some extra attention so that you don't knock over one of the trees with your head. Call the New York State Department of Environmental Conservation for specific hunting season dates.

Rescue index: You are only a few miles from well-traveled NY 86. The ascent trail to Scarface Mountain is a favorite among hikers, and if you

How about a child seat for my birthday?

didn't whiz past them on the trail, I'm sure they would be willing to lend you a hand if such an occasion should arise.

Land status: New York State Department of Environmental Conservation manages the forest.

Maps: The Adirondack High Peaks Region Area Map and the Adirondack Canoe Map published by Plinth, Quoin & Cornice Associates provide excellent topographical detail of the route and surrounding terrain and can be found at most outdoor-type stores in New York for $5.00.

Finding the trail: Take the New York State Thruway (Interstate 87) north to exit 24 (Albany). Take I-87 north to exit 30. Pick up NY 9 north, and follow it for 2 miles to NY 73. Continue on NY 73 for 28 miles to the Lake Placid area. Head toward Saranac Lake on NY 86, and turn left (south) onto Ray Brook Road. It is across from the state police barracks just past the Mobil gas station. One hundred or so yards down Ray Brook Road is a parking area on the left. This is the trailhead.

Sources of additional information:

Placid Planet Bicycles
51 Saranac Avenue
Lake Placid, NY 12946
(518) 523–4128
www.placidplanetbicycles.com

Backcountry utopia along the Scarface Trails.

Adirondack Park Agency
P.O. Box 99, Route 86
Ray Brook, NY 12977
(518) 891–4050

New York State Department of Environmental Conservation, Region 5
P.O. Box 296, Route 86
Ray Brook, NY 12977
(518) 897–1211

Lake Placid/Essex County Convention and Visitors Bureau
216 Main Street
Lake Placid, NY 12946
(800) 447–5224
www.lakeplacid.com

Notes on the trail: The first 1.5 miles take you through a dense, spruce-filled forest over undulating terrain. This portion of the trail is new and was rerouted in 1981 after a federal correctional facility was built nearby. The route is marked with red disks and is a lot of fun to ride. You will soon cross an abandoned railroad right-of-way. These were the Fairytale Railroad tracks, which ran between Remsen and Lake Placid. Left will take you on what could be a great ride to Lake Placid, but it is so overgrown it is considered a real disaster by some. Going right on the tracks will take you near the Adirondack Correctional Facilities. The chances are better than average that you will be questioned by people with guns about why you are there, even though it seems obvious by your Lycra shorts, jersey, and helmet that you are just cruising on your mountain bike (like anyone with more than two brain cells would intentionally go to a prison wearing Lycra). Anyway, go straight and cross an interesting walking bridge that crosses over an attractive pond into which the Ray Brook flows. It is an impressive-looking bridge, and a wooden plaque proclaims its construction history. At the far end of the bridge, a staircase takes you back into the woods. You will soon traverse an open meadow filled with blueberry bushes. The route proceeds southwest over fairly level ground. You will enter a majestic white pine forest and intersect a wood road at 1.3 miles.

Continue straight at 1.5 miles onto an old tote road whose width will narrow somewhat. The trail to the summit of Scarface leads to the left (south) at 1.7 miles. Continue straight through the mixed deciduous and conifer forest. Bear left at the next fork, and descend for about half a mile. At the T intersection, turn left. You may take this for another 1.5 miles to Roger Brook, but then you must return along the same route. After returning from this short spur, pedal past the first trail and take a right (east) onto the second trail, a few hundred yards later. This trail will reconnect with the original trail you came in on. At the time of this writing there were no posted signs indicating private property. If there are, don't trespass. It is a privilege to ride on these lands. Just turn back and head down another trail.

The Peninsula Trails

This small network of interconnecting doubletrack and singletrack trails provides an excellent mountain bike warm-up if you are staying in the village of Lake Placid and plan on riding the many trails in the area described by this guide. The distance only adds up to about 3 miles. The trails are conveniently located at the northern end of the village of Lake Placid, so while some of your party may want to shop the town, you can head on out to the trail. I rode them after a big pasta dinner one evening just before sunset, and it was a great way to end the day. This small maze consists of four named trails.

The easy-cruising, wide, hard-packed dirt Access Road Trail is 0.7 mile long. The hard surface makes this a delight for families with small children and those new to the sport. The trail is also important for reaching the other more technical trails. There is an intermediate dirt road called the Ridge Trail. This 0.8-mile-long, hard-packed singletrack travels through a beech forest. The intermediate Boundary Trail is of the same character and provides another 0.6 mile. The Lake Shore Trail is the only advanced singletrack and is 0.4 mile long. Its condition is very rooty, and it meanders along the shore of Lake Placid. The views of Lake Placid (the lake) from the technical Lake Shore Trail singletrack are a sight to behold and worth the trail effort. Beautiful homes line the shores of the lake, and benches are located at key viewing locations. In the western horizon are also views of the 2,800-foot Mount Colburn and the smaller Mount Tamarac behind it to the right. The 3,861-foot McKenzie Mountain lies behind them. This network of trails is proof that good things can come in small packages.

General location: Northeastern New York on the north side of the village of Lake Placid.

Elevation change: The riding is fairly level with no major elevation changes or tough climbs.

Season: Mountain biking is allowed on these trails during all seasons, providing the trails are not too wet or covered by snow.

Services: All services can be found in Lake Placid. Bike rentals can be found at Placid Planet Bicycles and High Peaks Cyclery.

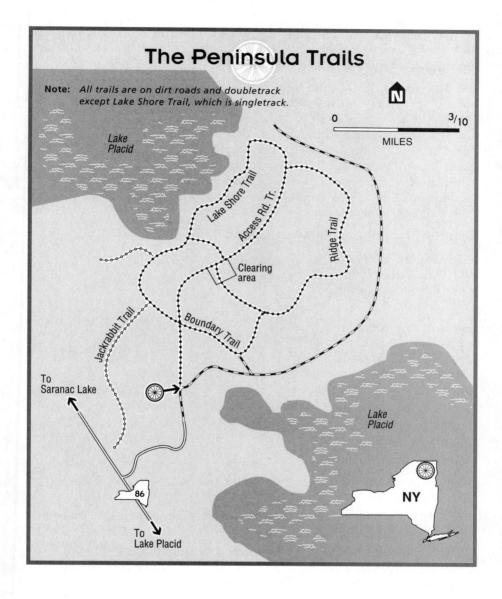

The Peninsula Trails

Note: All trails are on dirt roads and doubletrack except Lake Shore Trail, which is singletrack.

0   3/10
MILES

Lake Placid

Lake Shore Trail

Access Rd. Tr.

Ridge Trail

Clearing area

Jackrabbit Trail

Boundary Trail

To Saranac Lake

Lake Placid

86

To Lake Placid

NY

Hazards: The trail system is popular with hikers and joggers. Use caution on the fast, flat trails, and enjoy the serenity and beauty of the woods. This will minimize conflicts and provide mountain bikers with a good reputation.

Rescue index: The trails are all within 1 mile of Lake Placid.

Land status: New York State land.

Maps: The map accompanying this tour provides the best basic trail outline and is easy to follow. Trail signs along the route also give adequate indication of which way to go.

Finding the trail: Take the New York State Thruway (Interstate 87) north to exit 24 (Albany). Take I-87 north to exit 30. Pick up New York 9 north, and follow it for 2 miles to NY 73. Continue on NY 73 for 28 miles to the Lake Placid area. Pass through the village of Lake Placid on NY 86, and turn right (east) onto the paved road just after the Howard Johnson Restaurant. You will see a sign for Brewster Peninsula Trails. Turn in, and continue up the road for 0.3 mile. The road will swing to the right, and the parking will be on the left, just before a yellow metal gate with a stop sign. The trail begins beyond this gate.

Sources of additional information:

High Peaks Cyclery
331 Main Street
Lake Placid, NY 12946
(518) 523–3764

Placid Planet Bicycles
51 Saranac Avenue
Lake Placid, NY 12946
(518) 523–4128
www.placidplanetbicycles.com

Adirondack Park Agency
P.O. Box 99, Route 86
Ray Brook, NY 12977
(518) 891–4050

New York State Department of Environmental Conservation, Region 5
P.O. Box 296, Route 86
Ray Brook, NY 12977
(518) 897–1211

Lake Placid/Essex County Convention and Visitors Bureau
216 Main Street
Lake Placid, NY 12946
(800) 447–5224
www.lakeplacid.com

Notes on the trail: The Access Road Trail begins north of the gate. As you pass through a clearing with a picnic bench, notice the singletrack that leads east into the woods. This trail connects with the Ridge Trail. Continue straight through the clearing. Pass another trail to your left. This trail leads down to the Lake Shore Trail. Don't turn here yet. The end of the Access Road Trail turns into Lake Shore Trail, and you may return along this trail to your left. Continue northeasterly along the Access Road Trail.

It ends at a T intersection with the Lake Shore Trail and Ridge Trail. Turning left will take you along the blue-marked, advanced singletrack that twists and turns through a dark conifer forest over many exposed roots and rocks, and meanders along the shore of Lake Placid. The trail is 0.4 mile in length and leads back in a southwest direction. Near its end it leads into the Boundary Trail. You can take the red-marked Boundary Trail, crossing over the Access Road Trail into the Ridge Trail in 0.6 mile. Turn left onto the yellow-marked Ridge Trail. This trail winds through a beautiful hardwood forest mixed with hemlock and balsam and traverses rolling terrain. The higher ground the trail passes over is ideal for the hardwoods growing on it versus the conifers near the lake's shoreline. The trail ends at the Access Road Trail. Turn left (south) onto the Access Road Trail back to the parking area.

A Day at the Races

Mount Van Hoevenberg was the Olympic Cross Country Ski center during the thirteenth Winter Olympic Games in 1980. More than 30 miles of wide, well-graded trails are open to the public on this state-owned and -operated ski area. The ride-challenge index ranges from easy cruising to hard hill climbs. It is not a technical singletrack dream, although you can put together some good mileage on the wide, doubletrack paths. The beauty of Mount Van Hoevenberg is the multitude of trails to choose from and the terrain the routes traverse.

The area is named after Henry Van Hoevenberg, who in 1910 began constructing the system of trails and shelters for hikers in the High Peaks area. These trails and shelters are now maintained by the New York State Department of Environmental Conservation. Van Hoevenberg was also the original builder of the Adirondack Lodge during the late nineteenth century. A trail leading up to Mount Marcy is named after him, too.

The ski trails at Mount Van Hoevenberg were created in the early 1960s and first used for competition in 1969. Additional loops were put in for the biathlon events, and another expansion created more trails suitable for Olympic competition. The successive expansions of this large cross-country trail's complex have led to a crazy-quilt nature in the trail layout. Fortunately signs along the trail and detailed maps available at the Mount Van Hoevenberg ski center help you navigate the maze. For cross-country skiers these courses are considered equal to any in the world, and they offer a supreme test of a skier's ability. The labyrinthlike trail layout furnishes mountain bikers with endless excitement and a full day of riding.

General location: Northeastern New York, about 5 miles south of the village of Lake Placid on New York 73.

Elevation change: The trail system resides on a low mountain, compared with the high peaks that surround it. The multitude of trails traverses a whole range of minor elevation changes. It is a hilly area, and there are many trails. You could accumulate a bunch of vertical after a full day of riding.

Season: Mount Van Hoevenberg officially opens sometime in late June. It all depends on the conditions of the trail and their moisture content. I would call the Lake Placid Chamber of Commerce before heading out. You can ride around the trails before the area's opening, but the routes tend to be soft and soggy.

A Day at the Races

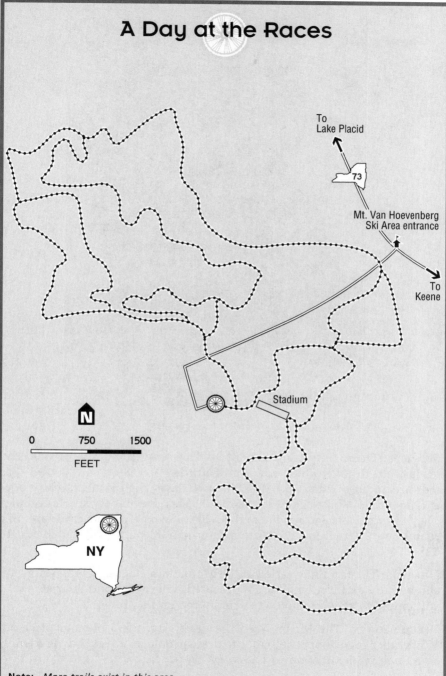

To
Lake Placid

73

Mt. Van Hoevenberg
Ski Area entrance

To
Keene

Stadium

N

0   750   1500
FEET

NY

Note: More trails exist in this area
than can be shown on this map.

Crossing a field at Mount Van Hoevenberg.

Services: Open daily from Sunday to Thursday, 10:00 A.M. to 5:00 P.M.; Friday, 10:00 A.M. to 8:00 P.M.; and Saturday, 9:00 A.M. to 8:00 P.M. Trail fees are $4.00 per day and $6.00 for two days. High Peaks Cyclery operates a mountain bike center in the Mount Van Hoevenberg sports complex. They offer rentals and repairs and advice on where the hot trails are. Bike rentals are $20 per day. For further information call the bike shop at (518) 523–3764.

Hazards: The terrain is varied at the Mount Van Hoevenberg Ski Area and can be hilly and challenging. Be prepared with water and nourishment if you intend to spend many hours riding the myriad trails.

Rescue index: The Mount Van Hoevenberg area is a popular place and offers other recreational activities to draw people in. Everybody is friendly, and a helping hand is never far away.

Land status: New York State Department of Environmental Conservation manages the forest as a multiple-use area.

Maps: Maps of the mountain bike trail system can be picked up after paying the day-use fee.

Finding the trail: Take the New York State Thruway (Interstate 87) north to exit 24 (Albany). Take I-87 north to exit 30. Pick up NY 9 north, and follow it for 2 miles to NY 73. Continue on NY 73 for 23 miles to the Lake Placid area. There will be a sign for the Mount Van Hoevenberg Ski Area on NY 73. Turn left (west) into the complex. You'll see several parking areas as you ride along the access road. Proceed straight to the stadium and park there.

Sources of additional information:

High Peaks Cyclery
331 Main Street
Lake Placid, NY 12946
(518) 523–3764

Placid Planet Bicycles
51 Saranac Avenue
Lake Placid, NY 12946
(518) 523–4128
www.placidplanetbicycles.com

Adirondack Park Agency
P.O. Box 99, Route 86
Ray Brook, NY 12977
(518) 891–4050

New York State Department of Environmental Conservation, Region 5
P.O. Box 296, Route 86
Ray Brook, NY 12977
(518) 897–1211

Lake Placid/Essex County Convention and Visitors Bureau
216 Main Street
Lake Placid, NY 12946
(800) 447–5224
www.lakeplacid.com

Notes on the trail: A large array of trails awaits the energetic mountain biker at Mount Van Hoevenberg. A tremendous number of riding configurations can be created on the maze of trails and will fill up an entire day of bike riding and exploration. Check in at the office, grab a map, pick a trail, and just begin riding. The routes are well marked, and a large map of the trail system at the stadium will help you determine and plan which trail to take.

54

Whiteface—A Place in the Sun

Mountain biking has come to Whiteface Mountain's alpine ski area. The year 1996 marked the first time mountain bikes could be hauled up by chairlift and riders could disembark and descend onto a variety of intermediate and advanced utility road bike trails. Two chairlifts are used to open up 2,100 feet of vertical descent. Wide, hard-packed, dirt maintenance roads, ranging from 1 to 3 miles in length, crisscross the 4,867-foot mountain and make for some very fast riding. Make sure your brakes are in good condition.

Whiteface Mountain stands sentinel above Lake Placid. Its massif is isolated from the other mountains that belong to the High Peaks and lie farther south. Its face is carved by challenging alpine ski trails and ancient landslides that have left vertical, treeless strips of exposed bedrock. Excessive moisture and rains peel off the thin layer of soil, plants, and trees from the steep, smooth bedrock. This phenomenon occurs on many Adirondack mountains.

It is a busy mountain. The summit is used by the Atmospheric Sciences Research Center. An auto-toll road ascends to the summit where a restaurant, tunnel, and elevator have become popular tourist attractions. The mountain also hosted the 1980 Olympic alpine events.

During its turbulent past, settlers cleared the lower slopes for agricultural purposes. The mountain's upper hillsides were logged for its abundance of hardwoods. Logging was rampant throughout the Adirondacks, and the forests were decimated. Whiteface Mountain has gone through its reforestation and recovered with a diversity of tree species not found on any other mountain in the Adirondacks. More than nineteen types of trees have repopulated the areas the old-growth virgin woodland once occupied. In summary Whiteface inspires awe in all who visit it. Whether you hike it, climb it, or ski or bike down it, this mountain will guarantee you full-blown fun.

General location: Northeastern New York, about 10 miles northeast of the village of Lake Placid on New York 86.

Elevation change: The second Little Whiteface chairlift leaves you at a point where you can descend 2,100 feet. That's vertical.

Season: Whiteface Mountain Ski Center officially opens sometime in late June. Call the Lake Placid Chamber of Commerce before heading out.

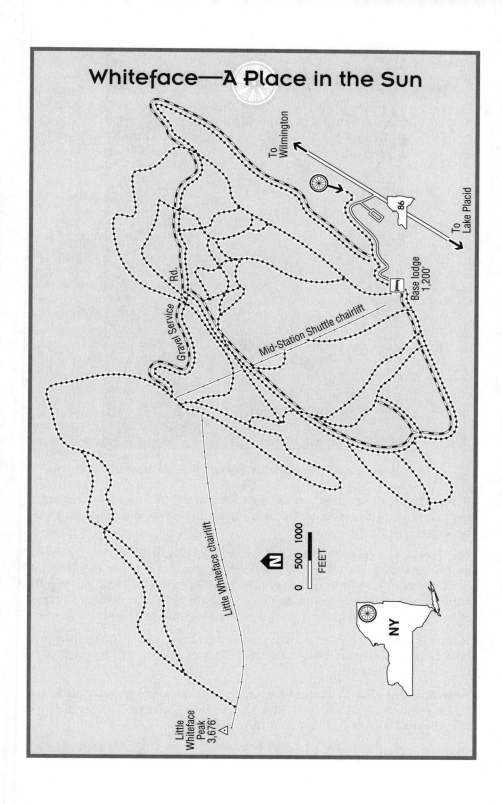

Whiteface—A Place in the Sun

To Wilmington

To Lake Placid

86

Base lodge
1,200'

Gravel Service Rd.

Mid-Station Shuttle chairlift

Little Whiteface chairlift

Little Whiteface Peak
3,676'

N

0 500 1000
FEET

NY

West branch of the Ausable River near Whiteface Mountain.

Before the area's opening you can ride around the trails that wind through the valley along the river at the base of the mountain, but the routes may be soft and soggy.

Services: Open from June 15 to October 14, 9:00 A.M. to 4:00 P.M. Fees for trail access only are $5.00 per day for adults and $3.00 per day for children. Chairlift and trail access fees are $15.00 per day or $8.00 per trip for adults and $10.00 per day or $6.00 per trip for children. Bike and helmet rentals are available in Base Lodge, as are food and beverages.

Hazards: This is an intermediate-to-advanced mountain. Make sure your bike is tight and your brakes are in good working order. You will need them on your descent.

Rescue index: The Whiteface Mountain Ski Center is a popular place and offers other recreational activities that draw people to it. Everybody is friendly, and a helping hand is never far away.

Land status: The area is managed by the Olympic Regional Development Authority.

Maps: Maps of the mountain bike trail system can be picked up after paying the day-use fee.

Finding the trail: Take the New York State Thruway (Interstate 87) north to exit 24 (Albany). Take I-87 north to exit 30. Pick up NY 9 north, and follow it for 2 miles to NY 73. Continue on NY 73 for 28 miles to the Lake Placid area. From Lake Placid it's approximately another 10 miles. Follow the signs for Whiteface Mountain Ski Center.

Sources of additional information:

Whiteface Mountain Ski Center
P.O. Box 1980
Route 86
Wilmington, NY 12997
(518) 946–2223

Adirondack Park Agency
P.O. Box 99, Route 86
Ray Brook, NY 12977
(518) 891–4050

New York State Department of Environmental Conservation, Region 5
P.O. Box 296, Route 86
Ray Brook, NY 12977
(518) 897–1211

Lake Placid/Essex County Convention and Visitors Bureau
216 Main Street
Lake Placid, NY 12946
(800) 447–5224
www.lakeplacid.com

Notes on the trail: Whiteface offers some great trails along the ski mountain's maintenance roads. To get the most out of this area, begin by taking the Mid-Station Shuttle chairlift. An array of intermediate bike trails can be accessed from this point. If you're brave and want something more challenging, take the Little Whiteface chairlift, and descend the advanced terrain for a full 2,100 feet. A large network of trails awaits the energetic mountain biker. Check in at the office, grab a map, pick a trail, and begin your riding.

55

The Flume Fall

A combination of old roads and cross-country ski trails provides up to 5 miles of well-maintained doubletrack and singletrack mountain bike riding. Portions of the trails have been used for competition mountain bike races. This maze of trails can be found just past 1 mile north of the entrance to the Whiteface Mountain Ski Area. The trails are adjacent to Whiteface Mountain and parallel the clear, bouldered West Branch of the Ausable River. The trailhead begins just beyond a bridge that spans a gorge known as the Flume Fall.

For thousands of years the Ausable River has tumbled and carved a wide path through the solid rock, and the area makes an impressive spot to sit, think, relax, and have a bite to eat. This mountain stream flows through a zone of geologic phenomenon known as the Wilmington Notch. More than 500 million years ago, the bedrock buckled and faulted, causing a series of northeast-trending fracture zones. This notch, which lies within one of those zones, extends from Lake Placid to Wilmington. This fracture zone had become the preferred drainage route for rivers and glaciers and causes rapids, waterfalls, and small pools to occur as the Ausable River flows through it. In other parts of the Adirondacks, these fracture zones have become deep, lake-filled valleys. The grandeur of the Adirondacks deserves special attention. They are filled with geologic and ecological wonders that have inspired study and awe.

General location: The trailhead lies just north of Lake Placid in the High Peaks area of Adirondack Park in northeastern New York, and about 1 mile past the entrance to Whiteface Mountain Ski Area.

Elevation change: The tour traverses gently rolling terrain. There are some minor climbs, but nothing too challenging. The trails near the Ausable River are the most level and can be found by bearing left after the parking area. They are part of the Riverview Loop.

Season: During the winter these trails are used as cross-country ski trails, but as the spring season opens up and the trails dry out, the riding can begin and continue until the first snowfalls. Remember, the blackflies can be fierce in late spring.

Services: The area offers convenient camping near the beautiful West Branch of the Ausable River. Two miles south is a public campground on

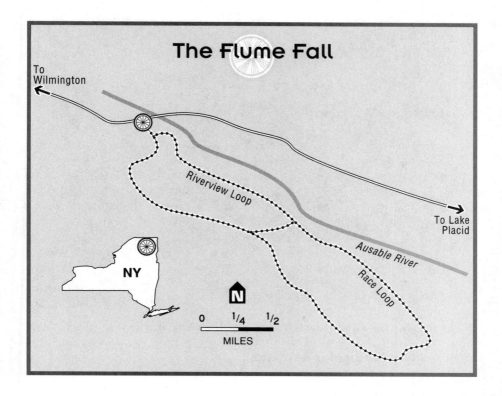

The Flume Fall

To Wilmington

Riverview Loop

To Lake Placid

Ausable River

Race Loop

NY

N

0   1/4   1/2

MILES

the banks of the Ausable, which makes a great spot to park your car and pitch a tent.

Hazards: Some sections of the trail are prone to flooding after periods of wet weather. They may be muddy and crossed by small streams. When I rode during one Memorial Day weekend, a 100-foot section of trail had been flooded. So be prepared for nature's surprises.

Rescue index: You are within earshot of New York 86, and help is never far away.

Land status: The trails are within the Saranac Lakes Wild Forest on New York State land.

Maps: There are currently no maps available for these trails.

Finding the trail: Take the New York State Thruway (Interstate 87) north to exit 24 (Albany). Take I-87 north to exit 30. Pick up NY 9 north, and follow it for 2 miles to NY 73. Continue on NY 73 for 28 miles to the Lake Placid area. Take NY 86 past the Whiteface Ski Area, and after about 1 mile you will see the Hungry Trout Motor Lodge and Restaurant. Proceed over the bridge that spans the West Branch of the Ausable River, and pull into the parking area on the left.

Expert rider Dave Moin negotiates a beaver dam along the Flume Fall Trail.

Sources of additional information:

High Peaks Cyclery
331 Main Street
Lake Placid, NY 12946
(518) 523–3764

Adirondack Park Agency
P.O. Box 99, Route 86
Ray Brook, NY 12977
(518) 891–4050

New York State Department of Environmental Conservation, Region 5
P.O. Box 296, Route 86
Ray Brook, NY 12977
(518) 897–1211

Lake Placid/Essex County Convention and Visitors Bureau
216 Main Street
Lake Placid, NY 12946
(800) 447–5224
www.lakeplacid.com

Notes on the trail: Route-finding is fairly straightforward. The trail network consists of two basic loops. Two hard-packed dirt roads lead from the parking area. The first loop, known as the Riverview Loop, is the beginner-level loop. The second, more advanced Race Loop follows the Riverside Loop.

The Riverview Loop should be ridden in a clockwise direction. Begin at the parking area and bear left (west) onto the leftmost hard-packed dirt road that parallels the river. You will soon pass a beaver pond on your right. The trail leads in a southwest direction. After about half a mile, turn right onto a singletrack leading north. You will begin a 0.2-mile gradual ascent, passing over a few stream crossings, and then you'll connect with a wider, hard-packed woods road. To complete this 1.3-mile loop and return to the parking area, turn right (northeast) onto the smooth, needle-covered dirt road. Some trails lead to your left. Continue straight, and descend to the parking area.

The second loop, known as the Race Loop, is mostly singletrack and can be accessed by continuing straight on the first half-mile of the Riverside Loop. Go past two large boulders, and climb gently in a westerly direction. Some sections may be rocky. You approach a small parking area. Turn right (north) onto a dirt road at the parking lot, and go past the maintenance building. Climb steeply onto a singletrack for about half a mile, and connect to an upper trail. Turn right (east), and descend on a somewhat rocky trail, crossing several streams. You will join the Riverview Loop in approximately 1 mile.

56

The Bloomingdale Bog Trail

This tour along an abandoned railroad bed is a great ride for novice mountain bikers and provides access into a remote, scenic wilderness. The 20-mile, out-and-back (10 miles one way) route is wide, flat, and smooth. The doubletrack trail passes over level, grassy sand flats and through an interesting bog and wetland environment. Two meandering brooks, the Two-bridge and Negro, provide the open water areas filled with wildlife, trees, and plants in the relatively dry area. The straight route was used in 1887 by the Chateaugay Division of the Delaware and Hudson Railroad to connect Plattsburgh to Saranac Lake. The sandy flats and level terrain were ideal for a rail bed. The trail is straight. You can see where the path leads on the horizon, which gives you a feeling of space and distance. Contrary to many of the winding trail systems in the heavily wooded Adirondack forests, this trail has a slightly western flavor. The railroad grade makes an easy cruising bike path walk and introduces you to an abundance of fauna and flora. I spotted otters and osprey along one section of the route. In winter the route is an excellent ski trail. Several roads cross the railroad and provide more territory in this unusual corridor to explore.

As you pedal along the trail, look for the clumps and mounds rising out of the bogs; these are known as leatherleaf. Several other trees and plants distinctive to bogs can be seen along the way. Rhododendron, cranberries, black spruce, and tamarack grow in the wetter areas, whereas the pines and balsams grow on the dryer borders. Early settlers drained portions of these bogs to grow vegetables.

This tour is long, flat, and usually smooth. Riders of all levels will enjoy experiencing the solitude of the forests and fast-cruising doubletrack.

General location: North of the village of Saranac Lake, Franklin County, in the Adirondack Park of northeastern New York.

Elevation change: The trail travels along an old, abandoned railroad bed and is relatively flat with little elevation gain.

Season: The route travels through wetlands and is best ridden during early summer after the blackflies have found better things to do with themselves. You can ride well into the winter providing there is no snow on the ground.

Services: Most services can be found in the village of Saranac Lake, approximately 7 miles from the trailhead on New York 86.

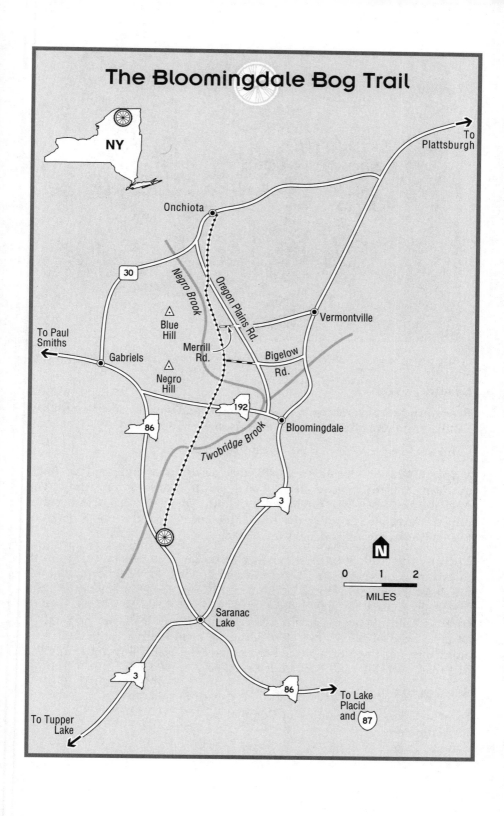

The Bloomingdale Bog Trail

NY

To Plattsburgh

Onchiota

30

Negro Brook

Oregon Plains Rd.

Vermontville

Blue Hill

Merrill Rd.

Bigelow Rd.

To Paul Smiths

Gabriels

Negro Hill

192

86

Bloomingdale

Twobridge Brook

3

N

0   1   2
MILES

Saranac Lake

3

86

To Tupper Lake

To Lake Placid and 87

Wandering brooks meander through the evergreen-lined Bloomingdale Bog.

Hazards: Bugs.

Rescue index: Several roads cross the route, and you are never more than 5 miles from one of these roads. Help is never too far away.

Land status: New York State Forest Preserve.

Maps: USGS 7.5-minute series, Saranac Lake quadrangle and St. Regis quadrangle provide good detail for these unimproved dirt roads. The Adirondack Canoe Map published by Plinth, Quoin & Cornice Associates provides excellent detail of the route and can be found at most outdoor-type stores in the Adirondacks for $5.00.

Finding the trail: Take the New York State Thruway (Interstate 87) north to exit 24 (Albany). Take I-87 north to exit 30. Pick up NY 9 north, and follow it for 2 miles to NY 73. Continue on NY 73 for 28 miles to the Lake Placid area. Pass through Lake Placid, and continue on NY 86 toward Saranac Lake. Look for a dirt road 1.3 miles north of the hospital in Saranac Lake on NY 86. NY 86 makes a big bend to the west, and there is a dirt road heading north at the beginning of the bend. Turn right onto the dirt road, bear left, and park your vehicle at the gate.

Sources of additional information:

Saranac Lake Area Chamber of Commerce
30 Main Street
Saranac Lake, NY 12983
(800) 347–1992, (518) 891–1990

Placid Planet Bicycles
51 Saranac Avenue
Lake Placid, NY 12946
(518) 523–4128
www.placidplanetbicycles.com

Notes on the trail: In this easy ride on the level railroad bed, the bog and wetlands are interesting to peruse. These wetlands arise from Twobridge and Negro Brooks. At 3.7 miles you'll intersect with NY 192. There is a short stretch of exposed roots, but generally it's smooth riding. At 4.2 miles intersect with the gravel Bigelow Road. After Bigelow Road you will see Negro Hill at 1,800 feet to the west. You will encounter some deep sandy spots north to Merrill Road. At 6.1 miles intersect Merrill Road (dirt). Looking west notice Blue Hill at 2,300 feet. At 7.8 miles intersect Oregon Plains Road (paved). At 9.8 miles arrive at County Road 30 (near Buck Pond State Campground).

Note: Several shorter loops are possible by parking at other access roads and returning on Oregon Plains Road.

57

The Deer Pond Odyssey

An 8-mile loop through pristine wilderness leads the rider past three attractive ponds. The first part of the loop is composed of an old semi-paved road. The path changes into an up-and-down singletrack as it passes Deer Pond and the little-frequented Mosquito Pond. You ascend a number of ridges on the way, but the overall relief change is minimal. An optional 1-mile spur trail leads to Lead Pond. The riding is moderately challenging and not too technical. The undulating terrain provides a pleasant roller-coaster ride for mountain bikers. The trails are well marked, and Deer Pond makes an idyllic spot for a picnic. This tour comes highly recommended from the folks at Placid Planet Bicycles.

General location: Sixteen miles west of the village of Saranac Lake, in Franklin County in Adirondack Park, northeastern New York.

Elevation change: The trail skirts around three hills with elevations of 1,600, 1,700, and 1,800 feet. There is no climbing of these hills on this tour, and the riding is moderately easy over undulating terrain.

Season: The blackflies can be fierce in late spring. The trails are available from late spring, when they dry out, through September 14. Hunting season begins in mid-September, and although you may don an orange hunting vest, it is still risky to be moving through the forest at the speed of a young buck.

Services: The village of Saranac Lake is about 16 miles east of the trailhead on New York 3.

Hazards: Bugs can be fearsome foes in late spring as the area thaws and dries out. Bring plenty of bug repellent in May and June.

Rescue index: The tour is fairly close to well-traveled NY 3, and help is not far away.

Land status: The route follows roads and trails in the Saranac Lakes wild forest. The wild forest classification on this state public land of Adirondack Park is available for mountain biking. Mountain biking is presently prohibited in designated wilderness areas of Adirondack Park and where signage is posted.

Maps: USGS 15-minute series, Saint Regis quadrangle provides good detail for this route. The Adirondack Canoe Map published by Plinth,

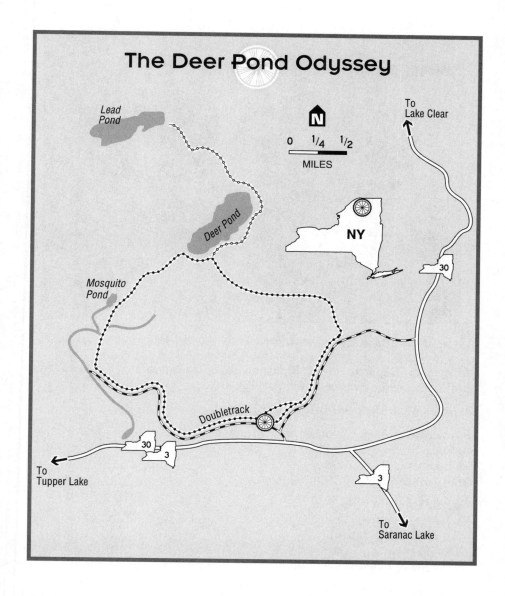

The Deer Pond Odyssey

Lead Pond

N

0   1/4   1/2
MILES

To Lake Clear

NY

30

Deer Pond

Mosquito Pond

Doubletrack

30
3

To Tupper Lake

3

To Saranac Lake

Quoin & Cornice Associates provides excellent topographical detail of the route and surrounding terrain and can be found at most outdoor-type stores in New York for $5.00.

Finding the trail: Take the New York State Thruway (Interstate 87) north to exit 24 (Albany). Take I-87 north to exit 30. Pick up NY 9 north, and follow it for 2 miles to NY 73. Continue on NY 73 for 28 miles to the Lake Placid area. Continue through Lake Placid west on NY 86. At Saranac Lake take NY 3 west for about 16 miles. At 0.6 mile west of the junction of NY 3 and NY 30, turn right (north) onto Old Wawbeek Road. A New

One of the 3,700 lakes and ponds found in the Adirondack Preserve.

York State Department of Environmental Conservation trailhead sign marks the road entrance to the parking area.

Sources of additional information:

Saranac Lake Area Chamber of Commerce
30 Main Street
Saranac Lake, NY 12983
(800) 347–1992, (518) 891–1990

Placid Planet Bicycles
51 Saranac Avenue
Lake Placid, NY 12946
(518) 523–4128
www.placidplanetbicycles.com

Notes on the trail: Continue from the parking area west on Old Wawbeek Road for 2.3 miles, paralleling NY 30 for about 1 mile. The road is full of potholes, and sections are heaved up from freezing and thawing.

After 2.3 miles turn right (north) onto a technical singletrack. The trail passes through a thick plantation of European spruce, and you begin to descend to a small beaver pond. The vegetation around the beaver pond is in stark contrast to the barren understory of the heavily shaded conifer plantation. Traverse another ridge before the trail dips again to skirt the east shore of Mosquito Pond. Begin a small ascent out of Mosquito Pond to a ridge crowned with mature beech and sugar maples. The route then drops from this hill to the shores of Deer Pond. The trail leads you along the southern shore of Deer Pond and intersects with another trail at 4.4 miles. The trail to your left leads north and passes along the eastern shore of Deer Pond and some nice picnic spots. Continuing farther on this spur trail will lead you to the western shore of Lead Pond.

To continue on the loop, bear right at this intersection, and head east. After about half a mile, you must cross wetland. A stringer bridge several hundred feet long crosses the area and then connects to a truck trail. Turn right (south), following the truck trail for another 1.5 miles back to the trail head.

58

Moss Lake

This moderate 5-mile loop includes 3 miles of wide, flat, doubletrack trails and about 2 miles of challenging snowmobile trails. The area is popular among hikers and passes by two attractive ponds. The trail begins at the Moss Lake trailhead on Big Moose Road. A 3-mile loop around the attractive lake with spurs down to the lakeshore will warm you up, and then another out-and-back (1 mile, one way) snowmobile trail leads to Bubb and Sis Lakes.

Moss Lake was the site for the Moss Lake Camp for Girls between 1923 and 1972. More than 3,000 girls attended this tiny haven. In 1929 the 600-acre property consisted of three separate camps spread along the lake's northern and eastern shores. Each of these camps had its own sleeping bungalow, dining room and recreation hall, archery range, dance studio, and craftshop. Moss Lake provided a perfect waterfront for swimming, canoeing, and sailing. The property was sold to the Nature Conservancy in 1973. Later that year the tract was sold to New York and became a part of the Adirondack Park and Forest Preserve. The buildings are long gone, and the lakeshore is now a public campground. The hard-packed surface of the 3-mile trail around the lake, built in 1924, is the camp's former bridle path and makes an ideal track for beginning mountain bikers. The tour doesn't require any special technical skills, allowing beginners an opportunity to get into some secluded woods and test their emerging skills without being too technically challenged. More experienced riders will appreciate the surrounding old-growth woodland, interesting spur trails, and lake scenery.

General location: Northeast of the village of Eagle Bay near Big Moose Lake, in Herkimer County in the west-central region of Adirondack Park, northeastern New York.

Elevation change: The loop around Moss Lake, elevation 1,758 feet, traverses gently rolling terrain. The snowmobile trail climbs moderately to Bubb Lake, elevation 1,815 feet, and Sis Lake, elevation 1,821 feet.

Season: You can ride after the wet season ends in April or May. It all depends on the amount of snow and rain in prior months. You can then ride until mid-September, when hunting season commences. You may don an orange hunting vest, but it is still risky to move through the forest at the speed of a young buck. The fall is a beautiful time to ride through the mixed hardwood and conifer forests, though.

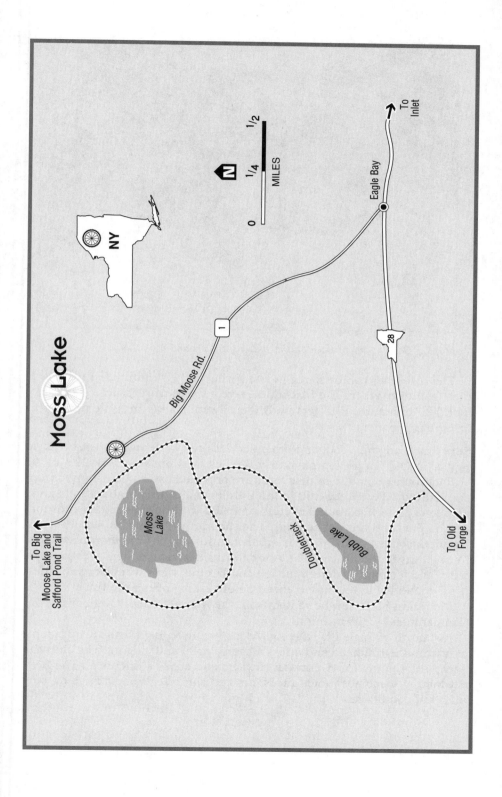

Moss Lake

NY

MILES
0 1/4 1/2

To Inlet

Eagle Bay

28

To Old Forge

Big Moose Rd.

1

To Big
Moose Lake and
Safford Pond Trail

Moss Lake

Doubletrack

Bubb Lake

My dog, Shogun, keeps pace on the snowy trails around Moss Lake.

The blackflies can be fierce in late spring and last until late June. Deer-flies take over where the blackflies leave off and can last into July. They look like miniature F-15 jets with their swept-back wings. Remember to bring bug repellent.

Services: Lodging, food, and other services can be found in nearby Eagle Bay or in Old Forge, approximately 5 miles west on New York 28.

Backcountry mountain bike tours are provided by Ted Christodaro from the bike store Pedals & Petals in Inlet. Daily and overnight tours are a great way to explore this abundant trail area. Ted is a good source for information on the condition of the trails. The shop provides repairs, supplies, and mountain bike sales. Call Pedals & Petals for any information on clinics, tours, festivals, and races. The Adirondacks has independent weather systems, and it's hard to determine the condition of trails from faraway cities. It's a good idea to telephone ahead before taking off on the trails.

Mountain bikes can be rented from the Mountainman Outdoor Supply Company on NY 28 in Inlet.

Just north of Eagle Bay, the Big Moose Inn along Big Moose Road is minutes from the trailhead and offers a hearty meal and lodging. The chef has been with the inn for twenty-seven years and cooks a fine meal. The Bennet family welcomes mountain bikers and can offer some advice on current trail conditions.

Hazards: This trail is popular with hikers, and care should be taken when descending along sections of the route to keep control of your bike.

Rescue index: The trail's popularity among hikers and its proximity to the well-traveled Big Moose Road makes this tour close to civilization. Help is never far away.

Land status: Old Forge and the central region of Adirondack Park offer a variety of terrain with exceptional natural beauty. The route follows roads and trails with the wild forests classification in Adirondack Park. They reside on state public land and are available for mountain biking. Mountain biking is presently prohibited in designated wilderness areas of Adirondack Park and where signage is posted.

The town of Web has expanded the use of its well-maintained snow-mobile trails and opened the well-marked routes for mountain bikers. The potential use of the diverse Old Forge/Web trail system is limitless and is an exciting opportunity for mountain bikers to explore.

Maps: USGS 7.5-minute series, Eagle Bay quadrangle provides good detail for this route. The Adirondack West-Central Wilderness Area Map published by Plinth, Quoin & Cornice Associates provides excellent topographical detail of the route and surrounding terrain and can be found at most outdoor-type stores in New York for $5.00. It is based on the USGS 15-minute series, at a scale of 1:62,500 and a contour level of 20 feet, where 1 inch = 0.98 mile.

Finding the trail: Take the New York State Thruway (Interstate 87) north to exit 24 (Albany). Take I-87 north to exit 25, Route 8/Chestertown and Hague. At the end of the exit ramp, turn left (west) onto NY 8 toward Loon Lake. After passing through Wevertown turn right (west) at the stop sign onto NY 28. This scenic highway takes you through the towns of North Creek, Indian Lake, and Blue Mountain Lake. White-water rafting on the Hudson River is very popular, and there are many outfitters in the Indian Lake area. Continue on NY 28 west toward Inlet and Old Forge.

Northern access is from the west side of Big Moose Road, 2.2 miles north of Eagle Bay on the left. There is a New York State Department of Environmental Conservation sign and a large parking area.

Sources of additional information:

Pedals & Petals
Route 28, P.O. Box 390
Inlet, NY 13360
(315) 357–3281

Old Forge Tourist Information Center
P.O. Box 68
Old Forge, NY 13420
(315) 369–6983

New York State Department of Environmental Conservation, Region 6
317 Washington Street
Watertown, NY 13601
(315) 785–2239

The Big Moose Inn
Big Moose Road
Eagle Bay, NY 13331
(315) 357–2042

Mountainman Outdoor Supply Company
Route 28, P.O. Box 659
Inlet, NY 13360
(315) 357–6672

Notes on the trail: From the parking area continue straight to the loop, and turn left onto it. You will pass through a hardwood forest that was logged years ago, resulting in the small trees you currently see. The trail is fairly level, and as you continue to circle around the lake, the forest becomes more mature and richer with older deciduous trees and some conifer hemlocks. You soon encounter the intersection with the trail to Sis and Bubb Lakes. They are approximately 1 mile away. Continue on this loop to complete it, and then come back around and pedal the trail to Bubb Lake.

Continuing the loop you will soon cross a bridge that spans the outlet in the southwest section of Moss Lake, about halfway around. This outlet eventually drains into the north branch of the Moose River. The stream leading away from Moss Lake is a typical Adirondack high-country stream that winds its way through an extensive marsh area. Follow the clear, open trail as it curves around the pond. Just before reaching the parking area, notice the open area on the right. This is where the camp was located.

59

Safford Pond Trail

The trip follows a snowmobile trail for a total distance of 10 miles and puts you in contact with two beautiful, wild, and uninhabited ponds. Located in the Fulton Chain Wild Forest, the dense conifer trees make the primeval woods dark and mysterious. This out-and-back route is 5 miles in one direction and begins at the Safford Pond trailhead on Big Moose Road. The trail traverses fairly level terrain along a wide singletrack. West Pond, a small pocket of fresh water with an attractive waterfall at the drainage point, is reached in just about 1 mile. Look for the old beaver dam and swamp. Safford Pond is a little farther along at 4 miles. The pond has a fine pebble beach and good swimming. The route ends at Lake Rondaxe 5 miles later.

General location: Northeast of the village of Eagle Bay near Big Moose Lake, in Herkimer County in the west-central region of Adirondack Park, northeastern New York.

Elevation change: The beginning of the trail climbs slightly to about 1,900 feet. After the spur trail to West Pond, the trail descends moderately to 1,800 feet for about 2.5 miles until you reach Safford Pond. It is all level riding after Safford Pond to the trail's end at Lake Rondaxe.

Season: This is a low drainage area and an inviting home for insects. Blackflies thrive under these conditions, and their season to swarm is usually in late spring (May). Try to avoid them if possible. The little buggers can be a fierce foe to fight in the woods. The trails are available from late spring, when they dry out, through September 14. Hunting season begins in mid-September, and although you may don an orange hunting vest, it is still risky to be moving through the forest at the speed of a young buck.

Services: Lodging, food, and other services can be found in nearby Eagle Bay and Old Forge, approximately 5 miles west on New York 28.

Backcountry mountain bike tours are provided by Ted Christodaro from the bike store Pedals & Petals in Inlet. Daily and overnight tours are a great way to explore this abundant trail area. Ted is a good source for information on the condition of the trails. The shop provides repairs, supplies, and mountain bike sales. Call Pedals & Petals for information on clinics, tours, festivals, and races. The Adirondacks has independent weather systems, and it's hard to determine the condition of trails from faraway cities. It's a good idea to telephone ahead before taking off on the trails.

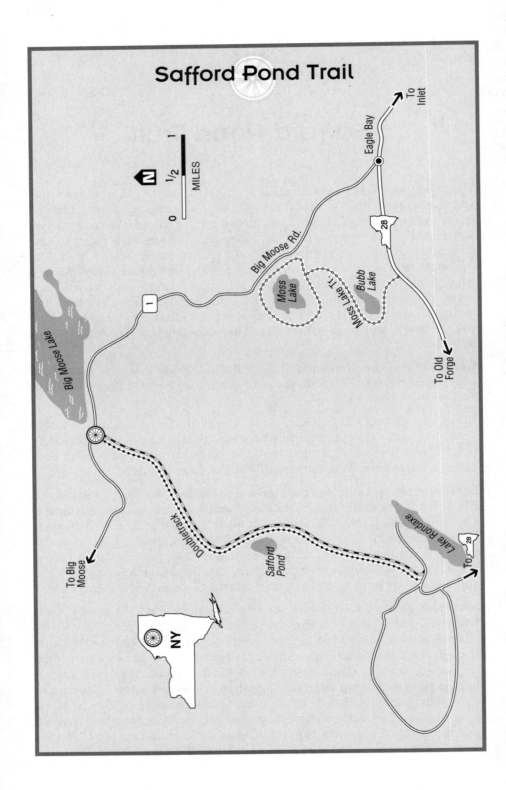

Mountain bikes can be rented from the Mountainman Outdoor Supply Company on NY 28 in Inlet.

Just north of Eagle Bay, the Big Moose Inn along Big Moose Road is minutes from the trailhead and offers a hearty meal and lodging. The chef has been with the inn for twenty-seven years and cooks a fine meal. The Bennet family welcomes mountain bikers and can offer some advice on current trail conditions.

Hazards: In July 1995 a severe storm swept through this terrain and caused many large, old-growth trees to blow down. Many huge trees lie across the trail, making passage difficult. The trail is slowly being cleared of these trees at the time of this writing. It is a good idea to check with the New York State Department of Environmental Conservation on the condition of this trail before you attempt to ride it.

Before the storm, Safford Pond Trail was popular with hikers and snowmobile enthusiasts. Care should be taken when descending along sections of the route to keep control of your bike. The snowmobile trails are maintained on a regular basis, but the heavy forest can set down new wooden obstacles at any time.

Rescue index: The trail is close to the well-traveled Big Moose Road, and help can be found in Eagle Bay.

Land status: Old Forge and the central region of Adirondack Park offer a variety of terrain with exceptional natural beauty. The route follows roads and trails in the wild forests classification of Adirondack Park. They reside on state public land and are available for mountain biking. Mountain biking is presently prohibited in designated wilderness areas of Adirondack Park and where signage is posted.

The town of Web has expanded the use of its well-maintained snowmobile trails and opened the well-marked routes for mountain bikers. The potential use of the diverse Old Forge/Web trail system is limitless and is an exciting opportunity for mountain bikers to explore.

Maps: USGS 7.5-minute series, Eagle Bay quadrangle provides good detail for this route. The Adirondack West-Central Wilderness Area Map published by Plinth, Quoin & Cornice Associates provides excellent topographical detail of the route and surrounding terrain and can be found at most outdoor-type stores in New York for $5.00. It is based on the USGS 15-minute series, at a scale of 1:62,500 and a contour level of 20 feet, where 1 inch = 0.98 mile.

Finding the trail: Take the New York State Thruway (Interstate 87) north to exit 24 (Albany). Take I-87 north to exit 25, Route 8/Chestertown and Hague. At the end of the exit ramp, turn left (west) onto NY 8 toward Loon Lake. After passing through Wevertown, turn right (west) at the stop sign onto NY 28. This scenic highway takes you through the towns of North Creek, Indian Lake, and Blue Mountain Lake. White-water rafting on the

Hudson River is very popular, and there are many outfitters in the Indian Lake area. Continue on NY 28 west toward Inlet and Old Forge.

In the town of Eagle Bay, turn right (north) onto Big Moose Road. Proceed about 5 miles. Access is from the Safford Pond trailhead at the Orvis parking area on Big Moose Road.

Sources of additional information:

Pedals & Petals
Route 28, P.O. Box 390
Inlet, NY 13360
(315) 357–3281

Old Forge Tourist Information Center
P.O. Box 68
Old Forge, NY 13420
(315) 369–6983

New York State Department of Environmental Conservation, Region 6
317 Washington Street
Watertown, NY 13601
(315) 785–2239

The Big Moose Inn
Big Moose Road
Eagle Bay, NY 13331
(315) 357–2042

Mountainman Outdoor Supply Company
Route 28, P.O. Box 659
Inlet, NY 13360
(315) 357–6672

Notes on the trail: From the parking area, follow the blue-marked, wide, singletrack south through a dark, mature conifer forest. Several small streams crisscross the trail but are easily forged. Safford Pond is approximately 3 miles from the trailhead and is the next pond you will encounter. A spur trail leads west to the pond. The main trail skirts the eastern edge of the wetland that lies east of Safford Pond. Another spur trail leads east to Goose Pond. The trail crosses a wide, wet area and then skirts the base of a hill. The trail is flat and continues to Lake Rondaxe. After reaching Lake Rondaxe (approximately 5 miles), you must return to the trailhead along the same route.

The Uncas Tour

This ride means many things to many people. The 18-mile loop can be ridden in total or broken up into segments you may wish to ride at different times. Along the way you will be challenged by moderate, hilly terrain but charmed by the lake, pond, and river scenery you pass. The combination of double- and singletrack winds through dark, primeval forests. The tour is invigorating and provides a riding experience for just about every level of biker.

Uncas Road is an easy 9-mile, cruising, scenic dirt road and is perfect for family fun and novice mountain bike riders. A 4-mile singletrack winds through a majestic forest, past ponds and brooks. The remaining mileage traverses hard-packed dirt roads that were built sometime in the nineteenth century. They were the old roadways that connected the great camps and summer homes of J. P. Morgan and Alfred G. Vanderbilt.

A popular singletrack leading from Eighth Lake Public Campground traverses hilly terrain for almost 4 miles, connecting scenic Eagle's Nest Lake and Bug Lake, and terminates at Uncas Road. From the village of Eagle Bay, Uncas Road parallels Eagle Creek, passing by the small Upper Pond and terminating at Raquette Lake. The wide, 9-mile, hard-packed dirt ride provides for some easy cruising, and its smoothness, good condition, and relatively flat grade give you the freedom to enjoy nature's canvas, which surrounds you all the way. It was constructed during the late nineteenth century and provided passage for Adirondack camp owners and their guests, who were traveling between Eagle Bay on Fourth Lake and Raquette Lake.

Once at Raquette Lake you have the options of taking it easy for the rest of the afternoon, going on a luncheon cruise on the *WW Durant,* and touring the lakeshores. If you want to continue on the circuit and finish the loop, pedal from Raquette Lake to New York 28 and then take the hard-packed, fast-cruising Sagamore Road to Sagamore Lake. Tours at the historic Sagamore Lodge are available. From the Sagamore Lodge ride 5 more miles on another part of Uncas Road back to NY 28. Pedal across NY 28 into the Eighth Lake Public Campground, where you began your loop. The campground is an excellent spot to establish your base camp, so bring a tent and some sleeping bags and immerse yourself in these pristine woodlands.

General location: Near the town of Inlet, in Herkimer County, in the west-central region of Adirondack Park in northeastern New York.

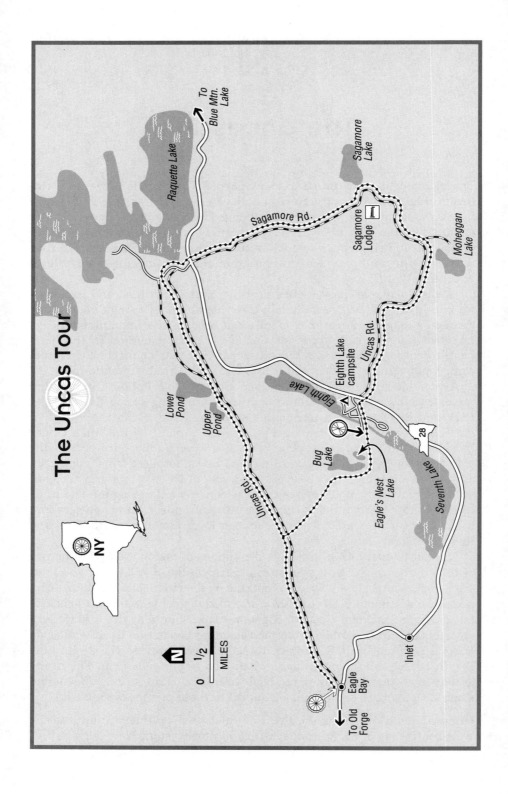

The Uncas Tour

N

0 1/2 1
MILES

NY

To Old Forge

To Blue Mtn. Lake

Raquette Lake

Sagamore Lake

Sagamore Rd.

Sagamore Lodge

Moheggan Lake

Uncas Rd.

Eighth Lake campsite

Eighth Lake

Lower Pond

Upper Pond

Uncas Rd.

Bug Lake

Eagle's Nest Lake

Seventh Lake

28

Eagle Bay

Inlet

Elevation change: The Uncas Road section is mostly level. Sagamore Road to the Sagamore Lodge traverses gently rolling terrain with no major climbs. The ride from the Sagamore area back to NY 28 on the "other" Uncas Road is more demanding, with elevation changes between 1,900 and 2,200 feet, and might take your breath away, but it's just for 5 miles. A 3-mile singletrack from the Eighth Lake Public Campground is a little more demanding but extremely exciting as it ascends from 1,800 to 2,200 feet and then descends back to the first Uncas Road.

Season: You can ride after the wet season ends in April or May. It all depends on the amount of snow and rain from prior months. You can then ride until mid-September, which is when hunting season commences. You may don an orange hunting vest, but it is still risky to be moving through the forest at the speed of a young buck. Autumn is a beautiful time to ride through the mixed hardwood and conifer forests, though.

The blackflies can be fierce from late spring until late June. Deerflies take over where the blackflies leave off and can last into July. They look like miniature F-15 jets with their swept-back wings. Remember to bring bug repellent.

Services: Lodging, food, and other services can be found in Inlet, approximately 6 miles west on NY 28.

Ted Christodaro from the bike store Pedals & Petals in Inlet provides daily and overnight backcountry mountain bike tours throughout this area and is a good source for information on the condition of the trails. The shop provides repairs, supplies, and mountain bike sales. Call Pedals & Petals for any information on clinics, tours, festivals, and races. The Adirondacks has independent weather systems, and it's hard to determine the condition of trails from faraway cities. It's a good idea to telephone ahead before taking off on the trails.

Mountain bikes can be rented from the Mountainman Outdoor Supply Company on NY 28 in Inlet. There is a state campground at Limekiln Lake if you are interested in camping out and sampling the Limekiln Trail and Moose River Plains Trails.

Hazards: The loop is long, and you must be in reasonable shape to attempt it. Of course you can ride this tour in sections and thereby enjoy it at a different pace. Care should be taken when crossing the sometimes busy NY 28, and you should pay attention to the occasional vehicle that might be driving by on Uncas or Sagamore Roads.

Rescue index: There are several bailouts, and you are never actually committed to the ride as in some other tours in this book. Help can be found by driving back to well-traveled NY 28, as well as in Raquette Lake and Inlet.

Land status: Old Forge and the central region of Adirondack Park offer a variety of terrain with exceptional natural beauty. The route follows roads and trails in the wild forests classification of Adirondack Park. They reside

Taking a break at Bug Lake.

on state public land and are available for mountain biking. Mountain biking is presently prohibited in designated wilderness areas of Adirondack Park and where signage is posted. This tour follows public roads, and the singletrack passes through state land.

Maps: The Adirondack West-Central Wilderness Area Map published by Plinth, Quoin & Cornice Associates provides excellent topographical detail of the route and surrounding terrain and can be found at most outdoor-type stores in New York for $5.00. It is based on the USGS 15-minute series, at a scale of 1:62,500 and a contour level of 20 feet, where 1 inch = 0.98 mile.

Finding the trail: Take the New York State Thruway (Interstate 87) north to exit 24 (Albany). Take I-87 north to exit 25, Route 8/Chestertown and Hague. At the end of the exit ramp, turn left (west) onto NY 8 toward Loon Lake. After passing through Wevertown turn right (west) at the stop sign onto NY 28. This scenic highway takes you through the towns of North Creek, Indian Lake, and Blue Mountain Lake. White-water rafting on the Hudson River is very popular, and there are many outfitters in the Indian Lake area. Continue on NY 28 west toward Inlet and Old Forge.

Approximately 6 miles east of Inlet on NY 28 is the entrance to the Eighth Lake Public Campground. Turn into the campground past the registration booth and park. Pedal straight ahead (west) in the campground on the paved road. The road turns into a doubletrack through a conifer forest. Follow the yellow Department of Environmental Conservation markers.

Sources of additional information:

Pedals & Petals
Route 28, P.O. Box 390
Inlet, NY 13360
(315) 357-3281

Old Forge Tourist Information Center
P.O. Box 68
Old Forge, NY 13420
(315) 369-6983

New York State Department of Environmental Conservation, Region 6
317 Washington Street
Watertown, NY 13601
(315) 785-2239

Mountainman Outdoor Supply Company
Route 28, P.O. Box 659
Inlet, NY 13360
(315) 357-6672

Notes on the trail: After leaving the campground proceed on the doubletrack. It soon crosses a small bridge spanning the inlet of Seventh Lake and begins a small climb for 0.6 mile. Bear left at a fork in the trail. The right fork is the spur trail to Eagle's Nest Lake. Continue riding, and cross the outlet stream of Bug and Eagle's Nest Lakes. The trail continues along the west side of Bug Lake as a steady climb. Continue straight past a snowmobile trail that leads to the left in a southwest direction at 2.3 miles. You soon cross a long bridge over the inlet to the Brown's Tract Ponds, and at 2.7 miles you pass the Black Bear Mountain yellow-marked hiking trail. Continue straight in a northwest direction to reach the dirt Uncas Road at 3.5 miles.

Turn right onto the wide, flat Uncas Road and pedal for about 3 miles to approach Upper Pond. Soon after this body of water, bear right at a fork and proceed on the dirt road. This is an easier route to Raquette Lake. The left fork leads you to a steep climb around Fox Mountain. Raquette Lake is reached in 2.5 miles.

Once in Raquette Lake turn right (south) toward NY 28. Cross NY 28, and begin riding on Sagamore Road, which is directly across the road. Sagamore Road is a wide, hard-packed road used by vehicles heading to Sagamore Camp. Sagamore Lodge is reached in just more than 3 miles. If you have time, check out the tours of this great Adirondack camp.

From the Sagamore pedal past the parking area, bearing right to a junction in 0.2 mile. Two barricades block two routes. Proceed past the barricade to the right. Don't worry, it is state land; the road is just off limits to vehicles. The left route proceeds into private land.

The road continues southwest, climbs one hill and then the contours of another, and reaches a fork in 1.6 miles from the Sagamore. Bear right. The

Snowfall adorns a grove of evergreens along the Uncas River.

left route leads to private land and Moheggan Lake, the site of nineteenth-century Camp Uncas. Camp Uncas contained the summer homes of J. P. Morgan and Alfred G. Vanderbilt. The road you just traveled was built to connect Sagamore and Uncas Camps. Continue on the main dirt road for about 2 miles out of Sagamore, and encounter a pile of bulldozed debris. Continue straight ahead. The route to your left leads down to the southern shore of Moheggan Lake.

Continue past the debris onto old, abandoned Uncas Road. The road leads gently downhill for more than 2.5 miles to NY 28. At NY 28 make a right and a quick left and you have returned to the Eighth Lake Public Campground. An exciting circuit has been completed!

The Limekiln Loop

Despite all the sleek frames, scientifically designed suspension systems, and technically enriched accessories (gadgetry), mountain biking is still a low-technology, low-impact, and take-your-time sport. Each push of the pedals expands our universe because we take the time to examine the world through which we pass. In doing so we rediscover just how much fun it is to explore the wilderness and embrace its environment. The Limekiln Loop tour is one such ride you shouldn't be in a hurry to complete. This 13-mile loop combines wide, grassy, compact snowmobile, hiking, and old-woods road trails. The riding is moderately challenging and suitable for intermediate beginners to advanced riders.

The tour begins at Limekiln Lake, passing through the woodlands surrounding Limekiln Swamp and Third Lake. Loggers used the terrain around the swamp to stockpile logs. The logs were then tossed into the stream, which carried them into the Moose River. The last 6 miles of the loop travel along the hard-packed, dirt, South Shore Road, which skirts the shores of the Fulton Chain of Lakes system's Fourth Lake. The trails pass through an area of attractive deciduous and conifer forests, lakes, and streams. Limekiln Lake is a great spot to observe wildlife or stop and have a picnic. I spotted several loons paddling in the lake during one ride. Nearby Limekiln State Campground, located on the shores of this scenic lake, is a good place to set up a base and camp out. Build a campfire, eat under the stars, and watch the moon rise. Wake up early and ride, come back for breakfast, and have coffee by the lake. It's your own piece of paradise.

Thanks to a large federal grant in the 1970s, the town of Inlet constructed and improved a cross-country ski trail system near Limekiln Lake. Currently the cross-country ski trails are off limits to mountain biking. According to the local word, there is a lobbying effort under way to make these wonderful trails open to mountain biking, and this would expand the Limekiln Loop immensely. Let's keep our fingers crossed.

General location: Near the town of Inlet, in Herkimer County, in the west-central region of Adirondack Park in northeastern New York.

Elevation change: Most of the elevation fluctuations occur at the beginning of the loop. Elevations vary between 1,800 and 2,000 feet. At 3.5 miles the riding levels out after you come out of the hills. From that point on, the riding follows the level of the land.

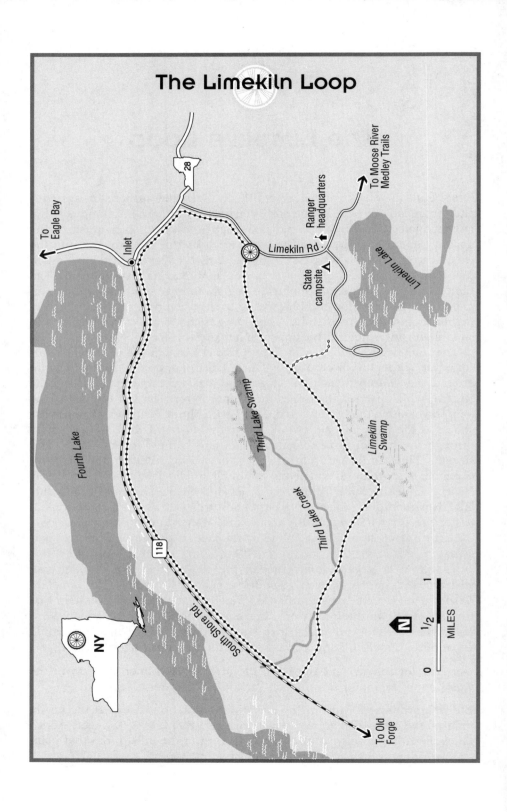

The Limekiln Loop

NY

To Eagle Bay

28

Inlet

Fourth Lake

118

South Shore Rd.

Limekiln Rd.

Ranger headquarters

To Moose River Medley Trails

State campsite

Limekiln Lake

Third Lake Swamp

Third Lake Creek

Limekiln Swamp

To Old Forge

N

MILES

0   1/2   1

Season: You can ride after the wet season ends in April or May. It all depends on the amount of snow and rain from prior months. You can then ride until mid-September, which is when hunting season commences. You may don an orange hunting vest, but it is still risky to be moving through the forest at the speed of a young buck. The fall is a beautiful time to ride through the mixed hardwood and conifer forests, though.

The blackflies can be fierce in late spring and last until late June. Deerflies take over where the blackflies leave off and can last into July. They look like miniature F-15 jets with their swept-back wings. Remember to bring bug repellent.

Services: Lodging, food, and other services can be found in Inlet, approximately 1 mile north on New York 28.

Ted Christodaro from the bike store Pedals & Petals in Inlet provides daily and overnight backcountry mountain bike tours throughout this area and is a good source for information on the condition of the trails. The shop provides repairs, supplies, and mountain bike sales. Call Pedals & Petals for any information on clinics, tours, festivals, and races. The Adirondacks has independent weather systems, and it's hard to determine the condition of trails from faraway cities. It's a good idea to telephone ahead before taking off on the trails.

Mountain bikes can be rented from the Mountainman Outdoor Supply Company on NY 28 in Inlet. There is a state campground at Limekiln Lake if you are interested in camping out and sampling the Limekiln Trail and Moose River Plains Trails.

Hazards: This trail is close to the town of Inlet and is popular with hikers and other mountain bikers. Care should be taken on any blind curves and bends. The section of the route known as the Third Lake Creek Trail passes through wet, swampy areas and can be laden with mosquitoes until the end of June. Bring bug repellent.

Rescue index: The route is only 1 mile from the town of Inlet, where help can be found. The excellently maintained snowmobile trails are well marked with orange circular discs and are easy to follow.

Land status: Old Forge and the central region of Adirondack Park offer a variety of terrain with exceptional natural beauty. The route follows roads and trails in the wild forests classification of Adirondack Park. They reside on state public land and are available for mountain biking. Mountain biking is presently prohibited in designated wilderness areas of Adirondack Park and where signage is posted.

The town of Web has expanded the use of its well-maintained snowmobile trails and opened the well-marked routes for mountain bikers. The potential use of the diverse Old Forge/Web trail system is limitless and an exciting opportunity for mountain bikers to explore.

Maps: USGS 7.5-minute series, Eagle Bay and Big Moose quadrangles, and USGS 15-minute series, Old Forge quadrangles provide good detail for this route. The Adirondack West-Central Wilderness Area Map published by Plinth, Quoin & Cornice Associates provides excellent topographical detail of the route and surrounding terrain and can be found at most outdoor-type stores in New York State for $5.00. It is based on the USGS 15-minute series, at a scale of 1:62,500 and a contour level of 20 feet, where 1 inch = 0.98 mile.

Finding the trail: Take the New York State Thruway (Interstate 87) north to exit 24 (Albany). Take I-87 north to exit 25, Route 8/Chestertown and Hague. At the end of the exit ramp, turn left (west) onto NY 8 toward Loon Lake. After passing through Wevertown, turn right (west) at the stop sign onto NY 28. This scenic highway takes you through the towns of North Creek, Indian Lake, and Blue Mountain Lake. White-water rafting on the Hudson River is very popular, and there are many outfitters in the Indian Lake area. Continue on NY 28 west toward Inlet and Old Forge.

Just before you get to the town of Inlet, you will find signs for Limekiln Road and Moose River Recreation Area. Turn left (south) onto Limekiln Road. Proceed for about 1 mile. Look for the trailhead on the right side of the road. This is the Limekiln Swamp trailhead. There is limited parking along the road near the trailhead.

Sources of additional information:

Pedals & Petals
Route 28, P.O. Box 390
Inlet, NY 13360
(315) 357–3281

Forest Ranger
Limekiln Lake
Inlet, NY 13360
(315) 357–4403

Old Forge Tourist Information Center
P.O. Box 68
Old Forge, NY 13420
(315) 369–6983

New York State Department of Environmental Conservation, Region 6
317 Washington Street
Watertown, NY 13601
(315) 785-2239

Mountainman Outdoor Supply Company
Route 28, P.O. Box 659
Inlet, NY 13360
(315) 357–6672

Notes on the trail: Pedal along a wide, hard-packed, grassy road and follow the New York State Department of Environmental Conservation's yellow cross-country ski markers. You will pass some trails that lead to your

Winter beckons the adventurous rider to discover its silent beauty.

right (north). These connect with the town of Inlet's network of cross-country ski trails. At this writing these trails were closed to mountain biking. A little farther on you will pass an intersecting snowmobile trail. At 1.5 miles another yellow-marked trail leads left (south) to the Limekiln Lake Public Campground. Continue straight, following the route as it traverses mostly southwest. Pass through some tall conifers and parallel Limekiln Creek and its wetland. The route terminates after 3 miles of riding at the intersection with a trail known as the Limekiln Creek–Third Lake Trail. Turn right (north), and follow this generally level trail along Third Lake Creek almost 3 miles to South Shore Road. The route passes by several beaver meadows and small waterfalls as it follows above the Third Lake Creek. After about 1 mile on this trail, you cross a small bridge that spans the creek. The route traverses some majestic hardwoods and fields of ferns. After another half mile the trail travels over a grassy snowmobile trail. Follow it for about 100 feet and then turn left. You enter a dark, coniferous forest after another 0.3 mile, and the trail crosses a bridge that spans the outlet of Limekiln Swamp. After reentering the woods, you pass a ski trail on your right. Continue in a northwesterly direction through a mixed hardwood and coniferous woodland over mostly flat, semiswampy terrain. The route follows a vehicle track on and off through dense conifers. Bear right onto a jeep road past a chain barrier; pedal through a hardwood forest to the end of the trail at South Shore Road. Turn right (east) onto the road. Follow South Shore Road almost 6 miles to its end at NY 28. Turn right onto NY 28, and then right again onto Limekiln Road. Follow Limekiln Road 1 mile to your parking area.

Moose River Medley

In 1963 New York purchased a 50,000-acre tract of remote land from the Gould Paper Company. At the heart of this acreage is the flat floodplain of the South Branch of the Moose River, known as the Moose River Plains. The plains are flat and mostly open, with grass, bushes, and expanses of wetland. They are surrounded by mixed hardwood and pine forests interspersed with many lakes and ponds. Moose River Plains is the largest natural open space in the Adirondack Park and Forest Preserve and has a wide-open look with low hills discernible in the distance. The area was extensively logged before the state purchased it, but you can still find plantations of virgin white pine and balsam fir in areas the state purchased before the logging. The majority of the forest consists of second- and third-growth woodland.

A myriad of well-graded and well-maintained, abandoned logging roads form a maze throughout the plains, leading to ponds and lakes. The routes are not technically demanding, but some endurance is required to cover the vast mileage of the rolling terrain of the Moose River Plains. More than 27 miles of mountain bike trails abound, and in winter the place is a snow-mobiler's heaven. An exciting day awaits the energetic rider.

A great way to explore the plains is by establishing a base camp and spending the night, camping at one of the lakes. There are many campsites (all primitive) throughout the area, situated in scenic spots near ponds and lakes. A variety of out-and-back trails can be configured to fill several days of exploration.

General location: Near the town of Inlet in Herkimer County, in the west-central region of Adirondack Park in northeastern New York.

Elevation change: The Moose River Plains Recreation Area has some sizable hills and even a mountain range. Little Moose Mountain tops out at 3,620 feet, and many of the ponds and lakes are at unusually high elevations and claim to be the highest bodies of water in the Adirondacks. Most of the riding is along gently rolling terrain, where the maximum elevation gain or loss is only a few hundred feet.

Season: You can ride after the wet season ends in April or May. It all depends on the amount of snow and rain from prior months. The plains officially open on Memorial Day, and you can then ride until mid-September, when hunting season commences. You may don an orange hunting vest, but it is still risky to be moving through the forest at the speed of a young buck. The fall is a beautiful time to ride through the mixed hardwood and conifer forests, though.

The blackflies can be fierce from late spring until late June or early July. Deerflies take over where the blackflies leave off and can last into July. They look like miniature F-15 jets with their swept-back wings. Remember to bring bug repellent.

Services: Lodging, food, and other services can be found in Inlet, approximately 1 mile north on New York 28.

Ted Christodaro from the bike store Pedals & Petals in Inlet provides daily and overnight backcountry mountain bike tours throughout this area and is a good source for information on the condition of the trails. The shop provides repairs, supplies, and mountain bike sales. Call Pedals & Petals for any information on clinics, tours, festivals, and races. The Adirondacks has independent weather systems, and it's hard to determine the condition of trails from faraway cities. It's a good idea to telephone ahead before taking off on the trails.

Mountain bikes can be rented from the Mountainman Outdoor Supply Company on NY 28 in Inlet. There is a state campground at Limekiln Lake if you are interested in camping out and sampling the Limekiln Trail and Moose River Plains Trails.

Hazards: Be aware of the hunting seasons that begin in mid-September. Call the forest ranger at Limekiln Lake for any further information on hunting season and trail conditions.

Rescue index: The Limekiln forest ranger is on duty usually after Memorial Day weekend. The well-defined roads are excellently maintained, straightforward, and easy to follow, minimizing the chances of getting lost over such a long distance. The route is only 2 miles from the town of Inlet, where help can be found. The excellently maintained snowmobile trails are well marked with orange circular discs and are very easy to follow.

Land status: The trail resides on state public land and is available for mountain biking. Mountain biking is presently prohibited in designated wilderness areas of Adirondack Park and where signage is posted.

Maps: The Adirondack West-Central Wilderness Area Map published by Plinth, Quoin & Cornice Associates provides excellent topographical detail of the route and surrounding terrain and can be found at most outdoor-type stores in New York for $5.00. It is based on the USGS 15-minute series, at a scale of 1:62,500 and a contour level of 20 feet, where 1 inch = 0.98 mile.

Finding the trail: Take the New York State Thruway (Interstate 87) north to exit 24 (Albany). Take I-87 north to exit 25, Route 8/Chestertown and Hague. At the end of the exit ramp, turn left (west) onto NY 8 toward Loon Lake. After passing through Wevertown turn right (west) at the stop sign onto NY 28. This scenic highway takes you through the towns of North Creek, Indian Lake, and Blue Mountain Lake. White-water rafting on the Hudson River is very popular, and there are many outfitters in the Indian Lake area. Continue on NY 28 west toward Inlet and Old Forge.

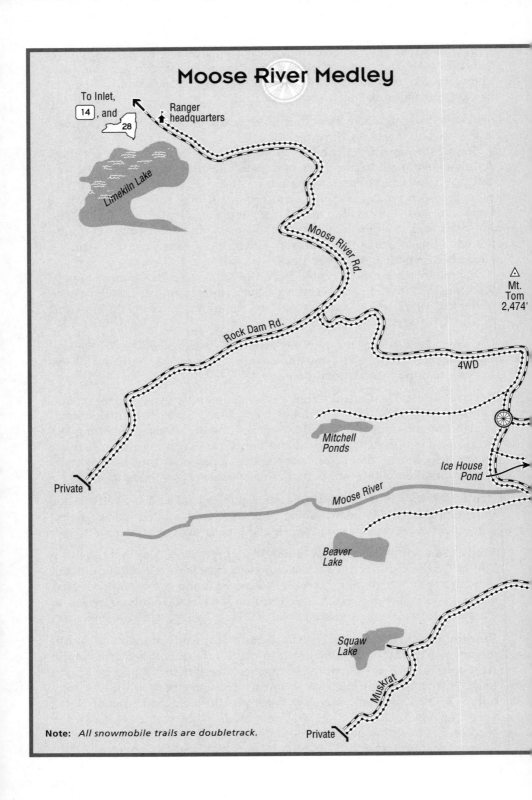

Moose River Medley

To Inlet, 14, and 28

Ranger headquarters

Limekiln Lake

Moose River Rd.

Rock Dam Rd.

Mt. Tom 2,474'

4WD

Private

Mitchell Ponds

Ice House Pond

Moose River

Beaver Lake

Squaw Lake

Muskrat

Private

Note: *All snowmobile trails are doubletrack.*

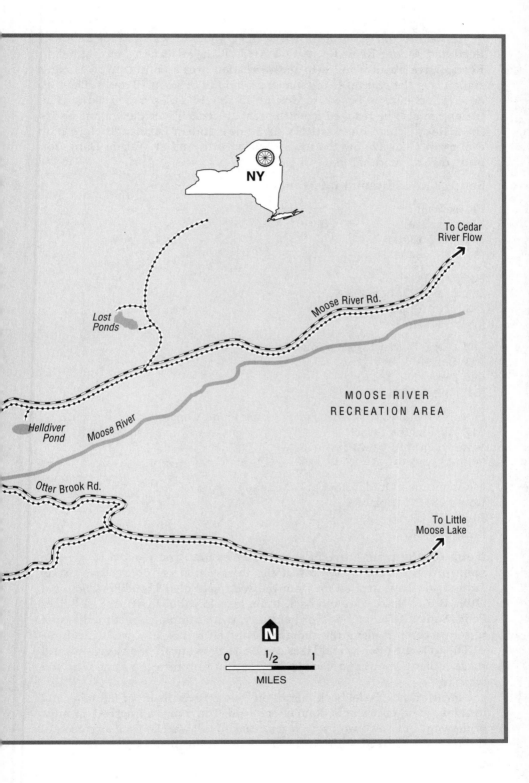

NY

To Cedar
River Flow

Moose River Rd.

Lost
Ponds

MOOSE RIVER
RECREATION AREA

Helldiver
Pond

Moose River

Otter Brook Rd.

To Little
Moose Lake

N

0   1/2   1

MILES

Just before you get to the town of Inlet, you will see signs for Limekiln Road and Moose River Recreation Area. Turn left (south) onto Limekiln Road. Drive about 3 miles to the recreation area's entrance. The ranger station is at the entrance. You may park here or drive in 10 miles. The trail description here is based on driving in the 10 miles and parking. The plains can also be reached from the east at Cedar River Flow along Cedar River Road, which intersects NY 28/30 near Indian Lake and before Blue Mountain Lake. Follow the town road until its end at Wakely Dam. You must register at either gate.

Sources of additional information:

Forest Ranger
Limekiln Lake
Inlet, NY 13360
(315) 357-4403

Pedals & Petals
Route 28, P.O. Box 390
Inlet, NY 13360
(315) 357-3281

Old Forge Tourist Information Center
P.O. Box 68
Old Forge, NY 13420
(315) 369-6983

New York State Department of Environmental Conservation, Region 6
317 Washington Street
Watertown, NY 13601
(315) 785-2239

Mountainman Outdoor Supply Company
Route 28, P.O. Box 659
Inlet, NY 13360
(315) 357-6672

Notes on the trail: Drive in about 10 miles until you reach a fork in the main dirt road. Park your car at the intersection of Moose River Road (which you have arrived on from the west gate near Limekiln Lake) and Otter Brook Road. Out-and-back trails lead to Mitchell Ponds, Helldiver Pond, Squaw Lake, and Beaver Lake. If you are camping, an attractive spot to set up camp is along the shores of Mitchell Ponds.

The following ponds and lakes can be accessed from this base point. All these routes are out and back, requiring you to return the same way you went in.

Mitchell Ponds: Pedal back (north) on Moose River Road for 0.3 mile, and turn left (west) onto an old doubletrack road. The trail is unmarked for most of the way, but don't worry; it is very easy to follow. The final approach to the ponds is marked with New York State Department of Environmental

The snowy solitude of Moose River Plains.

Conservation yellow markers. The trail skirts a rushing stream and comes into a junction in an open, grassy area at about 2 miles. Bear left (west) from the junction, and follow the northern contour of Mitchell Pond. The trail terminates at 2.8 miles at the pond's outlet stream.

Helldiver Pond: Head east on Moose River Road for 0.8 mile and turn right (south) onto a small dirt road. Bear right through an open woodland that soon turns into a dark forest. The pond is reached in 0.2 mile. It's a short trip, but the woods are exciting to ride through.

Beaver Lake Trail: Pedal south on Otter Brook Road for 1.2 miles. Turn right (west) onto a small dirt road that lies immediately past a small bridge spanning the South Branch of the Moose River. An estate was built down this road in 1904, but all the buildings are long gone. Proceed through a majestic forest of large white pines. These large species of pine were a common sight before logging started in the nineteenth century. Now the state's constitution protects the forest on state land.

After 2 miles and past the pines, you approach a clearing and the site of an old sawmill. Turn down a short road that descends to the shore of the lake. This scenic lake is another great spot to set up a campsite. If you do camp by the lake, stay far enough away from the shore to prevent pollution of the lake's waters. Old camping rule!

Squaw Lake: Pedal south on Otter Brook Road for 1.3 miles and fork right onto Indian River Road just after crossing Otter Brook. Proceed along Indian River Road for 4.9 miles past some small ponds and spur trails. Go past the barrier at the end of the road and head in for another 4.9 miles, whereupon you reach the eastern shore of Squaw Lake.

Journey to Stillwater Reservoir

The 24-mile, out-and-back (12 miles one way), gravel Big Moose Road extends from the village of Big Moose to the Stillwater Reservoir. This tour is composed of a wide, hard-packed dirt road with some roller-coaster hills and provides fast, easy, nontechnical riding. The Big Moose Road provides a good surface for someone new to off-road riding, allowing beginners to get used to the feel of the bike. More experienced riders should enjoy the fast-paced, cruising track and diverse scenery. The route leaves Big Moose and cuts through the Independence River Wild Forest. It traverses moderately rolling terrain, through forests of conifers and hardwoods, and past spruce-balsam fir swamplands, terminating at the western shore of the Stillwater Reservoir. The reservoir has more than 117 miles of shoreline and is a camper's delight. The Stillwater Hotel, which is basically the sole establishment at the reservoir, provides accommodations and a hearty menu. Stay overnight, rent a canoe and cruise the miles of shoreline, and then pedal back.

Two miles to the east of Big Moose, on Big Moose Road, lies Big Moose Lake. The lake was the setting for *An American Tragedy*, Theodore Dreiser's 1924 book about a young man's desire for riches. Big Moose Lake's notoriety was also expanded when Chester Gillette presumably killed his pregnant sweetheart, Grace Bond, in order to marry the boss's daughter. The infamous crime was researched and written about by Craig Brandon in his book, *Murder in the Adirondacks*. Although the names of those involved were changed, the murder has become part of American folklore.

This is a great ride to start in the morning so you can arrive in Stillwater by lunch. The hamlet of Stillwater, population twenty-five, offers boat and canoe rentals. Grab some grub at the Stillwater Hotel, and take a boat ride on the Norridgewock Ferry after lunch. The boat tours through the Stillwater Reservoir, passing many of the tiny islands dotting the waters. You can take your bikes on board and disembark at the village of Beaver River. Take a quick jaunt on a 6-mile, level gravel road from Beaver River. The riding is easy, and the lake scenery is exhilarating. Another option is to pedal and paddle. Pedal to Stillwater, leave your bike at the hotel, and rent a canoe at one of the forty-six primitive campsites that dot the reservoir's shoreline.

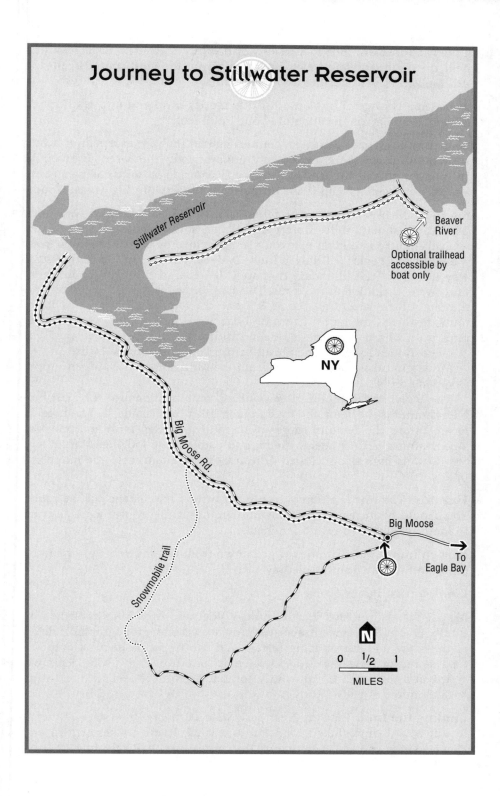

General location: About 8 miles north of the village of Eagle Bay and near the town of Inlet in Herkimer County, in the west-central region of Adirondack Park in northeastern New York.

Elevation change: Big Moose Road is mostly level and courses through the landscape at an elevation of about 1,600 feet.

Season: These roads can be ridden throughout the year except after heavy snows. Of course there are no boat cruises along Stillwater Reservoir in the winter, but Big Moose Road can be fun to ride on with compact snow and bike-tire chains. Fall is the prime season to explore Big Moose Road.

Services: Most services can be found in Eagle Bay and Inlet on New York 28, located about 5 miles from the trailhead in Big Moose.

Backcountry mountain bike tours are provided by Ted Christodaro from the bike store Pedals & Petals in Inlet. Daily and overnight tours are a great way to explore this abundant trail area. Ted is a good source for information on the condition of the trails. The shop provides repairs, supplies, and mountain bike sales. Call Pedals & Petals for any information on clinics, tours, festivals, and races. The Adirondacks has independent weather systems, so it's hard to determine the condition of trails from faraway cities. It's a good idea to telephone ahead before taking off on the trails.

Mountain bikes can be rented from the Mountainman Outdoor Supply Company on NY 28 in Inlet.

The Stillwater Hotel offers seasonal accommodations for the snowmobiler, hunter, fisherman, mountain biker, hiker, and canoeist. The hotel is located along the tranquil shores of the Stillwater Reservoir and provides a cozy atmosphere, a hearty menu, and comfortable lodging. Marian and Joe Romano own this secluded Adirondack lodge and welcome mountain bikers.

Hazards: The ride is strenuous only because of the distance of the route. You should be in reasonable shape to attempt it. Big Moose Road is open to motor vehicles, so watch for them.

Rescue index: Help can be flagged down from passing vehicles or can be found in Stillwater and Eagle Bay.

Land status: Public roads.

Maps: The Adirondack West-Central Wilderness Area Map published by Plinth, Quoin & Cornice Associates provides excellent topographical detail of the route and surrounding terrain and can be found at most outdoor-type stores in New York for $5.00. It is based on the USGS 15-minute series, at a scale of 1:62,500 and a contour level of 20 feet, where 1 inch = 0.98 mile.

Finding the trail: Take the New York State Thruway (Interstate 87) north to exit 24 (Albany). Take I-87 north to exit 25, Route 8/Chestertown and Hague. At the end of the exit ramp, turn left (west) onto NY 8 toward Loon

The remote Stillwater Reservoir.

Lake. After passing through Wevertown, turn right (west) at the stop sign onto NY 28. This scenic highway takes you through the towns of North Creek, Indian Lake, and Blue Mountain Lake. White-water rafting on the Hudson River is very popular, and there are many outfitters in the Indian Lake area. Continue on NY 28 west toward Inlet and Old Forge. In Eagle Bay turn right (north) onto Big Moose Road. In about 6.5 miles the road bears left (west) at a T intersection. A road to the right leads east along the northern shores of Big Moose Lake. Continue for another 2 miles into the village of Big Moose. Park at Big Moose station and bear right, heading out of town in a northwest direction along Big Moose Road.

Sources of additional information:

Pedals & Petals
Route 28, P.O. Box 390
Inlet, NY 13360
(315) 357–3281

Old Forge Tourist Information Center
P.O. Box 68
Old Forge, NY 13420
(315) 369–6983

Stillwater Hotel
Star Route Box 258M
Lowville, NY 13367
(315) 376–6470

New York State Department of Environmental Conservation, Region 6
317 Washington Street
Watertown, NY 13601
(315) 785–2239

Mountainman Outdoor Supply Company
Route 28, P.O. Box 659
Inlet, NY 13360
(315) 357–6672

Notes on the trail: After about 3 miles of pedaling on the moderately hilly Big Moose Road, there will be another dirt road that forks right. Continue straight. Another road is passed on your left after half a mile. Keep straight, skirting a small hill on your left and passing several streams on your right. You will pass two more dirt roads, on your right and then your left, but continue straight. Birch Creek, the drainage from Polack Swamp, parallels the road. A little more than 7 miles from where you started, you will begin to approach the southeastern end of Stillwater Reservoir. From this point the road passes along the eastern shore of the reservoir, and in about 1 mile you'll pass Stillwater Mountain, elevation 3,264 feet, on your left (west). Stillwater is reached in another 2.5 miles. Keep in mind that you must return along the same route you have just traveled.

Bloodsucker Passage

A rigorous 18-mile loop passes through attractive forests, meandering streams, sparkling ponds and lakes, and even a small waterfall. The riding is along snowmobile trails that are maintained year-round. During the winter snowmobile enthusiasts pay a permit fee to ride in the area. The funds are then used to keep the trails in shape, repairing washouts and cutting up blowdowns that block the routes.

The terrain is rugged and not for the fainthearted. Though not a technical ride, the doubletrack snowmobile trails will test an intermediate rider's endurance. A strong rider will be challenged by the length of the ride and rolling terrain, but charmed by spectacular woodland scenery. The mixed deciduous and conifer forest provides a dense woodland environment that is a pleasure to ride through. In the nineteenth century wildlife such as moose, cougars, wolves, and lynx were all hunted to extinction.

Fortunately over the last 100 years, these forests have been given a chance to recover, largely through protections by the state for the Adirondack Park and Forest Preserve. Bald eagles, moose, and peregrine falcons have returned to this unique topography of rivers, lakes, mountains, and forests.

The tour begins just outside of the historic village of Old Forge. The area was known for its rustic hotels, lodges, and private camps built in the late nineteenth century. Hunters and tourists explored the region's waterways in the famous Adirondack guide boat. These boats, an Adirondack creation, resembled a sleeker version of a rowboat. They were fast and light and provided a major industry for Old Forge between 1890 and 1940.

Bloodsucker Passage is a demanding, stimulating, and rewarding trail. The deep, dark, quiet woodlands, streams, and falls provide enough sensory overload for a full day of riding.

General location: Near the town of Old Forge in Herkimer County, in the west-central region of Adirondack Park in northeastern New York. Old Forge is a quiet New England kind of town. It is located at the beginning of the Fulton Chain of Lakes and is the starting point for the infamous 75-mile canoe trip through the heart of the Adirondack wilderness.

Elevation change: There is one major hill toward the end of the ride near Little Roundtop. The majority of the route traverses a rolling, sometimes hilly terrain. The route levels out for a short distance and then continues to undulate over several short hills.

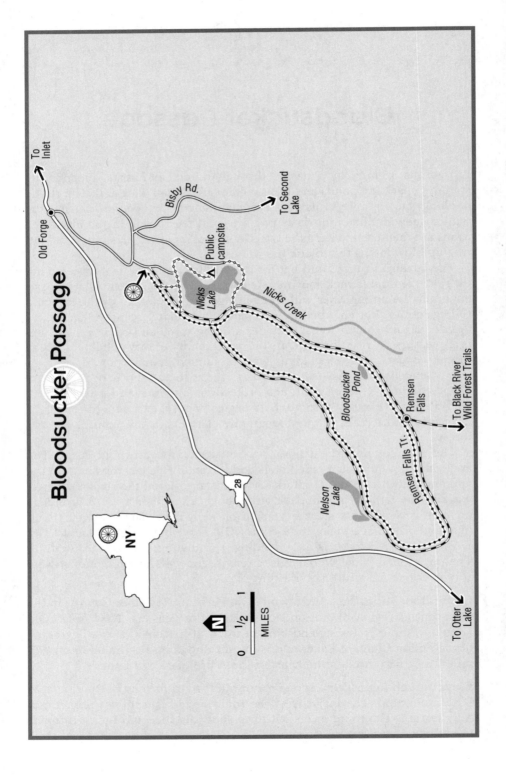

Bloodsucker Passage

NY

N

0   1/2   1
MILES

To Inlet

Old Forge

Bisby Rd.

To Second Lake

Public campsite

Nicks Lake

Nicks Creek

Bloodsucker Pond

Nelson Lake

Remsen Falls Tr.

Remsen Falls

To Black River Wild Forest Trails

To Otter Lake

28

Season: You can ride after the wet season ends in April or May. It all depends on the amount of snow and rain from prior months. You can then ride until mid-September, which is when hunting season commences. You may don an orange hunting vest, but it is still risky to be moving through the forest at the speed of a young buck. The fall is a beautiful time to ride through the mixed hardwood and conifer forests, though.

The blackflies can be fierce in late spring and last until late June. Deerflies take over where the blackflies leave off and can last into July. They look like miniature F-15 jets with their swept-back wings. Remember to bring bug repellent.

Services: Old Forge offers a wide range of accommodations, including food, restaurants, hotels, motels, camps, and even homes that can be rented.

Backcountry mountain bike tours are provided by Ted Christodaro from the bike store Pedals & Petals in Inlet. Daily and overnight tours are a great way to explore this abundant trail area. Ted is a good source for information on the condition of the trails. The shop provides repairs, supplies, and mountain bike sales. Call Pedals & Petals for any information on clinics, tours, festivals, and races. The Adirondacks has independent weather systems, and it's hard to determine the condition of trails from faraway cities. It's a good idea to telephone ahead before taking off on the trails.

Mountain bikes can be rented from the Mountainman Outdoor Supply Company on New York 28 in Inlet.

Hazards: This trail is challenging, so be prepared with spare tubes, patches, water, energy bars, and bug repellent.

Rescue index: At its greatest distance the trail is only 6 miles from Old Forge, making this route fairly close to civilization. You can bail out after reaching Nelson Lake on the dirt road that leads down to NY 28. The excellently maintained snowmobile trails are well marked with orange circular discs, and they are very easy to follow.

Land status: Old Forge and the central region of Adirondack Park offer a variety of terrain with exceptional natural beauty. The route follows roads and trails in the wild forests classification of Adirondack Park. They reside on state public land and are available for mountain biking. Mountain biking is presently prohibited in designated wilderness areas of Adirondack Park and where signage is posted.

The town of Web has expanded the use of its well-maintained snowmobile trails and opened the well-marked routes for mountain bikers. The potential use of the diverse Old Forge/Web trail system is limitless and an exciting opportunity for mountain bikers to explore.

Maps: USGS 15-minute series, McKeever and Old Forge quadrangles provide good detail for this route. The Adirondack West-Central Wilderness Area Map published by Plinth, Quoin & Cornice Associates provides excellent topographical detail of the route and surrounding terrain and can be

Miles of doubletrack lie ahead.

found at most outdoor-type stores in New York for $5.00. It is based on the USGS 15-minute series, at a scale of 1:62,500 and a contour level of 20 feet, where 1 inch = 0.98 mile.

Finding the trail: Take the New York State Thruway (Interstate 87) north to exit 24 (Albany). Take I-87 north to exit 25, Route 8/Chestertown and Hague. At the end of the exit ramp, turn left (west) onto NY 8 toward Loon Lake. After passing through Wevertown, turn right (west) at the stop sign onto NY 28. This scenic highway takes you through the towns of North Creek, Indian Lake, and Blue Mountain Lake. White-water rafting on the Hudson River is very popular, and there are many outfitters in the Indian Lake area. Continue on NY 28 west toward Inlet and Old Forge.

After reaching the town of Old Forge, go down Main Street (NY 28), and turn left at the large brick school onto Gilbert Street. Turn right at the next stop sign, following the sign for NICKS LAKE PUBLIC CAMPGROUND. Bear left at the next stop sign, continuing to follow the signs for the campground. Turn left onto Bisby Road. Park at the second snowmobile trailhead about 100 yards on your right.

Sources of additional information:

Pedals & Petals
Route 28, P.O. Box 390
Inlet, NY 13360
(315) 357–3281

Old Forge Tourist Information Center
P.O. Box 68
Old Forge, NY 13420
(315) 369-6983

New York State Department of Environmental Conservation, Region 6
3174 Washington Street
Watertown, NY 13601
(315) 785-2239

Mountainman Outdoor Supply Company
Route 28, P.O. Box 659
Inlet, NY 13360
(315) 357-6672

Notes on the trail: Pedal southwest on a wide, wooded snowmobile trail. About half a mile southwest of the lake, a trail will join the one you're on. This trail to your left leads east along the north end of Nicks Lake. Continue on the main trail in a southwest direction, and in 0.3 mile you approach a fork. Continue straight for another mile, whereupon you reach an intersection with the snowmobile trail that leads around Nicks Lake. The path straight ahead is known as the Remsen Falls Trail and is the main loop. Taking the snowmobile trail (left), you will soon climb a small hill just south of the lake. As you crest the hill a trail leads off to the left and terminates at the Nicks Lake Campground and beach. Return to the main trail and bear right.

The trail proceeds south, descending and winding closer to Nicks Creek, which drains from Nicks Lake into the South Branch of Moose River. At 4.8 miles Bloodsucker Pond is passed. Ascend a small hill, and descend to Remsen Falls at 6 miles. The falls are created by a natural rock dam across the stream. The falls are on a small spur trail that leads south into the Black Forest Trail system. Continue to bear right (west), paralleling the South Branch of the Moose River. The trail remains mostly in the woods.

Two miles past the falls the trail turns right (north) up a small hill and then down again, crossing a stream. The south shore of Nelson Lake is reached in 2.2 miles (12.2 miles total). A little more than a mile past the southern end of Nelson Lake, you reach an intersection with a dirt road that leads west to NY 28. Stay on the snowmobile trail heading east, and after 0.6 mile the trail bears northeast, ascending a large hill. After descending from the hill, pass the snowmobile trail that leads in from the left, and bear left at the next fork. This is the same trail you rode on from your parking area. Pedal back along the trail for about 1.8 miles to Bisby Road.

65

Black River Wild Forest

More than 23 miles of singletrack and doubletrack trails await the energetic intermediate rider in the mood for adventure. An interesting network of snowmobile trails connects three beautiful lakes. Woodhull Lake, shaped like a half-moon, is the largest (with its own island in the middle) and resides at an elevation of 1,875 feet. This lake overflows into and creates Sand Lake at a slightly lower elevation of 1,825 feet. Gulf Lake, which you pass later in the ride, sits at an elevation of 1,173 feet.

The woodlands are fairly flat with few distant views, but visiting these bodies of water is great fun. Bring some snacks and have a mountain biker picnic along the shores of these remote bodies of water. Toward the end of the eighteenth century, hunters, trappers, and others came through the Black River Valley and discovered its rivers and chains of lakes. The valley provided an easier passage into the west-central Adirondacks and soon became the main passage for many settlers in the Fulton Chain of Lakes area. The Oneida Indians occupied the land during this era and ended up selling more than 4 million acres to the white settlers. Logging took hold by 1850, making New York the leading timber-producing state in the nation. After the Civil War the Adirondack region was popular for recreation, and most of the thoroughfare came through the forested and hilly Black River Valley. As you ride throughout this territory, imagine what it must have been like for Native Americans to hunt and fish the land and waters, and think about the trepidation of the first settlers as they traveled through these dense woodlands and the awe inspired by the natural beauty of the lake-riddled landscape. This ride takes you past many such bodies of water. Happy trails.

General location: Near the town of Old Forge in Herkimer County, in the west-central region of Adirondack Park in northeastern New York. The trailhead is located in the town of McKeever, about 10 miles southwest from Old Forge on New York 28.

Elevation change: The ride has hilly ascents on the approach to Woodhull Lake and Sand Lake. One of the trails that leads into the Little Woodhull Lake area is a bit more hilly, and riding varies between 1,800 and 2,000 feet.

Season: You can ride after the wet season ends in April or May. It all depends on the amount of snow and rain from prior months. You can then ride until mid-September, which is when hunting season commences. You

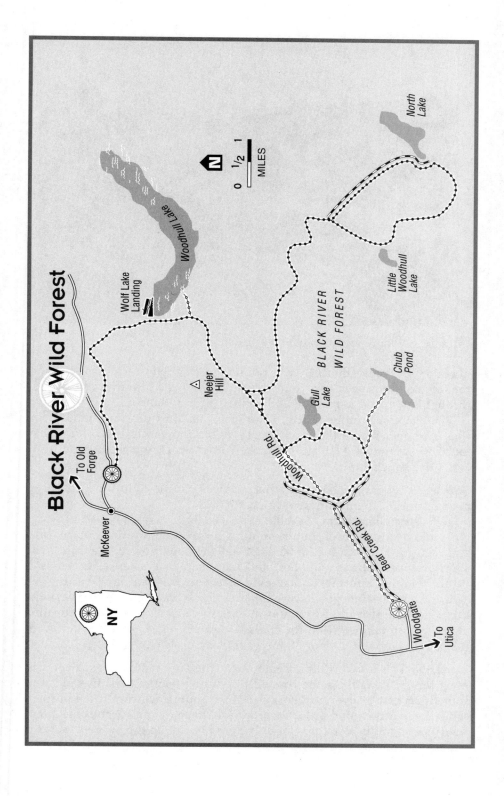

The Moose River passes through the Black River Wild Forest.

may don an orange hunting vest, but it is still risky to be moving through the forest at the speed of a young buck. The fall is a beautiful time to ride through the mixed hardwood and conifer forests, though.

The blackflies can be fierce in late spring and last until late June. Deerflies take over where the blackflies leave off and can last into July. They look like miniature F-15 jets with their swept-back wings. Remember to bring bug repellent.

Services: Lodging, food, and other services can be found in Old Forge, approximately 10 miles northeast on NY 28.

Ted Christodaro from the bike store Pedals & Petals in Inlet provides daily and overnight backcountry mountain bike tours throughout this area and is a good source for information on the condition of the trails. The shop provides repairs, supplies, and mountain bike sales. Call Pedals & Petals for any information on clinics, tours, festivals, and races. The Adirondacks has independent weather systems, and it's hard to determine the condition of trails from faraway cities. It's a good idea to telephone ahead before taking off on the trails. Mountain bikes can be rented from the Mountainman Outdoor Supply Company on NY 28 in Inlet.

Hazards: This is a long trail. Remember, whatever mileage you cover, you must return along the same route. Bring water, energy bars, first aid, and something that I never go into a forest without: a whistle. It is indispensable if you are injured or lost and need to reach out and grab some attention. The sound is piercing. Not only does it wake up the beavers, but it is better at attracting human attention than yelling.

Rescue index: The trail's proximity to well-traveled NY 28 at the beginning of the ride should be of some comfort, but as you get further into the ride, you must return the same way you came in. Along NY 28, the towns of McKeever, Otter Lake, and Woodgate are your closest bets for help. Seven miles into the ride, past Woodhull Lake, if you need to bail out, you can take the snowmobile trail out to Woodhull Road. This leads directly into Bear Creek Road and into the town of Woodgate, about 8 miles south on NY 28 from McKeever. The excellently maintained snowmobile trails are well marked with orange circular discs and are very easy to follow.

Land status: Old Forge and the central region of Adirondack Park offer a variety of terrain with exceptional natural beauty. The route follows roads and trails in the wild forests classification of Adirondack Park. They reside on state public land and are available for mountain biking. Mountain biking is presently prohibited in designated wilderness areas of Adirondack Park and where signage is posted.

The town of Web has expanded the use of its well-maintained snowmobile trails and opened the well-marked routes for mountain bikers. The potential use of the diverse Old Forge/Web trail system is limitless and is an exciting opportunity for mountain bikers to explore.

Maps: USGS 15-minute series, McKeever, North Wilmurt, Ohio, and Old Forge quadrangles provide good detail for this route. The Adirondack West-Central Wilderness Area Map published by Plinth, Quoin & Cornice Associates provides excellent topographical detail of the route and surrounding terrain and can be found at most outdoor-type stores in New York for $5.00. It is based on the USGS 15-minute series, at a scale of 1:62,500 and a contour level of 20 feet, where 1 inch = 0.98 mile.

Finding the trail: Take the New York State Thruway (Interstate 87) north to exit 24 (Albany). Take I-87 north to exit 25, Route 8/Chestertown and Hague. At the end of the exit ramp, turn left (west) onto NY 8 toward Loon Lake. After passing through Wevertown, turn right (west) at the stop sign onto NY 28. This scenic highway takes you through the towns of North Creek, Indian Lake, and Blue Mountain Lake. White-water rafting on the Hudson River is very popular, and there are many outfitters in the Indian Lake area. Continue on NY 28 west toward Inlet and Old Forge.

From Old Forge proceed another 10 miles to the town of McKeever. Turn left onto McKeever Road toward McKeever. Proceed 0.3 mile, and turn left onto a dirt road past the old railroad station. Cross the tracks, and park in the first parking area 0.6 mile from NY 28.

Sources of additional information:

Pedals & Petals
Route 28, P.O. Box 390
Inlet, NY 13360
(315) 357–3281

Old Forge Tourist Information Center
P.O. Box 68
Old Forge, NY 13420
(315) 369–6983

New York State Department of Environmental Conservation, Region 6
317 Washington Street
Watertown, NY 13601
(315) 785–2239

Mountainman Outdoor Supply Company
Route 28, P.O. Box 659
Inlet, NY 13360
(315) 357–6672

Notes on the trail: There are two access points. You can begin in McKeever and follow the Sand Lake Falls snowmobile trail. It leads south into the network. You can also begin in Woodgate and follow the Bear Creek Road to Woodhull Road, and follow the trails north to McKeever. The route description below begins at the McKeever–Sand Lake Falls trailhead.

The trail heads east, parallels a dirt truck road for about 3 miles, and then comes to a T intersection with another trail. The trail to your left leads to Remsen Falls about 1 mile north. Turn right (south), and cross a small stream. These are some of the drainage streams from Woodhull Lake. They lead farther north into Moose River. The trail begins to ascend and, in 1.3 miles from the last intersection, reaches the shore of Woodhull Lake at Wolf Lake Landing. Continue south, and soon another trail leads off to your right in a westerly direction. Ignore this trail, and remain on the main trail. After 0.6 mile bear right, and head southwest. The trail to your left leads back to Woodhull Lake. After 2.2 miles you come to a fork. The small mountain to your right (west) is known as Neejer Hill. The trail to your left leads to a 12-mile loop to Little Woodhull Lake. This loop is optional, and the map clearly describes its passage.

Bearing right will connect you to Woodhull Road. Continuing straight, ignore the next 3 trail intersections, and at 1.3 miles from the fork to Little Woodhull Lake, you'll come to a four-way intersection. Turning left or right will eventually lead you back to where you are standing. It is a 5.5-mile loop. Turn left, and pass by the west shore of Gull Lake. Continue past, and you will soon cross the Gull Lake Outlet, a small drainage stream from Gull Lake. You will begin riding on a dirt road. Take that for approximately 1 mile, and turn right (north) at the next intersection. Continuing north on the dirt road, you will again pick up the snowmobile trail, and you will soon reach the intersection where you started this little loop. To return proceed north on the snowmobile trail toward Woodhull Lake and back out to McKeever.

Cedar River Flow

Cedar River Flow provides the eastern access into the Moose River Plains Recreation Area. A 22-mile, out-and-back (11 miles one way), doubletrack dirt road penetrates into the eastern section of the Moose River Plains. The riding is fast and easy, and there is plenty of mileage to take advantage of. Only one steep pitch over the saddle between Sturges Hills at 2,700 feet and Cellar Mountain at 3,447 feet may make your knees wobble, but the rest is all easy to moderate pedaling. At the beginning of the tour, views of Cedar River open up and are then followed by the towering cliffs to the west of Roundtop and then Sugarloaf Mountains. The challenging ascent over Sturges Hill is your final obstacle, and the only item remaining is some great cruising on rolling terrain. The terrain is ideal for mountain bikers of all levels, and during the colder months the lack of foliage extends your views to the wide-open surrounding hills and mountains.

Cedar River Road was established to provide access into a popular hunting and fishing region during the latter part of the nineteenth century. W. D. Wakely built a hotel around 1870 near Cedar River Falls and advertised that boats were available for use. They were kept 14 miles farther inland in the Moose River Plains. The hotel burned down, as did so many other of the hotels and camps in the Adirondacks during the late nineteenth and early twentieth centuries.

General location: Near the towns of Blue Mountain Lake and Indian Lake in the west-central Adirondacks.

Elevation change: The old logging road begins a 1.5-mile climb up Sturges Hills from about 2,300 to 2,600 feet, where the route crests at the pass between Cellar Mountain and Sturges Hills. From the pass it's all downhill until you reach the level of the Cedar River Flow at 2,100 feet.

Season: You can ride after the wet season ends in April or May. It all depends on the amount of snow and rain from prior months. You can then ride until mid-September, which is when hunting season commences. You may don an orange hunting vest, but it is still risky to be moving through the forest at the speed of a young buck. The fall is a beautiful time to ride through the mixed hardwood and conifer forests, though.

The blackflies can be fierce in late spring and last until late June. Deerflies take over where the blackflies leave off and can last into July. They look like miniature F-15 jets with their swept-back wings. Remember to bring bug repellent.

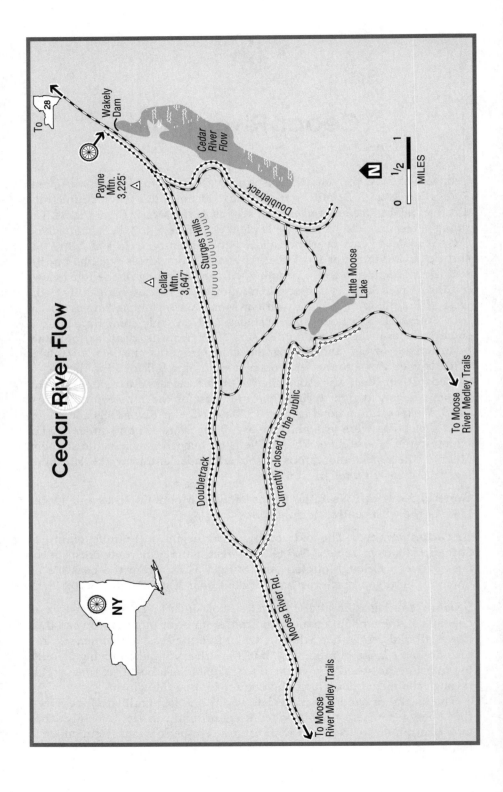

Cedar River Flow

NY

To 28

Wakely Dam

Payne Mtn.
3,225'

Cedar
River
Flow

Cellar
Mtn.
3,647'

Sturges Hills

Doubletrack

Little Moose
Lake

Doubletrack

Currently closed to the public

Moose River Rd.

To Moose
River Medley Trails

To Moose
River Medley Trails

N

0   1/2   1
MILES

Services: Blue Mountain Lake is nearby and offers the nationally acclaimed Adirondack Museum showcasing the region's history. Ted Christodaro from the bike store Pedals & Petals in Inlet provides daily and overnight backcountry mountain bike tours throughout this area and is a good source for information on the condition of the trails. The shop provides repairs, supplies, and mountain bike sales. Call Pedals & Petals for any information on clinics, tours, festivals, and races. The Adirondacks has independent weather systems, and it's hard to determine the condition of trails from faraway cities. It's a good idea to telephone ahead before taking off on the trails.

Hazards: Hunting season begins in mid-September, so if you do venture out on these roads, wear the appropriate hunter-orange colors. Call the Limekiln Ranger for further details on road conditions and the bug index.

Rescue index: Help can be flagged down on the well-traveled New York 28/30 and in Indian Lake.

Land status: New York State park land. The Department of Environmental Conservation manages the forest as a multiple-use area. The excellently maintained snowmobile trails are well marked with orange circular discs.

Maps: The Adirondack West-Central Wilderness Area Map published by Plinth, Quoin & Cornice Associates provides excellent topographical detail of the route and surrounding terrain and can be found at most outdoor-type stores in New York for $5.00. It is based on the USGS 15-minute series, at a scale of 1:62,500 and a contour level of 20 feet, where 1 inch = 0.98 mile.

Finding the trail: Take the New York State Thruway (Interstate 87) north to exit 24 (Albany). Take I-87 north to exit 25, Route 8/Chestertown and Hague. At the end of the exit ramp, turn left (west) onto NY 8 toward Loon Lake. After passing through Wevertown, turn right (west) at the stop sign onto NY 28. This scenic highway takes you through the towns of North Creek and Indian Lake. White-water rafting on the Hudson River is very popular, and there are many outfitters in the Indian Lake area. Continue on NY 28 west.

After passing through the village of Indian Lake, turn left onto Cedar River Road, which intersects NY 28/30 near Indian Lake and before Blue Mountain Lake. You may park here or drive in on the town road until its end at Wakely Dam in roughly 12 miles.

Sources of additional information:

Pedals & Petals
Route 28, P.O. Box 390
Inlet, NY 13360
(315) 357–3281

Cedar River.

Forest Ranger
Limekiln Lake
Inlet, NY 13420
(315) 357-4403

The Adirondack Museum
Route 30
Blue Mountain Lake, NY 12812
(518) 352-7311

Notes on the trail: You should register at the cabin near Wakely Dam to go into the plains or if you're just hanging out in the Wakely Dam area, for which currently there is no charge. Pedal past the gate, heading west on the well-defined, hard-packed dirt road. Bear right at a fork in a little more than 1 mile, and begin your ascent up and over the pass at Sturges Hills. Sturges Hills lie to your south, and Cellar and Payne Mountains are to the north. After descending from the pass, bear right at the next fork, and just ride to your heart's content. Remember that the distance you ride in on, you must return on that day, unless of course you are planning to spend the night camping. If you are planning an overnight, you might want to pedal toward Otter Brook Road and Moose River Road; most of the neat campsites are located along the shores of the lakes and ponds. See the Moose River Plains tour description for campsite recommendations.

Sargent Ponds Wild Forest

Sargent Ponds Wild Forest offers a 4-mile loop of double- and singletrack trails with an 8-mile, out-and-back trail (4 miles one way) tacked onto the end. The route begins as an eroded singletrack and continues along the well-marked snowmobile trails connecting two scenic ponds rimmed with evergreens. The first pond, known as Upper Sargents Pond, is a great spot for camping. The tiny islands in the middle of the lake add great beauty to the scenery. A lean-to can be found on the second pond, Lower Sargents Pond, and makes another great place to camp. From these base camps you can then set out to explore the 8-mile, out-and-back trip to Tioga Point on Raquette Lake. Tioga Point is located at about the center portion of the lake. The fairly level ride through a mature woodland of conifer and hardwood makes this out-and-back trail a pleasant and enjoyable trip. There are several lean-tos used for canoe camping, but anyone can camp in them. Reservations must be made ahead of time for the lean-tos by calling the New York State Department of Environmental Conservation at (800) 456–2267. Fifteen lean-tos and ten campsites are administered from the small Department of Environmental Conservation office at Tioga Point.

The view from Tioga Point of Raquette Lake is impressive. Although the lake is only 6.5 miles long, its many bays and peninsulas give Raquette Lake 99 miles of shoreline.

Lying west of this small jewel of a trail system is the majestic, 3,759-foot Blue Mountain and Blue Mountain Lake. Blue Mountain has a great hiking trail system, and views from the summit are something to seek out. Considered to be one of the most beautiful in the Adirondacks, Blue Mountain Lake is filled with a variety of islands.

This is a great ride, and its location is amid great canoeing, camping, and hiking.

General location: Near Blue Mountain and Long Lakes on County Route 3 in the west-central Adirondacks.

Elevation change: There is a minor ascent after leaving CR 3 and then a descent to the level of the ponds. From there it is mostly level riding. The last section of the loop you will take to leave this area requires another small ascent, followed by a short descent back to CR 3.

Season: You can ride after the wet season ends in April or May. It all depends on the amount of snow and rain from prior months. You can then

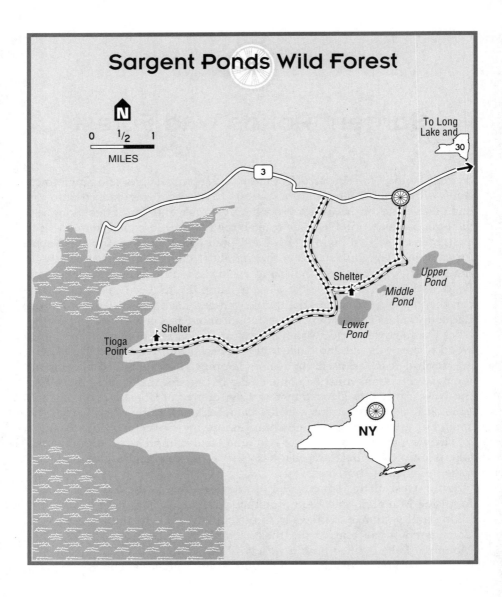

ride until mid-September, which is when hunting season commences. You may don an orange hunting vest, but it is still risky to be moving through the forest at the speed of a young buck. The fall is a beautiful time to ride through the mixed hardwood and conifer forests, though.

The blackflies can be fierce in late spring and last until late June. Deerflies take over where the blackflies leave off and can last into July. They look like miniature F-15 jets with their swept-back wings. Remember to bring bug repellent.

Upper Sargent Pond in the Sargent Ponds Wild Forest.

Services: Blue Mountain Lake is nearby and offers the nationally acclaimed Adirondack Museum, showcasing the region's history. Ted Christodaro from the bike store Pedals & Petals in Inlet provides daily and overnight backcountry mountain bike tours throughout this area and is a good source for information on the condition of the trails. The shop provides repairs, supplies, and mountain bike sales. Call Pedals & Petals for any information on clinics, tours, festivals, and races. The Adirondacks has independent weather systems, and it's hard to determine the condition of trails from faraway cities. It's a good idea to telephone ahead before taking off on the trails.

Hazards: Hunting season begins in mid-September, so if you do venture out on these roads, wear the appropriate hunter-orange color.

Rescue index: Help can be found in Blue Mountain Lake.

Land status: New York State park land. The Department of Environmental Conservation manages the forest as a multiple-use area. The excellently maintained snowmobile trails are well marked with orange circular discs.

Maps: The Adirondack Central Mountain Area Map published by Plinth, Quoin & Cornice Associates provides excellent topographical detail of the route and surrounding terrain and can be found at most outdoor-type stores in New York for $5.00. It is based on the USGS 15-minute series, at a scale of 1:62,500 and a contour level of 20 feet, where 1 inch = 0.98 mile.

Finding the trail: Take the New York State Thruway (Interstate 87) north to exit 24 (Albany). Take I-87 north to exit 25, Route 8/Chestertown and Hague. At the end of the exit ramp, turn left (west) onto New York 8 toward Loon Lake. After passing through Wevertown, turn right (west) at the stop sign onto NY 28. This scenic highway takes you through the towns of North Creek and Indian Lake. White-water rafting on the Hudson River is very popular, and there are many outfitters in the Indian Lake area. Continue on NY 28 west.

Turn right (north) at Blue Mountain Lake onto NY 30. Drive about 8 miles to Deerland. Deerland is located at the southern end of Long Lake. Turn left onto North Point Road (CR 3), and park near the New York State Department of Environmental Conservation trailhead 6.3 miles on your left.

Sources of additional information:

Pedals & Petals
Route 28, P.O. Box 390
Inlet, NY 13360
(315) 357–3281

Forest Ranger
Limekiln Lake
Inlet, NY 13420
(315) 357–4403

The Adirondack Museum
Route 30
Blue Mountain Lake, NY 12812
(518) 352–7311

Notes on the trail: Pedal south over level ground, and then ascend a small hill at 1 mile. The trail descends steeply to an intersection. A trail to the left (east) leads to the campsite on the shore of the upper pond.

Bear right (west) at the intersection to continue the ride. The trail meanders along the contours of the hills to your right (north), crossing the stream that connects the upper and lower ponds. In about 1.5 miles the trail comes to a T intersection with another trail. Turning right (north) will return you to CR 3 (1.5 miles west on CR 3 from where you parked and began riding). This is the loop. To begin the out and back, turn left (south). A small, yellow-marked trail leads 0.4 mile east to the Sargent Pond lean-to on your left.

Continuing on the snowmobile trail, remain straight ahead as the trail hugs the eastern shore of the lower pond.

The Osgood/Jackrabbit Run

This tour is great if you come with some people who would like to visit the Adirondack Park Visitor Interpretive Center at Paul Smiths. They can drop you off at the trailhead and go on ahead to the Interpretive Center. You can meet them there later, after you have completed a 9-mile, moderately level doubletrack that exits at the doors of the center. Very convenient. The route travels over the famed Jackrabbit Cross-Country Ski Trail and passes by the very scenic Osgood Pond. A small detour toward the end of the route, from the Jackrabbit Trail, brings you to an incredible singletrack that skirts the shores of Osgood Pond. Several lean-tos dot the shoreline and make for excellent campsites. The route passes over mostly old back roads and logging roads that are wide and well defined.

The Jackrabbit Ski Trail was constructed in 1986 to improve the cross-country skiing in the Lake Placid–Saranac Lake area. It is named in memory of Herman "Jack Rabbit" Johannsen, who laid out many of the trails himself. He was a pioneer of Lake Placid skiing from 1916 to 1928 and died in 1987 at 111. The trail described in this route travels on a small portion of the Jackrabbit Trail system from Lake Clear Junction to the Adirondack Park Visitor Interpretive Center at Paul Smiths. You will also pass White Pine Road, which leads to the 1907 White Pine Camp that served as the summer White House for President Calvin Coolidge in 1926. Located on thirty-five acres of majestic pines and wetlands, this "great camp" has 3,900 feet of shoreline on Osgood Pond.

The area has an abundance of wildlife. We saw the eastern chipmunk and some loons near Osgood Pond. The forest around Osgood Pond is mostly red pine. This tall conifer reaches heights of 80 feet and has a diameter of 3 feet. The bark is made of diamond-shaped plates. The needles from these majestic trees carpet the singletrack that borders the Osgood Pond shoreline.

General location: North of the village of Saranac Lake in Franklin County in the Adirondack Park of northeastern New York.

Elevation change: The route follows terrain that is slightly hilly. There is more flat terrain than hills.

Season: The route travels through wetlands and is best ridden during early summer after the blackflies have found better things to do with

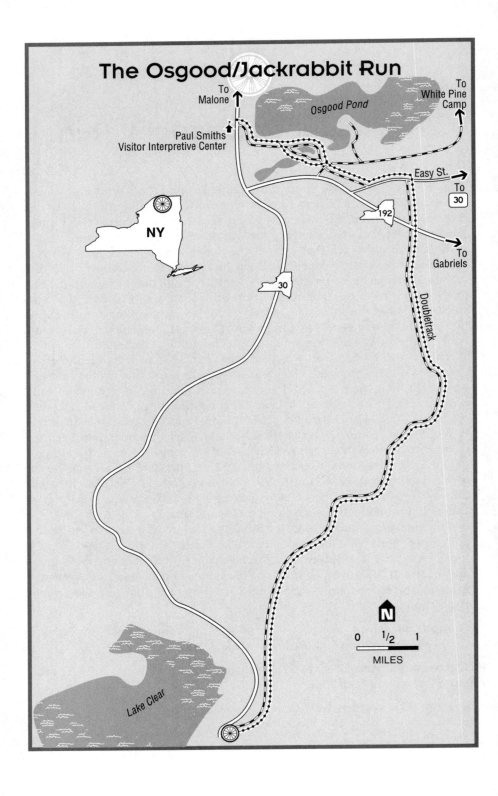

The Osgood/Jackrabbit Run

To Malone

Osgood Pond

To White Pine Camp

Paul Smiths Visitor Interpretive Center

Easy St.

To 30

192

To Gabriels

NY

30

Doubletrack

N

0   1/2   1

MILES

Lake Clear

Singletrack surrounded by dense wilderness on the Osgood/Jackrabbit Trail.

themselves. You can ride well into the winter, providing there is no snow on the ground.

Services: Most services can be found in the village of Saranac Lake, approximately 7 miles from the trailhead on New York 86. The Visitor's Interpretive Center offers rest-room facilities, water, picnic tables, and ranger information. It also has exhibits on the human and natural history of Adirondack Park. Wildlife and ecological processes are described along a network of interpretive nature trails on the 2,800-acre tract.

Hazards: This is a long trail, and in the summer it's quite dry. Bring water and bug repellent.

Rescue index: Vehicles flagged down on the well-traveled NY 30 can be a source of help. Help can also be found at the Adirondack Park Visitor Interpretive Center at Paul Smiths.

Land status: New York State Forest Preserve.

Maps: The Adirondack Canoe Map published by Plinth, Quoin & Cornice Associates provides detail of the surrounding area and can be found at most outdoor-type stores in the Adirondacks for $5.00.

Finding the trail: Take the New York State Thruway (Interstate 87) north to exit 24 (Albany). Take I-87 north to exit 30. Pick up NY 9 north, and follow it for 2 miles to NY 73. Continue on NY 73 for 28 miles to the Lake Placid area. Pass through Lake Placid, and continue on NY 86 toward Saranac Lake. Continue on NY 86 through Saranac Lake and past Lake Colby. Turn left (west) onto County Route 186 toward Lake Clear Junction. At Lake Clear Junction turn right (north) onto NY 30. Travel about half a mile north of the junction. A small parking area and dirt road are directly across the roadway from the Lake Clear Elementary School. You may park your car here or have someone drop you off and then continue north for about 9 miles on NY 30 to the Adirondack Park Visitor Center at Paul Smiths. You can meet up with them later.

Sources of additional information:

Saranac Lake Area Chamber of Commerce
30 Main Street
Saranac Lake, NY 12983
(800) 347–1992, (518) 891–1990

Placid Planet Bicycles
51 Saranac Avenue
Lake Placid, NY 12946
(518) 523–4128
www.placidplanetbicycles.com

Adirondack Park Visitor Interpretive Center
Route 30, Box 3000
Paul Smiths, NY 12970
(518) 327–3000

Notes on the trail: The hard-packed doubletrack follows the power line for 0.1 mile to a main transmission line. Turn left at the main transmission line. You will then pass over two gravel roads. At about 2.8 miles the Jackrabbit Trail makes a sharp right away from the transmission line. The route now follows a wide lumber road. You reach a gravel pit at 4.2 miles. The Jackrabbit Trail now follows an old woods road for a short distance and goes right onto a narrow trail, reaching Montou Clearing at 5 miles. NY 86 is reached in just less than 6 miles. Cross NY 86, ascend for a short distance, and descend to Jones Pond Road (CR 31) at 6.7 miles. The trail continues across the road. Continue up a small incline, and soon the trail intersects with White Pine Road. White Pine Road leads to the White Pine Camp. Continue on the Jackrabbit Trail, crossing over a small bridge that spans the channel between Little Osgood and Church Ponds. The route joins a trail with red paint splashes, known as the Red Dot Trail. Continue straight through a four-way intersection at 8 miles. In 0.3 mile turn right at another intersection, and descend to a small open field in 0.4 mile on the western end of Osgood Pond. Some dirt roads lead to the shore of Osgood Pond. The yellow-blazed Osgood Pond shoreline trail is located along the pond and makes a great intermediate singletrack. The trail is carpeted with pine needles and hugs scenic Osgood Pond. The lean-tos along the shore can be reached with this trail.

From the open field a doubletrack trail leads to NY 30. Continue for a short distance north on NY 30 to the Interpretive Center at 9 miles.

Sweet Oseetah

About 4 miles of interesting beginner and intermediate dirt roads and singletrack weave through the dense conifer Saranac Lakes Wild Forest. This small network of interconnecting trails provides an excellent opportunity to sample a combination of singletrack and doubletrack mountain bike trails. Though the mileage only adds up to about 4 in total, the trails provide you with great scenery and a small test of your skills.

The easy-cruising, wide Oseetah Marsh snowmobile trail is 0.7 mile long. The surface is carpeted with the fallen needles of the tall, dense, red and white pine forest it passes through. The entire forest is filled with evergreens and is well shaded, with shafts of sunlight poking through openings in the canopy. Gliding silently on the bed of pine needles is an enjoyable treat. The trail's easy passage makes this a delight for families with small children and those new to the sport. The Oseetah Marsh Trail leads to the marshy shoreline of Lake Oseetah. Lake Oseetah is attractive, with many rocky islands sporting birch and pine trees on their tiny acreage in the lake. A 0.4-mile, beginner spur trail swings off the marsh trail and descends to another section of Oseetah Lake shoreline. Views of the lake, Ampersand Mountain, and the Sawtooth Range open up. The 0.4-mile-long Balsam Spur Trail singletrack winds over undulating terrain and requires intermediate skills to maneuver the many twists and turns. A 0.4-mile, beginner singletrack leads off the Oseetah Marsh Trail soon after leaving the parking area. The smooth, mostly flat trail arrives near the shoreline of the small Turtle Pond. This small network of trails offers a great opportunity to sample different types of trail riding for all levels.

General location: Seven miles west of the village of Lake Placid, Essex County, in the Adirondack Park of northeastern New York.

Elevation change: There is no appreciable elevation gain or loss. There are perhaps a few minor hills to climb, but the trails undulate over a generally flat terrain.

Season: The trails are open and available for riding throughout the year. Of course, if they are covered with snow, you might consider putting on some cross-country skis and exploring the trails. The dense evergreen forest causes most rains to be quickly absorbed into the porous, peaty soil.

Services: Most services can be found in the village of Saranac Lake.

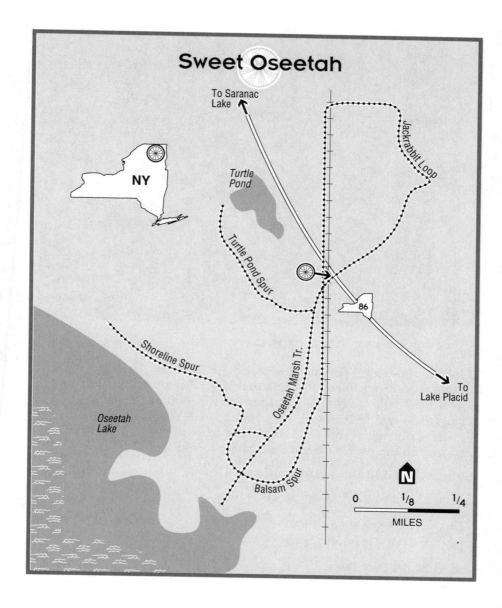

Sweet Oseetah

To Saranac Lake

Jackrabbit Loop

NY

Turtle Pond

Turtle Pond Spur

86

To Lake Placid

Shoreline Spur

Oseetah Marsh Tr.

Oseetah Lake

Balsam Spur

N

0   1/8   1/4

MILES

Hazards: Be careful when crossing busy New York 86.

Rescue index: The trails are all within a mile of NY 86, where help can be obtained from a passing motorist.

Land status: New York State land.

Maps: The Adirondack Canoe Map published by Plinth, Quoin & Cornice Associates provides some detail of the route and nearby vicinity. It can be found at most outdoor-type stores in the Adirondacks for $5.00.

Singletrack simplicity through the evergreen canyons of the Oseetah Lake Trails.

Finding the trail: Take the New York State Thruway (Interstate 87) north to exit 24 (Albany). Take I-87 north to exit 30. Pick up NY 9 north, and follow it for 2 miles to NY 73. Continue on NY 73 for 28 miles to the Lake Placid area. Pass Lake Placid, and continue on NY 86 toward Saranac Lake for approximately 7 miles. Pass over the railroad tracks after Ray Brook, and park in the parking area immediately to your left.

Sources of additional information:

Saranac Lake Area Chamber of Commerce
30 Main Street
Saranac Lake, NY 12983
(800) 347–1992, (518) 891–1990

Placid Planet Bicycles
51 Saranac Avenue
Lake Placid, NY 12946
(518) 523–4128
www.placidplanetbicycles.com

Notes on the trail: From the parking area, head south directly into the forest, where you will pick up and follow the orange-marked snowmobile trail. This is the Oseetah Marsh Trail. The route follows a wide, double-track path through a dense pine forest. An unmarked trail soon forks to the right. This is the flat, Turtle Pond singletrack spur. It is 0.4 mile in length, and at the end you must turn around.

After returning from Turtle Pond, continue south on the Oseetah Marsh Trail. At 0.4 mile, another doubletrack soon forks to the right in a westerly direction. This path is 0.4 mile in length also and leads down to the shore of Lake Oseetah. Beginners beware: The wide, inviting doubletrack deteriorates into an exposed-root singletrack as you approach the proximity of the lake's shoreline.

Return from this shoreline trail, and continue south along the Oseetah Marsh Trail to its terminus at the marshy shore of Lake Oseetah. During the winter cross-country skiers and snowmobile enthusiasts continue beyond this point across the lake.

There are two options for your return. Beginners ought to head back along the Oseetah Marsh Trail. Intermediate to advanced riders can tackle the Balsam Spur singletrack that appears to your right soon after returning from the terminus of Oseetah Marsh Trail. Fork right, and ascend the unmarked singletrack through a spruce-and-fir woodland. After winding through this attractive forest, you soon reach higher ground. The trail is 0.8 mile in length and leads back in a northerly direction to the parking area on NY 86.

There is still one more small, 1.1-mile trail to sample before leaving Sweet Oseetah. Across from the parking area, to the left of a silver-painted, metal transformer box, is another singletrack loop. Cross NY 86, and enter the woods to pick up an orange-marked snowmobile trail. In approximately 500 feet you may be required to dismount and carry your bike around a small, flooded section of trail. Afterward the route ascends to higher and drier ground, passing through an attractive pine forest. Continue along the snowmobile trail down a small hill. You will arrive in a red pine woodland. At 0.3 mile turn left onto the red-blazed Jackrabbit Trail. Follow this cross-country ski route, which soon descends to railroad tracks at 0.7 mile. Proceed over the tracks and turn left. Pedal along the sandy road back to NY 86 and your parking area.

Kushaqua Loop Trail

This tour traverses the rolling country of small mountains and is blessed with a lake-filled landscape. Pedaling along this 13-mile loop over doubletrack and quiet backcountry dirt roads is recommended for those who wish to spend a leisurely day cruising the countryside. While riding along the scenic shores of Lake Kushaqua, you will be enchanted by the bordering columns of tall, white birch trees that line the route. The hardpacked surface is a pleasure to ride on and makes this trip ideal for families and people seeking a day of easy pedaling. Buck Pond public campground, which is part of the tour, offers a full day of recreational possibilities. After completing the loop you may wish to swim at Buck Pond's wide sandy beach, stay overnight in the campground, or canoe on Lake Kushaqua and paddle to several other nearby ponds and lakes.

The Adirondack Park is the middle ground between the northern, largely coniferous forests, mixed with spruces and firs, and the hardwood, deciduous species like beeches, birches, and maples. This mixture of flora is very interesting to ride through. During the autumn the forests are filled with brilliant colors accented by the deep, rich, perpetual tones of the evergreens, as seen in the surrounding hillsides. The land was glaciated 10,000 years ago, smoothing out the much larger mountains that long ago eroded away. As you pedal along take a moment to study the lowland mountains, the sandy soils and beaches, and the many bodies of water that dot the land. These features were carved and deposited by the great Ice Age. As the climate warmed and the glaciers melted, the land was flooded with fast-flowing streams from the retreating glaciers. Sediments were carried and deposited. Lakes and ponds appeared and disappeared. Bike through geologic history, and imagine acres of ice a thousand feet thick moving over the land! It did happen.

General location: North of the village of Saranac Lake, Franklin County, in the Adirondack Park of northeastern New York.

Elevation change: About 2 miles of level doubletrack skirt the shoreline of Lake Kushaqua. The remaining dirt roads follow easy grades with no strenuous hill climbs or descents.

Season: You can ride this tour in most seasons. Of course if the trails are well covered with snow, you might want to choose another time. Blackflies come out in strength in late spring, from May to June, and it is advisable

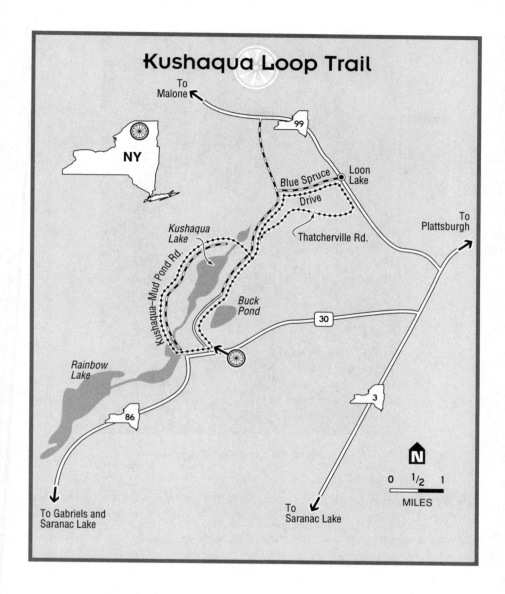

Kushaqua Loop Trail

to bring bug repellent. Fall is brilliant and shouldn't be missed in any part of the Adirondacks. The campground opens in May and remains open through Labor Day. The registration booth is open daily from 8:00 A.M. to 9:00 P.M.

Services: Most services can be found in the village of Saranac Lake. There is a small delicatessen 6 miles away in Gabriels.

Hazards: These backcountry roads occasionally see light traffic, so pay attention while cruising and looking at the scenery.

Cruising on the birch-bordered Kushaqua doubletrack.

Rescue index: A facility supervisor is on the premises at all times at Buck Pond public campground. Help can also be found in nearby Gabriels.

Land status: Buck Pond is on New York State land, and the roads are public.

Maps: USGS 7.5-minute series, Loon Lake and Debar Mountain quadrangles provide good detail of the surrounding countryside. The accompanying map should provide most of the detail needed for completing the loop. Buck Pond campground hands out a general map of the area after you pay a $4.00 day-use fee.

Finding the trail: Take the New York State Thruway (Interstate 87) north to exit 24 (Albany). Take I-87 north to exit 30. Pick up New York 9 north, and follow it for 2 miles to NY 73. Continue on NY 73, and pass through Lake Placid. Continue on NY 86 toward Saranac Lake. Follow the signs for NY 86 through Saranac Lake, and continue to Gabriels. In Gabriels take

County Route 30 6 miles to Buck Pond public campground. You can park along the access road or in one of the parking areas in the campground.

Sources of additional information:

Saranac Lake Area Chamber of Commerce
30 Main Street
Saranac Lake, NY 12983
(800) 347–1992, (518) 891–1990

Placid Planet Bicycles
51 Saranac Avenue
Lake Placid, NY 12946
(518) 523–4128
www.placidplanetbicycles.com

Buck Pond Public Campground
Franklin County Road 30
Onchiota, NY 12968
(518) 891–3449

Notes on the trail: Pedal back to CR 30, and turn right (west) toward Onchiota. Turn right (north) onto Kushaqua–Mud Pond Road. You will cross a small bridge at 3 miles. You may at this point return to Buck Pond campground by making a sharp right after the bridge beyond a metal barrier. This is a doubletrack that skirts the eastern shore of Lake Kushaqua.

Thatcherville Road intersects from the right with the route at 4 miles. You will return along Thatcherville Road later. Continue past Thatcherville Road and after approximately 1 mile, turn right (east) onto Blue Spruce Drive into Loon Lake. You will arrive at the intersection with NY 99 at 6.2 miles. Turn right onto this paved road, and cruise down a pleasant hill. At the bottom of the hill, turn right onto Thatcherville Road. The ride along this dirt road is extremely interesting, as it meanders with and parallels the north branch of the Saranac River. After about 3.5 miles from the intersection of NY 99, you will arrive back at Kushaqua–Mud Pond Road. Turn left (southwest), and continue for about 1 mile. Just before the small iron bridge, turn left onto the doubletrack that leads around the eastern shore of Lake Kushaqua and into the Buck Pond public campground.

The Great Santanoni

The 5-mile, hard-packed dirt road to Newcomb Lake in the 12,000-acre Santanoni Preserve is a great one-day adventure. The road is easy to ride. Those new to mountain biking who have not ventured beyond the lower mileage trips will find this tour a pleasure. The well-graded surface, easy pedaling, and scenic assets provide a fun and fulfilling package. The 10-mile (total) out-and-back tour is along a well-maintained road that traverses a mixed deciduous and coniferous forest. The wide road is not technically challenging, and its smoothness, good condition, and gentle, rolling grade facilitate a sort of out-of-saddle experience. On this trail you do not have to try hard to feel great and ride at one with nature. The preserve was once a very large private estate. The one-way, 5-mile route leads you up a gentle grade and near its end descends to the shores of the very scenic and remote Newcomb Lake, surrounded by majestic mountains. The imposing Santanoni Peak at 4,607 feet can be seen beyond the northern shores of the lake. Two smaller mountains, Baldwin and Moose Mountains, just less than 3,000 feet, fill in the western horizon.

You will pass by the remains of a barn, silo, stone milking house, and great camp that were owned and built by the well-to-do Pruyn family of Albany. Situated amid a cedar grove along the rocky southeastern shores of the lake, their great camp, built in the classic Adirondack architectural style, consisted of an enormous rustic lodge, boathouse, and lakeside studio. Many of the "great camps" constructed during this bygone era were located on some remote lake and were created as family retreats. Increasing affluence toward the end of the nineteenth century and a desire to pursue leisure activities in the wilderness led many wealthy individuals to build rustic inns, lavish hotels, and family retreats in the Adirondacks. Trains and steamboats ferried families from New York and Boston spending entire summers. The years from 1870 to 1910 were called the Gilded Years. They represented the burgeoning, socially trendy pursuits of relaxation, adventures in the wilderness, and the quest for spiritual and physical well-being. The idyllic mountain and lake atmosphere and camping, fishing, and boating became vacation pastimes for many New Yorkers and Bostonians.

The sounds and sights of this bygone era have been replaced by the chatter of wildlife, and the overgrown environment is a return to the natural solitude. This old forest road provides an opportunity to experience a historical, pristine, and enchanting forest environment.

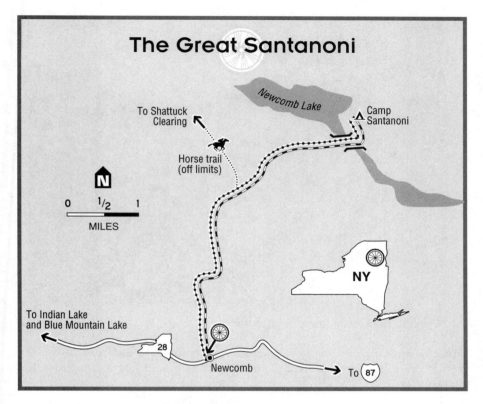

The Great Santanoni

To Shattuck Clearing

Newcomb Lake

Camp Santanoni

Horse trail (off limits)

0 1/2 1

MILES

NY

To Indian Lake and Blue Mountain Lake

28

Newcomb

To 87

General location: Just outside the village of Newcomb in the central area of Adirondack Park in northeastern New York.

Elevation change: The route gradually ascends for a little more than 3 miles and then gently descends to the shores of Newcomb Lake.

Season: The blackflies can be fierce in late spring. I passed by several hikers and canoeists sporting bug netting that covered their heads and arms. One tends to avoid the little buggers cruising on a mountain bike, but when you stop they swarm all over you as if you were sent as a special, alluring bug gift.

Services: The nearby town of Newcomb has some services, but you should stock up on picnic supplies before you set out for the day if you intend to spend time around Newcomb Lake. Camping at one of the lean-tos overlooking the lake is available by obtaining a camping permit from the ranger on duty at the gatehouse.

Hazards: Equestrians, walkers, and bikers gladly share the trails. You will encounter horses and hikers on the same trails, so display a mutual respect and courtesy for each other, and this beautiful preserve will remain a recreation area for all to enjoy. A passing hello has always been met with one in return from equestrians and hikers. They are glad to see you enjoying the preserve, too.

Newcomb Lake in the Santanoni Preserve.

Rescue index: You are not far from well-traveled New York 28N. The return route is mostly downhill, making it easy and fast to return to the parking area.

Land status: The preserve was first sold to another family who then sold it to the Nature Conservancy in 1972. In 1973 the land was transferred to New York. The New York State Department of Environmental Conservation now manages the property with special restrictions on fishing, camping, and motorized vehicles, but it's fortunately open to bicyclists.

Maps: The Adirondack High Peaks Region Area Map published by Plinth, Quoin & Cornice Associates provides excellent topographical detail of the route and surrounding terrain and can be found at most outdoor-type stores in New York for $5.00. It is based on the USGS 15-minute series, at a scale of 1:62,500 and a contour level of 20 feet, where 1 inch = 0.98 mile.

Finding the trail: Take the New York State Thruway (Interstate 87) north to exit 24 (Albany). Take I-87 (Adirondack Northway) north to exit 29. Pick up Blue Ridge Road, and follow it for about 40 minutes. Continue on NY 28N west, passing the Harris Lake Campsite in 3.1 miles and crossing the Hudson River in 3.4 miles. The entrance to the preserve is in Newcomb. A small sign just down from the main road marks the narrow access road. Cross a narrow iron bridge, pass the gatehouse on your right, and proceed to the top of the hill, where you will find a small parking lot. The only requirement for riding on this property is that you register your name at the kiosk near the parking area.

Sources of additional information:

Placid Planet Bicycles
51 Saranac Avenue
Lake Placid, NY 12946
(518) 523–4128
www.placidplanetbicycles.com

Adirondack Park Agency
P.O. Box 99, Route 86
Ray Brook, NY 12977
(518) 891–4050

New York State Department of Environmental Conservation, Region 5
P.O. Box 296, Route 86
Ray Brook, NY 12977
(518) 897–1211

Lake Placid/Essex County Convention and Visitors Bureau
216 Main Street
Lake Placid, NY 12946
(800) 447–5224
www.lakeplacid.com

Notes on the trail: A forest of large hemlock, spruce, tamarack, cedar, and birch greets you just beyond the gatehouse. The road alternates between flat and gentle grades for 0.9 mile to a group of old farm buildings with stone walls edging the fields. You will pass the abandoned homes of the farm families who kept the Pruyn family dairy herd and gardens. An interesting stone building was the milk house, and the smaller stone shed beyond the last cottage was the smokehouse. Proceed past the buildings, swinging left and gradually up to the crest of a hill at 1.1 miles. A 1-mile descent brings you to a beautiful stone bridge. From the bridge you will climb gently to the intersection with Moose Pond Road. Keep to the right because the Moose Pond Trail, which connects with the Cold River horse trails, is not open to bikes. You will climb gently for another quarter-mile to where the road flattens out and begins to descend to the south shore of Newcomb Lake, to a promontory where a picnic table overlooks the lake. Beyond this the bridge carries you over a narrow neck of the lake. Continue along the road, which turns west, past some numbered campsites for 0.4 mile to the old estate and boathouse. The massive log architecture of these old buildings, with their wide porches and covered breezeways, represents a bygone era of Adirondack history. Rustic logs geometrically pattern the doors, and enormous fieldstone fireplaces heated the numerous rooms. This was the typical building style of the late-nineteenth- and early-twentieth-century Adirondack retreats. Position yourself at the boathouse where you can see Moose Mountain in the west with Santanoni Mountain. Return along the same route.

Perkins Clearing

A combination of snowmobile trails and old forest roads provides access throughout 16,000 acres of New York State and International Paper Company (IP) land. An entire network of logging and forest roads branches to remote, scenic places and encompasses anywhere from 10- to 20-mile trips. The well-conditioned roads are wide and smooth and a joy to ride on. You can spend a half to a full day exploring these old logging and forest roads. The riding is moderately challenging as you pedal on hard-packed surfaces and over small hills.

Perkins Clearing was historically known as the place on the way to another place. During the early part of the nineteenth century, a state road passed through Perkins Clearing, crossing the southern Adirondacks and connecting Albany to an area navigable by a boat near the St. Lawrence River. The route, called Albany Road, became a state road in 1812. One of the trails described below traverses part of that route and follows the old forest trail from Perkins Clearing to Sled Harbor. The route then continues along Old Military Road and follows through a pass to the north of Pillsbury Mountain. Sled Harbor was the point at which lumber supplies were unloaded from horse-drawn wagons and loaded onto sleds destined for the lumber and hunting camps in the remote wilderness of the West Canadas. The West Canadas are a region of high-altitude lakes and forests favored for their hunting and fishing.

A 1984 land swap between IP and New York State provided access for recreationalists through IP land into state land. The constitutionally approved deal opened up some serious off-road opportunities for the adventure-seeking mountain biker.

General location: Near Indian Lake in Hamilton County, eastern-central region of Adirondack Park in northeastern New York.

Elevation change: The moderately hilly terrain is potentially challenging for an intermediate rider.

Season: The blackflies can be fierce in late spring. Avoid Perkins Clearing during hunting season or you may find more excitement than you bargained for.

Services: Services can be found in the town of Speculator, farther south on New York 30.

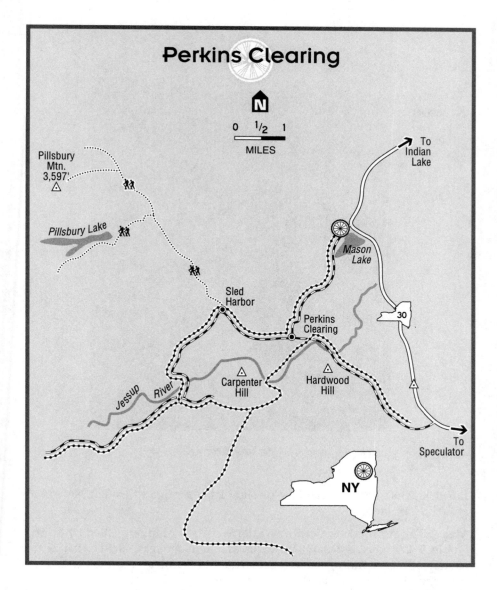

Hazards: Call the New York State Department of Environmental Conservation for information on hunting regulations. The season begins in mid-September. Pay attention to vehicle traffic that occasionally uses these dirt roads. Your tendency to bomb down some hill should be tempered by an awareness for blind turns. You never know when a car, animal, or other biker could be rounding the bend.

Rescue index: There is not a whole lot out here, and the nearest and largest town is Speculator, 7 miles to the south on NY 30. Remember to bring the proper provisions for first aid, food, and water.

Creeks and bogs near Perkins Clearing.

Land status: These secondary public dirt roads pass through New York State and IP land.

Maps: The Adirondack Central Wilderness Area Map published by Plinth, Quoin & Cornice Associates provides excellent topographical detail of the route and surrounding terrain and can be found at most outdoor-type stores in New York for $5.00. It is based on the USGS 15-minute series, at a scale of 1:62,500 and a contour level of 20 feet, where 1 inch = 0.98 mile.

Finding the trail: Take the New York State Thruway (Interstate 87) north to exit 24 (Albany). Take I-87 north to the exit for Warrensburg and NY 28. Take NY 9 into NY 28. Follow NY 28 for 10 miles to Wevertown. Turn left (west) onto NY 8 for 30 miles to Speculator. Follow NY 30 north from Speculator, and take the dirt road at the north end of Mason Lake. Park anywhere along the road and start to ride.

Source of additional information:

Hamilton County Tourism
County Office Building
White Birch Lane, Box 771
Indian Lake, NY 12842-0771
(518) 648–5239

The Downtube
466 Madison Avenue
Albany, NY 12208
(518) 434–1711

Notes on the trail: Continue on the dirt road south past Mason Lake for about 3 miles. The dirt road parallels the Mason Lake Outlet Stream. Soon you approach a fork at Perkins Clearing. Bear right (west) onto Forest Trail, past the gate, for 2 miles. You will reach the small hamlet of Sled Harbor. You may continue straight after Sled Harbor and take an optional day-hike to Pillsbury Lake or Pillsbury Mountain at 3,597 feet.

Turn left (southwest) at Sled Harbor, continuing on the dirt road for 3.5 miles and crossing several streams and the Jessup River; you'll reach a T intersection. An optional dirt road that heads into the wilderness can be your choice by turning right (west) at this intersection. It is a 7-mile, one-way dirt road you must return on, bringing your total distance for this dirt road spur to 14 miles. Turning left at the intersection takes you along another dirt road that runs up and over Carpenter Hill. In 1.6 miles the dirt road ends, and you can follow two snowmobile trail options, one of which takes you back to Perkins Clearing.

You may turn right and continue south on one snowmobile trail. It meanders for about 6.5 miles into the Jessup River Wild Forest, paralleling the Mossy Vly Brook and eventually reaching Fawn Lake. This route tends to skirt swamp areas and may be extremely wet, so keep that in mind.

Turn left onto the snowmobile trail, and continue north for about 2 miles to arrive at an intersection with Perkins Clearing. At this point you may return to your vehicle by turning left to Perkins Clearing, and then right at the Perkins Clearing intersection back to your parking area.

If you are in the mood for some more riding, turn right (southeast) onto the dirt road, and proceed up and over Hardwood Hill. Upon descending from Hardwood Hill, notice another dirt road to your right. Turn right onto this dirt road past a gate heading south. This route continues for another 4.5 miles, meandering into the wilderness and paralleling Place Brook. You must return along the same road to get back. If you have completed this dirt road spur, you can now return to Perkins Clearing by turning left after the gate and heading over Hardwood Hill. At Perkins Clearing turn right to return to your parking area.

Lapland Lake

Lapland Lake, located in the low, rugged mountains and valleys of the southern section of the Adirondack Park and Forest Preserve, is a self-enclosed mountain bike mecca. More than 16 miles of well-maintained, wide, rolling, doubletrack trails traverse and network through hundreds of pristine, wooded acres of a private resort. During the winter months the Lapland Lake Vacation Center is one of the Northeast's finest cross-country ski centers. During the summer months the well-configured cross-country ski trail network provides a variety of mountain bike routes that will appeal to all levels and is a work of trail art. Novice riders will enjoy the easy cruising trails and scenic beauty of the countryside, and intermediate riders can test their endurance and skills over the more challenging routes. This oasis of trails is surrounded by vast mountain ranges and accented by a serene, seventy-acre, spring-fed wilderness lake. If you decide this is where you want to ride, there is only one requirement: You must stay at the Lapland Lake Resort to use their trail system.

This rustic, cozy setting, reminiscent of Finland, combines solitude and relaxation with exciting mountain biking. It is owned and operated by former Olympic skier Olavi Hirvonen and his family. Ann and Olavi Hirvonen are your hosts and the owners of the Lapland Lake Visitor Center. The experienced staff is eager to help you enjoy your time there.

Stay in one of their tupas, or cottages, with wood-burning stoves and screened porches, and ride the trails. These facilities are available exclusively to overnight guests.

Tervetuloa (welcome)!

General location: Northeastern New York, in the southeastern section of Adirondack Park.

Elevation change: The trails traverse hilly terrain with no appreciable or difficult ascents and descents.

Season: The trails are available for riding after spring thaws, sometime in late May when the land dries out, until late fall. Call the Lapland Visitor Center for more details on the condition of the trails.

Services: Overnight lodging includes free use of rowboats, canoes, beach and swimming facilities, lawn games, hiking, and a Finnish wood-burning sauna. There are ten private two-, three-, and four-bedroom tupas. Immaculately maintained, each tupa contains a living room, separate bedrooms, a bathroom with shower, and a fully equipped kitchen. An 1800s farm-house can also be reserved for large groups and families. Mountain bike rentals and children's bike trailers are also available on the premises. The village of Northville, 9 miles away, offers golf, tennis, antiques, and coun-try stores.

At day's end, cool off your tires and head into the sauna. Afterward, you can say only one thing: *Kiitos saunasta* (thank you for sauna).

Hazards: The routes are well maintained, and the only hazard may be that you are enjoying yourself too much and might not return to work on time.

Rescue index: All trails lead back to the visitor center where help can be found.

Land status: Private land.

Maps: The visitor center provides the most detailed map of all the trails. Pick one up before heading out. All trails are marked with the standard cross-country ski trail marking system, and there are trail signs and cor-responding numbers at most intersections. Most of the Lapland trails are designated as one way.

Finding the trail: Lapland Lake is just over an hour's drive from Albany and 4 hours from New York City. Take the New York State Thruway (Inter-state 87) to exit 27 at Amsterdam, and follow New York 30 north 27 miles. Turn left onto Benson Road for 5.2 miles. Take a right onto Storer Road for the remaining 0.7 mile, bearing right.

Source of additional information:

Lapland Lake Nordic Vacation Center
139 Lapland Lake Road
Northville, NY 12134
(518) 863–4974
www.laplandlake.com

Notes on the trail: A large array of trails awaits the energetic mountain biker at Lapland Lake. A tremendous number of riding configurations can be created on the maze of trails and will fill up an entire day of bike rid-ing and exploration. Check in at the office, grab a map, pick a trail, and just begin riding. The routes are well marked and impeccably maintained. The printed map of the trail system will help you to determine and plan which trail to take.

To begin with you might want to warm up with the easier, flat trail net-work, consisting of the Lake Trail, Talvi Tie (Winter Road), and Era Polku (Forest Trail). If you wish to head for the more challenging and scenic trails, Sisu (Determination) provides 3 miles of rolling, grass-covered trails that pass along the rocky Grant Stream and through stands of giant pine.

Lapland Lake

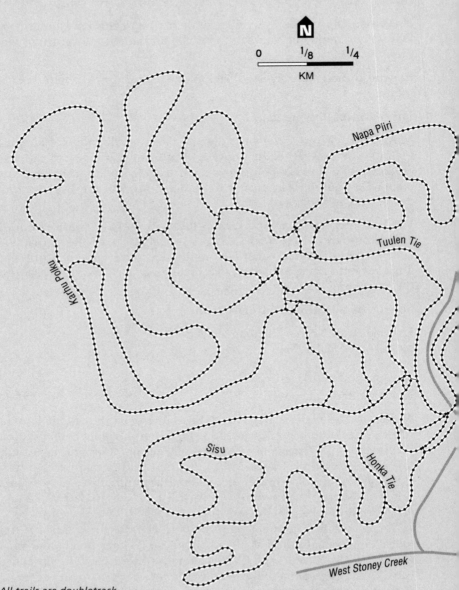

Napa Piiri

Tuulen Tie

Kahu polku

Sisu

Honka Tie

West Stoney Creek

Note: *All trails are doubletrack.*

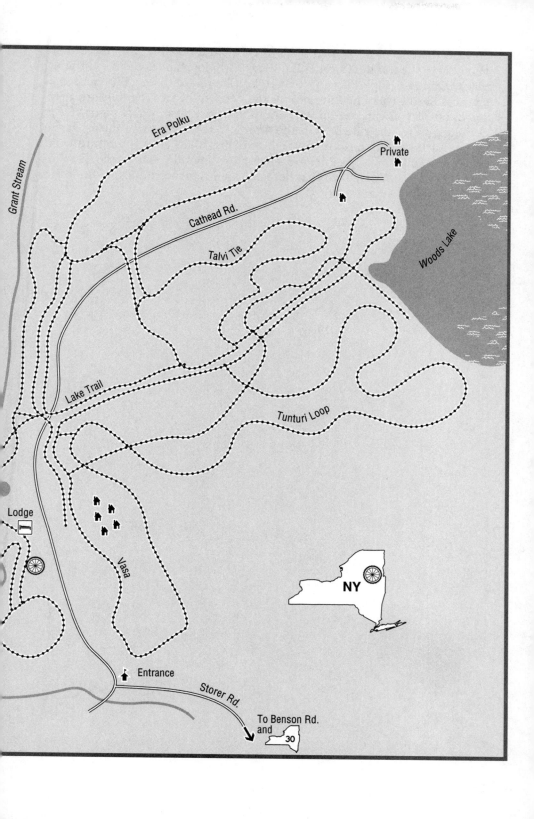

Toward the end of Sisu, turn off at the Leilan Latu link, which will connect you to the 3-mile Karhu Polku (Bear Path) loop and the more difficult, black diamond Napa Piiri (Arctic Circle). There are three hilly loops that spur off Karhu Polku and are not for the weak of heart. The hills are gruesome, but if you can put up with more than a little physical pain, you're definitely in for the ride of your life. If you're ready for more thrills, at the end of Karhu Polku, head up to the Napa Piiri. Make sure you return from the Karhu Polku or Napa Piiri trails along the 0.6-mile, exhilarating Tuulen Tie (Way of the Wind) Trail that descends and returns you to the ski lodge and bike rental shop.

74

The Inner Circle

Many of the best, most exciting trails are shared by the inner circle of cyclists, the esoteric group of riders who know the lay of the land and are obsessed with discovering the best escapes, the most remote routes unknown to the masses. They want these routes left relatively untraveled. They want these routes to themselves.

Garnet Hill Lodge is where you'll find the inner circle. The obsessive ones. But they come to this great riding area even though it's no longer undiscovered. Riders of all abilities and at all levels of commitment to the sport share in the wealth of this mountain biking terrain. More than 25 miles of well-maintained, double- and singletrack trails form a maze that winds through the attractive, rolling countryside around the lodge in the southern Adirondacks' North River. In the winter the lodge area is laced with a network of cross-country ski trails. Once the snow melts the skiers may be gone, but the trails remain perfect for mountain bikers and have broad enough appeal to meet the requirements of any kind of rider. Novice riders can explore the easy cruising trails and backcountry dirt roads and witness the scenic beauty of the woodland landscape. Expert riders can rough it through some steep, challenging singletrack. Indeed the trails are a mixed bag, beckoning beginning, intermediate, and expert riders. The terrain around the lodge has a seemingly endless network of trails. These vary from flat, wide, and smooth to narrow and steep. Follow the inner circle and explore Garnet Hill Lodge.

General location: Northeastern New York, in the southern section of Adirondack Park.

Elevation change: The hilly terrain provides challenging riding. Trail riding is helped by the skill-level trail markers that designate the wintertime cross-country ski trails.

Season: The trails are available for riding after spring thaws, sometime in late May when the land dries out, until late fall. Call Garnet Hill Lodge for more details on trail conditions.

Services: Overnight lodging is available at Garnet Hill's lovely and attractive inn. Mountain bike rentals and sales are available on the premises. Inquire at Garnet Hill to see if they are running their "bike downhill–ride back" shuttle bus service. Riders can tour the trails and roads at Garnet

The Inner Circle

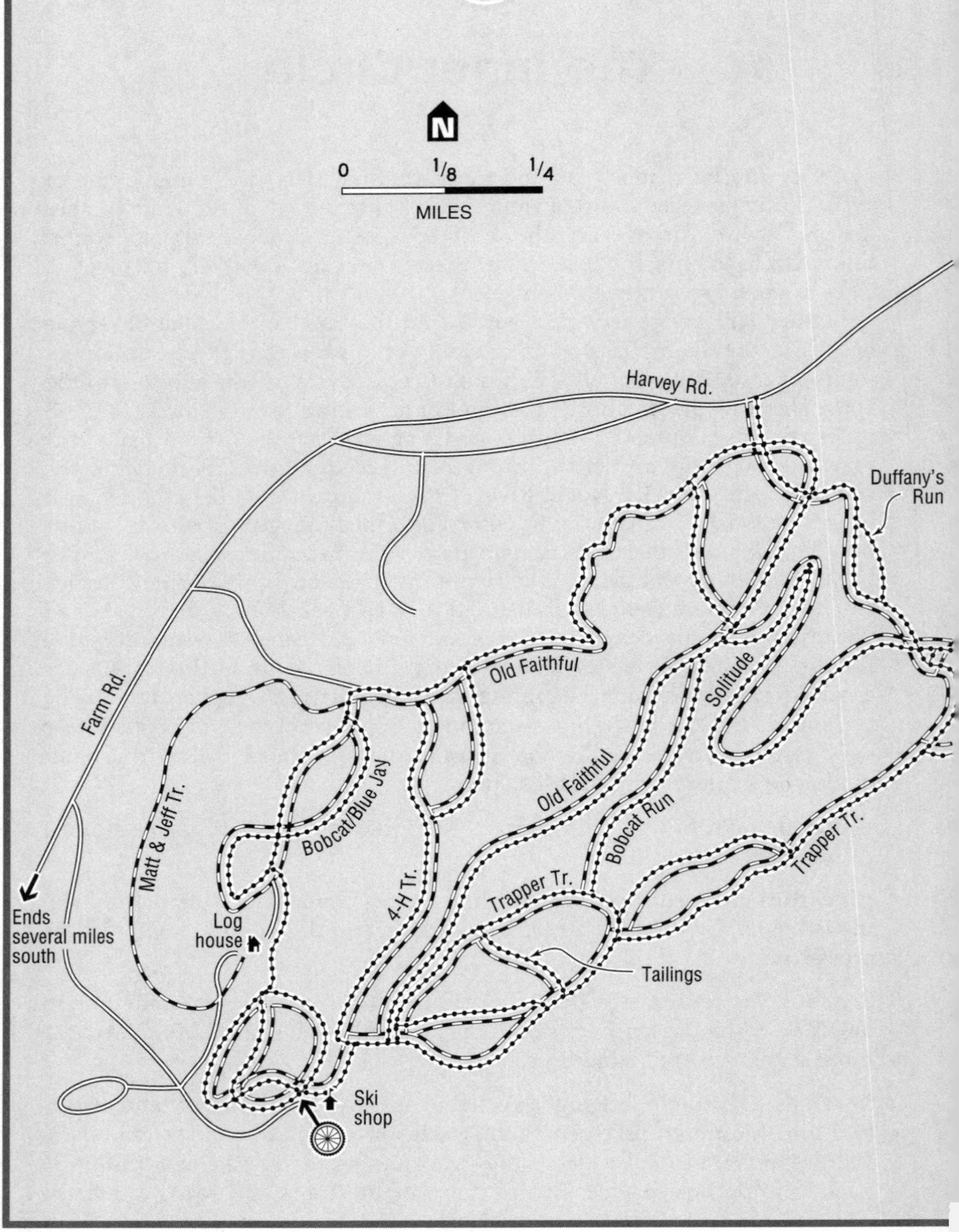

N

0   1/8   1/4

MILES

Harvey Rd.

Duffany's Run

Old Faithful

Solitude

Farm Rd.

Matt & Jeff Tr.

Bobcat/Blue Jay

Old Faithful

Bobcat Run

Trapper Tr.

4-H Tr.

Trapper Tr.

Ends several miles south

Log house

Trapper Tr.

Tailings

Ski shop

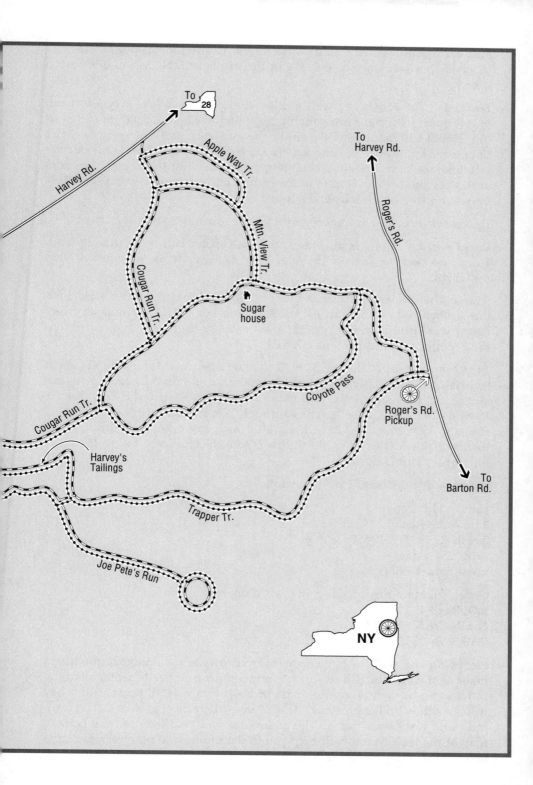

Hill and eventually ride into North Creek to the pickup point. The distance is approximately 10 miles, and the trip is suitable for all but novice bikers.

Hazards: The routes are well marked and easy to follow. Not all of the cross-country ski trails are suitable for mountain bike riding. As stated in the Garnet Hill mountain bike guide, the novice ski trails are generally the novice bicycle trails, and the expert ski trails become expert-only mountain bike trails. If you are a beginner, it may be wise to attempt the trails at the beginner level. Stop in at the mountain bike center to get the latest update on trail conditions and suggestions.

Rescue index: You are never more than a few miles from the lodge.

Land status: Public land. Many trails at Garnet Hill cross private land. Please do not wander off the trail near houses, barns, or other private buildings.

Maps: The ski center provides the most detailed map of all the trails. Pick one up before heading out. All trails are marked with the standard cross-country ski trail marking system, and there are trail signs and corresponding numbers at most intersections.

Finding the trail: Take the New York State Thruway (Interstate 87) north to exit 24 (Albany). Take I-87 north to exit 25, Route 8/Chestertown and Hague. At the end of the exit ramp, turn left (west) onto New York 8 toward Loon Lake. After passing through Wevertown, turn right (west) at the stop sign onto NY 28. This scenic highway takes you through the towns of North Creek and North River. After North River, follow the signs for Garnet Hill Lodge.

Sources of additional information:

Garnet Hill Lodge
13th Lake Road
North River, NY 12856
(518) 251–2444
www.garnet-hill.com

Gore Mountain Region Chamber of Commerce
P.O. Box 84
North Creek, NY 12853
(518) 251–2612

Notes on the trail: A large array of trails awaits the energetic mountain biker at the Garnet Hill Resort. A tremendous number of riding configurations can be created on the maze of trails and will fill up an entire day of bike riding and exploration. Check in at the office, grab a map, pick a trail, and just begin riding. The routes are well marked, and the printed map of the trail system will help you to determine and plan which trail to take.

The Garnet Hill mountain bike guide provides the following riding advice for the different levels of riders that come and visit the area.

The easiest riding for beginners is on the roads in the area. The best of these rides is the Old Farm Road, returning the same way. (Ride only to the yellow barrier!) 4-H Road and Harvey Road are also easy riding. The Old Faithful Trail connects both these roads and makes for a nice loop.

For intermediate riders Trapper Trail to Harvey's Tailings is a good route. At Harvey's Tailings cross the stream to the Cougar Run Trail. Take Cougar Run left past the Sugarhouse Trail, and left at the driveway to Harvey Road. Turn left onto Harvey Road to 4-H Road, and then take the Bobcat/Blue Jay Trail to the lodge. Mountain View and Apple Way Trails are at the end of Cougar Run. These are open field trails with great views of the High Peaks. Another intermediate loop is Sugarhouse Trail and Coyote Pass, both of which branch off Cougar Run after Harvey's Tailings. Sugarhouse Trail ends at Roger's Road. You can ride left on Roger's Road to Harvey Road and left on Harvey Road and eventually back to Garnet Hill. This is a very hilly ride.

The expert trails are Bobcat, Matt & Jeff Trail, Joe Pete (open to the ravine only), Solitude, and Duffany's Run.

Glossary

This short list of terms does not contain all the words used by mountain bike enthusiasts when discussing their sport. But it should serve as an introduction to the lingo you'll hear on the trails.

ATB All-terrain bike; this, like "fat-tire bike," is another name for a mountain bike

ATV All-terrain vehicle; this usually refers to the loud, fume-spewing three- or four-wheeled motorized vehicles you will not enjoy meeting on the trail—except, of course, if you crash and have to hitch a ride out on one.

bladed Refers to a dirt road that has been smoothed out by the use of a wide blade on earth-moving equipment; "blading" gets rid of the teeth-chattering, much-cursed washboards found on so many dirt roads after heavy vehicle use.

blaze A mark on a tree made by chipping away a piece of the bark, usually done to designate a trail; such trails are sometimes described as "blazed."

blind corner A curve in the road or trail that conceals bikers, hikers, equestrians, and other traffic.

BLM Bureau of Land Management, an agency of the federal government.

buffed Used to describe a very smooth trail.

catching air Taking a jump in such a way that both wheels of the bike are off the ground at the same time.

clean While this may describe what you and your bike won't be after following many trails, the term is most often used as a verb to denote the action of pedaling a tough section of trail successfully.

deadfall A tangled mass of fallen trees or branches.

diversion ditch A usually narrow, shallow ditch dug across or around a trail; funneling the water in this manner keeps it from destroying the trail.

doubletrack The dual tracks made by a jeep or other vehicle, with grass or weeds or rocks between; mountain bikers can ride in either of the tracks, but you will of course find that whichever one you choose, and no matter how many times you change back and forth, the other track will appear to offer smoother travel.

dugway A steep, unpaved, switchbacked descent.

feathering	Using a light touch on the brake lever, hitting it lightly many times rather than very hard or locking the brake.
four-wheel-drive	This refers to any vehicle with drive-wheel capability on all four wheels (a jeep, for instance, has four-wheel drive as compared with a two-wheel-drive passenger car), or to a rough road or trail that requires four-wheel-drive capability (or a one-wheel-drive mountain bike!) to negotiate it.
game trail	The usually narrow trail made by deer, elk, or other game.
gated	Everyone knows what a gate is, and how many variations exist upon this theme; well, if a trail is described as "gated," it simply has a gate across it. Don't forget that the rule is if you find a gate closed, close it behind you; if you find one open, leave it that way.
giardia	Shorthand for *Giardia lamblia,* and known as the "backpacker's bane" until we mountain bikers expropriated it. This is a waterborne parasite that begins its life cycle when swallowed, and one to four weeks later has its host (you) bloated, vomiting, shivering with chills, and living in the bathroom. The disease can be avoided by "treating" (purifying) the water you acquire along the trail (see "Hitting the Trail" in the Introduction).
gnarly	A term thankfully used less and less these days that refers to tough trails.
hammer	To ride very hard.
hardpack	A trail in which the dirt surface is packed down hard; such trails make for good and fast riding, and very painful landings. Bikers most often use "hardpack" as both a noun and adjective, and "hardpacked" as an adjective only (the grammar lesson will help you when diagramming sentences in camp).
jeep road, jeep trail	A rough road or trail passable only with four-wheel-drive capability (or a horse or mountain bike).
kamikaze	This once referred primarily to those Japanese fliers who quaffed a glass of sake, then flew off as human bombs in suicide missions against U.S. naval vessels, but it has more recently been applied to the idiot mountain bikers who, far less honorably, scream down hiking trails, endangering the physical and mental safety of the walking, biking, and

equestrian traffic they meet; threatening to get us all kicked off the trails.

multipurpose A BLM designation of land that is open to many uses; mountain biking is allowed.

out-and-back A ride in which you will return on the same trail you pedaled out. This might sound far more boring than a loop route, but many trails look very different when pedaled in the opposite direction.

portage To carry your bike on your person.

quads Bikers use this term to refer both to the extensor muscle in the front of the thigh (which is separated into four parts) and to USGS maps. The expression "Nice quads!" refers always to the former, however, except in those instances when the speaker is an engineer.

runoff Rainwater or snowmelt.

signed A "signed" trail has signs in place of blazes.

singletrack A single, narrow path through grass or brush or over rocky terrain, often created by deer, elk, or backpackers; singletrack riding is some of the best fun around.

slickrock The rock-hard, compacted sandstone that is great to ride and even prettier to look at; you'll appreciate it even more if you think of it as a petrified sand dune or seabed, and if the rider before you hasn't left tire marks (from unnecessary skidding) or granola bar wrappers behind.

snowmelt Runoff produced by the melting of snow.

snowpack Unmelted snow accumulated over weeks or months of winter—or over years in high-mountain terrain.

spur A road or trail that intersects the main trail you're following.

switchback A zigzagging road or trail designed to assist in traversing steep terrain: mountain bikers should not skid through switchbacks.

technical Terrain that is difficult to ride not because of its grade (steepness) but because of its obstacles—rocks, logs, ledges, loose soil, etc.

topo Short for topographical map, the kind that shows both linear distance and elevation gain and loss; "topo" is pronounced with both vowels long.

trashed A trail that has been destroyed (same term used no matter what has destroyed it—cattle, horses, or even mountain bikers riding when the ground was too wet).

two-wheel-drive	This refers to any vehicle with drive-wheel capability on only two wheels (a passenger car, for instance, has two-wheel drive); a two-wheel-drive road is a road or trail easily traveled by an ordinary car.
washboarded	A road that is surfaced with many ridges spaced closely together, like the ripples on a washboard; these make for very rough riding, and even worse driving in a car or jeep.
water bar	An earth, rock, or wooden structure that funnels water off trails to reduce erosion.
wilderness area	Land that is officially set aside by the federal government to remain natural—pure, pristine, and untrammeled by any vehicle, including mountain bikes. Although mountain bikes had not been born in 1964 (when the United States Congress passed the Wilderness Act, establishing the National Wilderness Preservation system), they are considered a "form of mechanical transport" and are thereby excluded; in short, stay out.
wind chill	A reference to the wind's cooling effect upon exposed flesh; for example, if the temperature is 10 degrees Fahrenheit and the wind is blowing at 20 miles per hour, the wind chill (that is, the actual temperature to which your skin reacts) is minus 32 degrees; if you are riding in wet conditions, things are even worse—the wind chill would then be minus 74 degrees!
windfall	Anything (trees, limbs, brush, fellow bikers) blown down by the wind.

About the Author

Michael Margulis and his wife Barbara; his two children, Alize and Chloe; and their Norwegian Elkhound, Shogun; live in Forest Hills, New York. His passion for the outdoors has drawn him to a multitude of state and national parks in the Pacific Northwest, the Southwest, and the Northeast, particularly in New York. His unrelenting drive to explore natural locations has taken him to the French and Swiss Alps, where he led hiking tours.

Michael and his family have a philosophy that life in New York should be balanced by the pursuit of the great outdoors. They camp, hike, bike, or cross-country ski almost every weekend, despite his busy schedule working as a software architect for Canterbury Financial Group in Connecticut. He has been a student and teacher of Okinawan Shorin-Ryu Karate-do for more than fifteen years and has earned the rank of third-degree black belt. His other pastimes include photography, carpentry, and piano. In addition, he has organized and participated in fundraising endurance rides for the Ronald McDonald House in New Hyde Park, New York.

The writing of this book has been a passion fulfilled. It's his way of sharing with other outdoor enthusiasts the challenging and rewarding sport of mountain biking in New York.

FALCON GUIDES®

From nature exploration to extreme adventure FalconGuides lead you there. With more than 400 titles available, there is a guide for every outdoor activity and topic including essential outdoor skills, field identification, trails, trips, and the best places to go in each state and region. Written by experts, each guidebook features detailed descriptions, maps, and expert advice that can enhance every outdoor experience.

You can count on FalconGuides to lead you to your favorite outdoor activities wherever you live or travel.

MOUNTAIN BIKING

These guides selectively cover the best rides in a state or region. Mountain bikers of all abilities will enjoy the assortment of rides that vary in length and difficulty and are appropriate for a variety of skills and fitness levels.

6 x 9" • paperback • maps • photos elevation graphs

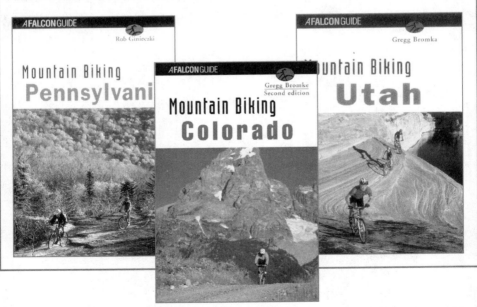

A FALCON GUIDE
Rob Ginieczki

Mountain Biking
Pennsylvani

A FALCON GUIDE
Gregg Bromke
Second edition

Mountain Biking
Colorado

A FALCON GUIDE
Gregg Bromka

Mountain Biking
Utah